THE GREAT REFORM BILL
IN THE BOROUGHS

The Great Reform Bill in the Boroughs

English Electoral Behaviour, 1818–1841

JOHN A. PHILLIPS

CLARENDON PRESS · OXFORD
1992

Oxford University Press, Walton Street, Oxford OX2 6DP
Oxford New York Toronto
Delhi Bombay Calcutta Madras Karachi
Petaling Jaya Singapore Hong Kong Tokyo
Nairobi Dar es Salaam Cape Town
Melbourne Auckland
and associated companies in
Berlin Ibadan

Oxford is a trade mark of Oxford University Press

Published in the United States
by Oxford University Press, New York

British Library Cataloguing in Publication Data
Data available

Library of Congress Cataloging in Publication Data
Phillips, John A., 1949–
The great reform bill in the boroughs: English electoral
behaviour, 1818–1841 / John A. Phillips.
p. cm.
Includes bibliographical references and index.
1. Elections—Great Britain—History—19th century. 2. Voting—
Great Britain—History—19th century. 3. Great Britain—Politics
and government—19th century. I. Title.
JN951.P483 1992
324.941'074—dc20 91–45438
ISBN 0–19–820296–2

Typeset by Hope Services (Abingdon) Ltd.
Printed and bound in
Great Britain by Biddles Ltd.,
Guildford and King's Lynn

For Ginny

ACKNOWLEDGEMENTS

I have incurred many debts in my pursuit of England's voters. I am particularly grateful to Richard W. Davis for years of support that amount to a splendid example of patronage in its best sense. His work helped shape my decision in graduate school to pursue electoral behaviour. No one who works with this period can avoid massive intellectual obligations to John Brewer. H. T. Dickinson's work has taught me much about Hanoverian England. Donald Ginter has kept me aware of the limitations of my quantitative skills, while John Money has on occasion made me despair of ever managing to learn enough about England to deserve to have an opinion. Frank O'Gorman's magnificent study of the unreformed electoral system provides an essential backdrop for this book; his work informs virtually all of what follows. I have also benefited greatly from the work of Ian Newbould, James Bradley, and Penelope Corfield. J. C. D. Clark's work has forced me, along with almost everyone else interested in the period, to reconsider much.

Though occasionally dejected by my inability to live up to the impossibly high standards set by my colleagues Edwin Gaustad and Ron Tobey, my spirits have been rescued time and again by their joint example. The members of the editorial staff of *Parliamentary History*, Eveline Cruickshanks, David Hayton, Clyve Jones, and Carole Rawcliffe, have made my trips to England over more years than I care to admit extraordinary, both from their collective friendship that has made London seem as hospitable as southern California, and from their example of superb scholarship. I appreciate their willingness to allow portions of two articles that appeared in *Parliamentary History* to be included here. I am particularly indebted to two members of the staff of the 1820–32 section of the History of Parliament, Martin Casey and Howard Spencer, for steering me straight on a number of matters. My daughter Jennifer made a significant, though unwitting, contribution. By monopolizing the car that we 'shared', she kept me at my desk when I might have been tempted to spend my time at the Santa Anita Racetrack or the Normandie Casino. Lou Masur provided a countervailing influence for a time, but his departure for the East Coast along with Jani and Benjamin left me to finish the book with too few distractions.

Without the facilities available in the Laboratory for Historical Research and the guidance, advice, criticism, and assistance of its Director, Charles Wetherell, this project would have perished at a relatively early stage. The cumulative weight of more than 25,000 individual voters and hundreds of thousands of records would have crushed this effort without the assistance of the Lab. I was also ably assisted with data processing and analysis at various stages by Richard Turner, Thomas Thompson, Michael Ikeda, and Laurie Curtis. The data gathered, processed, and analysed for this book are available from the Laboratory for Historical Research, UC Riverside, CA 92521, USA.

A number of institutions must be acknowledged of which the University of California has been the most generous. Year after year, the Committee on Research of the University of California, Riverside has, in its various manifestations, lent support to this research. The National Endowment for the Humanities took a shorter-term interest, but I am very grateful for their support in the form of a research stipend. The Institute of Historical Research of the University of London also played an important role at times.

I would like to thank the staffs of the Bedfordshire Record Office, Birmingham University Library, Bodleian Library, Bristol Record Office, Bristol Central Library, Colchester Local History Central Library, Cornwall Record Office, Dr Williams's Library, East Sussex Record Office, Essex Record Office, Friends Library, Guildhall Library of the City of London, Humberside Record Office, Huntington Library, Kent Archives Office, London School of Economics Library, National Register of Archives, Norfolk Record Office, Northamptonshire Record Office, Public Record Office (Portugal Street and Kew), Shrewsbury Local History Library, and Shropshire Record Office.

I am most indebted to my wife Ginny, to whom this book is dedicated with love and admiration. If she failed to eliminate my abuse of subordinate clauses, she improved the manuscript in countless ways, not least in helping me to keep it all in perspective.

CONTENTS

TABLES

ABBREVIATIONS

AR	*The Annual Register of World Events*
BL	British Library
BRO	Bristol Record Office
CJ	*Journals of the House of Commons*
CLHL	Colchester Local History Library
CRO	Cornwall Record Office
ERO	Essex Record Office
ESRO	East Sussex Record Office
HRO	Hertfordshire Record Office
HumRO	Humberside Record Office
KAO	Kent Archives Office
MoP	J. H. Barrow (ed.), *The Mirror of Parliament*
NRO	Norfolk Record Office
NtRO	Northamptonshire Record Office
Parl. Deb.	*Parliamentary Debates*, 3rd series
Parl. Pap.	*Parliamentary Papers*
PRO	Public Record Office
SLHL	Shrewsbury Local History Library
SRO	Shropshire Record Office

Introduction
1832 and All That

Historians hold few things sacred, least of all the work of their predecessors. As revisionists scurry about wreaking havoc on a once well-ordered historical landscape, very few judgements of previous generations of scholars have proven impervious to assault. Attributions of significance to a specific year (or years) have been particularly susceptible to revision. Few years once identified as 'watersheds' have retained the global significance accorded them in the past. Years for which far less grandiose claims have been made have usually succumbed even more quickly to historiographical affrays.

At one time there seemed little doubt that 1832 should be counted among England's most distinguished years. Though Sellar and Yeatman failed to select it as one of their two 'genuine' dates, it featured prominently in their list of 103 'good things'.[1] W. N. Molesworth believed that 1832 marked the point at which 'the nation . . . triumphed after a desperate struggle over the most powerful aristocracy in the world, and tore from them the rights which they [the aristocracy] had not the wisdom to concede'.[2] Sounding much like Molesworth, G. M. Trevelyan's 1920 biography of Lord Grey extolled 1832 as the point at which the whole spirit of England's polity finally diverged 'from that of aristocratic Germany', just as in 1793 it had diverged from that of Jacobin France. 'We all', Treveyan exclaimed, 'rejoice at both divergences.'[3] Just before the First World War, G. S. Veitch echoed John Bright in arguing that though 'the Reform Bill was not a good Bill, it was a great Bill when it passed. It was a first and necessary step in parliamentary reform'.[4]

The Reform Bill introduced by Lord John Russell in 1831 proposed a revision of England's political order drastic enough to

---

[1] W. C. Sellar and R. J. Yeatman, *1066 and All That* (London, 1931). They included 103 good things, 5 bad things, and 2 genuine dates.
[2] W. N. Molesworth, *The History of the Reform Bill of 1832* (London, 1865), 1–3.
[3] G. M. Trevelyan, *Lord Grey of the Reform Bill* (New York, 1920), 350–1.
[4] G. S. Veitch, *The Genesis of Parliamentary Reform* (London, 1913), 355.

Intro

seem important at the time. After considerable alteration, it planned to disfranchise fifty-six boroughs completely, while thirty-one others were to lose one of their two Members of Parliament. Twenty-two towns completely unrepresented in the old system were to be given two MPs, and another nineteen were slated to receive one. The Bill promised to double the representation of twenty-six counties, and intended a 50 per cent increase for eight others. More controversially, the Bill enfranchised householders inhabiting houses valued at a minimum of £10 per annum in all parliamentary boroughs. It coupled that urban increase with the enfranchisement in counties of £50 tenants-at-will. The thousands to be enfranchised and the thousands more already possessing the franchise were to be formally registered prior to voting. For the first time it would be possible to know before an election who could and who could not vote. At the same time, thousands of others were disfranchised; non-resident borough voters, however previously qualified, were to lose their rights. Residents kept their franchises, however acquired, for their lifetimes, but in the future, with a few exceptions, new voters would qualify only as £10 householders. Lord John and the Whigs could only guess at the effects of these changes in the franchise, but the Bill promised (and delivered) a substantial overall increase in the already large number of Englishmen who had the right to vote.[5] The more than 400,000 men who held the franchise just before the Reform Act grew to more than 650,000 in 1833.[6] Through such radical measures, the grosser inequities in the old system would be eliminated, electoral corruption would be reduced, borough mongers would lose their undue influence, and purity and virtue would be restored to the entire electoral process. Or would they?

Attitudes towards the significance of 1832 have been shaped by perceptions of the unreformed political system, particularly the Hanoverian electorate. At the beginning of this century the prevailing image of the unreformed electorate was shaped by the historical accounts of John Grego (1892) and Edward and Annie Porritt (1909), which were in turn based upon contemporaneous Radical and Whig

[5] Actually 55 lost two MPs and Higham Ferrers lost its sole delegate. Thirty boroughs lost one MP and Weymouth and Melcombe Regis lost two of their conjoint four. The Isle of Wight also became a county with one MP. The most recent and most accurate estimate of the changes in the franchise suggests that 1832 resulted in a net increase of just over 200,000 voters. F. O'Gorman, *Voters, Patrons, and Parties* (Oxford, 1989), 179–80.

[6] Ibid. 179.

attacks upon the political system.[7] These combined efforts did everything possible to besmirch the system in the interest of attracting support for Reform. The 1793 attack on the state of England's representation by the Society of the Friends of the People was followed by T. H. B. Oldfield's condemnation of the parliamentary boroughs. These exercises in political propaganda, sufficiently damning by themselves, were reinforced by William Cobbett, Henry Hunt, George Wade, and others who maintained a continuous, highly visible assault on the political system in general and the electoral system in particular in the years leading up to 1832.[8] After Reform, the denigration of the old system continued through the efforts of Joseph Parkes and the Whig-appointed commissioners who, in examining England's municipal corporations, prepared a fresh vilification of the old political order.

With the reputation of the Hanoverian electorate already destroyed, Lewis Namier applied the *coup de grâce* to the unreformed political system by insisting that neither ideology nor party politics contributed to parliamentary activity in 1761, much less events in the constituencies.[9] Robert Walcott's extension of Namier's interpretation backwards into the early eighteenth century and Norman Gash's projection of it into the post-Reform era left very little to stand in the way of an exclusive focus on high politics and the men who scrambled for the spoils of office.[10] The field was ripe for D. C. Moore's reinterpretation of 1832. While in one sense merely continuing 'the tendency of modern scholarship . . . to question whether the Reform Act deserved the epithet "Great"', Moore actually went much further by portraying the Act as little more than a trick perpetrated by the aristocracy in its successful bid to retain political control. In Moore's scenario, the Act's only 'Great' quality was its remarkable success in maintaining aristocratic dominance in

[7] J. Grego, *History of Parliamentary Elections and Electioneering* (London, 1892); E. and A. Porritt, *The Unreformed House of Commons*, 2 vols. (Cambridge, 1909).

[8] T. H. B. Oldfield, *The History of the Boroughs*, 2 vols. (London, 1794); id., *Representative History of Great Britain and Ireland*, 6 vols. (London, 1816); J. Wade, *The Extraordinary Black Book*, 2 vols. (London, 1820).

[9] L. Namier, *Monarchy and the Party System* (Oxford, 1952); id., *The Structure of Politics at the Accession of George III* (London, 1929); id., *England in the Age of the American Revolution* (London, 1930). See also K. Thomas, 'The Brilliant Misfit', *New York Review of Books*, 37 (1990), 46–8.

[10] R. Walcott, *English Politics in the Early Eighteenth Century* (Oxford, 1956); N. Gash, *Politics in the Age of Peel* (London, 1953).

Parliament and in the country.[11] Thus both Gash and Moore implied that English popular politics hardly warranted serious attention either before or after 1832.

Just when all traces of an open political system seemed to have been eradicated, however, J. H. Plumb, Geoffrey Holmes, and others destroyed Walcott's thesis by resurrecting party and popular participation in their accounts of Augustan England. In their view, widespread political participation was the rule rather than the exception in the early years of the century. During the 'rage of party' under Anne, parties and principles engaged the attentions and actions of tens of thousands of Englishmen at a rash of contested elections.[12] The political frenzy with which the century began gave way to a somewhat protracted hiatus under Walpole because of George I's proscription of the Tories, the passage of the Septennial Act, and the Whig assault on the broadly interpreted franchise, but in many ways Walpole's England was shaped as a response to the dangers posed by such widespread political power. The England described so effectively by Plumb et al., was not an *ancien régime*, but a very new one emerging swiftly in the decades following the Glorious Revolution, replacing an old world lost for ever. Continuities could be found between the old and new worlds, but that it was a new world could not be doubted.

Almost simultaneously, Frank O'Gorman and Donald Ginter began an equally important restoration of party, principle, and popular politics at the other end of the eighteenth century, a restoration subsequently extended by John Brewer and others.[13] In

[11] J. Cannon, *Parliamentary Reform, 1640–1832* (Cambridge, 1973), 254; D. C. Moore, 'The Other Face of Reform', *Victorian Studies*, 4 (1961); id., 'Concession or Cure: The Sociological Premises of the First Reform Act', *Historical Journal*, 9 (1966); id., *The Politics of Deference* (Hassocks, 1976).

[12] J. H. Plumb, *The Growth of Political Stability in England, 1675–1725* (London, 1967); G. Holmes, *British Politics in the Age of Anne* (London, 1967); W. A. Speck, *Tory and Whig* (London, 1970).

[13] D. Ginter, *Whig Organization in the General Election of 1790* (Berkeley, Calif., 1967); F. O'Gorman, *The Whig Party and the French Revolution* (London, 1967); id., *The Rise of Party in England* (London, 1975). The year 1967 was a notable one for 18th-cent. historiography. Ginter and O'Gorman built upon a foundation established by G. Rude, *Wilkes and Liberty* (Oxford, 1962), E. C. Black, *The Association* (Cambridge, Mass., 1963), and E. P. Thompson, *The Making of the English Working Class* (London, 1963). J. Brewer, *Party Ideology and Popular Politics at the Accession of George III* (Cambridge, 1976). More recent accounts are contained in F. O'Gorman, *The Emergence of the British Two-Party System* (London, 1982) and B. W. Hill, *British Parliamentary Parties* (London, 1985).

their versions of the later eighteenth century, issues, principles, and participation (quite a bit of it extra-parliamentary) re-emerged under George III and continued, albeit possibly on a reduced scale, into the new century. The England described by Ginter and O'Gorman was much like the England revealed by the work of Plumb, Holmes, and Speck. From the frantic attacks on Henry Sacheverell in the years following 1709 to the remarkable celebration of the number 45 in honour of John Wilkes in the years following 1763, this new political world included the many, not just the few. Subaltern studies were essential for an understanding of political and social realities at either end of the eighteenth century.

Those who would dismiss the importance of formalized electoral behaviour must now contend with Frank O'Gorman's magisterial study of the Hanoverian electorate which solves the maze of the unreformed system; it captures the system's essentials while never ignoring its complexity and variety. O'Gorman never underestimates the deficiencies of the unreformed electoral system; elections often involved venality, corruption, and a variety of influences that seem indefensible to modern eyes. Moreover, contested elections often signified disputes among local élites, ineffectual or rejected patrons, ambitious families, or the changing fortunes of a particular MP rather than anything resembling a modern political contest. The great majority of constituencies could not be considered 'open' by the most generous interpretation of that term. Even worse, electoral activity declined over the century, reaching abysmal levels in many kinds of constituencies by 1800.

All of these qualifications and limitations notwithstanding, it is clear that the electoral system played far more than a marginal political role. Local élites aside, the electoral system was never really closed. And if most electoral contests tended to be expressions of local conflicts, national issues could make themselves felt at almost any time. Many general elections inflamed political imaginations and provoked debates over national issues in a wide range of constituencies. In stark contrast to the conclusions of Moore and others, O'Gorman identifies an electorate capable of much independence of thought and action.[14] Local rifts often generated intense partisan loyalties early in the century. Party voting engendered more by national

---

[14] For discussion of the 'depersonalization of influence' that O'Gorman thinks influenced these developments, see M. Kishlansky, *Parliamentary Selection* (Cambridge, 1986).

Introduction

issues re-emerged in the years just before and during the war against first Jacobin and then Napoleonic France. By the end of those wars, 'the day of party . . . voting was dawning', based on neither 'republicanism or fundamental disaffection', but on less divisive, substantive political issues and party organization. Put broadly, 'before 1832 party attachments may have been less formal and more intermittent than they later became, but they were not noticeably less assertive nor less popular'.[15]

If parties existed both in Westminster and in the countryside well before 1832, and there was already a relatively open electoral system in England, what impact could Reform have had on English popular politics? A great number of the Reform Bill's contemporaries had no doubts about its potential impact. Their great expectations in 1831 and 1832 serve to introduce this study. No bill could have measured up to some of the grandiose claims made for the Bill, but the projections of Reform as a constitutional panacea provide an important context for understanding the Bill's role in popular perceptions of politics, a role potentially as important as its actual restructuring of the electoral system. This book seeks answers to questions about the impact of Reform not by examining the whole of England's electoral system, but by focusing more narrowly and also more thoroughly on some of its parts, specifically the electorates of eight borough constituencies at general elections before and after 1832. Restricting this analysis to individual voters in just a handful of boroughs between 1818 and 1841 required the consideration of a massive database including tens of thousands of electors and hundreds of thousands of pieces of information.

England's boroughs, reformed and unreformed, present a bewilderingly diverse array of differences of size and political development. Moreover, the urban electorate grew commensurately with England's towns in the nineteenth century. This growth, added to the Reform Act's artificial augmentation of the electorate, creates gargantuan analytical problems for a study of nineteenth-century electoral behaviour. More than 50,000 votes were recorded at elections in Bristol alone between 1812 and 1841; a comprehensive look at nineteenth-century elections in Liverpool before the secret ballot in 1872 eliminated these windows into the political lives of

---

[15] O'Gorman, *Voters*, 383, 388, 357.

individuals would involve more than 200,000 specific votes from tens of thousands of electors. The need to translate data on this scale into machine-readable form imposed a potentially crushing burden on a quantitative analysis of electoral behaviour in this period. Chapter 1 explains the ways in which the size and complexity of the problem dictated restrictions on both the number of constituencies and the number of electors subjected to comprehensive statistical analyses.[16] The first chapter also considers the meaning of partisan behaviour and its measurement. The act of voting, a complex phenomenon under most circumstances, was vastly complicated in this period by the fact that most voters at parliamentary elections possessed two votes that could be cast simultaneously. The implications of the double vote are critical to the analyses of voting behaviour that follow. The following chapters analyse the behaviour of individual electors at both unreformed and reformed elections, thus permitting a critical comparative perspective. Simple questions such as electoral turnout and occupational structure can be answered much more intelligibly in comparative focus. Many more complex questions about behaviour can be addressed only comparatively. Dunbabin's assertion that 1868 is 'probably about as far back as we can safely employ modern psephological techniques' is correct in the sense that summary statistics for early elections usually raise more questions

[16] The primary technique used to reduce the data requirements of this study, letter–cluster sampling, is explained in J. A. Phillips, 'Achicving a Critical Mass while Avoiding an Explosion', *Journal of Interdisciplinary History*, 9 (1979), 493–508. In brief, random sampling, a staple of cross–sectional analysis, cannot be used in conjunction with nominal record linkage, an essential component of longitudinal analysis. By using clusters of letters consistently and generating a sample that has elements of a stratified sample and elements of a random sample, a large enough group of individuals can be selected at each relevant point (a poll book for example) to permit statistical analyses and at the same time the members of one sample can be traced in a subsequent or previous sample. Thus data from the sample for 1818 that contains John Smith's vote can be combined with data from the sample of 1820 or 1826 or 1830, all of which will also contain John Smith's votes if he participated in those years. For a similar approach, see J. E. Bradley, *Religion, Revolution, and English Radicalism* (Cambridge, 1990). For other recent discussions, see J. Elkit, 'Nominal Record Linkage and the Study of Non–Secret Voting', *Journal of Interdisciplinary History*, 15 (1985), 419–43; A. Abbott and J. Forrest, 'Optimal Matching Methods for Historical Sequences', *Journal of Interdisciplinary History*, 16 (1986), 471–94. The boroughs selected for intense scrutiny were chosen on the basis of (1) representativeness in a number of areas including size, franchise-type, and location, (2) electoral activity, and (3) available data. The resulting selection may be unscientific, but it is defensible and unavoidable.

than they answer.[17] Efforts to apply standard aggregate analytical techniques are more likely to mislead than to clarify. Yet, at the level of the individual voter, English electoral data before 1868 are among the richest and most revealing available; they permit far subtler analyses than the aggregate data available after the veil of secrecy lowered by the Ballot Act in 1872.

After the first chapter identifies many of the pertinent questions and establishes the popular context of Reform, Chapters 2 to 6 measure the popular impact of Reform by examining quantitative and qualitative evidence concerning electoral behaviour and the underlying political systems in the provinces. Each chapter employs both simple and complex statistical evaluations conducted in the context provided by the full range of traditional historical evidence, including private papers, newspapers, pamphlets, broadsides, and election speeches. These chapters demonstrate the powerful popular impact of Reform even in towns such as Bristol and Maidstone, where political parties had long played critical roles in elections. Voters in Colchester were also affected by Reform despite the town's conservative political complexion. In all three of these boroughs, altered electoral behaviour can be traced to the Reform Act itself: pronounced differences separated voting behaviour at the last unreformed election in 1831 and the first reformed election only a year later.

In Shrewsbury and Northampton, on the other hand, the implementation of the Reform Act seems to have been no more important than the preceding months of political debate and popular agitation over the Bill's fate. Voting patterns at the elections of 1830 and 1831 in these two towns differed dramatically from patterns evident at the election of 1826 and before; the enhanced partisan behaviour and party loyalty discernible at reformed elections only extended the trend clearly begun during the last two unreformed general elections. The temporal component of the popular impact of Reform, then, varied considerably. Reform transformed voting behaviour in these towns, but the popular debate over the Reform Bill sometimes proved as powerful a catalyst for political change as the Act itself.

Qualifying somewhat the conclusions that might be drawn from the evidence of Reform's extensive impact in the first five towns

[17] J. P. D. Dunbabin, 'Parliamentary Elections in Great Britain, 1868–1900', *English Historical Review*, 81 (1966), 83.

considered, Chapters 5 and 6 examine three towns largely unaffected by 1832. Reform proved to be redundant in Lewes and Great Yarmouth; voters in both towns engaged in fiercely partisan, open political struggles well in advance of 1832. The zeal with which Lewes residents petitioned Parliament over political issues, from the fate of Queen Caroline to the slave trade, translated electorally into rigid partisan divisions camouflaged by the unwillingness of Lewes's Tories to plump before Reform. Reform cast Lewes's partisan rift into higher relief, but it had little impact on the already intensely partisan behaviour of Lewes's voters. Great Yarmouth differed only in that its long-standing partisan rift was readily apparent. Yarmouth's voters occupied two exclusive camps; virtually every enfranchised townsman cast a strictly partisan vote in 1818 and continued to do so at every subsequent election. Nothing could have heightened partisanship in Yarmouth; there was no room for improvement. Party rigidity and loyalty preceded Reform. In both towns, then, 1832 helped broaden already flourishing local partisan political struggles into unmistakably national orientations.

At the other end of the spectrum, Beverley required more than a single Reform Act to eliminate the town's older, apolitical forms of electoral behaviour. Elections in Beverley before and after 1832 had little or nothing to do with national parties, issues, or identifiable principles. Beverley's voters were not sufficiently politicized until 1837 to behave in the partisan fashion achieved in so many other places in 1830/1 or 1832. The Municipal Corporations Act finally dragged Beverley's electorate, reluctantly even then, into the modern political arena.

The development of partisan, issue-oriented electoral behaviour in these towns cannot be linked to 'class', defined occupationally or economically, either before or after Reform. Using very detailed data that might have been expected to reveal differences if they existed, Chapter 7 searches in vain for a systematic relationship between socio-economic variations and partisan alliances in the electorate. Occupations were occasionally related to party preferences, but occupational and economic differences in the electorate appeared too spasmodically to be taken seriously. Differences appeared at one election, only to evaporate or reverse themselves at the next, or appeared in one town and not in another. Members of the commercial élite, for example, ordinarily supported Whig candidates in Northampton after 1830, yet the same sorts of men in Beverley supported Tory candidates. Members of Lewes's commercial élite shifted politically from most conservative in 1818 to least conservative in 1837. The labouring men were among the most conservative voters in Northampton, yet their counterparts made up the least conservative group in Lewes. These do not constitute meaningful patterns. Moreover, the probability of a particular occupational category voting for a specific party encompassed a meaninglessly wide range. The commercial élite in Northampton, for instance, tended not to vote for Tory candidates, but the actual odds of their tendency not to do so ranged between the unhelpful extremes of 0.15 in 1831 and 4.6 in 1835. With this much diversity within a single group, generalizations are impossible. Every effort to identify some larger, meaningful socio-economic divisions in these towns failed.

Conversely, the connection posited equally often between religion and politics appeared wherever sought. Chapter 8 examines those voters who could be tied to particular Nonconformist denominations and compares some specific congregations within denominations. The evidence points almost without qualification to a link between Nonconformity and Whig/reformist politics. Robert Southey suggested in 1829 that Nonconformists threw their weight uniformly behind the Whigs.[18] Voters in these towns repeatedly corroborated his assessment. Nonconformists may have deserted the Whigs at particular times in particular places, but both before and after Reform Dissenters tended to be Whigs. If anything, that tendency may have increased after 1832, particularly among groups such as the Methodists, but the weakest evidence indicates a decided Tory minority among Nonconformists from 1818 onward.

Nicholas Rogers has shown the degree to which England's political élite could ignore popular politics only at their peril.[19] O'Gorman has extended that vision and described an unreformed political system that encompassed many active, sometimes issue-oriented, and increasingly partisan electorates. Yet despite what was by any standard a remarkable degree of popular political participation before 1832, the ultimately successful two-year agitation for Reform helped orient popular politics more consistently around national issues. The Great Reform Bill failed to reform much that needed reforming, and some of its more important effects, such as the boost voter registration gave to partisan activity, were unintentional.

[18] R. Southey, *Sir Thomas More* (London, 1829), ii. 44.
[19] N. Rogers, *Whigs and Cities*, (Oxford, 1989).

Nevertheless, both the Bill and the intense political agitation leading to its passage altered the nature of parties, partisanship, and politics generally. Popular political behaviour in the 1830s was distinctly different in many ways from that of earlier periods, even those in which parties and elections played an important role. England contained a vibrant 'political nation', to use Burke's phrase, well before 1832, much of it unenfranchised, but the Reform Act expanded the ranks of the enfranchised, and more importantly, catalysed partisan politics and reshaped the political process in constituency after constituency across England.

PART I
THE PROMISE OF REFORM

1
Great Expectations

O F the many men and women in England who anxiously awaited the passage of the Great Reform Bill during the months of delay in 1831 and 1832, few had more reason to feel gratified by the country's widespread, increasingly vociferous concern than Thomas Hardy, one of the founders of the London Corresponding Society in 1792.[1] Hardy, the guiding force behind the growth of the Society, was arrested with four others on charges of high treason in 1794 and tried for his determination to discuss and promote parliamentary reform.[2] Though Hardy's trial began just ten days after the execution of a Scottish Jacobin, Thomas Erskine's skilful defence and a sympathetic jury resulted in Hardy's acquittal on Guy Fawkes Day, 1794 after a remarkable nine-day trial.[3] Attorney General Sir John Scott's nine-hour opening statement was matched by an equally extreme three-hour jury deliberation capped by the foreman fainting from the strain immediately after delivering the 'not guilty' verdict. Following these exceptionally protracted and intense proceedings, London dissolved into celebrations of Hardy, Erskine, the jurors, and what Londoners perceived as the triumph of English justice.

The crowds heralding Hardy's release from Newgate were notably less enthusiastic about Hardy's concern for parliamentary reform. In fact, most of them appear not to have shared his concern at all. Thus

[1] The eight decided to become a society with dues of a penny a week to permit the purchase of paper and ink to admit a wider circle of correspondents; Hardy returned home with the initial war chest, 8 pennies, in his pocket. T. Hardy, *Memoir of Thomas Hardy, Written by Himself* (London, 1832), 107–10.

[2] Twelve men were taken in charge, but only five accused of treason. The Attorney General, Sir John Scott, decided that Fox's recent Libel Act rendered charges of seditious libel too susceptible to sabotage from a sympathetic jury who could now decide law as well as fact. See J. A. Phillips and T. C. Thompson, 'Jurors v. Judges in Later-Stuart England', *Law and Inequality*, 4 (1986), 189–229.

[3] Robert Watt was executed for high treason on 16 Oct. 1794. David Downie, found guilty along with Watt, escaped death through a last-minute reprieve. Hardy, *Memoir*, 110; T. Howell (ed.), *State Trials* (London, 1817), xxiii. 859, xxiv. 198; *Gentleman's Magazine*, 102 (1832), 480–1.

Hardy escaped the executioner only to fall victim to the fate of so many popular heroes, precipitous obscurity. Hardy had been forgotten by the end of the Napoleonic wars. He still held a commemorative dinner every Guy Fawkes Day, but few attended. Nor could he have afforded to host very many because he had fallen into penury a few years after retiring in 1815, mistakenly expecting imminent death.[4] By 1823, the 72-year-old Hardy had exhausted his small capital and had to be rescued from destitution by Sir Francis Burdett.[5] At the point of his financial rescue in 1823, it is difficult to imagine what would have surprised Hardy more, simply that he would live for nearly another decade, or that in living so long he would witness the formation of a Government determined to reform Parliament. Hardy recognized the irony of these changes in 1831, writing to Sir Francis: 'perhaps you may smile when I tell you that I am now for the first time, in my humble measure, a supporter of Ministers.'[6] He seems not to have realized the double irony that Burdett himself was moving in the opposite direction.

E. P. Thompson was undoubtedly correct in noting that 'throughout the war years there were Thomas Hardys in every town and in many villages throughout England, with a kist or shelf full of Radical books, biding their time . . . waiting for the movement to revive'. It is also true, however, that most of those 'Hardys' who waited so impatiently could not have guessed the wait would be so long, too long for many of them to see it through.[7] Most of those waiting died in the wait or at the very least were too old and infirm to participate in the events of the 1830s except vicariously. Sydney Smith, born two decades after Hardy, complained in January 1831: 'I am too old to fight or to suffer.'[8] Hardy himself noted in 1816 that

---

[4] Having lost all his children to early deaths and his wife, tragically, just before his trial, Hardy had settled in Fleet Street with his sister in 1797 where he became a freeman of the Cordwainers Company and a liveryman of the Needlemakers Company. His health failing, Hardy liquidated for £700. He assumed that he and his sister could live on £100 p.a., and that after his imminent demise, she could live on the remainder. His return to health immediately after retirement caused the financial crisis.

[5] Hardy, *Memoir*, 89–110. See also Thompson, *English Working Class*, 17–20, 123–37.

[6] Hardy, *Memoir*, 94.

[7] Thompson's village politician in 1849 would have been a very youthful revolutionary in 1792. Thompson's claim that the movement was *their own* certainly is not literally true. *English Working Class*, 183.

[8] Lady Holland, *A Memoir of the Reverend Sydney Smith* (London, 1869), 483, Smith to John Murray, 3 Jan. 1831.

half of the twelve men with whom he had been arrested in 1794 were dead. All of the remainder but one died during the subsequent decade. Only an aged John Thelwall was left by the end of 1832 to emerge from his obscurity in Bath and deliver Hardy's eulogy.[9]

Thus it was an entirely unexpected and unusual fate that awaited Hardy. He could never have guessed in 1823 that he would end his days corresponding with the Marquis de Lafayette about the return of ideas belonging to those heady, revolutionary times they had known thirty years earlier. Hardy also could not have dared to hope that he would emerge from decades of anonymity into a modest but no less welcome light of public interest. Hardy's anniversary dinners ceased to be small, private affairs; 150 attended in 1830. And at long last he was able to present his formal version of the events leading to his trial. The publication in 1832 of the chronicle that he had written thirty-four years earlier detailing the activities of the London Corresponding Society capped his renewed fame. Within a week of examining the page proofs of his story, Hardy died, having realized his greatest expectations at the age of 81.[10]

Hardy may have been one of the few survivors of an earlier age able to rekindle his great expectations in 1831, but many younger people shared his aspirations in the months immediately prior to Reform. A virtually forgotten issue as late as 1829 despite the various bills perversely proposed by Sir Francis Burdett and Lord John Russell over the years, Reform had begun to attract a little more attention in the early part of 1830 when in February Russell introduced a bill to enfranchise Manchester, Birmingham, and Leeds. Even in 1830, though, most constituencies paid little attention to such measures. The *Shrewsbury Chronicle* reported in July on the tranquillity pervading the general election. After long

---

[9] The financial disaster of the *Champion*, the journal Thelwall purchased in 1818 as the vehicle for his premature reopening of the campaign for constitutional change, forced him into embarrassed retirement. Mrs C. (Boyle) Thelwall, *Life of John Thelwall* (London, 1837), 430–6; C. Cestre, *John Thelwall* (London, 1906); *Gentleman's Magazine*, 104 (1834), 549. Thelwall's death in Feb. 1834 failed to attract the attention given to Hardy's in Oct. 1832. Ironically, the nemesis of the reformers, Sir John Scott (Earl of Eldon), also lived to see this new age, but his expectations, while great enough, were of a different nature altogether. Scott was a year older than Hardy yet survived to swear allegiance to Victoria.

[10] Hardy's funeral cortège to Bunhill Fields, complete with flags and banners bordered with crêpe displayed from houses and lining some streets, attracted thousands according to Thelwall, who believed that 20,000 to 40,000 people listened to his funeral oration. *Life*, 431.

decades of political unrest stemming in large part from the French Revolution:

the Jacobins are defunct, the Radicals are moderates, the Papists, being no longer kicked and abused, have become excellent subjects, the Tories have become Whigs, or something very like it.[11]

The resurgence of Reform later that year caught more than the *Chronicle* by surprise. Few can have imagined the number of men who championed Reform before the end of the year.

LOYAL REFORMERS

William IV himself partly accounted for this rapid change. After his accession, Englishmen could proudly champion Reform and claim to be expressing their loyalty to the King in doing so. The Reform Bill was the King's as well as Lord Grey's. Thomas Hardy noted that 'the King and his Ministers are now turned Parliamentary Reformers'.[12] Colchester's voters were deeply suspicious of change of any kind, yet they now accepted Reform largely as a result of the royalist guise in which it was presented. Those advocating Reform in Colchester called the election of 1831 a referendum in which 'for the first time in our history, *the Sovereign* has put the sincerity of his People to the test by calling upon them to declare whether our laws and liberties . . . shall be confided any longer to a vile and profligate Oligarchy . . . or whether the Commons of England shall hereafter be . . . a full and fair Representative of the People'.[13] Colchester's Radical MP, Daniel Whittle Harvey, assured voters that 'the grandchildren of your far-distant descendants will delight to trace back their pedigree to the men, who stood by their KING in the hour of their country's fate'.[14]

---

[11] *Shrewsbury Chronicle*, 16 July 1830. Dickinson has recounted recently the poignant episode of Major Cartwright dining with only three other members of the Hampden Club in 1814, and alone the next year. H. T. Dickinson, *British Radicals and the French Revolution* (Oxford, 1985), 76.

[12] Hardy, *Memoir*, 95.

[13] CLHL, Rebow Collection, E. COL. 1/9579, 49 (emphasis added).

[14] A. F. J. Brown, *Colchester, 1815–1914* (Chelmsford, 1980), 80, citing broadsheet, 5 June 1831.

Stressing the King's involvement, placards in Shrewsbury played upon Lord Nelson's famous appeal to 'duty'. The King had 'done his duty' in dissolving Parliament, and 'it now remains with you [the voter] to do yours. He [the King] relies upon your zealous support and trusts you will not disappoint his just expectations.' Another poster urged men to 'give each your sovereign, (if you will permit me a bad pun in good sense) to support your sovereign'.[15] If the King supported the measure and actually contributed to its creation, then opposition smacked of disloyalty or even treason. The *Shrewsbury Chronicle* mentioned the King's support at every opportunity, and reformist candidates covered the town with announcements about the Bill, 'sanctioned by HIS MAJESTY'. One placard, advertising 'Russell's Purge: A sovereign remedy for Aristocratic stomachs . . . that effectually exercises the spirit of Rebellion to a King's command', ended with the claim that the elixir was 'patronised by HIS MAJESTY!!'[16] At the 1831 election in Northampton, R. Vernon Smith argued that reformers who the year before had been 'friends of the people alone' now were 'friends of the King and the people'.[17] Ironically, even some of the more violent threats demanding Reform assumed an unmistakably loyalist tone. Weavers in Glasgow threatened that if the Lords 'should still persevere in their wicked purpose' in defeating the Bill, they would 'willingly arm themselves to a man in defence of the Throne and His Majesty's patriotic councillors'.[18]

Great Yarmouth's reformers announced in April 1831 'a glorious victory by the H.M.S. Reform', adding that 'whilst the ROYAL WILLIAM remains on the station, a stopper will be put upon their [the enemy's] unconstitutional practices'. Nottingham repeated this royal, nautical theme. A crowd met Sir Stephen Denman five miles out of town with Whig flags, 'at the top of one a figure of His Majesty as a true British tar, with the Reform Bill in his hand'.[19] Another Yarmouth placard announced a Reform Festival held 'UNDER THE AUSPICES OF WILLIAM IV'.[20] George Eliot reflected this attitude when she portrayed a slightly drunk farmer Dagley confronting Mr Brooke by saying: 'An' I meean as the King 'ull put a stop to 't

[15] SLHL, DA45/1170, 28 Apr. 1830. [16] Ibid., DA45/1170.
[17] E. G. Forrester, *Northamptonshire County Elections and Electioneering, 1695–1832* (Oxford, 1941), 132.
[18] *Westminster Review* (July 1831), 161.
[19] Sir J. Arnould, *Lives of the Chief Justices* (London, 1881), v. 249–50, 273.
[20] BL, N. TAB 2021/6/1. 21, 71.

[abuse], for them say it as knows it, as there's to be a Rinform.'[21] Dagley's vision of a 'Rinforming' King improving the country was a widespread and remarkably persistent image. As late as 1837 references were still being made to 'William the Reformer'.[22]

This vision of a reforming King also held sway among some of Reform's opponents who pointed bitterly to the results of the King's alleged support. The freeholders from the Isle of Portland who branded the Bill a trick in October 1831 claimed to have been 'deceived into support of the Bill in the first instance by the abuse of the King's name'.[23] The Portland freeholders had awakened to their mistake in time, but many took far longer to question the relationship between Reform and William IV. One particularly prescient attack in 1831 anticipated the King's actual role as it forecast him threatening 'to *swamp* the House of Lords' by 'peremptorily' creating 'a sufficient number of peers to nullify' all opposition.[24]

Partly as a result of the King's support, expectations raised by Reform among thousands of Englishmen in 1830 and 1831 exceeded Hardy's. Many felt that only the Reform Bill could save England from catastrophe. Some of their expressions of hope were couched in language inspired by or likely to inspire fear. George Whiting, the Whig editor of the *Maidstone Gazette*, professed to 'tremble for the consequences' if Reform failed.[25] Macaulay gave fuller expression to fears like those of Whiting and others when he told that Commons that if Reform were not forthcoming, 'I pray to God that none of those who concur in rejecting it may ever remember their votes with unavailing regret, amidst the wreck of laws, the confusion of ranks, the spoliation of property, and the dissolution of social order.'[26] If Macaulay's warning was in part the hyperbole of a Commons debate, incendiary activity in many counties, widespread hunger after successive bad harvests, and evidence of some extremely hostile

[21] G. Eliot, *Middlemarch* (New York, 1985), 361.

[22] *Maidstone Gazette*, 28 July 1835. The *Gazette*, now calling for municipal reform, held high hopes of 'William the Reformer' retaining 'sufficient firmness' in backing his Whig ministers. Writing to his fellow electors at the time of the King's death in 1837, an 'Old Elector' reminded Lewes's reformers of how 'kind a benefactor . . . [William IV] was to his people *by giving them the Reform Act*'. BL, Add. MSS 64813/ 53, Pelham MSS, press clipping of 10 July 1837, 'An Old Elector to the Electors of Lewes'.

[23] *Parl. Deb.* 8 (20 Oct. 1831), 932.

[24] *Great Britain in 1841, or The Results of the Reform Bill* (London, 1831), 11.

[25] *Maidstone Gazette*, 2 Feb. 1830.   [26] Veitch, *Parliamentary Reform*, 355.

public opinion in petitions for Reform lent credence to his distress.[27] Carlyle had in the previous year cautioned against the common view that society 'is fast falling in pieces; and a time of unmixed evil is come'.[28] That he did not share this bleak outlook seemed less important than its wide currency.

Francis Place expected parliamentary reform to lead to nothing less than 'a better administration of the Poor Laws, a repeal of the Corn Laws, of all laws restricting trade and commerce, economy in the administration of the public revenue, decrease of taxation', and the 'reform of the laws, especially those which relate to the administration of justice'.[29] If few commentators were as precise, many shared these expectations. William Cobbett felt that Reform would be 'the means of removing our poverty and misery and delivering our country from this mass of crime and disgrace'.[30] Lewes petitioners in 1831 were hardly less optimistic in expecting the prompt passage of Reform to alleviate 'the great distress at present existing among all the productive classes of the community ... [that may] be attributed to the corrupt state of Representation'.[31]

Many shared this vision that political change would somehow correct England's social and economic woes. Montagu Gore, trying to avoid hyperbole, wrote: 'When then, I am asked, will this Bill give clothes to the naked and food to the hungry? I reply, no; nor will it assure favourable seasons, nor avert pestilence, nor promote our discovery of the stone to which alchymists have attached so much virtue. These idle wishes and ideas I leave to the ultras of either party.'[32] And absurd views were not limited to party ultras. William Holsworthy dismissed as 'ridiculous' the views he heard expressed so often that:

'Farmer so and so who thinks that the Reform Bill will abolish all rent and tithes;'—'this or that mechanic thinks that henceforth bread will be had for nothing, and that there will be no further necessity for labour;' 'such and

[27] Bedfordshire, Oxfordshire, Sussex, and Westmorland contested three of the five elections. Along with Devonshire and Huntingdonshire, then, only 15% of England's counties participated in a majority of the general elections while 25% participated in none.

[28] Cited in B. Hilton, *The Age of Atonement* (Oxford, 1988), 213–14.

[29] G. Wallas, *The Life of Francis Place* (New York, 1919), 288, 254–5.

[30] W. Cobbett, *Cobbett's Twopenny Trash* (London, 1851), 241.

[31] V. Smith (ed.), *The Town Book of Lewes, 1702–1837*, (Sussex Record Society, 69; 1972–3), 270–90. 26 Jan. 1831.

[32] M. Gore, *What Will Be the Practical Effects of the Reform Bill?* (London, 1831), 22, 14–15.

such an Irishman thinks it will lead to an equalization of property',—and such like unfounded and senseless notions, which it is by no means improbable that a few poor ignorant fellows may entertain.

In recording these anecdotes, however, Holsworthy both confirmed the prevalence of wildly optimistic expectations of 'Rinform' and unintentionally fuelled the already wild fire by answering his question, 'What Will Reform Do?' with the claim that it would lead to 'the removal of a mass of iniquity and crime, . . . the gradual, but inevitable abolition of all other abuses and corruptions both in Church and State, both in our foreign and domestic policy', and the ultimate banishment 'to a very considerable extent, poverty and vice'.[33] While stopping short of claiming that Reform would guarantee good weather, cure scrofula, and turn lead into gold, Holsworthy closely approximated the views belittled by Gore. Enthusiasm for Reform led Holsworthy into hyperbolic nonsense despite himself.

Nor, of course, were Reform's proponents alone in their hyperbole. The excesses of the doomsayers may have surpassed those of the heralds. One Tory pamphleteer described a Rip Van Winklish hero falling into a decade-long slumber in 1831. Waking from his ten-year nap, the story's hero encountered his prematurely aged brother who explained that Reform had killed their mother by breaking her heart and had forced their clergyman father into a penurious exile. These familial disasters stemmed from the general calamities brought on by Reform. In reformed England, Oxford and Cambridge had been attacked, dispossessed, and opened to all religions, tithes had been abolished, and the Church disestablished. The £10 franchise had swamped the electorate with labourers who quickly transformed MPs into mere delegates who now shared a chamber, the House of Delegates, with the remnants of the House of Lords. Primogeniture had been eliminated, and all wealth had been redistributed. The repeal of the Corn Laws had imposed free trade. The results had been as devastating to trade and commerce as the elimination of tithes had been destructive of the Church. Ireland had been lost. Topping off this catalogue of horror was the King's flight to Hanover, an entirely just fate for the 'Patriot King' whose reformist stance in 1831 had critically assisted England's collapse.[34]

---

[33] C. Croxall, *What Will Reform Do?* (Birmingham, 1832), 14–21.
[34] *Great Britain in 1841*, 3–25.

Projecting as fearsome a scenario of reformed England, another popular pamphlet forecast twentieth-century England as a place destroyed by deceptively mild Whig reforms.[35] This pamphlet described a reign of terror complete with a 'new patent British guillotine'. The King was blamed for not resisting 'Radical Reform'. The House of Lords had survived the mêlée, but its complete destruction might have sounded less frightening to many readers than a revamped aristocracy containing the likes of Viscount Cobbett and Lord (Daniel Whittle) Harvey. Daniel O'Connell and Henry Hunt remained in the lower house, but as Secretary for Ireland and Home Secretary respectively. Few more generally horrifying possibilities existed in 1831.

Others observers thought that it was either too late, or that Reform was a principal component of the disease rather than the cure. The Duke of Wellington predicted lugubriously that 'in a short time . . . nothing will remain of England but the name and the soil'.[36] Lord Wharncliffe believed that England was 'gravitating towards a revolution' as a result of Reform, because the influence of the 'respectable persons of the middle class' was 'overwhelmed by the numerical strength of the low voters, who want to go to all lengths'.[37] A Doyle cartoon of 4 April 1831 foretold the death of the Constitution within a decade of Reform on a tombstone inscribed:

> Here lyeth the British Constitution,
> which, after a rapid decline of ten years,
> departed this world, 1841.
> I was well;
> wishing to be better,
> here I am.
> *Sic transit gloria mundi.*[38]

---

[35] This pamphlet sold more than 12,000 penny copies. *A Leaf from the Future History of England* (London, 1831), 1–12. Roake and Varty, the publishers of *A Leaf,* proudly listed their best-selling pamphlets on the last page of *Hints to Electors* (1831). The *Real Character and Tendency of the Proposed Reform* (1831) led the field by a wide margin with sales of 58,000, but *A Leaf* ranked fifth, just after two other penny pamphlets about Reform and, at tuppence, *The Life and Death of Swing.* See also *Weekly Political Register,* 19 Mar. 1831.

[36] A. Aspinall (ed.), *Three Early Nineteenth Century Diaries* (London, 1952), p. xxxi.

[37] C. F. Greville, *The Greville Memoirs,* ed. H. Reeve (London, 1896–9), ii. 55–6.

[38] *A Very Prophetical and Pathetical Allegory,* in *A Catalogue of Prints and Drawings in the British Museum. Division 2: Political and Personal Satires,* comp. F. G. Stephens, E. Hawkins, and M. D. George, 11 vols. (London, 1879–1954), xi. 462.

In the midst of so much hope and fear the ardently reformist *Northampton Free Press* perceived the situation more realistically. It did 'not regard the reform bill as a panacea which will or can cure the countless ills which the people have become heir to from the rule of the Tories, and the system of misgovernment which has been pursued particularly since the year 1790', but believed the Act would 'stay further ills'.[39]

GREAT EXPECTATIONS MET?

Opinions about Reform since its passage have been as diverse as those expressed in the tense days of 1831. Many heralded Reform as everything its advocates had promised. In 1836 the *Westminster Review* saw Reform as 'our taking of the Bastille; it was the first act of our great political change; and like its precursor', the *Review* confidently predicted, 'it is a sample of the character of all that will follow'.[40] Conversely, many dismissed it as ineffective. In Karl Marx's eyes, the Reform Act was, 'by a series of the most extraordinary tricks, frauds, and juggles . . . calculated not for increasing middle-class influence, but for the exclusion of Tory and the promotion of Whig patronage'.[41] Benjamin Disraeli and his sister Sarah agreed that Reform was nothing more than a political ploy devised by the Whigs with the sole objective of dishing the Tories. Whig swindlers intended Reform 'to root up the power of their opponents; and to destroy the happy balance of parties in the state, which in an aristocratic country is indispensable to the freedom and felicity of the mass'.[42] Some of those who thought more highly of the Act felt that it would prove inadequate in the absence of additional changes, notably the secret ballot, without which 'the representative system is utterly defeated', because 'if bribery and

[39] *Northampton Free Press*, 7 Jan. 1832.
[40] *Westminster Review*, 25 (4 Apr.1836), 271, 276.
[41] Karl Marx, 'Lord John Russell', in *Karl Marx and Frederick Engels on Britain* (Moscow, 1962), 451–4. George Eliot also refers to the trick in *Felix Holt* (Harmondsworth, 1972), 396. D. C. Moore, *Politics of Deference, passim*.
[42] B. and S. Disraeli, *A Year at Hartlebury* (London, 1834), 104–5. For recent accounts of the debate see I. D. C. Newbould, *Whiggery and Reform 1830–1841* (Stanford, Calif., 1990), particularly chs. 2 and 3, and E. A. Smith, *Lord Grey, 1764–1845* (Oxford, 1990), ch. 6.

intimidation are not effectually restrained, the Reform Bill will prove worse than a nonentity—a positive curse'.[43]

Much of the subsequent debate over 1832 has stemmed from the prevailing harsh perceptions of the electoral system that it replaced. Those who accepted the negative image of an entirely venal and corrupt unreformed system as popularized by William Hogarth's mocking paintings and prints were predisposed to champion Reform. If one believed with the Porritts, Joseph Grego, and others, that the unreformed electoral system was a cesspool reeking of undiluted corruption, unmitigated coercion, and unsurpassed chicanery of every imaginable kind, then any process that began to drain the foul sump was of necessity a 'good thing'.[44] Any political system would seem virtuous in comparison to the one described by the Porritts. Histories that damned the unreformed electoral system with impressive unanimity tended to glorify Reform for its role in diminishing the spectre of borough mongers, corruption, and unreformed elections 'determined by a small minority of the voters'.[45] And since this harshly negative view of the old system has proven to be 'one of the most powerful orthodoxies in modern British historiography', 1832 became a great watershed virtually by default.[46]

The dominant interpretation of 1832 in recent years, however, has been shaped by Norman Gash's contention that 'we have for the most part attributed, not perhaps too much, but the wrong kind of importance to the Reform Act of 1832'. By highlighting the unbroken influence of political patrons, the many unaltered local political climates in which electoral violence and corruption still flourished, and the continuing influence of the Court in elections after 1832, Gash simultaneously cast reformed and unreformed

---

[43] A. Buller, 'Bribery and Intimidation at Elections', *Westminster Review*, 25 (1836), 485–513. Buller, a barrister, became an MP with a speciality in electoral corruption. W. E. Houghton, *The Wellesley Index to Victorian Periodicals 1824–1900*, 5 vols. (Toronto, 1966–89), iii. 573.

[44] W. Hogarth, *Four Prints of an Election*, 1755–58; Grego, *History*; Porritt and Porritt, *Unreformed House*. [45] Trevelyan, *Lord Grey*.

[46] F. O'Gorman, 'Electoral Deference in "Unreformed" England, 1760–1832', *Journal of Modern History*, 56 (1984), 393. Molesworth thought that the Reform Bill could 'be regarded by every Englishman with feelings of unmixed pride and satisfaction', a feeling that many shared for at least a century after the Bill's passage. He recognized that England's *menu peuple* 'no doubt . . . greatly exaggerated the effects which that measure would produce, and overlooked many causes of distress which it would not remove, but still they were right in their belief that it would tend to ameliorate their condition, as the event has abundantly proved'. *Reform Bill*, 1.

electoral systems in a harshly negative light.[47] Gash limited Reform's benefits primarily to party activity at the national level. He minimized its local impact, claiming that by the mid-1840s, 'party [in Berkshire and by inference other places] was still only a vague and half-recognized element' in local politics. Gash saw little reason to believe that local politics had improved and cited in support of his contention a Maidstone MP's claim that Maidstone's reformed voters were 'if possible worse than the old'.[48] Gash also paid much attention to allegations of bribery at Great Yarmouth in 1835 when the Tories allegedly bought both seats by paying 2 guineas for each double vote. Gash argued that 'when the reversion to the old technique of electioneering brought such immediate success, few candidates or agents could long withstand the temptation to concede to the prejudices of the electorate in favour of material inducements'.[49] Unreformed and reformed England stood condemned equally.

Certainly corruption in various forms survived Reform. Before the end of the century, Parliament disfranchised for corruption two of the eight boroughs considered in the following chapters. The reputations of the remaining six were far from untarnished; reputations for electoral integrity were all too rare in nineteenth-century England. The allegations of corruption in Yarmouth are undoubtedly correct. Many of the town's voters were 'fond of seeing the king's picture', preferably against a gold rather than a silver background.[50] Gash's conclusions, however, are suspect. The notoriety of Yarmouth's corruption prompted an investigation by the House of Commons. Paradoxically, while confirming its existence, the investigatory committee concluded that such wholesale and standardized corruption failed to negate the electoral process. If votes in Yarmouth (and elsewhere) were worth a set price payable by either side regardless of the outcome of the election, electors operated as freely as if no money had been offered at all. Differential payments for votes and other more serious forms of corruption marred some elections in some boroughs, but the bulk of the evidence from the boroughs examined in the following chapters suggests that however visible corruption may have been at times, it was on the whole politically irrelevant.[51]

[47] *Age of Peel*, pp. ix–x. [48] Greville, *Memoirs*, iii. 132–3, 1 Jan. 1835.
[49] Gash, *Age of Peel*, 124.
[50] Buller, 'Bribery and Intimidation', 485–513.
[51] Surprisingly few boroughs were disfranchised for corruption over the century.

THE POLITICS OF DEFERENCE?

Should deference be dismissed along with corruption? D. C. Moore has argued for the persistence and power of 'deference' in reformed England. His revisionist thesis, built upon the work of Victor Turner, rests upon the assumption that post-Reform politics merely continued older modes of behaviour.[52] In 1840, as in 1740, Englishmen carried on the 'politics of deference'; traditional modes of behaviour dominated both old and new voters after 1832. Moore argued that 'when the continued existence of the traditionally structured deference communities and deference networks was . . . threatened, steps were taken to perpetuate them and thus to perpetuate the roles and status of traditional élites'.[53] Far from conceding power to the masses, Moore's Reform Act preserved aristocratic control, both over the electorate and in Parliament. Moore also stressed the pre-eminence of the county electorates, though the counties usually did not contest general elections prior to Reform and continued their relative inactivity after 1832. Richard Davis's close examination of Buckinghamshire politics, however, is one of many that reached the opposite conclusion. If voters in Buckinghamshire were any indication, 'the importance of landed influence has been vastly over-rated, more especially, if, as with Moore, "influence" and "control" often seem to be used interchangeably'. Of the three potential factors behind votes (influence, principle, and party), 'landed influence, as such, was the least important'.[54]

The quality and quantity of Moore's evidence is suspect. His

Grampound began the process in 1821, followed by Sudbury (1844), St Albans (1852), Lancaster, Reigate, Totnes, and Great Yarmouth (1867), and finally Beverley, Bridgwater, Cashel, and Sligo (1869).

[52] See e.g. V. Turner, 'Variations on a Theme of Liminality', in S. F. Moore and B. Myerhoff (eds.), *Secular Ritual* (Amsterdam, 1977), 36–52; S. F. Moore, 'Political Meetings and the Simulations of Unanimity', ibid. 151–72.

[53] *Politics of Deference*, 15–23. Moore examined Huntingdonshire (1826, 1830, 1831, and 1837), Cambridgeshire (1826, 1830, 1831 by-election, 1833 by-election and 1835), and Northamptonshire (1831), along with its subsequent divisions in 1832, 1835, and 1837. He cites another dozen poll books, but provides no detailed analyses of them.

[54] R. W. Davis, *Political Change and Continuity, 1760–1885* (Newton Abbot, 1972), 98; id., 'Toryism to Tamworth: The Triumph of Reform, 1827–1835', *Albion*, 12 (1980), 132.

reference to 'all the voters' in Lowick voting Tory in 1835, for example, seems less impressive when the *all* is translated into the grand total of four men that it represented. Moore pointed to the initial refusal of candidates in Oxfordshire to conduct a joint campaign in 1831 as evidence of the lack of partisan feeling in the county, yet failed to acknowledge the candidates' rapid acquiescence to a political reality that mandated a coalition.[55] In fact the partisan unity of the 1831 Oxfordshire contest against the initial wishes of the candidates argues for a political environment in counties as well as towns quite unlike Moore's vision. J. R. Fisher has pointed to the many other influences affecting county voters.[56] Aside from pointing to the inaccuracy of some of Moore's extremely rare percentages, Fisher argued that if the independent electors of South Nottingham-shire, one of England's most aristocratic counties, were able to command one county Member until the reforms of the 1880s, it seems unreasonable to dismiss the power of independent county electors.[57]

Moore's argument was ostensibly limited to the county electorates and the period before the Reform Act of 1867, but it was extended both spatially and chronologically by Patrick Joyce. Rather than ending with the second Reform Act as new influences such as class began to redefine voting groups, Joyce's view mirrored *Vanity Fair*'s: 'counties are naturally the appanage of the landowners and the cities of millowners and merchants.' Joyce concluded that 'in industrial Lancashire at least, for decades after 1867, class lines had not become 'too sharp' nor interest groups 'too jumbled', nor had

[55] J. Cannon, *Parliamentary Reform*, 246–8, 293–8; D. Eastwood, 'Toryism, Reform, and Political Culture in Oxfordshire, 1826–1837', *Parliamentary History*, 7 (1988), 114. Edwin Jaggard's detailed study of Cornwall also rejects Moore's hypothesis: 'Cornwall, it seems, provides "another face of reform" markedly different from that originally suggested by Professor Moore.' Moore's 'model is irrelevant to developments in Cornwall'. Jaggard's Cornwall also failed to resemble Davis's Buckinghamshire, indicating something of the complexity of politics during the Reform era. Davis, *Change and Continuity*, 98; E. Jaggard, 'Cornwall Politics, 1826–1832: Another Face of Reform?', *Journal of British Studies*, 22 (1983), 81, 96; id., 'The Parliamentary Reform Movement in Cornwall, 1805–1826', *Parliamentary History*, 2 (1983), 113–29.

[56] J. R. Fisher, 'Issues and Influence: Two By-Elections in South Nottinghamshire in the Mid-Nineteenth Century', *Historical Journal*, 24 (1981), 155–63.

[57] Fisher's scrutiny reduced Moore's 24% rate of unanimity by half, and his estimate of 56–92% in which overwhelming patterns existed to little over a third. The inclusion of outvoters would have reduced the percentages further. 'Issues and Influence', 156.

social and economic categories 'ceased to overlap'. In his scenario, the 'politics of deference' continued to dominate politics in the urban, post-1867 world.[58]

Davis's emphasis on continuity in Aylesbury across the Reform era was predicated upon an unusually favourable assessment of unreformed popular politics in Buckinghamshire that involved local party activity before and after 1832. As such, Davis's work helped restore to England's much maligned voters a large measure of the integrity previously denied them. A range of eighteenth-century specialists have supported this position and shown that corruption, coercion, and chicanery notwithstanding, England's voters could, and with increasing frequency did, play an integral part in the nation's political processes. O'Gorman's reminder that unreformed electoral politics often involved a 'reciprocal concept of deference', where deference was involved at all, highlighted much work that has demonstrated the existence of considerable freedom of choice in the electorate well in advance of 1832. Emphases on continuity across the unreformed and reformed political systems have been positive as well as negative, and Reform's potential impact takes on an entirely different perspective if the emphasis on continuity rests upon a positive assessment of the Hanoverian electorate.

THE STRUCTURE OF ELECTORAL POLITICS

The renewed focus on the unreformed electoral system has permitted answers to many fundamental questions about its composition, greatly facilitating a fully informed evaluation of Reform's impact. Two interrelated questions concerning the physical impact of Reform at its most basic level are the size of the electorate across these years and the extent of electoral turnout. The absence of electoral registers prior to 1832 prevents precise answers for the unreformed electorate, but reasonably accurate comparisons of the electorates of unreformed and reformed England are possible.

Electoral size is the simpler of the two issues. The unreformed electoral system increased from approximately 338,000 in the later

[58] *Vanity Fair*, 29 Mar. 1873, 97; P. Joyce, 'The Factory Politics of Lancashire in the Later Nineteenth Century', *Historical Journal*, 18 (1975), 528; id., *Work, Society, and Politics* (New Brunswick, NJ, 1980).

years of the eighteenth century to just over 439,000 on the eve of Reform. Since the reformed electorate is known to have numbered 656,000, the Reform Act increased the electorate overall by nearly 50 per cent.[59] Much of the increase, of course, stemmed from the addition of £10 householders in England's borough constituencies, which generated a wide variety of alterations across England's electoral landscape. Newly qualified householders in Maidstone outnumbered the 'ancient-right' voters (freemen in this instance) from the beginning. Maidstone's new electoral register listed only 456 ancient-right freemen who shared political power with 652 newly enfranchised householders. And following the pattern common in all boroughs, the gradual elimination of the ancient-right voters through death and migration led to a slowly but steadily increasing proportion of householders in the electorate. By 1841 householders accounted for 63 per cent of Maidstone's electoral register. The residency requirement of the new Act most affected freeman boroughs such as Maidstone; approximately 80,000 non-resident freemen across England lost their votes to Reform.[60] The changes in electoral boundaries that accompanied Reform also reduced the number of freemen by excluding those who lived near some towns but not near enough to be counted as a resident.[61] Colchester, greatly affected by the disfranchisement of non-resident

[59] Davis, *Change and Continuity*, 15–105; id., 'Toryism to Tamworth', 132. O'Gorman's revised figures settle the question. *Voters*, 178–80.

[60] The new residency requirement disfranchised more than 40% of the total number of freemen. C. Seymour, *Electoral Reform in England and Wales* (New Haven, Conn., 1915) 27–44. The percentage of 'old' voters in the boroughs examined here varied from 20% at Great Yarmouth and 24% at Beverley, to 57% in Lewes and Bristol. Shrewsbury and Northampton both contained 47% 'old' voters, while Maidstone and Colchester contained 34% and 36% respectively. J. H. Philbin, *Parliamentary Representation 1832* (New Haven, Conn., 1965), 193–4.

[61] The Boundary Act, (2 & 3 William IV, c. 64) did not change the parliamentary boundaries of Colchester, Northampton, and Maidstone. The five other boroughs, however, experienced change, some of it massive. The number of houses in Bristol e.g. increased from 9,700 to 17,842. Yarmouth, on the other hand, experienced a modest increase from 5,075 to 5,578. Beverley's increase was smaller, an addition of fewer than 200 to the original 1,740. According to Seymour, properties valued at less than £10 ordinarily were not assessed scot and lot. *Electoral Reform*, 35–8, 255–7. Only in London would a £10 house be occupied by someone who might by any stretch of the imagination be considered working class. Lindert and Williamson suggest that the bottom chargeable house was £5 in 1820, rising to £10 by 1830. P. Lindert and J. G. Williamson, 'Reply to N. F. R. Crafts', *Journal of Economic History*, 45 (1985), 146. See also T. J. Nossiter, *Influence, Opinion, and Political Idioms in Reformed England* (Hassocks, 1975), 162–76; J. R. S. Vine, *English Municipal Institutions* (London, 1879), 25.

freemen, also experienced an immediate householder majority, while freemen constituted only a third of Liverpool's new electoral register.[62] Reform might have been expected to enfranchise only a handful of householders in Bristol since the town's unusual 'county' status already enfranchised 40-shilling freeholders, but the more than 4,000 'ten-pound renters' added in 1832 constituted more than a third of the total. Householders comprised only 14 per cent of Beverley's new electorate. Similarly, Yarmouth's freemen contributed almost two-thirds of the town's voters a decade after Reform. Urban property values as well as franchise requirements could dramatically affect the implementation of the new £10 qualification. Lewes's 'scot and lot' franchise had generated a relatively inclusive electorate prior to Reform; ancient-right voters constituted almost 80 per cent of the 1832 electorate.

Altogether, the electorates of the eight boroughs examined in the following chapters contained more than 20,000 voters in 1832 out of a combined population of just over 203,000, meaning that roughly 40 per cent of their adult males were enfranchised. This percentage, while considerably higher than that of the country as a whole, reflected a change from unreformed levels in these towns only in the sense that the percentage of enfranchised *residents* rose considerably. The total number of electors remained surprisingly stable because the broad unreformed franchise of towns such as Northampton left little room for increases, and the disfranchisement of non-resident freemen in other towns often offset the addition of £10 householders. Northampton's electorate actually decreased in 1832, as did Beverley's. The number of voters participating in elections in Bristol, Great Yarmouth, Lewes, and Colchester changed little. Only Maidstone registered an appreciable overall increase.[63]

---

[62] Using the poll books, freeholders cannot be distinguished positively from 'ancient-right' freemen in Maidstone until the election of 1835, but the uniformity of the proportion of freeholders at the elections of 1835 (59.3%), 1837 (59.9%), and 1841 (62.4%) suggests that the first reformed electorate contained the same proportions. Lindert estimates an average annual rental of £3 to £4 for untaxed houses in 19th-cent. towns. Lindert and Williamson, 'Reply to Crafts', 146.

[63] Householders were not distinguished in Bristol elections after 1832, but their proportional increase probably would have been more rapid than in other towns since those who otherwise would have qualified as freeholders prior to Reform would have been added as householders after 1832. The figures reported for these constituencies were calculated from precise identifications in the relevant poll books.

ELECTORAL TURNOUT AND THE REFORM ACT

Voter turnout in unreformed England has recently attracted much attention. J. C. D. Clark has discounted the quarter of a million enfranchised Englishmen who went to the hustings with such frequency under William III and Anne, and who continued to poll in very large numbers if less often under the first four Georges. Despite their sheer numbers, Clark has suggested that the irregularity of their participation raises questions about the degree to which Augustan electors were politically involved. As Clark notes, 'in the late twentieth century we are accustomed to regular turnouts in general elections of nearly 80 per cent of those on the electoral register'.[64] Yet by this very standard, the unreformed borough electorate measured up very well indeed.

Turnout rates for unreformed electors at specific elections can usually only be estimated, but contemporary accounts often identified non-voters meticulously. Measuring turnout in more than two dozen boroughs and three counties over the ninety years following 1741, O'Gorman found turnout rates consistently high, often exceeding Clark's 80 per cent standard. Ninety-six per cent of Oxfordshire's voters cast ballots in 1747, yet they were outdone by Lincolnshire's electors in 1818. Minehead's virtually complete participation in 1754 and in 1790 could not be improved upon, but many other boroughs regularly achieved turnouts above 90 per cent. Maidstone's 90 per cent in 1774 was topped by Derby's 97 per cent. Rochester's 88 per cent in 1806 fell short of Oxford's 90 per cent that year. While a general figure cannot be derived from such sporadic evidence, there can be little doubt that very high turnouts characterized many unreformed elections. Moreover, participation levels tended to increase somewhat in the half-century leading to Reform. Much additional data could be mustered to corroborate O'Gorman's, including figures for the towns in this study. Maidstone's poll books contained very precise accounts of those entitled to vote who were absent. Only 75 per cent of the town's qualified voters participated in 1826, possibly because of a lack-lustre campaign, but in 1830 nearly 85 per cent turned out, followed by more than 90 per cent in 1831.[65]

[64] J. C. D. Clark, *English Society, 1688–1832* (Cambridge, 1985), 17.

[65] Electoral participation in contemporary American Presidential elections rose

Many other towns achieved similar heights. Turnout at Northampton's elections between 1818 and 1831 consistently topped 70 per cent. Lewes's meticulously kept poll books indicate turnouts between 80 per cent and 94 per cent. The logistical problems encountered by boroughs as large as Bristol, notably the expense of bringing in outvoters, failed to keep two-thirds or more of all electors from participating ordinarily. Turnout in Beverley before 1832 usually topped 80 per cent. Any constituency could experience a low participation rate on occasion as a result of a prematurely closed poll, the resignation of a candidate, or some other reason unrelated to the desire of the voters to record their choices, but most normal polls generated very high turnouts. An election as unusual as the 1819 by-election in Shrewsbury that pitted a hard-drinking, fox-hunting gambler against the son of an archdeacon who had 'never brought a blush to his father's face' managed to elicit votes from more than half of the enfranchised.[66]

Reformed turnout rates were even higher, in part because of structural changes occasioned by Reform that inadvertently encouraged participation. The 1832 expansion of the electorate would have caused difficulties if the old system of polling had been maintained. The reduction of the polling period from a maximum of fifteen days, Sundays excluded, first to only two days, and then to a single day between 8 a.m. and 4 p.m., would have crushed the old system.[67] The provision of annually revised electoral registers by the Act, however, vastly increased the speed with which electors could be handled; obstreperous parties could no longer obstruct elections by objecting to electors from the camp of the opposition. The process of casting one's vote could be extremely time-consuming at

from an anaemic 26.9% in 1824 to 57.6% in 1828, and reached an impressive 80.2% in 1840. State and local contests had attracted a higher participation rate from earlier in the century. For the rest of the century, the range remained between 66% and 84%. R. L. McCormick, 'New Perspectives on Jacksonian Politics', *American Historical Review*, 65 (1960), 288–301.

[66] E. Edwards, *Parliamentary Elections of the Borough of Shrewsbury* (Shrewsbury, 1859), 21.

[67] O'Gorman agrees that post-Reform rates were often even higher. F. O'Gorman, 'Electoral Behaviour in England, 1700–1832', in P. Denley et al. (eds.), *History and Computing II* (Manchester, 1989), 225. The maximum of 40 days established in 1696 had been reduced to 15 in 1785. For a full account of polling, poll books, and related topics see O'Gorman, *Voters*, 129–41. The Polls at Elections Act (5 & 6 William IV, c. 36) reduced the Reform Bill's two days to a single day between 8 a.m. and 4 p.m. No oaths were to be administered and no more than 300 voters were to be handled by one polling booth, thus making this abbreviated election time possible.

unreformed contests. Without the remarkably careful orchestration of a substantial portion of Bristol's electorate by the White Lion party, for example, the relatively high turnouts of the unreformed period would not have been possible. The party showed considerable skill in ensuring that voters arrived at the hustings willing to wait as long as necessary and prepared to defend their right to vote with copies of their freedoms.[68]

Voter registration helps explain high turnouts after 1832. However intense efforts before Reform might have been, they were invariably hobbled by the lack of registration lists. Canvassers typically had to rely on poll books from the most recent contested election. With the ready availability of published, comprehensive, lists of electors after 1832, however, canvassers' efforts could be much more thorough. And thorough they appear to have been. The determination with which canvassers scoured constituencies for every available elector is often reflected in the poll book itself; a vote from every name on the registration list was expected, and poll books often listed reasons for a registered voter's failure to participate. The Lewes poll book of 1835 explained that of the thirty-eight voters who did not appear at the hustings, ten had left town, fourteen had died since the last revision of the register, and 14 were duplicate entries. Only thirteen unexplained non-voters marred the next election as actual turnout approached 99 per cent.[69] In this fashion, voter registration lists helped ensure some improvement after 1832, though great increases were impossible; the unreformed electorate turned out too fully to permit much change.

The Reform Act also tended to boost turnout by requiring constituencies to provide at least one polling-booth for every 600 electors. Some boroughs had bowed to the pressure of numbers before 1832 by establishing more voting-booths. Maidstone shifted from one location in 1826 that took each voter as he arrived, to two separate booths in 1830 that divided the electorate by surname at the letter L to improve the flow of votes. Yet even those boroughs with improved facilities before Reform benefited from improvements

[68] BRO, Stedfast MSS 12144.
[69] HumRO, DDBC/11/54/5–7. Of the 28 specific measurements of turnout reported by O'Gorman for these 11 towns prior to 1832, only 3 reached 90%, while 12 of the 31 instances reported for those same towns after 1832 equalled or exceeded 90%. By-elections also attracted extremely high participation levels after 1832, such as Beverley's 1840 by-election with 966 of the town's 1,054 registered voters. O'Gorman, *Voters*, 184, 189–90, 195.

after 1832. Maidstone's voters found four booths awaiting their pleasure in 1832. In 1835 they encountered twelve polling stations, three each in the town's four wards, set up to deal with the electorate in three groups divided at the letters D and O.[70]

Most constituencies experienced similar improvements. Beverley provided two voting-tables in 1835, dividing the town geographically (north and south) instead of alphabetically. By 1841 the number of booths had doubled again, far in excess of the demands of the Act; between 224 and 269 voters used each of the polling-stations in 1841. Lewes shifted to two booths in 1830, and four in 1835 to serve an electorate of 800. The ratio of 200 voters per booth in Lewes and Beverley after Reform should have been sufficient, but Great Yarmouth went further in 1837. There, sixteen voting compartments handled roughly 1,600 registered electors. To speed the use of these voting-stations, Yarmouth divided voters (1) geographically, (2) into freemen and freeholders, and (3) alphabetically at the letter J. It is hardly surprising that Yarmouth's polling could be accomplished easily in a single day with a turnout of over 85 per cent.[71]

The alacrity with which these towns improved their physical facilities may be explained in part by the profitability of poll-booth construction. Candidates were assessed all costs associated with the erection of these structures, less any proceeds from the sale of the wood for scrap afterwards. In the days before the mandated increases, Colchester provided a single booth, erected at a cost of £82 in 1830. After the election the booth was sold at auction for £31, leaving the candidates to make up the £51 difference. More booths, justified by law, meant more profits for locals, and in an era of generally declining electioneering revenues, such opportunities were not likely to be missed. Candidates were not always subject to abuse of this sort. Approximately 10 per cent of Colchester's electorate cast their votes in the Conservative Committee Rooms in 1837 and saved the expense of yet another booth.[72]

These improvements led to extremely high turnouts. Participation rates in Shrewsbury, which had been high but spasmodic prior to Reform, settled into the consistent 90 per cent range after 1832. Northampton's turnouts had reached 90 per cent as early as 1784

---

[70] *The Poll for Electing Two Burgesses* (Maidstone, 1832), 37; *The Poll for Electing Two Burgesses* (Maidstone, 1835), 41.

[71] *Norwich Mercury*, 8 Jan. 1835; BL, N. TAB 2012/6, Aug. 1837.

[72] *The Poll* (Colchester, 1837), 23; *Colchester Gazette*, 4 Aug. 1837.

before falling to less complete albeit very respectable levels thereafter. Following Reform, every Northampton election involved approximately 95 per cent of the electorate. Similarly, Beverley's turnouts never fell below 95 per cent at elections following 1832. The degree of increased participation, however, is less impressive than the greater consistency of extraordinarily high turnouts achieved after Reform.[73] Still, variations occurred after Reform as well as before. After achieving a rate of 92 per cent in 1832, Maidstone's turnout fell to 74 per cent in 1835, only to rise again to about 87 per cent at the last two elections. Northampton, able to boast a rate of 97 per cent in 1835, could account for only 77 per cent of its electors in 1841.[74]

REFORM IN THE BOROUGHS

Instead of testing for Reform's impact among England's often somnolent county voters, this analysis examines politics in parliamentary boroughs. It does so by using poll books as a pathway into the political realities of individual English voters. The potential value of these rather mundane sources is now well known. John Cannon attracted wider attention to poll books nearly thirty years

[73] *The Poll for Electing Two Burgesses* (Maidstone, 1832, 1835, 1837, 1841); *The Poll at the Election* (Northampton, 1835); *Northampton Borough Election* (Northampton, 1841). Caution must be exercised in measuring turnout from electoral registers after 1832 because double entries for freemen who were also qualified as £10 householders exaggerated the size of the electorate in some boroughs. Beverley's electoral register contained 1,284 names in 1841 e.g., but 211 of those were double entries. Another 17 men still registered in 1841 had died between the revision in 1840 and the actual poll in 1841, reducing the actual potential electorate to 1,056. Of these, only 20 freemen and 24 householders failed to vote. Turnout measured by a straightforward comparison of the number voting with the number registered without making this correction would be grossly inaccurate. The 966 men who voted in the parliamentary election of 1837 actually constituted nearly 92% of all Yarmouth voters rather than the 76% indicated by a comparison to the total number of registered names.
[74] BL, N. TAB 2012/6, Aug, 1837. An 1837 Shrewsbury poll book used for a canvass book in 1841 marked 16 deaths, 4 who had 'left town', 18 whose addresses had changed, and 21 whose names were struck through without explanation. SLHL, *A Correct Alphabetical List of the Electors* (Shrewsbury, 1837). Newark poll books indicate 16%, 4%, and 11% missing from the elections of 1826 through 1831 respectively, while only 4% and 5% were absent in 1832 and 1841. *An Alphabetical List of the Poll* (Newark, 1826–41).

ago.[75] Several years later, studies by John Vincent and D. C. Moore employed nineteenth-century poll books to great advantage. Almost simultaneously, several studies demonstrated the enormous potential of eighteenth-century poll books.[76] Such has been their conjoint success that poll books now hardly need an introduction.

Printed poll books developed rapidly from an Act passed in the first session of William III's third Parliament (7 & 8 William III, c. 25) for preventing 'irregular proceedings of sheriffs and other officers' at contested elections. The Act failed to eradicate irregular proceedings, but its requirement that returning officers keep copies of polling-lists resulted almost immediately in the publication of poll books in some constituencies. An immediate ready market for these lists, coupled with the relative ease with which they could be produced, led local publishers to seize upon poll-book publishing as a new source of revenue. Printed poll books survive for roughly a third of all contested English elections between the reigns of William III and Victoria and for nearly half of all nineteenth-century contests.[77] Occasional gaps in the printed record can be filled in some instances by surviving unpublished poll books. The Bristol general election of 1820 failed to generate a poll book because no publisher sensed a market for a record of Henry Baillie's anaemic challenge to R. H. Davis and Henry Bright. Only 127 Bristolians voted for Baillie while nearly 3,000 voted for Davis and Bright. Fortunately, however, in this and a number of other instances, the manuscript poll book kept by the returning officers under the requirement of the Act of 1696 reveal the choices of voters.[78]

Poll books are remarkable documents. They varied widely from constituency to constituency, but at their most complete they recorded a voter's full name (including all given names), address (street and parish), occupation (as described by the voter himself), voting qualification (including the location of qualifying properties for freeholders and householders), and, of course, votes for the

---

[75] J. Cannon, 'Poll Books', *History*, 47 (1962), 166–9.

[76] For a fuller discussion, see O'Gorman, 'Electoral behaviour', 220–38. See also J. Gibson and C. Rogers, *Poll Books, 1696–1872* (Birmingham, 1989).

[77] J. Sims (ed.), *A Handlist of British Parliamentary Poll Books* (Leicester, 1984), pp. v–vii.

[78] The 1820 Bristol manuscript poll survives, but no one printed a poll book in 1818, and the manuscript disappeared in the 1970s after serving as the basis for J. Williams for 'Bristol in the General Elections of 1818 and 1820', *Transactions of the Bristol and Gloucestershire Archaeological Society*, 87 (1968), 173–201.

election in question. A broadly inclusive picture of electors can be built upon the base provided by the poll books. And by merging the information available for each elector from election to election, poll books permit electoral behaviour to be examined over the long term as well as cross-sectionally. If John Smith voted for Whig/reformer candidates in 1831, did he continue to vote for them in 1832 or did he defect to the Tories? If John Bull supported the Tories in 1826, did he continue to vote Tory well into the next decade? Did the ability of parties to attract and retain voters vary over time? Were voters who split their support between parties at a particular election likely to continue in their non-partisan ways? Questions such as these can be answered by the construction of what amount to panel surveys of voters.

At the same time, poll books provide the foundation for a more complete record of individual electors at specific elections. Poll books did not include information about each elector's economic status except indirectly through occupation. On the other hand, tax lists offer much information about the relative economic position of many voters, though such data are flawed and oblique. By joining the data concerning each voter from the poll books with available information about the amount each paid in poor rates and the like, the rental value of their dwellings, the total value of their real and personal property, the degree to which their tax assessments were in arrears, and other similar information contained in tax rolls, a remarkably comprehensive picture of individual voters can be created. These bits of information, systematically organized into comprehensive records for individual voters, can be augmented further with church and chapel membership rolls, baptismal lists, and burial records. The result is a set of comprehensive files containing dozens of variables about thousands of individual voters that permit cross-sectional and longitudinal analyses.

Employing extended and extensive records of this kind, the following chapters attempt a quantitative and qualitative assessment of the electoral system immediately before and after the Great Reform Act by systematically considering electoral behaviour in eight diverse English boroughs between 1818 and 1841. It cannot claim to provide generally inclusive answers to questions about the impact of Reform on England as a whole, but much is suggested by an analysis of the last five unreformed and first four reformed elections across a broad range of parliamentary boroughs, particularly in the context provided by O'Gorman's overview of the unreformed electorate. Gash recognized the difficulties inherent in drawing 'in anything like accurate detail the physiognomy of politics in an age so complex', but he was no less determined to draw exactly that.[79] This less ambitious analysis assesses the impact of 1832 upon the largest active segment of England's electoral system.[80]

No less true for reformed than unreformed England is O'Gorman's dictum that 'the study of electoral politics becomes the study of local communities'. Accordingly, this study takes the form of a series of local studies, usually in pairs. P. F. Clark has argued that 'national elections were essentially local in the late nineteenth century'.[81] I have argued elsewhere that some local elections were essentially national in the later eighteenth century.[82] J. P. Parry has concluded from Roland Thorne's study of the later Georgian Parliament that in the open boroughs, 'local interests had lined up behind national parties by 1818'.[83] But the way in which these interests had lined up, and the degree to which they did so can be revealed only by close analysis. The following analysis is conducted in the context of the local/national continuum in provincial England.

Of England's counties little will be said, in part because prior to the electoral registration requirements of the Great Reform Act the potential county electorate cannot be identified sufficiently well to measure even electoral basics such as turnout. Moreover, voters in the few counties where elections occurred sufficiently often to permit more than a single cross-sectional view are too poorly identified individually to permit a longitudinal study. County poll books never included occupations and suffer particularly from both large numbers of shared names and peripatetic populations. This dismissal of the county poll books has been called a 'counsel of despair', but impossible obstacles bar the way of a quantitative assessment of

---

[79] *Age of Peel*, p. xv.

[80] Letter-cluster sampling reduced the data requirements of this analysis. Nearly 26,000 voters were examined at all elections between 1818 (or 1812 in Bristol) and 1841. The entire electorates of Lewes and Shrewsbury were included; letter-cluster samples of approximately 25% were taken for the other towns. J. A. Phillips, 'Achieving a Critical Mass'.

[81] P. F. Clarke, 'Electoral Sociology of Modern Britain', *History*, 57 (1972), 31–55.

[82] J. A. Phillips, 'From Municipal Matters to Parliamentary Principles', *Journal of British Studies*, 27 (1988), 351.

[83] J. P. Parry, 'Constituencies, Elections, and Members of Parliament, 1790–1820', *Parliamentary History*, 7 (1988), 156.

county elections.[84] Even if the obstacles could be overcome, the potential rewards of a study of the county electorate would not be sufficient to justify the effort. Counties seldom contested elections to the point of a poll. At the five general elections preceding Reform, a quarter of England's counties permitted every election to pass unpolled. Another 40 per cent brought only one to a poll. Eight other counties polled only twice during these five opportunities, leaving four counties with three contests, and only two with four. None of England's counties polled all five general elections. Overall, a mere quarter of the county electorate voted in general elections during the first third of the nineteenth century, and the total fell at times as low as 10 per cent.[85] Nor was electoral activity common in England's sixty-eight reformed county constituencies. At the first four reformed elections, almost half of the county constituencies either failed entirely to mount a poll or staged only one; remarkably, only three counties contested all four general elections to the point of a poll.[86] Thus, tracing voters across elections in the counties is usually impossible for a variety of reasons, any one of which would be sufficient to stymie the exercise.

Both before and after 1832 most electoral activity occurred in the parliamentary boroughs. The counties may have contained a somewhat larger share of the nominal electorate, but the bulk of England's active voters resided in towns, partly because the boroughs controlled so many more seats. The English boroughs alone accounted for virtually half of the entire Commons.[87] English boroughs also reflected national political fluctuations much more accurately. Immediately after Reform, counties and boroughs alike returned nearly three times as many Whigs as Tories. By 1832 the national ratio of Whig to Tory victors fell to 0.8 (290:368), and

[84] S. W. Baskerville, '"Preferred Linkage" and the Analysis of Voter Behaviour in Eighteenth-Century England', *History and Computing*, 1 (1989), 118.

[85] Calculated from Cannon, *Parliamentary Reform*, 278–9.

[86] No polls occurred in 7 county constituencies during the first four reformed general elections; 24 others had only one. Only Buckinghamshire, South Essex, and East Norfolk polled all four times. Two-thirds of the new counties polled in 1832; one-third polled in 1835; half polled in 1837, and just over a quarter in 1841.

[87] The standard estimate of the unreformed electorate assigned nearly a quarter of a million (247,000) voters to the counties and 188,391 to the boroughs, proportions of 57% and 43% respectively. J. Lambert, 'Parliamentary Franchises Past and Present', *The Nineteenth Century* (Dec. 1889), 958. Cannon's estimate of the unreformed electorate reduced the total for both counties and boroughs, but his proportions remained almost identical at 55% and 45%. *Parliamentary Reform*, 290–2; Philbin, *Parliamentary Representation, passim*.

the borough ratio of roughly 1 was far more representative than the county ratio that fell to a pathetic 0.16 (20:124).[88] The decision to examine parliamentary boroughs exclusively forced a further selection. A systematic examination of surviving evidence for all boroughs would be impossible. The size of a single town like Bristol threatens a quantitatively based study, and the multiplication of problems of scale by the inclusion of all boroughs would prove fatal. If only some towns, then, which?

The eight constituencies in this study had very little in common other than their joint status as parliamentary boroughs. They ranged in size from Bristol, with more than 100,000 inhabitants in 1831, to Lewes, with fewer than 10,000. England's towns grew rapidly in these decades (the overall urban rate neared 23 per cent per decade). Bristol reflected the overall rate almost exactly. Absolute growth can be as dramatic as proportional growth, though, and if Bristol's growth was proportionately unremarkable, its explosion from 60,000 in 1801 to more than 120,000 in 1841 was impressive. Northampton and Maidstone grew more rapidly than the norm, but they both began the century with so few inhabitants that their rapid growth only allowed them to catch up with Shrewsbury and Colchester, both of which grew sluggishly. Beginning the century with 8,000 and 12,000 inhabitants respectively, Maidstone and Colchester both reached 18,000 in 1841. Only 7,000 people called Northampton home in 1801, but explosive growth allowed Northampton to reach 21,000 along with Shrewsbury in 1841, though Shrewsbury started with more than 15,000. Lewes, removed from the mainstream, also grew slowly, but not as slowly as Beverley and Great Yarmouth.[89]

[88] In England alone the Tories gained a lead in 1837. Overall election results in the first four reformed general elections were as follows:

Parliamentary seats

	1832		1835		1837		1841	
	Whig	*Tory*	*Whig*	*Tory*	*Whig*	*Tory*	*Whig*	*Tory*
UK	479	179	383	275	349	309	290	368
Boroughs*	244	83	192	135	185	142	167	160
Counties	104	40	74	70	47	97	20	124

* University seats included.
Source: C. Cook and B. Keith, *British Historical Facts* (New York, 1975), 138–9, based on *Constitutional Yearbook* (London, 1886).

[89] J. R. McCulloch, *A Statistical Account of the British Empire* (London, 1839), 405–6. For figures on Beverley and Bridgwater see J. Marshall, *Statistics of the British*

Geographically, these boroughs were scattered across the length and breadth of England. Beverley in the North balanced Lewes in the South. Great Yarmouth could not be further east, just as Bristol and Shrewsbury could not be much further west. Northampton occupies a central location, while Maidstone's proximity to London may have led to more influence from the capital. Substantial numbers of Maidstone's non-resident voters flocked in from London and its environs to participate in parliamentary general elections and occasionally in municipal elections.[90] The economic interests of these boroughs varied equally widely. Bristol and Yarmouth shared seafaring interests, but Bristol's commercial interests were so different from Yarmouth's that their common link to the sea resulted in few real similarities. Northampton's specialization in shoemaking was not matched by other towns, and the importance of paper manufacturing in Maidstone's economy was unique. Beverley's ancient connection with wool manufacturing, on the other hand, had long since evaporated, leaving the town without a particular purpose, much like Lewes.

Local government among the eight differed structurally as well as practically. Seven were governed by Corporations, but the range of local popular participation allowed by the Corporations could not have been more extreme. The Corporations of Bristol and Northampton were completely closed. Maidstone's was completely open and hotly contested; municipal elections there had rivalled parliamentary elections since at least the middle of the eighteenth century. The others fell somewhere in between, though on balance all were closed to meaningful popular participation. Beverley staged mayoral elections and allowed the town's capital burgesses to be 'shouted in', but neither process could be counted as an open election.[91]

These towns bestowed parliamentary franchises in somewhat varied fashion, but greater uniformity is apparent in this category than in any other. Borough franchise qualifications have usually

---

Empire (London, 1831). Measuring populations in these towns is complicated by the imposition of new electoral boundaries in 1832 as part of Reform.

[90] J. A. Phillips, 'Municipal Matters', *passim*.

[91] A. E. Cockburn, *The Corporations of England and Wales* (London, 1835). No report was filed for Colchester or Great Yarmouth. Lewes was not included because it had no Corporation to be investigated. For other towns: Beverley (Northern) 161; Bristol (Southern) 136; Maidstone (South-eastern) 109; Northampton (North Midlands) 197; Shrewsbury (North Midlands) 199. See also Vine, *English Municipal Institutions*, 25.

been grouped into five categories (freeman, scot and lot, burgage, Corporation, and potwalloper), but the actual variation among towns was far greater. Molesworth identified at least fifteen categories used to qualify voters.[92] Beverley, Bristol, Colchester, Maidstone, Shrewsbury, and Yarmouth shared freeman franchises. This heavy weighting in favour of freeman boroughs posed few analytical problems since 'freeman' boroughs contained the bulk of the electorate. And this common feature aside, many differences distinguished the six 'freeman' boroughs. All followed the norm and permitted non-resident freemen to vote, but in other ways their electorates were quite distinct. Bristol's rare administrative 'county' status permitted 40-shilling freeholders to vote. Shrewsbury was one of only five towns that permitted scot-and-lot paying householders to vote along with the freemen. Northampton, a potwalloper borough, was equally unusual in according the franchise to every resident adult male not on relief who possessed a 'pot to boil'. Though a scot and lot borough, Lewes also was unusual in possessing neither charter nor Corporation.

By O'Gorman's calculations, sixty-six of Engand's parliamentary constituencies were absolutely venal or proprietary (votes tied to pieces of property). These largely apolitical boroughs accounted for fewer than 12,000 voters (about 6 per cent of the borough electorate).[93] None of the eight towns examined in this book fell among those sixty-six. Four (Lewes, Beverley, Great Yarmouth, and Maidstone), however, fell among the eighty-one, containing 20 per cent of the electorate, that O'Gorman has identified as 'patronage boroughs'. Patron influence, often sporadic and frequently unsuccessful, permitted a fair amount of electoral activity. The other four (Bristol, Colchester, Northampton, and Shrewsbury) fell into O'Gorman's 'open' category, constituencies that more than made up for their relative scarcity by the size of their electorates. 'Open'

---

[92] He listed householders, resident householders, householders (scot and lot), inhabitants, resident inhabitants, inhabitants (scot and lot), burgesses, capital burgesses, burgage-holders, freeholders, freemen, resident freemen, Corporation members, potwallopers, and payers of poor rates. *Reform Bill*, 107. Examining individual voters makes the system seem even more complicated. In Bristol e.g. William Rickards, a labourer, qualified to vote in 1812 by virtue of a freehold of a rent charge of £13 issuing out of the dean and chapter lands, held for life. Robert Priest, an apothecary, voted in 1812 because he held the freehold of a fee farm rent of £9 p.a. issuing out of a messuage in Bridge Street, St Nicholas. The Bristol poll book provides full details. A fuller discussion is contained in O'Gorman, *Voters*, 28–67.

[93] Ibid. The size of unreformed electorates cannot be calculated precisely.

boroughs contained perhaps 125,000 voters, roughly two-thirds of the entire urban electorate.

These eight towns, therefore, reasonably represent England's hundred-odd borough constituencies that were either entirely open or subjected only to some limited degree of patronage, usually in decline.[94] As representatives of England's more open constituencies, they command the greatest interest since they contained relatively large numbers of voters and contested elections regularly. They do not represent England's parliamentary constituencies generally, nor could any selection of towns, however chosen, given their overall diversity. A more strictly scientific sampling procedure based upon size, location, franchise type, or the host of other variables that might be used to create a stratified sample, would generate a set of boroughs likely to be no more or less representative than these eight.

PARTISAN TERMINOLOGY

The use of party labels throughout the following analysis may seem to predispose the argument by assuming what many would argue must be proven. Substantial disagreements about the role and nature of parties characterize discussions of early nineteenth-century politics. The existence of a party system prior to Reform has been debated for some time.[95] Peter Fraser has dismissed the concept of party during the Liverpool administration, while O'Gorman has argued that such a dismissal underestimates considerably the party activity, rivalry, and identification in Parliament and in the country that had its immediate origins in the politics of the 1790s.[96] In this study, however, to agree that 'nothing resembling a modern "two-

[94] The law of available data played a part in the selection of these towns. After eliminating the towns for which data were not available either through a lack of contests or missing or inadequate poll books, the only towns that might have been added to the ones examined were Preston, Lincoln, Oxford, Southampton, Liverpool, Newcastle under Lyme, Cambridge, Rochester, and York.

[95] For summary discussions see J. C. D. Clark, 'A General Theory of Party, Opposition, and Government, 1688–1832', *Historical Journal*, 23 (1980) and I. Newbould, 'The Emergence of a Two-Party System in England from 1830 to 1841', *Parliaments, Estates, and Representation*, 5 (1985), 25–32.

[96] P. Fraser, 'Party Voting in the House of Commons, 1812–1827', *English Historical Review*, 98 (1983), 764–5; F. O'Gorman, 'Party Politics in the Early Nineteenth Century (1812–32)', *English Historical Review*, 102 (1987), 63–4.

party system" is discernible before the 1870s' is largely irrelevant.[97] Local party organizations, broadly or narrowly defined, parliamentarily or municipally focused, effective or ineffective, capable or incapable, successful or unsuccessful, were far too idiosyncratic to sustain analogies to modern systems. Nevertheless, party organizations often shaped popular politics in these boroughs, whatever their degree of idiosyncrasy.

Ian Newbould has recently underscored the vast differences between Whig and Radical political realities and has stressed the frequent co-operation of Whigs and Tories against Radicals during the Whig administrations of the 1830s.[98] The increasing popularity of Liberal/Conservative labels during that decade highlights these differences. The blurring of Whig/Tory distinctions confused a number of issues under Grey/Althorp, and the blurring worsened under Melbourne. But if an equation of Whigs and reformers is misleading in discussions of post-1834 parliamentary politics because Lord Melbourne, among others, clearly viewed Reform as *passé*, Reform was still very much *the* issue among many provincial electorates. The principles of Lord Melbourne could not be mistaken for those of Lord Durham, much less those of Daniel Whittle Harvey, but such subtleties did not concern the voters in Colchester who returned Harvey to Parliament year after year. In their eyes, Melbourne, Durham, and Harvey were all reformers. 'Reform could not be a terminus: the coach had to be driven on', and Lord Melbourne was Lord Grey's relief driver.[99] Distinctions appropriate for the rarefied atmosphere of Westminster had little meaning in Essex. Voters in Colchester found it equally difficult to distinguish between moderate Tories such as Huskisson or Wharncliffe and ultras such as Eldon and Sir Richard Vyvyan. A Tory was a Tory, and a Whig was a Whig, even if the Tory was actually an Ultra and the Whig was clearly a Radical.

Contemporary usage justifies the party labels applied in the following analyses. It seems pointless to cavil at usage that did not trouble voters in Shrewsbury, Bristol, Maidstone, and elsewhere.

[97] A. Hawkins, '"Parliamentary Government" and Victorian Political Parties, c.1830–c.1880', *English Historical Review* 104 (1989), 638–49.
[98] Newbould, *Whiggery and Reform*, ch. 2. The problem existed well before Melbourne's administration. The *Morning Chronicle* of 4 Feb. 1830 identified six different parties: Ministers, Old Whigs, High Tories, Althorp's, Huskisson's, and Independents.
[99] M. Bentley, *Politics without Democracy, 1815–1914* (London, 1984), 82.

They used the terms 'Whig', 'Tory', 'Liberal', 'Conservative', and 'reformer' unselfconsciously. This discussion continues that practice, though in a slightly more cautious fashion. The general election of 1818 in Colchester or Bristol cannot be discussed exclusively as 'Whig' and 'Tory', but these labels were a key component of discussions then, and therefore must be considered now. A relatively uniform terminology is a boon to understanding. The Liverpool poll book of 1832 made the equation of these terms quite clear in arguing that competition at English elections was 'one of party against party—of Whig against Tory—and Reformer against Conservative'.[100] Whig and Tory party labels may over-simplify local political environments, but parliamentary distinctions of the more esoteric kind concerned few local electors. Their grasp of the nuances of high or low politics did not match their grasp of the more basic Whig/Tory lines that were laden with meaning. Voters in Lewes thought, spoke, and voted along the Whig/Tory axis.[101] In Shrewsbury 'Whig' and 'Tory' serve best to describe events. Standing at election after election, Robert Slaney was a Whig. Standing almost equally often was Richard Jenkins, a Tory. Slaney and Jenkins admitted their party ties only reluctantly. Shrewsbury's voters knew and had no qualms about them.[102] As late as 1841, Barclay Fox was horrified at the candidacy of a complete stranger named Sartoris standing for Falmouth as a Tory. Fox found 'preposterous' the idea that a man 'without a shadow of a connection with Falmouth and being profoundly ignorant of our local interests' should be returned.[103] Yet while Fox thought local connections and local knowledge an essential qualification for candidates, he was very much aware of their parliamentary political connections. Sartoris's candidacy actually demonstrated the degree to which many voters were willing to

---

[100] *The Poll for the Election of Members of Parliament* (Liverpool, 1832), 1.

[101] M. Zimmeck, 'Chartered Rights and Vested Interests: Reform Era Politics in Three Sussex Boroughs', MA (Sussex, 1972).

[102] Jenkins introduced himself to Shrewsbury by promising his defence of 'Our Glorious Constitution in Church and State'. He did not need to use the word 'Tory'. *Shrewsbury Chronicle*, 6 Aug. 1830.

[103] O'Gorman, *Voters*, 9–10; R.L.Brett (ed.), *Barclay Fox's Journal* (Totowa, N.J., 1979), 234. J. Clark has argued that a Whig/Tory dichotomy did not emerge in the Commons until after 1827, or after 1832, or possibly after 1835. J. C. D. Clark, 'A General Theory of Party'. Nevertheless, a widespread perception of two parties existed in Lewes prior to the 1818 general election, whatever the shape of parliamentary divisions.

overlook a candidate's lack of local connections as long as he possessed the correct national party orientation.

Contemporaries described local political divisions in a variety of ways, however, and this analysis retains those local variations in all of their potential complexity. Discussions of local variations benefit from the use of more general terms, but when local parties are described using national labels, to some degree the label's local meaning is retained. Maidstone's two-party battles were distinguished as Whig versus Tory, Blue versus Purple, Opposition versus Corporation, or Liberal versus Conservative. Somewhat surprisingly, Maidstone's electorate often seems to have understood the occasionally subtle differences, but in a larger sense the terms were interchangeable. The parliamentary parties may have been more clearly defined after 1827 than before, but Maidstone's political battles had grouped voters into two antagonistic camps that continued their battles from parliamentary to municipal elections and back again. If 'party activity before 1832 revolved principally around great constitutional issues', these issues translated well in Maidstone. The fact that many party divisions 'had their immediate origins in the politics of the 1790s' facilitated party identification over time.[104] The Tories based their appeal upon reaction, repression, and a particularly intense form of patriotism. The Whigs hearkened back to the tradition of Fox and stood for peace and liberty. Peace may have lost its relevance after Waterloo, but the idea of liberty, particularly liberty of conscience, appealed as powerfully as ever. Voters knew the stances taken by the candidates well enough by whatever name. Maidstone's True Blues addressed the point in 1834 when they urged the voters to 'let not the names mislead you. Whig, Liberal, Radical all have a common enemy—the determined Tory.'[105]

The terms 'Whig' and 'Tory' though they never entirely disappeared had fallen on hard times before their revival in the general election of 1807. From that point, the terms regained their prominence in political debate. Yet before many individual electors came to terms with these party labels, Liberal and Conservative had begun to coexist with or perhaps replace them. On the other hand, for the

---

[104] L. Colley, 'The Apotheosis of George III: Loyalty, Royalty, and the British Nation', *Past and Present*, 102 (1984); ead., 'Whose Nation? Class and National Consciousness in Britain, 1750–1830', *Past and Present*, 113 (1986); O'Gorman, 'Party Politics', 67.
[105] *Maidstone Gazette*, 25 Nov. 1834.

early part of the period examined here, neither set of labels is as appropriate on occasion as the terms 'Government' and 'Opposition'. Since local concerns played a vital role in specific constituencies, and attitudes toward Corporations often vied for importance with attitudes toward the national government, Government/Opposition are particularly useful terms in the context of these provincial elections, complicated but not confused by the Government/party reversals in 1830 and in 1834/5. Norman Gash mirrored contemporaneous usage when he described the 1818 general election in terms of 'government' and 'opposition'.[106] Just before the election, Lord Granville felt that 'at present nothing can equal the flat insipidity of politics', but shortly after the contests a Somerset parson claimed never to have 'heard of more riots than there have been in this election'. Parson Holland was worried particularly about 'a desperate spirit among the lower People at this time' but trusted that 'a better kind of people will rouse themselves and quiet them'.[107] This milieu provided a perfect medium for the resurgence of party feelings and party terminology in the countryside, even in remote Somerset.

The generally high level of literacy among the population also aided the growth of partisan terminology. Parliamentary partisan divisions were highlighted by a growing provincial press that began to report regularly the voting records of local MPs and to take sides on issues in a partisan fashion likely to enhance local awareness of national political debates.[108] The *Maidstone Gazette* maintained a neutral tone politically until it assumed a Whig/reformist stance in 1830, partly in response to the challenge of the vehemently Tory *Maidstone Journal*. A similar newspaper rivalry developed in Colchester when in 1814 the mildly conservative *Colchester Gazette* emerged as a local supplement to the arch-conservative *Essex Standard*. The *Gazette* changed sides in 1829 as it changed editors, and vigorously battled the *Standard* in print for the next three years. By 1831 the editorials of the two newspapers had taken on an intensely combative tone, with the *Standard* as virulently anti-Catholic as it was fervently opposed to Reform. A variety of

---

[106] N. Gash, *Lord Liverpool* (London, 1984), 135.

[107] R. G. Thorne (ed.), *The House of Commons, 1790–1820*, 5 vols. (London, 1986), i. 253; J. Ayers (ed.), *Paupers and Pig Killers: The Diary of William Holland* (Harmondsworth, 1986), 297.

[108] By 1830 the *Gazette* included voting records in every issue published during a session. See e.g. 9, 16, and 23 Feb., 2, 16, 23, and 30 Mar. 1830.

newspapers of all political perspectives served Bristol, and one or two newspapers served most towns by the time Reform attracted the nation's interest.[109] Of the towns examined in this study, only Beverley lacked a local newspaper or an effective substitute for one. Beverley's failure to develop partisan divisions until well after Reform may be related to the absence of a local press battle. It is not necessary to agree with Burke's assertion that those who read newspapers daily for six months are invariably won to their opinions in order to recognize the potential political impact of the press.[110] The stamp tax limited the readership of newspapers to some extent, but many achieved wide circulations despite the levy.[111]

Lord Ellenborough feared that the Duke of Wellington neglected the press too much because he despised the rabble, 'but the rabble read newspapers' and were more of a threat for doing so.[112] By 1818 England contained almost 24,000 Sunday schools and claimed to have nearly a million pupils engaged in at least weekly instruction. To this total was added another substantial number in unendowed and endowed schools, for a total of one and a half million students from a total population of perhaps two million between the ages of five and twelve.[113] An underpriviledged community such as Bradford could claim in 1839 that two-thirds of adult weavers could read, though only a quarter could write. Northampton, another relatively depressed town, could echo Bradford's boast that between two-thirds and three-quarters of the town's bridegrooms could sign the marriage register in the initial decades of the nineteenth century. Among Nonconformists the rate exceeded 90 per cent.[114] The editor

---

[109] M. E. Speight, 'Politics in the Borough of Colchester, 1812–47', Ph.D. (London, 1969), 156–208.

[110] *The Companion to the Newspapers and a Journal of Facts* (London, 1834), 151.

[111] The press complained that the absence of stamp taxes in America meant that the proportion of newspapers to the population was 20 or 30 to one more than in the UK. Ibid. (1835), 208.

[112] E. Law, Lord Ellenborough, *A Political Diary*, 2 vols. (London, 1881), ii. 408–9; cited in A. Aspinall, 'English Party Organization in the Nineteenth Century', *English Historical Review*, 41 (1926), 389–411.

[113] J. Wade, *History of the Middle and Working Classes* (1833), 103–12. See also T. Laqueur, *Religion and Respectability* (New Haven, Conn., 1976). Wade concluded from his figures 'that no large portion of the children of the working population are now entirely without instruction'.

[114] D. G. Wright, 'Politics and Opinion in Bradford, 1832–1860', Ph.D. (Leeds, 1966), 70; V. A. Hatley, 'Literacy at Northampton, 1761–1900', *Northamptonshire Past and Present*, 5 (1976), 86; id., 'Literacy at Northampton, Some Interim Figures', *Northamptonshire Past and Present*, 4 (1971), 379–81. In the 1830s 95% of all

of the *Maidstone Gazette* claimed smugly at the news of the French Revolution of 1830 that unlike the English, the people of France 'although full of generous feelings, are of course easily misled', because 'half of the population of France cannot read'.[115] But if less easily misled, the English could be more easily politicized.

B. W. Hill has tracked the parliamentary re-emergence of the Whig/Tory dichotomy after 1811. By the election of 1820 Whig leaders counted on more than 200 'thick and thin' supporters.[116] Both Whig and Tory parties changed considerably over these years as the Whigs tried to define themselves as something other than merely Fox's party, or the party of 1688. A dead leader leads a party less capably than a live one, and though Fox served remarkably well as a dead party leader after 1806, Tierney tried to take the place of Fox's image and to inject more contemporary ideas into the fabric of Whiggery. At the same time, the Tories were moving away from such a close identification with their dead leader, though the power of Pitt's memory may have exceeded Fox's. Under these conditions, national party labels translated sometimes crudely and sometimes not at all in the countryside, but the occasional vagueness of the national parties did not necessarily impede the development of partisan awareness in particular constituencies. As in the later eighteenth century, many boroughs used colours in place of party names, but party loyalties and party continuities could be developed around a colour just as well. The Colchester election of 1820 involved considerable embarrassment for the supporters of Sir Henry Russell, whose son initially raised purple banners intending to indicate to the voters the true-blue principles his father professed. Only some time afterwards did he learn that purple alone actually stood for Reform; purple and white represented true-blue conservatism. This mix-up over colours may have confused the voters of Colchester to some degree until the proper colours were raised, but they were never in doubt about the underlying principles. The ordinary identification of James Wildman (conservative or true-blue MP) in Colchester through purple and white banners instead of through a Tory label created no difficulties for alderman William

Nonconformist grooms in Northampton and 82% of all Nonconformist brides signed the register. See also D. Vincent, *Literacy and Popular Culture* (Cambridge, 1990).

[115] *Maidstone Gazette*, 17 Aug.1830.

[116] Hill, *British Parliamentary Parties*, 203–16.

Smith who could claim no less certainly to be attached to Mr Wildman 'on principle'.[117]

Party principle was equally clear to electors at the first reformed election in Yarmouth, but even then Whig propagandists used a variety of designations in lieu of standard party labels. Trying not to lose a seat to split-voting, the Whigs attacked the Tories by begging voters not to vote for the 'Red' or 'Corporation' candidate. They referred neither to themselves nor to their enemies by conventional party labels, but the references to local colours and to the relationship of the candidates to the Corporation clarified the situation unmistakably. Their slogan 'Stand by your Colours! Stand by your Promises! Stand by Reform!' needed no national party labels to be absolutely clear.[118] Nor were Beverley's electors at all confused about the meaning of blue and orange in either local or parliamentary elections. Blue stood for the Tory/Corporation party while orange indicated Whigs, anti-corporationists, and eventually reformers. One of the more clever handbills issued in conjunction with the election of Beverley's mayor in 1824 coloured a vivid picture with its attack on the Corporation's candidate, the apothecary John Williams:

> See, as he comes, Coerulean hues arise,
> Blue are our ribbons, blue the azure skies,
> And blue are they who have to pay his bills;
> And blue our coats, and very blue his pills;
> Him, the Blue Boar, delighted grunts to see
> Where once were butter-cups now blue bells nod,
> And blue is every inch of Westwood's sod,
> And e'en the Burgesses fair cows, they say,
> Produce blue milk to grace this glorious day.

Williams's opponents did not lack for issues. They attacked his opposition to Queen Caroline, to civil rights and liberties, to 'the cause of the People', and his foreign origins. The Whigs also felt no compunction about using party labels, though they argued that in this case Whigs, Radicals, and Tories should all hate Williams. They were keenly aware of the relationship between this local contest and parliamentary politics. The 'anticipation of a General Election in the course of the ensuing Mayoralty' made the issue keener. Neverthe-

---

[117] *The Poll for Members* (Colchester, 1820), p. v. For a fuller account see Ch. 3.
[118] BL N. TAB 2012/6/1.

less, they were quite content to speak most often of the Blues and of the Orangemen in the course of the electioneering.[119]

The eighteenth-century stigma attached to party labels was a long time dying. Henry Fitzroy, the lone Conservative candidate at Lewes in 1835, took umbrage at a shout from the crowd, 'You're a Tory.' Rejecting the undeniably accurate but potentially damaging label in a borough that had returned two Whigs since 1831, Fitzroy denied the charge in one breath, only to accept it with the next. Fitzroy answered initially, 'No . . . I am not influenced by party motives', and argued that 'the nick names of Whig and Tory are forever at an end, and that the parties have ceased to exist'. Yet he simultaneously acknowledged that 'the principles' upon which he 'came forward are those which are called Conservative'.[120] Fitzroy's objections to the label given him were irrelevant in the context of politics in Lewes; the crowd's perception of Fitzroy as a Tory was sufficiently accurate whatever his semantics. When he exhorted the crowd to 'Sink each party designation, | In the spell word "Conservation"', he made his position clear enough to the voters in Lewes. Tory, Conservative, or simply the colour purple conveyed a clear enough message. Fitzroy was not Whig, Liberal, or Blue. He was also not elected. Despite his willingness to support a 'fair commutation of tithes', his only gesture towards Church reform, the crowd could see his political position clearly enough. They rejected him and continued to return Whigs for both seats as they had done since the town was swept away in its enthusiasm for Reform.[121]

Kentish and East Kentish elections reinforced the town of Maidstone's political battles, and colours continued to be used in both contexts for some time. A large number of politically minded and thrifty East Kent voters converging on Maidstone in 1832 to oust Sir Edward Knatchbull (who ultimately withdrew without a contest) planned to bivouac in a barn to save expenses for the reforming candidates. A Knatchbull (Tory) supporter, recognizing the futility of his position, argued that 'when this mania, this fever of reform, is over, you will find that light blue is not the only colour'. In this he proved correct. Blue, the traditional Whig colour for

---

[119] *Squibs and Handbills relating to a Mayor Choosing at Beverley* (Beverley, 1824), 21–2, 33.

[120] *A Poll for the Election of Members* (Lewes, 1835), 5–10.

[121] W. B. Hills, *The Parliamentary History of the Borough of Lewes* (Lewes, 1908), 38.

Maidstone and Kent, was challenged soon enough in both venues by the traditional purple of the Tories.[122]

The general stances of the parties, locally and nationally, were not in doubt, and vagueness on specifics permitted a flexibility locally that could be useful in developing party loyalties. The general election of 1826 may have presented an indistinct image of party to the electorate since 'corn rivalled Catholicism as the principal topic of public interest' at a series of relatively tepid contests. Corn did not carry all of the Whigs with it, while Catholicism drew as powerful a line within as between parliamentary parties.[123] It was not just the editor of the *Maidstone Gazette* who was struck by the 'extraordinary coincidence of opinion' prevailing 'upon all those questions which formerly involved the very existence of the two great political parties in the State'.[124] A Shrewsbury commentator at the next election (1830) also found the 'country is more tranquil than it has ever been in the memory of man'.[125] He may have suffered from a rather short memory or a very limited perception, but the election caused by the unmourned death of George IV appeared strangely quiet to many. Nevertheless, the basic division both in Parliament and in the countryside between the relatively progressive Whigs and the generally regressive Tories is hardly in doubt. Maidstone's reformist editor had no doubt about political divisions both within Parliament and within Maidstone. As O'Gorman has noted, 'the outlines of a stable and coherent party system were becoming visible' as early as the end of the Napoleonic wars, and the impact of a growing, nationally oriented press had begun to generate 'an increasingly homogenous political nation'.[126] By 1831 genuinely independent (or 'Liberal Tory') MPs such as Sir George Staunton, who voted for the second reading of the Reform Bill before reversing course and voting for General Gascoyne's obstructionist motion, accounted for only fifteen seats.[127] Recurring issues of constitutional, religious, and economic reform provided ample fuel to keep partisan fires burning across a wide spectrum of society as well as in Parliament.

This somewhat arbitrary bifurcation of the electorate ignores the Radicals, and in doing so raises a few problems nationally and

[122] Molesworth, *Reform Bill*, 196 n.
[123] Gash, *Lord Liverpool*, 239.   [124] *Maidstone Gazette*, 24 Aug. 1830.
[125] *Shrewsbury Chronicle*, 16 July 1830.
[126] O'Gorman, *The British Two-Party System* (1982), 61–3.
[127] Fifteen MPs behaved as Sir George. M. O'Neill and G. Martin, 'A Backbencher on Parliamentary Reform, 1831–1832', *Historical Journal*, 23 (1980), 539–40.

locally. It should be noted, however, that both George Crosby and Henry Stooks Smith treated MPs similarly in their independent 1841 listings of England's MPs for the preceding half-century. Daniel O'Connell may well have been unhappy with his categorization as a Whig by Crosby and by Smith, but their crude labels served their purposes effectively.[128] Daniel Whittle Harvey, who sat for Colchester during many of these years, was no Whig, but to refer to him as such places him on the correct segment of the political continuum, albeit imprecisely. An analysis of Colchester politics is not damaged by such an over-simplification. Further attention is given to local partisan variations, however, when the precise political preferences of candidates are critical to an assessment of voting patterns. Partisan divisions in Bristol, for instance, demand and receive much more complicated treatment. To call someone a Whig in Bristol prior to 1832 was to raise more questions than it answered. Usually, though, categorical partisan shorthands such as 'Whig' and 'Tory' are sufficient. *Ad hoc* arrangements successfully handled the very few maverick candidates and MPs who failed to meet even crude tests of party or principle.[129]

There is little need in this discussion for the sort of anachronistic divisions that help explain the development of Whiggery across the 1830s, but Richard Brent's general use of 'Liberal' to mean progressive is valuable because Liberals in both Westminster and the provinces can be understood as those who had come

to the conclusion that the exaggerated Tory principles, generated by hatred and deadly opposition to Jacobinism, were no longer fit to preside, when Jacobinism was no more. People grew sick of the affectation of exclusive honesty and wisdom, put forth by the ruling party; they grew ashamed of its narrow views, its common-placing, and its cant. They looked for rulers more adapted to circumstances, more congenial to the time.[130]

---

[128] See R. A. Sykes, 'Some Aspects of Working-Class Consciousness in Oldham, 1830–1842', *Historical Journal*, 23 (1980), 167–79. According to Sykes, Radicals must be distinguished from Whigs, but he admits that Oldham was exceptional in almost every way. For contemporary categorizations of MPs, see H. S. Smith, *The Register of Parliamentary Contested Elections* (London, 1841); G. Crosby, *Crosby's Parliamentary Record* (York, 1841).

[129] For another discussion of this sort of problem see G. Claeys, 'A Utopian Tory Revolutionary at Cambridge', *Historical Journal*, 25 (1982), 583–603. Newbould counted 100 Radicals in the first reformed Parliament, but their numbers declined thereafter, *Whiggery and Reform*, chs. 2 and 3.

[130] C. H. Normanby (Earl Mulgrave), *The English at Home* (London, 1830), 47. See also R. Brent, *Liberal Anglican Politics* (Oxford 1987).

Thus, extremists, oddities, and major and minor variations aside, a crude clumping of MPs into two general camps that might be labelled variously as Whigs and Tories, Liberals and Conservatives, reformers and anti-reformers, Government and Opposition (with the resulting shifts as parties gained and lost office), is an analytical device that usually serves well in the following chapters.

The Act of Voting

If party terminology presents relatively few problems, the protean nature of both reformed and unreformed partisan behaviour presents many. Partisan behaviour can often be understood only in the context of local political conditions. The nature of the franchise also obscures much that can be clarified only by careful contextual analysis. Each of these towns, along with virtually every other English parliamentary borough, returned two Members to Parliament. All eight also avoided Schedules A and B and continued to return two MPs after 1832. Accordingly, each elector controlled two votes at all general elections over these years, though he was under no obligation to cast both votes at an election and could instead 'plump' (cast only one) if he wished to. The possibility of plumping meant that if a party offered a pair of candidates to fill a constituency's two seats, a voter could vote for the party but not support it fully with both of his votes. Moreover, and more potentially distressing since most voters did not like to waste votes, the double vote meant that a voter could simultaneously support opposing parties at an election by 'splitting'. Many voters might have believed with George Eliot's Mr Wace that 'It's nonsense for . . . [Tory] voters to split for a Whig. A man's either a Tory or not a Tory.' But it was equally possible for voters to adopt an attitude like that of Eliot's Mr Timothy Rose, the independent gentleman farmer from Leek Malton, who explained his split vote at the first reformed election for North Loamshire by arguing: 'the most an independent man can do is try to please all . . . when you can vote for two, you can make things even.'[131]

---

[131] G. Eliot, *Felix Holt*, 305, 410.

The electorate may not have been fully aware of the potential damage done by split votes or unnecessary plumpers. An otherwise astute observer of the unreformed electoral process demonstrated confusion about the mathematical implications of plumping and splitting in a close election. Emily Eden's post-Reform *The Semi-Attached Couple* described a struggle for the two seats in Boroughford between two Blue candidates (Lord Teviot's men) and two Pinks standing on the interest of the Duke of Broughton. Even with two candidates standing together on each side and a relatively close contest, Eden saw nothing untoward in either a split vote for one Pink and one Blue or a plumper for the Blue candidate with the fewest votes. Near the end of her fictitious contest Eden described a 'very small pale-faced cripple' who might have stepped directly out of Hogarth being brought to the hustings with great fanfare by the Blues to cast a vote for the trailing Blue candidate. At the same time, however, he cast his other vote for one of the Pink candidates because he was a tinker for the leader of the Pink party. Remarkably, Eden believed that the split did the Blues 'no harm'. Similarly, the next voter's plumper for the trailing Blue candidate was greeted by the Blues with a 'low murmur of delight' even though the leading Blue candidate was not assured of victory at that point. More remarkably, at that point Eden had 'five or six voters who had hung back all [come] in on the winning [Blue] side'. These last voters could just as easily have created a Pink victory as a Blue one, and that possibility had been enhanced by both of the partial Blue votes Eden recorded with such delectation. She had no notion of the danger posed by less than full support.[132]

Nor, apparently, had many of Eden's enfranchised contemporaries, despite repeated, intensifying efforts to enlighten them. Without reference to candidates, issues, or parties, an 'independent elector' at the 1818 Northampton election warned his fellow voters to 'let no designing men persuade you to give a single vote, or as they are called plumpers, as by doing so you not only lose half your franchise and leave it to others to choose the other Member, but you deprive yourself of the gratification of pleasing other friends; and who is there among us that has not friends among all the parties?' He capped this line of reasoning with the rather bizarre but undeniable

[132] E. Eden, *The Semi-Attached Couple* (New York, 1979 [1831]), 226–7. See also the election account of H. Martineau in *Deerbrook* (London, 1839), 181–99.

truth that in a three-man contest, 'by giving two votes, you are sure to have one of your friends returned to Parliament'.[133]

An urgent tone had crept into some of the appeals to the voters by 1831. In Oxfordshire they were told 'above all things not [to] disfranchise your county by splitting your votes between a reformer and a corruptionist, nor throw away a chance by giving a plumper . . . Union is a sure forerunner of success.'[134] This urgency marked some reformed elections; quite a few party leaders still feared that potential or erstwhile supporters would be lured away from the partisan path by appeals for split votes. Great Yarmouth's three-man contest in 1832 raised fears that Whig electors would fail to recognize the danger posed by the single Tory candidate. The Tories (the Reds) were asking for single votes, arguing that 'it will do them [the Whigs] no harm'. Yarmouth's Blues (Whigs) responded with a detailed mathematical demonstration of the harmful consequences of a split. Using a hypothetical base group of 100 voters, the Whigs showed that if 30 of 70 voters who had promised both votes to the Whigs partially deserted to the Tories (assuming an equal number splitting with each Whig candidate), disaster would ensue. Whig calculations showed the account as follows:

	Anson (Blue)	Rumbold (Blue)	Colvile (Red/Corporation)
Promises (kept)	40	40	30
Split votes	15	—	15
Split votes	—	15	15
	55	55	60

[133] Bodleian Library, John Johnson Collection of Election Ephemera, Leicestershire and Northamptonshire, unfoliated, 20 Apr. 1818. Actually, Eden, other commentators, and participants cannot be blamed for not understanding fully the implications of single and double voting in a multi-member constituency. A single or double vote may not necessarily accomplish the expected. Hoffman has recently discussed the puzzling and often paradoxical implications of game theory for multi-member, multi-vote constituencies. P. Hoffman, *Archimedes' Revenge* (New York, 1988), 224–58. Brams and others have provided illustrations that raise serious questions about the mathematical soundness of voting. S. Brams, *Paradoxes in Politics* (New York, 1976), *passim*. See also J. Mitchell, 'Electoral Change and the Party System in England', Ph.D. (Harvard, 1977), 291–324; J.M. Kousser, 'Toward "Total Political History": A Rational-Choice Research Program', *Journal of Interdisciplinary History*, 20 (1990); and Kenneth J. Arrow, *Social Choice and Individual Values* (New York, 1951).

[134] Eastwood, 'Toryism, Reform, and Political Culture', 105–6.

Despite an overwhelmingly favourable (70 per cent / 30 per cent) canvass for the Whigs, 'the false friends of the Blues [would] give them [the Reds] the victory' because 'every split vote gives but half a vote to Anson and Rumbold but a whole vote to Colvile'. Far better '*not to vote at all*' than to be duped by the Tories and beaten as a result.[135] Yarmouth's Whig voters appear to have known this already. They were not in the habit of splitting their votes, and it seems very unlikely that they would have deserted the party in 1832. The anxiety of the Whig propagandists, however, as they urged the Blues to 'Stand by your Colours! Stand by your promises! Stand by Reform!', reveals the lingering fear of non-partisan behaviour.

These perceptions were further enhanced as the implications of registration began to be understood. When Maidstone's sole Tory candidate, Wyndham Lewis, fell far short of the large numbers of plumpers he expected in 1832, his failure was attributed to Maidstone's female 'blue devils'. Many men who had promised Tory plumpers were married to 'blue devils' (reformers). Succumbing to marital lobbying, these men compromised and cast their second votes as their wives demanded. Yet splitters were rare in reformed Maidstone. In 1835 the *Maidstone Gazette* illustrated the clear expectation that voters would behave consistently by publishing a 'black list' of twenty-four skilled labourers who had been registered with Liberal assistance, and who then betrayed their allegiance by voting Tory. To the list of twenty-four the *Gazette* appended another thirteen who voted Tory after having been defended against Tory objections during the revision of the electoral registers.[136]

These intensely partisan visions in Maidstone and elsewhere stand in stark contrast to the expectations of the later nineteenth century electioneering expert, Edward W. Cox, who even after the second Reform Act did not expect double (straight party) voting. He assumed in 1868 that if three Radicals stood against a single Conservative in a town with 700 Radical and 500 Conservatives voters, the Conservative would win one of the seats because of Radical splitting. Cox assumed the presence of partisans in the electorate, but he did not believe that voters could be made to toe the party line even under favourable circumstances, much less adversity. A lopsided contest spelled disaster, but not for the united pair; Cox argued that a solitary candidate actually held an advantage if he

---

[135] BL. N. TAB 2012/6/1ND (Nov. 1832).
[136] *Maidstone Gazette*, 21 Aug. 1832; 13 Jan. 1835.

stood against two opponents. Cox admitted the desirability of candidates standing together, but he did not believe joint candidacies to be possible ordinarily.[137]

D. C. Moore has dismissed the assumption that votes indicate either the 'wishes' or the 'opinions' of voters in favour of a belief that voters comprised elements within deference communities. Votes were not spontaneous expressions of either moral or intellectual positions.[138] Though completely at odds with Moore's assumptions about voters, the following analyses do not simply assume that voting behaviour necessarily reflected public opinion. Instead they seek, and find, compelling evidence of the meaning behind votes both in the comments of contemporary observers and voters and in systematic analyses of individual electoral behaviour in comparative perspective. The voters in these boroughs left both qualitative and quantitative evidence that their actions involved not deference but politics.

Quantitatively, both synchronic and diachronic analyses of voting patterns are critical to an evaluation of electoral behaviour. Synchronic analyses conducted against the backdrop of the local political environment reveal much about the nature of electoral behaviour. Comparing a series of synchronic analyses can also reflect elements of change and continuity in a political environment. Changes in levels of 'necessary' (or 'partisan') plumping, for example, reveal much about attitudes to party because most voters saw no reason not to exercise their franchises fully rather than discarding half of their voting rights. An increase in the willingness of voters to cast plumpers when required by the appearance of a solitary candidate in a particular election, therefore, suggests much about the popular meaning of party. Changes in levels of strictly party voting are also important indicators of party solidarity in a system that permitted neutrality. This book evaluates such changes in light of the constitutional revision of 1832.

Diachronic patterns are much rarer indications of the meaning of votes. Fortunately, rather than being forced to rely solely on comparisons of cross-sectional views of the behaviour of various electorates, the data supporting this study permit the voting choices of specific individuals to be examined over time. A decline in

---

[137] E. W. Cox, *Hints to Solicitors for the Conduct of Elections* (London, 1868); see also H. J. Hanham (ed.), *Dod's Electoral Facts* (Brighton, 1972).

[138] *Politics of Deference*, 10–11.

unnecessary plumping or an increase in straight party voting may indicate much about the degree to which votes reflected public opinion generally, but comparisons of the specific political choices of Nathaniel Palmer or Thomas Raney or Edmund Reeve Palmer at election after election in Great Yarmouth permit rare insights into popular political realities. Following the votes of Shrewsbury's William Hulme across eight elections, in the context of the voting choices of thousands of other Shrewsbury voters over these years, reveals much about Hulme and much about Shrewsbury politics. It is not necessary merely to assume that Hulme's votes had meaning; their meaning can be sought in the context of the political system. Were his votes at a particular election politically rational?[139] If they were politically rational (or partisan) at one point, was Hulme's political behaviour consistent across elections, and was its degree of consistency related to his partisanship?[140] These and similar questions are considered as the behaviour of Hulme and thousands of his fellows is examined to determine the popular impact of Reform.

The great expectations of so many Englishmen could hardly have taken more diverse forms in 1831. But whether they were rioting in Bristol, petitioning in Lewes, or just voting for reformers in Maidstone, the enfranchised (and many of the disfranchised) in these towns revealed levels of popular engagement and popular participation that reinforce the recent images of vibrant popular politics in Hanoverian England painted by Rogers and O'Gorman. If the agitation of some of these men stemmed from their mistaken impression that the King wanted the Bill to pass, their sense of the importance of their opinions and their determination to express them, belligerently if necessary, were no less evident than the

---

[139] An obvious danger lies in assumptions about the relationship of 19th-cent. voting patterns and modern electoral habits. Assumptions about changes in the direction of 'modern' patterns raise complex problems, not the least of which is the meaning of modernity. Elvin has cautioned against attempts 'to formulate "modernity" simply in terms of some sort of increased "rationality", whether in economics or politics or religion'. M. Elvin, 'A Working Definition of "Modernity"?', *Past and Present*, 113 (1986), 209–13.

[140] The debate about the meaning of 'floating votes' is not likely to be settled for some time. Speck is correct to question assumptions made by some, including myself, that 'floating' voters were likely to have been apathetic and uninformed. Such sweeping assumptions must be demonstrated, not assumed. See W. A. Speck, 'The Electorate in the First Age of Party', in C. Jones (ed.), *Britain in the First Age of Party, 1680–1750* (London, 1987), 51–2.

opinions of those who cared not what the King thought. The salient feature of these attitudes is less the motivation behind them than the degree to which they replicated episodes across the eighteenth and early nineteenth centuries involving local or national events. The intensity of the interest over Reform was unusual, to be sure, but an interest in political issues was not. England's very long tradition of popular political debate and popular participation could and did result in massive outpourings of public opinion. Reform as a political issue only mobilized and magnified what already existed in many settings across the country.

Reform in Bristol differed from Reform in Maidstone, which in turn differed markedly from Reform in Lewes. There were many faces of Reform, as the following chapters reveal. Yet underlying each face was a political system that already contained parliamentary political parties, local political parties that sometimes mirrored parliamentary parties, tens of thousands of active electors, relatively frequent elections for local and national political offices, and a degree of popular participation from enfranchised and disfranchised alike that already guaranteed that the political nation could not be ignored. If Reform in Bristol differed from Reform in Lewes, in both places, and in dozens of other relatively 'open' parliamentary boroughs, Reform occurred in a milieu already politicized and participatory. Not infrequently, it was also already and sometimes heavily, partisan. In such an environment what impact could Reform have? The search for the rather complicated answer begins at Bristol.

PART II
THE IMPACT OF REFORM

2
Reform and Reaction: Bristol and 1832

REFORM

Between the late afternoon of Saturday 29 October 1831 and the following Monday morning, a mob in Bristol caused King William IV 'the deepest affliction' by burning down a sizeable portion of the town.[1] During thirty-six hours of violence Bristol mobs stormed, emptied, and fired three gaols, sacked and burned the Mansion House, Customs House, and Bishop's palace, and destroyed dozens of private residences.[2] Before armed intervention from the 3rd Dragoons, 14th Hussars, and mounted elements of the local yeomanry stopped the riot, scores of people died or were seriously injured in the flames, in the crush of the crowd, or from sabre strokes and musket fire.[3]

---

[1] Cobbett referred to Bristol as England's third largest city in 1812, but it was in fact already in seventh place by the census of 1811, which Cobbett refused to believe. *Weekly Political Register*, 4 July 1812. National growth rates between the first five censuses were 14%, 18%, 19%, and 14%. Bristol's increases between those censuses amounted to 15%, 18%, 20%, and 19%. *Parl. Deb.* 9. 4.

[2] Perhaps the fullest account of the riot is provided by *The Bristol Riots by a Citizen* (Bristol, 1832), a collection of material collected by the Revd. T. Curme, Mayor Charles Pinney's chaplain at the time of the incident. Curme escaped with Pinney and Sir Charles Wetherell over Bristol's rooftops as the Mansion House burned. BL, LR277e, v. 2–3. Of the dozens of tracts describing the riots or the trials of those accused of participating in the rioting, see *Dreadful Riot. Destruction of Bristol New Gaol, Bridewell, Lawford's Gate Prison, Mansion House, Bishop's Palace, Customs House, Excise, and 42 Other Houses* (Bristol, 1831); *Full Particulars of the Dreadful and Tremendous Riots in Bristol* (London, 1831); *A Narrative of the Dreadful Riots and Burnings which Occurred in Bristol on 29, 30, 31 October 1831* (Bristol, 1831); *A Voice to Bristol* (Bristol, 1831); *A Full Report of the Trials of the Bristol Rioters* (Bristol, 1832); *Lamentation on those Five Unfortunate Men now Lying under Sentence of Death* (Bristol, 1832).

[3] Harrison has recently discussed the importance of timing in mob action. Since Monday was traditionally not just an 'idle' but an 'outside' day, failure to quell the riot in the early hours of Monday morning might have led to much greater damage. M. Harrison, 'Time, Work, and the Occurrence of Crowds, 1790–1835', *Past and Present*, 110 (1986), 134–68. Latimer's description indicates that only 14 Bedminster Yeomanry arrived to support the handful of Dragoons and Hussars, J. Latimer,

The Reform Bill caused Bristol's brush with disaster. Despite the extreme unlikelihood that they would in any way profit from it, many Bristolians vehemently championed parliamentary reform. The proposed redistribution of seats affected Bristol not at all, and the £10 franchise requirement promised to add few voters from the sort of men who made up the mob.[4] All 40-shilling freeholders in Bristol were already entitled to vote, along with all freemen.[5] More than a quarter and possibly nearly a third of Bristol's adult males possessed the franchise in 1830; after 1832 only a third of Bristol's initial reformed constituency owed their possession of the franchise to the new qualification. Nevertheless, whatever their voting status, many in Bristol fervently believed the Bill to be essential to their welfare. That their perception rested upon a delusion rendered their behaviour no less determined or dangerous.

Bristol's ultra-Tory senior alderman and recorder, Sir Charles Wetherell, KC, actually triggered this bloody Reform riot. The virtual defeat of the Reform Bill on its second reading in the Commons had been accompanied by a claim from Wetherell, Lord Eldon's favourite MP, that Bristolians were 'indifferent to reform'.[6] Wetherell's assessment reflected his usual tenuous grasp of reality. In stark contrast to his view, citizens in Bristol had set up a Reform Committee, and increasingly large numbers demanded the Bill's passage. They had made their concerns quite clear when fully eight months before the riot, more than 12,000 signed a petition supporting parliamentary reform and demanding the ballot.[7]

Annals of Bristol in the Nineteenth Century (Bristol, 1887), 147–9. According to the *AR*, 12 people died including 2 from gunshot wounds, 2 from sabre wounds, and 6 from burning while 94 were injured (10 from gunfire, 48 from sabres). *AR* 73. 294–5.

[4] Predictably, Wetherell argued that the £10 qualification would impose a caste system in England. *Parl. Deb.* 9 (17 Dec. 1831), 505.

[5] A survey published in 1834 listed 9,785 houses in Bristol valued at £10 or more. Wetherell told the Commons that these £10 householders were no better than paupers and that they did not merit the franchise. Cannon, *Parliamentary Reform*, 222; *The Companion to the Newspapers*, 186–7. Bristol was one of five among 16 'county' towns that enfranchised 40-shilling freeholders. Seymour, *Electoral Reform*, 23–32.

[6] *Parl. Deb.* 6. 698–9. William Carpenter called Wetherell 'the *primo buffo* of the anti-reformers'. *Carpenter's Monthly Political Magazine* (Sept. 1831), 1. Cannon has argued that Bristol's riot ultimately had little to do with Reform, though the issue of Reform and Wetherell's presence started it. *Parliamentary Reform*, 227 n. 1. The evidence of the trials after the riot supports Cannon's view.

[7] So mistrustful were the petitioners of Bristol's MPs that they included their petition among the hundred presented by Lord Althorp at the special meeting of the Commons held on 26 Feb. exclusively to receive petitions about Reform. Bristol's

Wetherell had been the darling of the Bristol mob as recently as 1829 for resigning his post as Attorney General in the Wellington administration to protest against Catholic emancipation.[8] Sitting as he did for Boroughbridge, however, a town scheduled for destruction by the Bill, Wetherell had more immediate concerns than his relative popularity in Bristol. The Bill's defeat in the Lords on 8 October 1831, coupled with Wetherell's new claim that 'Reform Fever has a good deal abated in Bristol', augured ill.[9]

Riots in Nottingham and Derby in the days immediately following the Lords' vote raised frightening prospects, and Bristol's past behaviour provided little reassurance for a worried magistracy. Mobs in Bristol often disrupted elections: a serious riot accompanied the Excise crisis; a grain riot of major proportions marked 1753; and damage from the turnpike riots of 1727, 1730, and 1749 paled in comparison to the dozen people shot to death by troops during the riot over the continuation of tolls on Bristol Bridge in 1793. The Riot Act itself stemmed from the Bristol accession riots in 1714.[10] Fears

petition lost something by its inclusion among much larger ones from Glasgow, Leeds, and Edinburgh, but the reformers had no choice since Davis would not submit it and they did not trust Baillie. The Manchester petition presented by Althorp contained 12,245 signatures, and the one from Bristol was 'signed by about an equal number'. *Parl. Deb.* 2. 994–7.

[8] Wetherell became a KC in 1816, was appointed Solicitor–General 1824, knighted the same year, appointed Attorney General 1826, resigned with Lord Eldon, reappointed by Wellington in 1828, and resigned again in 1829.

[9] *CJ* 27 Aug. 1831. Protheroe immediately repudiated Wetherell's assertion, which may have been based on reports in the 'local organ of ultra-Toryism', *Felix Farley's Bristol Journal*. Wetherell was known not only for the extravagance of his speeches in Parliament, but also for the gymnastics accompanying them that led frequently to his unbraced trousers slipping down. After his rantings against the second reading of the Catholic Emancipation Bill, one member said that Wetherell 'had no lucidity save the interval between his waistcoat and his breeches'. Latimer, *Annals*, 146. See also *Dictionary of National Biography*, xx. 1298. For a description of Wetherell's attack on Brougham's Bankruptcy Bill in 1831 see Arnould, *Lives of the Chief Justices*, v. 276. George Cruickshank singled out Boroughbridge for attack in his cartoon *The Boroughmongers Grinding Machine*. Stephens, Hawkins, and George (comp.) *Catalogue*, 16610, 21 Mar. 1831. Latimer counted 180 speeches by Wetherell in the *Mirror of Parliament* during 1831 alone, which certainly should have been enough to justify his reputation. The entry for Wetherell in the index to the *Mirror of Parliament* under the subheading 'Parliamentary Reform' occupies an entire paragraph. *MoP* (June–Oct. 1831). Widely unpopular for some time, Wetherell had been used as a weapon against Sir Edmund Lacon in the Great Yarmouth election of 1830 when Whigs suggested a Lacon and Wetherell ticket to discredit the Tory cause. *Election Budget or an Appendage to the Poll Book* (Great Yarmouth, 1830), p. iv.

[10] For Bristol's various riots see M. Harrison, '"To Raise and Dare Resentment": The Bristol Bridge Riot of 1793 Re-examined', *Historical Journal*, 26 (1983), 573–6;

occasioned by the Swing Riots the previous November had prompted Bristol's mayor, John Savage, to warn the new Secretary of State (Lord Melbourne had held office only five days) that while Bristol was 'peaceable and orderly' at the moment of his writing, it was 'impossible to say how soon this may cease'. He reminded Lord Melbourne that on previous occasions of 'violent outrage' the 'established Police has not been found adequate to preserve the peace', and requested that a military force, including cavalry, be made available in the city.[11] The Bristol assizes, scheduled for 29 October, posed a special threat since Wetherell's presence would be required. His popularity had declined since the previous April when his presence at the assizes almost incited a riot. The Corporation therefore asked Lord Melbourne either to postpone the assizes or to secure the town with troops in advance. Bristol's reformist MP, Edward Protheroe, jnr. simultaneously advised against heeding the Corporation's request. He believed the reformers would demonstrate peacefully, and he promised to escort Wetherell into town personally to ensure the good conduct of the crowd.[12] Reassured by Protheroe, Melbourne sent only a token force of cavalry (ninety-three men).

With this paltry response from the Home Office, Bristol's new mayor, Charles Pinney, a reformer himself, called a meeting aboard his ship *The Earl of Liverpool* to recruit respectable men (principally sailors) to maintain order during Wetherell's assize procession, but the sailors rejected Pinney's offer.[13] The Corporation's security arrangements having failed spectacularly, a delegation led by 'Perpetual' Under-Sheriff Hare asked Wetherell personally to postpone the assizes, but Wetherell, a slave to 'duty', determined to

id., *Crowds and History* (Cambridge, 1988); P. Langford, *The Excise Crisis* (London, 1975); R. Malcomsom, '"A Set of Ungovernable People": The Kingswood Colliers in the Eighteenth Century', in J. Brewer and J. Styles (eds.), *An Ungovernable People* (London, 1980), 85–127; P. D. Jones, 'The Bristol Bridge Riot and its Antecedents', *Journal of British Studies*, 19 (1980); B. Little, *The City and County of Bristol* (Bristol, 1967), 116; BRO, Hare MSS 8073.

[11] PRO, HO40/502, John Savage to Lord Melbourne, 27 Nov. 1830.

[12] PRO, HO40/28, Charles Pinney to Lord Melbourne, 4 Nov. 1831. See also *Morning Chronicle*, 7 Nov. 1831.

[13] Pinney, the 'odd sock in the Corporation's top drawer', was the only Whig mayor between 1820 and 1835, and one of only two to hold the office in Bristol until 1856. He chaired a meeting that supported the French Revolution of 1830. Little, *Bristol* 240; PRO, HO40/28/9–10, Lt. C. Claxton to Lord Melbourne, 17 Oct. 1831; G. Amey, *City under Fire* (London, 1979), 23.

earn his recorder's salary of 100 guineas and a hogshead of sherry.[14]
Facing disaster, Hare then recruited 300 special constables to assist
the city's hundred regulars. Such was Wetherell's unpopularity that
most respectable merchants and tradesmen refused service, leaving
largely young, zealous anti-reformers among the volunteers.[15] To
reach his goal of of 300, Hare was forced to hire nearly a hundred
men from the ranks of the truly unsavoury.[16]

On 24 October Bristolians rehearsed their greeting of Wetherell
by pelting the Bishop of Bath and Wells, one of those responsible for
the Lords' defeat of the Bill, with mud and stones when he arrived to
consecrate a new church.[17] The next day the Bristol Political Union
issued a broadside arguing that the Corporation's request for troops
to escort Wetherell demonstrated their incapacity, and demanding
their joint immediate resignation to 'prevent riot and perhaps
bloodshed'.[18] It came as no surprise to anyone, then, that
Wetherell's procession into town four days later met with a shower
of stones despite the unusually early hour (10 a.m.), the use of the
sheriff's carriage, the presence of Protheroe in the carriage, and an
escort of special constables. Protheroe and others such as William
Herapath of the Union had miscalculated the anger unleashed by
Wetherell's presence. The press of the mob so impeded Wetherell's
progress that the assizes had to be adjourned until the following
Monday, but the adjournment failed to placate the *enragés*. The
crowd soon laid siege to the Mansion House. By 5 p.m. Mayor
Pinney had read the Riot Act to its usual lack of effect. Pinney
therefore turned to Lieutenant Colonel Brereton and the cavalry to
restore order. Whether or not Pinney gave Brereton the order to use
firearms is unclear. Pinney certainly wanted to avoid gunfire in light
of the disastrous use of deadly force in the 1793 Bridge Riot. This
episode had been painfully resurrected during the 1812 election with
cries of 'No six and eightpence! No bloody bridge! No murderers!'

---

[14] They met independently to declare that their loyalty to the King notwithstanding,
they would not 'be made catspaws by the Corporation'. Latimer, *Annals*, 148.

[15] BRO, Dakin Papers, 'Arrangements for the Entry of Sir Charles Wetherell, 29
October 1831', unfoliated.

[16] H. Hunt, *Memoirs*, 3 vols. (London, 1821), ii. 500; iii. 126.

[17] Many shared Bristol's contempt for the Bishops for their role in the Bill's defeat.
L. G. Johnson, *The Man with Forty Crowns a Year* (London, 1957), 180.

[18] Joseph Kayes, the rioter who escaped death with perpetual banishment, said
afterwards that 'if the Corporation of Bristol had insisted on it [the Reform Bill] and
kept Sir Charles Wetherell back, . . . the Riot would never have occurred'. *Incidents in
the Life of Joseph Kayes* (Bristol, 1832), 7.

The Impact of Reform

John Cranidge dredged up the issue again in 1818 when he revealed that the Corporation had remunerated the troops who fired on the crowd to the amount of £105.[19] Any mayor, and certainly Bristol's only Whig mayor in the decades prior to Reform, would have been keen to avoid responsibility for the recurrence of such violence. Whatever the reason, Brereton not only refused to order his troops to fire, but he actually removed them from the scene at a critical juncture, effectively abdicating control to the mob as it stormed and burned the Mansion House. Wetherell barely escaped with his life by disguising himself as a postillion and scrambling over the rooftops of Queen Square as it was being destroyed by the flames.[20] The rioting continued until dawn on Monday when a handful of Dragoons and Hussars finally used force to crush the thinning ranks of the rioters.[21] Once called upon to act without restraint, the troops restored calm rather easily.

The deaths attributable to the riot did not end with the restoration of quiet in the early hours of 31 October. Sydney Smith, a recent addition to the Bristol clergy, would have had 'ten people hanged, and twenty transported, and thirty imprisoned'.[22] The Government did not quite meet his target, but four of the twenty-six men who received the death sentence for their part in the disorder actually died on the gallows.[23] Fifty-five others of more than 100 tried at the

[19] J. Cranidge, *A Mirror for the Burgesses of Bristol* (Bristol, 1818); J. Claridge, *Extracts from the City Cash Book* (Bristol, 1814). Pinney wrote to his sister soon after the event: 'I have forbore [*sic*] ordering the troops to fire.' Amey, *City under Fire*, 50. Latimer, on the other hand, asserts that Pinney did give the order, which both Brereton and the other soldiers resisted. *Annals*, 153.

[20] Wetherell continued as recorder until his death in a carriage accident in 1846 at the age of 76.

[21] *AR* 73. 294–5 lists casualties. For report of trials see AR 74. 51. Francis Place estimated that England contained only 11,000 troops all told at the time, with 7,000 of those stationed in London. The tiny contingent sent to Bristol may be a reflection of the mere 4,000 available for the rest of Great Britain. Wallas, *Francis Place*, 293–6. By the time reinforcements from the 11th Foot arrived, their presence proved superfluous.

[22] Lady Holland, *Memoir*, 492, Smith to Lady Grey, Oct. 1831.

[23] Three of the men hanged were workers, but one, Christopher Davis, was a 'man of superior station' worth £300 p.a. independently. A fifth man's sentence was commuted to perpetual banishment at the last minute. The remaining men against whom sentences of death were recorded for destroying property or assault had their punishment reduced to transportation for 14 years and were sent to Botany Bay. Seven others convicted of lesser crimes, mostly theft, were also sent to Botany Bay, though only one for the full 14 years. The other 43 served terms of years at hard labour. *A Full Report of the Trials of the Bristol Rioters; Charge to the Grand Jury by Sir*

assizes were convicted and punished. Wetherell wanted to judge the rioters himself, but the Government bypassed him with a special commission.[24] More than 10,000 Bristolians futilely signed a petition asking the Crown to commute the death sentences and more than one pamphlet denounced the incompetence of the magistracy.[25] A cartoon by Robert Seymour suggested that the scales of justice could be balanced only by hanging in equal numbers smock-clad rioters and bewigged, black-robed members of the Corporation.[26] In fact, the only member of the establishment to die was Lieutenant Colonel Brereton, who, facing certain conviction, shot himself after the fourth day of his court-martial. Another court-martial cashiered Captain W. H. Warrington, and subsequently two other officers involved in the riot left His Majesty's service prematurely.[27] Mayor Pinney easily survived prosecution in King's Bench for dereliction of duty. After twenty-three minutes of deliberation, a jury acquitted Pinney and added their belief that he had 'acted to the best of his judgment with the highest zeal and courage', thus ending the Government's intention of prosecuting all of Bristol's aldermen.[28]

REACTION

The riot notwithstanding, not every Bristolian favoured Reform. So alarmed were Bristol's anti-reformers by the 'spread of Revolutionary Principles' that the White Lion Club, Bristol's powerful Tory association, 'anxious to avert . . . the spread of Revolutionary Principles and anxious to avert . . . the calamities which a reckless

---

Nicholas C. Tindal (Bristol, 1832); *Narrative of Conversations held with Christopher Davis* (Bristol, 1832).

[24] Wetherell objected to the Government's issuance of a special commission, citing Judge Jeffreys in support of his claim to be permitted to resume his assize seat. *Parl. Deb.* 9 (6 Dec. 1831), 65–71; 'An Impartial Citizen', *The Magistracy of Bristol Brought to the Bar of Public Opinion* (Bristol, 1832).

[25] Pinney, *The Trial of Charles Pinney* (London, 1833); C. H. Walker, *The Petition of William Clark* (London, 1832); *Incidents in the Life of Joseph Kayes.*

[26] Robert Seymour, *The Balance of Justice*, 3 Nov. 1832, Stephens, Hawkins, and George (comp.), *Catalogue*, 17296; J. A. Sharpe (ed.), *Crime and the Law in English Satirical Prints, 1660–1832* (Cambridge, 1986). See also *A Letter to the Judges . . . upon the Impropriety of Punishing the Rioters with Death* (Bristol, 1832).

[27] *The Court Martial of Captain Warrington* (Bristol, 1832).

[28] *AR* 74. 51.

spirit of innovation is labouring to draw down upon this hitherto favoured land', petitioned the Commons to prevent this 'fatal error'. They opposed all change as a preliminary step to 'the next object of Radical Reform—Universal Suffrage'. Their petition asserted: 'We *will* not that the laws of England should be changed.'[29]

Richard Hart Davis presented the White Lion petition on the same day (26 February) that Althorp presented Bristol's far more numerous petition in favour of Reform. In offering Parliament the only sizeable anti-Reform petition of 1831, Davis argued that the 5,000 signatures on his petition proved that Bristol's more respectable citizens agreed with him that 'Reform sought out of doors meant neither more nor less than revolution'. Henry Hunt, erstwhile candidate for Bristol now sitting for Preston, dismissed Davis's offering as 'a hole and cover' petition, devised by a handful in Bristol and then sent clandestinely to parishes up to fourteen miles from the city for signatures to augment its strength. Davis denied that 'above 700 signatures were obtained out of Bristol', and claimed that 'he owed his return, in a great degree, to the sentiments he had professed against Parliamentary Reform'.[30] He scorned Lord John Russell's prediction of 'a sort of Millennium' approaching, warning instead that the King, Lords, and Commons would be 'melted down in the crucible of Parliamentary Reform' into 'one fearful power, under the denomination of the United Commons House of Parliament, in which democracy would reign triumphant'.[31]

During the eight days between the dissolution of Parliament on 22 April 1831 and the entrance into the city of R. H. Davis, Bristol's Tory, anti-Reform incumbent of nearly twenty years, however, the anti-reformers lost all credibility in Bristol. Davis's once nearly unanimous support vanished. At the election only a year earlier, his total vote had reached the unprecedented level of 5,000, a total not achieved again by any candidate until 1865, and a thousand votes more than ever before in Bristol's electoral history. Fully four-fifths of the electorate supported Davis in 1830. Barely nine months later, most of them had changed their minds. The results of the White Lion's canvass were so dismal that a contest would only have

[29] A printed petition resulted from the meeting at the White Lion with senior alderman Thomas Daniel in the chair. BRO 38699 (1–2).

[30] *Parl. Deb.* 2. 996–7. *AR* recorded 19 petitions in 1821, 12 in 1822, 29 in 1823, none between 1824 and 1829, and only 14 in 1830.

[31] *Parl. Deb.* 2. 1302–4.

highlighted Tory unpopularity. Forced to eat his parliamentary boasts, Davis withdrew.[32] The extremely powerful, well-organized local Tories did not bother to propose a candidate, and without a White Lion to stand for the first time in half a century, Bristol returned two Whigs (though only one dedicated reformer).[33]

The White Lions were defeated but unbowed. Forced to concede the 1831 election, they had no intention of relinquishing their traditional control of one of Bristol's seats. One stunning upset would not destroy an organization that had been carefully constructed over a century of electoral activity. Nor would a mere riot intimidate the anti-reformers. A month after the fires had been extinguished, alderman Daniel chaired a White Lion meeting that promised the King their support against the 'anarchists, atheists, robbers, and incendiaries' who constituted Lord Grey's allies.[34] The White Lions also began to search for a new candidate since Davis refused to stand again. Their confidence in the future was justified; they quickly found a candidate and almost as quickly regained their hegemonic position in Bristol politics.

BRISTOL'S UNITED TORIES: THE WHITE LION PARTY MACHINE

At every Bristol election except 1831, the White Lion Club wielded enormous power and orchestrated its efforts with remarkable efficiency and skill. The Tories focused formally on a single candidate whom they invariably sent to Parliament at the head of the poll. The White Lion's power survived the fires of 1831 virtually unchecked. A bare thirteen months after the October riot, Bristol's old and new voters assembled at the hustings erected in the ruins of

---

[32] The White Lion presented Davis with a gift of plate worth £750 when he refused to stand again in 1832.

[33] The Stedfast Society was founded in 1737 as a direct successor to the True Loyal Club of 1710 vintage. Only one of the two Whigs, however, Edward Protheroe, jnr., was a liberal reformer; the other was a conservative Whig and the candidate of Bristol's large West Indian interest, James Evan Baillie. BRO 12144, fo. 57. The Stedfast Society controlled the White Lion Club which was still more exclusive than the Loyal and Constitutional Club. In a typical meeting schedule on 17 Feb. 1812 the Stedfast met in the morning, the White Lion Club at 1 pm., and the Loyal and Constitutional Club at night.

[34] Latimer, *Annals*, 175.

Queen Square to choose their representatives for the first reformed
Parliament. This election marked the beginning of the White Lion
Club's resurgence after their momentary stumble.

The death from Reform fever of the White Lion candidate of
nearly two decades led to the acquisition of a new ultra-Tory
candidate, Sir Richard Vyvyan, recently ousted from his Cornwall
seat by Reform fever every bit as virulent as the Bristol variety.[35]
Vyvyan had played a very visible role in the Commons debates of
1831/2. His speeches on 21 April 1831 tried to twist Reform into an
issue of Protestantism against popery. He prophesied revolution the
next day in the charged atmosphere heightened by the sound of
cannons announcing the King's arrival. Forced into a seat at
Okehampton by his rout at the hands of Cornwall's thousands of
reformist voters in 1831, Vyvyan might have been chary of another
populous constituency.[36] The expansion of Bristol's parliamentary
boundaries in 1832 had added more than 50,000 citizens to the town,
with no fewer than 10,315 appearing on the new electoral register.
But the White Lion Club was well accustomed to masses of voters.
Bristol's electorate probably exceeded 8,000 in the later years of the
eighteenth century. The expansion of the constituency's formal
parliamentary boundaries did not translate directly into votes and
was partially offset by the elimination of non-resident freemen. Thus
the maximum number of voters in Bristol during the 1830s exceeded
the maximum at later eighteenth-century elections by no more than
10 per cent, an increase that did not tax the White Lion
organization. Roughly as many voters participated in the Bristol
elections of 1774 and 1784 as in 1835.[37]

An offer from the Tory White Lion Club would have tempted any
man in search of a parliamentary seat, whatever the size of Bristol's
electorate. Active since the first half of the eighteenth century, the
White Lion had become a sophisticated, efficient party machine.
Overseen by the Stedfast Society, and assisted by both the Loyal and

[35] Vyvyan received barely 900 votes to his opponents' totals of more than 1,800.
See Jaggard, 'The Parliamentary Reform Movement in Cornwall', and id., 'Cornwall
Politics'; Molesworth, *Reform Bill*, 184–94.

[36] Vyvyan sat first for Cornwall, then Okehampton, Bristol, and Helston.
B. Disraeli, *Letters*, iii, ed. M. G. Wiebe et al. (Toronto, 1987), 351.

[37] The number of actual voters at Bristol elections had remained relatively stable
for decades. Actually casting ballots were 6,631, 5,879, and 6,375 electors in 1832,
1835, and 1837 respectively. J. Vincent and M. Stenton, *McCalmont's Parliamentary
Poll Book* (Brighton, 1971), 34. The reports of returns that list the leading candidate
with more than 5,000 votes are incorrectly reporting a total that should be 4,193.

Constitutional Club and the relatively new (post-riot) Operative Conservative Association and the Friends of Conservative Principles, the White Lion men staged campaigns with exceeding care and attention to detail.[38] After several ruinously expensive contests, the White Lion and its rival, the Whig Union or Independent Club, split Bristol's representation between them without contests for twenty years after 1754, and again from 1784 until the Whigs broke the truce in 1812.[39] The White Lion proved itself more than equal to the renewed electioneering. Well justified was Vyvyan's assertion after the 1832 contest that 'there are few places in the Kingdom where the organization is so perfect, none where it has been productive of effects so serviceable to the cause of order'.[40] The Whigs in Bristol had good reason to regret the inefficacy of Vyvyan's prayer, uttered only a year earlier, for God to 'defend this country against Political Clubs'.[41]

The White Lion's electoral activities for Vyvyan in 1832 were neither more nor less thorough than at preceding Bristol contests. Its preparations were exhaustive, its efforts relentless. The White Lion's preliminary preparation for an unreformed election entailed creating as many freemen voters as possible. The cost of freedom for those qualified through birth, marriage, or apprenticeship averaged £3, a bargain in comparison to the average of £42 for those otherwise unqualified individuals who had to purchase a freedom outright.[42] Helped by White Lion subsidies, 1,689 men took up their freedoms between 29 September and 28 October 1812, 44 per cent of the total number of participants during the election. After 1832 the committee served the same end by attending scrupulously to the annual revision of Bristol's electoral registers. By defending their own and attacking Whig registrants, the White Lion tried to ensure victory in advance of the actual contest.

From the first intimation of an impending contest, the White Lion leapt into action. The general committee appointed parish committees of two to nine men, usually churchwardens, to conduct canvasses,

---

[38] CRO, Vyvyan MSS, DDV/BO/61/8.

[39] Bristol's polls in 1790 and 1796 resulted from disagreements among Whig factions and never seriously threatened the compromise between the two parties. Whig and Tory had become standard terms of reference in Bristol by 1780. *The Bristol Contest* (Bristol, 1781); BRO, B6979, 'Bristol Elections 1774–1790'.

[40] CRO, Vyvyan MSS, DDV/BO/61/10.   [41] *Parl. Deb.* 8. 912–13.

[42] *An Authentic Report of the Evidence and Proceedings before the Committee . . . on the Bristol Election* (London, 1813), 243.

organize residents, and guarantee the appearance of the voters at the hustings. Before Reform, the Blue election committee ordered copies of the previous election's poll book for use in the canvass of the voters. After Reform, the committee was able to use ward lists from the registration books for their canvasses. The committee also ordered special canvassing books for officers appointed in each parish, who were also given detailed instructions and a deadline by which the completed book was to be returned.[43] Letters from these parish officers to the central committee reported the progess of the canvass.[44] The committee mailed hundreds of letters to members of the Stedfast Society requesting their attendance, complete with carriage, at their candidates' public entry into the city. Additional letters requested specific numbers of men from each parish, ranging from ten from large parishes such as St James to only one from tiny St Ewen's, to serve as special constables for the procession. Care was to be exercised in obtaining only 'stout able bodied decent freemen' to serve in this capacity. Yet more letters to 'managers' assigned each parish a quota of 'sidesmen and carriers', to be filled exclusively from the ranks of those freemen who had 'always been true to the Party'. Even dress could not left to chance. Sidesmen were to 'have clean white shirts over their waistcoats, black breeches, and good white stockings'. Yet more letters authorized parish managers to requisition enough cockades to decorate the hats or breasts not only of the sidesmen, carriers, and special constables, but of all voters in the parish.

The committee organized candidates' schedules as carefully. During both of his elections in 1812 R. H. Davis spent from an hour and a half to six hours in each parish, depending on its size. Whether the Club was orchestrating Davis's election in 1812 or Sir Richard Vyvyan's personal tour in 1832, the committee timed arrivals to the minute to ensure formal and impressive receptions. Intense canvassing both before and after reinforced the candidate's personal visit. So well organized was the committee that even the initial absence of a candidate caused no difficulty. Letters to Vyvyan in several Continental cities kept him well informed of the excellent progress of the canvass made in his absence in the winter of 1834, though every

---

[43] BRO, MSS 22225, Ward Lists for 1834 used as canvass books for the election of 1835. See also BRO 04736.

[44] A letter from St George's parish in 1832 reported 'that our cause in this part appears certain'. CRO, Vyvyan MSS, DDV/BO/61/6/1, 6 Nov. 1832.

effort was made to dramatize his entry into the city when he returned to England at the end of December.[45] The activity in each parish more than warranted the Webbs' claim that the select vestries in Bristol were nothing more than 'Tory electioneering clubs'.[46] During the polling the White Lion tallied each parish two or three times daily and sent lists of those who had voted to parish managers so that they might ensure the appearance of the remainder in proper order.[47]

Bristol's actual polling process was reformed two years in advance of 1832. Traditionally, every voter had registered his choices at the Guildhall, which tended to delay the process and had on occasion been the cause of serious disturbances. The problems inherent in this exclusive reliance on the Guildhall were eliminated at the general election of 1830 with the construction of ten 'commodious' polling-booths in Queen Square.[48] The new procedure worked well enough that year, and since the election of 1831 never reached the polling stage, the general election of 1832 was only the second Bristol election conducted in booths. The Reform Act restricted the election to only two days, but booths permitted effective and efficient polling. The constant tallies kept by the White Lion Committee were actually more important during these two-day (and then one-day) polls since they left far less time to ensure a complete turnout. Prior to Reform each Bristol elector might have to prove his right to vote. Freeholders could do so with evidence of taxpaying, but both political clubs tried to ensure that freemen brought copies of their freedoms to the hustings.

The White Lion had less control over the oaths. At the by-election of 1812, for example, the White Lion could not prevent Henry Hunt's insistence that each voter swear the several oaths requisite to voting despite the inevitable delay. As a result each voter had to deny his receipt of a bribe, affirm his qualification as freeholder or freeman, and attest his allegiance to King and Church before voting. The committee responded to Hunt's demand by organizing the

---

[45] Ibid., DDV/BO/62/9–11.

[46] S. and B. Webb, *English Local Government* (London, 1913), 227, 242.

[47] Parish managers, however, were to 'always have in reserve a Tally of Gentlemen . . . to be in readiness when wanted'. BRO, Stedfast Society MSS 12144/92, 96, 106–7.

[48] *The Bristol Poll Book* (Bristol, 1830), p. xv. The 1826 election was the last poll taken in the Guildhall, 'access to which was by a steep flight of stone steps' that invited intimidation. BRO, Rose Collection, 1826.

swearing of the electors as well as their voting. Each parish sent freemen with 'their copies [of their freedoms] in their pockets' in batches at particular times to the Tailors' Hall in order to swear the requisite oaths in advance, thereby eliminating all but the inevitable delay and confusion caused by the Guildhall's narrow flight of steps.[49] The White Lion used similar obstructionist tactics if appropriate. At the 1812 general election the White Lion objected to virtually every potential voter for the Independent Whig candidate Sir Samuel Romilly. Their objections, each of which had to be resolved by the returning officers on the spot, obstructed the process so badly that only fifty men voted on the first day of the poll. After two more days of obstruction Romilly's supporters began to refuse to attend the hustings again unless they could be assured of voting. So hobbled was Romilly by these well-orchestrated delays that after seven days he faced failure without a large London contingent of non-resident freemen whose support he could not afford. He gave up.[50]

White Lion obstructions could be more dangerous than mere delaying tactics. The True Blues were accused of hiring large groups of 'bludgeon' men during the general contest in 1812. The committee's vigorous denials notwithstanding, expense accounts recorded £114 paid to ten men of 'Lockley's gang' along with 104 men listed as their 'Cronies'. Another group of thugs received £20 for their services. However thin the line separating legitimate employment from bribery, in this instance the White Lion stepped over it. The complaints to the Lords of the Admiralty about the involvement of regular naval officers in this business were sufficiently serious to lead to a formal investigation. Perhaps not surprisingly, the accused officers escaped punishment.[51]

Once a potential voter's qualification was verified, and the requisite oaths sworn if demanded, polling was the same before and after Reform. Each elector possessed two votes to use, or not, as he pleased. He could cast a plumper for a single candidate if he wished. The normal practice of casting both votes, however, carried with it the potential for the simultaneous support of political opposites.[52]

[49] BRO, Stedfast Society MSS 12144/13, 85, 86.

[50] The polling dragged on for the full 15 days, however, as at the by-election, because Hunt kept the hustings open by polling the minimum one voter per hour.

[51] BRO, Hare MSS 8033/24/g; Stedfast Society MSS 12144/97–103.

[52] Nossiter, *Influence, Opinion, and Political Idioms*, 177–92 ; J. A. Phillips, *Electoral Behaviour in Unreformed England* (Princeton, NJ, 1982), 20–2.

Theoretically, the White Lion Club sought only one of each elector's two votes. The Club did not violate officially the pre-1812 compromise between the parties by supporting two Tory candidates until 1835. Nevertheless, the White Lion committee usually had a decided preference for one of the two (or three) Whig candidates and occasionally mounted an overtly joint campaign with one of them.

Following the actual polling, the committee continued to decide matters such as whether or not to chair the victorious candidate. They decided not to chair Vyvyan in 1832. The chairing of the unopposed reformists in 1831 turned out to be Bristol's last, depriving a number of men of the periodic opportunity to earn a wide range of sums. Chair carriers earned £1 2s. 6d. and a new hat.[53] Umbrella carriers earned 7s. 6d. These fees, small enough in themselves, could add up quickly. The White Lions spent £2,500 for the 1812 chairing ceremony.[54] The White Lion committee also synchronized bell-ringing to celebrate victory, again by letter to all churchwardens whose churches were 'supplyed with bells', and displayed the party's colours from church towers during the ringing and chairing. The bells had been denied the reformers after the final passage of the Reform Bill in June 1832. The clergy locked their churches rather than permit the celebratory pealing of the sort the White Lion Club could command as a matter of course. Bristol's reformers were either less imaginative or more law-abiding in this instance than their counterparts in Northampton. Refused entry to the belfry for the purpose of celebrating the Reform Act, men in Northampton's All Saints parish had a local whitesmith 'open' the door for them, allowing them to ring for hours.[55]

The general committee in 1812 authorized during both elections a pre-election 'Supper and Drink . . . to the amount in the whole of 5 shillings' to be given to 'all those freemen in your parish who have their freedoms (but *not* those who are only entitled to it [freedom])'.[56] Having dispersed other refreshment tickets during the electioneering, usually valued at 5 shillings and redeemable at local inns, the Blue committee distributed 10s. 6d. tickets after the election in 1832 for a public dinner celebrating their victory. They also continued to

---

[53] F. O'Gorman, 'Election Ritual', *Past and Present*, (forthcoming).
[54] BRO, Rose Collection, unfoliated, citing 1831; BRO, Stedfast MSS 12144/112–13, 124.
[55] *Northampton Herald*, 9 June 1832.
[56] BRO, Stedfast Society MSS 12144/123, 125.

give out the 5-shilling tickets to reward loyal voters after the fact. The Blues requested the names of those particularly active in each parish so that they might be thanked personally by the successful candidate(s). Finally, accounts payable from the election had to be settled, from charges for barrels of beer to fees for hired musicians. Not receiving their £18 from the committee promptly, a band headed by James Filer and John Stockwell, 'the most of whom woted [*sic*] at the late Election', wrote directly to Vyvyan, but most settled their accounts with the committee, not the candidate.[57]

The extraordinary level of organization achieved by Bristol's Tories was not unrelated to the amount that the White Lions could and did spend, but vast sums were expended in many constituencies without creating the party structure that permitted the White Lion to orchestrate Bristol's elections so carefully and effectively. The Reform Act affected this aspect of Bristol politics not at all. The White Lion's activities on behalf of Vyvyan in 1832 matched their efforts for Davis beginning in 1812, and continued unabated during the 1830s. The White Lions won both of Bristol's seats in 1835, and retained their single seat at the two subsequent elections. Their orchestration of election victories for P. W. S. Miles became as customary as the ones they had achieved for R. H. Davis.

The Reform Bill did nothing to restrict the river of Tory gold. The committee warned parish managers before and after 1832 specifically against bribery, treating, or any suspicious behaviour in case one of the losing candidates petitioned against the return. Managers were 'not to give any Voter even a Glass of Beer or the smallest Trifle or Promise whatever' in exchange for a promise to vote.[58] Managers did not always obey. T. J. Manchee's Whiggish edition of the 1832 poll book included an analysis of the vote by qualification that showed (without editorial comment) Vyvyan's losing to Edward Protheroe, jnr. among Bristol's new £10 householders and winning only by six votes among the previously enfranchised freeholders. The bulk of Vyvyan's great lead stemmed from the old freeman voters, among whom he outpolled Protheroe by nearly 800 votes. The Tory version of the poll book, printed by J. Wansbrough, countered Manchee's insinuation by pointing out that many freemen could have qualified

---

[57] BRO, Stedfast Society MSS 12144/121; CRO, Vyvyan MSS., DDV/BO/61/41.

[58] The election committee decided that Romilly's forces had been most guilty in paying for freemen to take up their freedoms. BRO, Stedfast Society MSS 12144/88. See also J. Belchem, *'Orator' Hunt*, (Oxford, 1985), 40–1.

to vote as £10 householders had they wished.[59] To Tory eyes the daily polling figures afforded 'pretty convincing proof that the Reformers . . . were virtually beaten early on the first day of the Poll'.[60] Wansbrough did not believe that the various qualifications of the voters in either camp had anything to do with the election outcome. His allegations notwithstanding, a substantial number of Bristolians had rushed to qualify under the new law.[61]

Since Vyvyan's win could be traced to the theoretically more susceptible freemen, Manchee's insinuation of corruption cannot be dismissed lightly. But Tories were not the only ones spending heavily, and electioneering ordinarily required the collection and distribution of substantial amounts in a constituency as large as Bristol. In the face of the thousands of pounds being spent by the Tories in 1826, the adamant refusal of the Whig Edward Protheroe, snr. to spend any money should have eliminated him from competition from the outset, but his supporters raised and spent on his behalf and without his knowledge more than £7,000 during the contest. More than £2,000 purchased freedoms for Protheroe's potential supporters. In keeping with tradition, £1,250 reimbursed non-resident freemen voters for their travel expenses, £1,000 hired toll clerks to keep track of Protheroe's voters, and hundreds of additional pounds were expended in other very ordinary, completely legitimate, ways. True to his word, Protheroe had nothing to do with these expenses. The Independent and Constitutional Club defrayed the costs by subscription lists drawn up on the first day of the poll. James Cropper contributed £1,000 and George Wright £700 towards

[59] *The Poll Book* (Bristol: T. J. Manchee, 1833), p. ix. The *Bristol Mercury* claimed that the White Lion Committee distributed bribes after the close of the poll from 8 King Street. The Radicals also claimed that the Conservative Operative Association was nothing more than a device through which 1,200 freemen might be bribed with offers of assistance in times of need and 7 lb. of Blue beef at Christmas. The Tory *Felix Farley's Bristol Journal* responded that the moneys changing hands after the poll were neither illegally given nor received, but rather were legitimate payments to those paid to attend nominations and to assist in the election in other ways.

[60] *The Bristol Poll Book* (Bristol: J. Wansbrough, 1833), 20.

[61] Freedoms could be earned through birth, marriage, or apprenticeship, but those qualified still paid £3 upon admission. Without these qualifications freedoms could be purchased, but the average fees paid to a number of men including the mayor averaged £42 pounds. The electorate in 1832 contained 5,301 freemen, 862 freeholders, and 4,215 £10 householders. By 1835 only 500 additional freemen had been added, along with more than 4,000 householders. See *An Authentic Report of the Evidence and Proceedings before the Committee on the Bristol Election* for a discussion of Bristol freedoms.

the return of Protheroe as the 'free, warm, and spontaneous choice of the Electors' of Bristol, and another group of ten men contributed £200 each, but most men contributed far less. Nine men, including one anonymous donor, gave £100 each. Thirteen gave £50 each, with one of them promising 'a further £25 if needful' and another 'a further £50 if successful'.[62] Dozens of smaller contributors gave a pound, a guinea, or a slightly larger sum to pay the costs of the Independent candidate. Bristol's Whigs also contested other elections with money against the wishes of their candidates, but excessively scrupulous candidates hurt the party's chances. As his father before him, Edward Protheroe, jnr. proudly refused to pay for his election in 1830; he canvassed without any personal expenditure. He meant it when he said: 'There shall be no mistake, gentlemen: I will expend nothing, nor will I ever repay one shilling, if others, in opposition to my express desire, should be drawn into expense supporting me.'[63] Protheroe jnr. paid for this attitude dearly just as in 1812 Romilly had paid for a similar stance. Both refused all compensation to the voters, and both lost their bids for office.

If money or the lack of it influenced some voters, the behaviour of many Bristolians and the actual words of a few highlight the role of ideas, issues, and partisanship among electors. After the 1832 election, three men responded to the White Lion committee's request for a list of names of those active on behalf of Richard Vyvyan with relatively long discussions of their political beliefs. These three, James Chanter, linen-draper, of St Mary le Port; Preston Edgar, coppersmith, of St Thomas; and Henry Lloyd, brush-maker, of Castle Precincts, are indistinguishable from their fellows except for their willingness to set down their conservative principles in detail. Chanter claimed that 'a Very, Very Great proportion of those who voted for' Vyvyan gave their votes 'from the purest and most conscientious of motives; that of supporting the cause which *they* as well as *myself* believed to be for the welfare of the country'. Edgar swore never to 'swerve from the support of our Constitution in Church and State', while Lloyd believed Vyvyan to

[62] BRO, Hare MSS 8033/25(*a*)–34(*a*).

[63] John Hare served as Protheroe's election manager, and his correspondence demonstrates the care with which he oversaw Independent efforts in the face of such potent opposition. See also Broadsheet, 15 July 1830, reprinted in *Bristol Gazette*, 15 July 1830 and in *The Bristol Poll book* (Bristol, 1830) p. xviii, indicating the effort to raise other issues.

embody 'the Only Chance of Restoring the Once good name of the Loyal City of Bristol'.[64]

BRISTOL'S DIVIDED WHIGS: INDEPENDENT DISARRAY

Facing the finely tuned White Lion political machine was a Whig organization of comparable vintage, but not comparable talent. The principal Whig organization, the Independent and Constitutional or Union Club had grown out of the old Hanoverian Club at the same time that the White Lion emerged from the old True Loyal. By 1790 it represented the more radical, Foxite Whigs in Bristol.[65] Bristol's united Whigs had compromised with the strongly organized Tories and prevented polls in Bristol altogether in the early nineteenth century. Thus Bristol returned a split delegation at election after election as both parties avoided expense and the dangers of electioneering. A compromise over two seats, however, is difficult to arrange if one of the two groups arranging the compromise cannot agree among themselves. The Whigs ceased to agree in 1812 and were unable nominate a single candidate to fill their seat under the terms of the compromise. Divided into increasingly hostile camps, the Whigs effectively ceded control of Bristol to the White Lions.

Bristol's 1812 general election illustrated the complex cross-currents of Whiggery in Bristol and also indicated the general pattern of Bristol elections. The resumption of two Whig candidates seeking seats in Bristol should have raised the spectre of a joint Whig return, but the enmity between the two Whig factions coupled with the talent of the White Lion ensured absolute safety of Bristol's Tory seat. The White Lion candidate in 1812, R. H. Davis, began the year with an easy by-election victory over Henry Hunt that had nevertheless cost the White Lions more than £14,000. Davis had hardly finished paying his £10,000 share of this amount when Lord Liverpool dissolved Parliament, leaving Davis to face the voters

---

[64] Chanter lived in Bridge Street in 1830 and cast a plumper vote for Davis, as he did in each of the other unreformed elections. CRO, Vyvyan MSS, DDV/BO/61/21, 23, 36.

[65] Charles H. Walker, *Address to the Electors of Bristol* (Bristol, 1818). In pleading for support for Hugh Baillie against Edward Protheroe, Walker called for the true Whigs to rally around the Bristol Concentric Society in order to reject the Blues, 'for there the true poison lurks'.

again.[66] Bristol's Independent Whigs rejected the candidacy of Edward Protheroe in 1812, leading the undaunted Protheroe to offer himself without their backing as the 'enemy of tyranny and corruption whether exercised by a Court, an Aristocracy, or a Club'. Protheroe explained his unorthodox stand as a refusal to sell himself to the 'paltry patronage of a Political Club' that no longer represented the 'Old Whig' interest in Bristol.[67] The Independents responded by recruiting Sir Samuel Romilly whose principles could hardly have been more sharply attuned to an Independent Whig audience. Romilly proudly cited the memory of Fox and reminded the voters at every opportunity of his abolitionist views. While Protheroe's statements about Reform were extremely vague, Romilly demanded parliamentary reform in order 'to render more perfect the representation of the People in Parliament'.[68] War and peace in America drew particular attention in Bristol. The press gangs operating in the city added direct local relevance to Romilly's concerns about enlistment in the armed forces for a term of years instead of life. Romilly openly supported Catholic emancipation; Protheroe evaded the issue. Protheroe professed his loyalty to the Church, but also espoused religious liberty. Protheroe knew the danger of antagonizing Dissenters. As one contemporary described it: 'No town abounds with more seats of Religion than this; they [Dissenters] keep unto themselves teachers of every Denomination.'[69] From the Unitarians of Lewins Mead to the relatively few but powerful Quakers, Bristol was extremely heterodox. Catholicism raised particularly sticky questions since many Dissenters placed Catholics well outside the protection of religious liberty. Protheroe waffled on the issue before suggesting when pressed that a repeal of the punitive laws against Catholics would be acceptable only if they were required to swear an oath to the Constitution.[70]

At his second 1812 contest, therefore, Davis faced in addition to the troublesome Hunt, a reforming Whig, Romilly, and an

---

[66] *Bristol Times*, 2 Aug. 1862. The election papers of the White Lion Committee (or Stedfast Society) recorded £29,429 14s. 7d. spent in returning Davis twice in 1812. The by-election cost just over £14,000 and the general election approximately £15,000.

[67] BRO 04728(1), p. xxvi; Sir S. Romilly, *Memoirs*, 3 vols. (London, 1840) iii. 59.

[68] BRO 04728(1) pp. xxix, xix; Stedfast Society MSS 12144/36, 38.

[69] Ayers (ed.), *Paupers and Pig Killers*, 223.

[70] Romilly, *Memoirs*, iii. 58; BRO, Stedfast Society MSS 12144/40; 04728 (1).

extremely moderate Whig, Protheroe.[71] Originally Davis presented himself as the solitary White Lion candidate, but so pronounced were the differences between Protheroe's very 'mild' Whiggery and Romilly's reforming zeal that Davis united with Protheroe on the third day of the poll. Protheroe's abandonment by the Whigs left him little recourse. He needed the alliance with the Tories despite the extremely poor fit of his principles and those of his new-found friends. If Protheroe was not an 'advanced' Whig like Romilly, he was on most issues no Tory. Protheroe may have waffled on emancipation, but Davis had announced more than once his utter hostility to any concession to Catholics. Protheroe, like Romilly, advocated peace with France; Davis supported the war. Only by papering over major disagreements of this sort between Tories and mild Whigs could Protheroe join his orange banners with Davis's blue ones.[72]

The vote reflected the broad but unsuccessful appeal of Romilly's politics. Despite his refusal to canvass personally, Romilly attracted 767 plumpers (roughly 17 per cent of the total vote cast) before withdrawing from the contest.[73] Romilly may not have won the election, but an extraordinary number of those to whom his principles appealed were willing to make the political sacrifice of plumping. The Independents succeeded in identifying their candidate's stand on the issues so clearly that another 9 per cent of the voters coupled Romilly with Hunt, a commonsensical pairing of the two most radical candidates regardless of Romilly's official condemnation of Hunt.[74] Undaunted, Hunt's supporters called for Hunt/Romilly doubles, and many responded. Only 10 per cent of the voters cast unequivocally split votes by coupling the diametrically opposed Davis and Romilly, and even fewer (3 per cent) ignored the division among the local Whigs and doubled for Romilly and

---

[71] Gash, *Lord Liverpool*, 96.

[72] For a discussion of war or peace as an issue in 1812 see R. M. Stewart, *Henry Brougham, 1778–1868* (London, 1985), 82. See also, BRO 04728. Davis had scrupulously avoided parliamentary reform, war and peace, and other subjects of contemporary interest in his speech to his Bristol supporters in Apr. 1812, but such issues were unavoidable in Oct. Romilly, *Memoirs*, iii. 56–62.

[73] Romilly was returned in Dec. 1812 for Arundel, the Duke of Norfolk's borough. Romilly refused to canvass personally. *Memoirs*, iii. 22, 54–5. See also BRO 04728 (1), 23.

[74] The Independents accused Hunt of trying to 'disunite the ties by which society in a religious, moral, and political point of view is cemented'. Belchem, *'Orator' Hunt*, 40.

Protheroe. Virtually no one plumped for Davis, but no one asked voters to do so, and indeed there was no reason for it. Nearly half (48 per cent) of the electorate doubled for Davis and Protheroe, and another 10 per cent split their support between Davis and Romilly, placing Davis at the top of the poll by more than 500 votes over Protheroe, who won Bristol's second seat, and by more than 1,000 votes over Romilly. Davis's subsequent claim of full credit for Protheroe's victory seemed justified at least in part since nearly 90 per cent of Protheroe's votes were doubled with a vote for Davis.

From a national perspective, a Romilly/Protheroe vote made more sense than any other vote except a plump for Davis, the sole Tory. Bristol's two sets of Whigs, however, dismissed their similarities as irrelevant. The Whig Independents wanted Romilly to fill 'their' seat and fully expected the Tories to fill the other one. Many of the Independents refused actually to vote for a Tory, but at the same time spurned the opportunity to use their second votes to support Protheroe. They had as a group rejected his candidacy earlier in the year, and they ignored him at the hustings. Their unwillingness to double for Romilly and Protheroe illustrates the unbridgeable Whig rift and the primacy of local politics in 1812.

The Whig division in Bristol also determined the 1818 election as Whig again fought Whig, leaving the White Lion candidate virtually unopposed. The Independents rejected Edward Protheroe, snr. a second time, declaring that his parliamentary behaviour was 'directly opposed to his original [Whig] professions'. So tepid was Protheroe's support for parliamentary reform that many Independents were convinced that Protheroe had sold himself to the Government. His support of Sidmouth's repressive measures in 1817 which included the suspension of habeas corpus enhanced those suspicions. His vote against the Government's revision of the Corn Laws did nothing to help his reputation among the Independents. Davis had also voted against the new Corn Law. Protheroe defended his absence from 'the lists of the opposition' by rejecting the role of delegate. The Independents wanted 'a decided party man', but he had never intended to serve 'in that character' and would continue to vote according to his conscience.[75]

[75] Thorne (ed.), *House of Commons*, i. 254; Sir H. Protheroe, *A Full Account of the Late Election for Bristol Vindicating the Conduct of Edward Protheroe* (Bristol, 1819); *An Impartial Statement of All Proceedings connected with the Progress and Result of the Late Elections* (Bristol, 1819); C. A. Elton, *An Apology for Colonel Hugh Baillie* (Bristol,

Rank-and-file Whigs as well as the party's leaders suspected Protheroe's principles.[76] It was relatively easy for ordinary citizens to be well informed. Bristol's several newspapers mirrored the wide political spectrum of its electors, and a deluge of broadsheets issued daily during the most intense electioneering raised most political issues bluntly and clearly. *Felix Farley's Bristol Journal* catered to Bristol's White Lions; the *Mirror* and the *Observer* covered moderate Whig interests well; and the *Mercury* reflected Independent Whig policy. The Bristol *Gazette* served radical voters before the term 'Radical' entered Bristol's political vocabulary two years later.[77]

Dismissing Protheroe as a Tory in Whig clothing, the Independents adopted Colonel Hugh Baillie in 1818. Baillie's politics also left much to be desired. A prominent Independent lawyer argued for Baillie only in comparison to Protheroe because Baillie had 'never openly and publically [*sic*] avowed his political sentiments in favour of a Constitutional Reform of Parliament, nor had he pledged himself to the support of that cause'.[78] Having no personal voting record in the Commons to which he could refer, Baillie claimed that his brother James Evan Baillie's (Member for Tralee) record was identical to the one he would have accumulated had he been in Parliament.[79] Walker suspected that Baillie adopted this unusual tactic in order to avoid clear avowals or pledges on the issues of the day. Anxious from the beginning to avoid a fight and afraid that his Presbyterianism would pose an impediment, Baillie announced his belief in religious toleration and his desire to admit Roman Catholics to political power, but hedged his position by declaring himself 'bound, upon this subject to obey any instructions unequivocally

1818); *A Summary View of the Public Conduct of Edward Protheroe, Esq., MP* (Bristol, 1818); *A Full Detail of the Facts relative to the Late Election of Edward Protheroe* (Bristol, 1819).

[76] During Protheroe's nomination speech, he defended his support of the Home Secretary's proposals by arguing that the first Commons secret committee had unanimously recommended the suspension of habeas corpus. A member of the crowd called Protheroe a liar and in the process revealed a detailed knowledge of the Commons' actions on this and other matters. *The Late Elections* (London, 1818), 41–2. *An Authentic Account of the Evidence Given to the Committee . . . on the Bristol Election* (Bristol, 1819).

[77] Charles Elton, a banker with pronounced views in support of religious toleration, edited the *Mercury* soon after its purchase by the Independent Whigs in 1818. A substantial number of broadsides augmenting Bristol's newspapers during these years has been collected. BL 1880.c.12; BL 1880.c.20. Williams, 'Bristol in the General Elections of 1818 and 1820', 176.

[78] Walker, *Address to the Electors*, 3–7.   [79] *The Late Elections*, 27–30.

expressed to be the general voice of my constituents'.[80] Partly mollified by his promises and having no real choice, Walker and the Independents backed Baillie. Protheroe had 'aided a corrupt Ministry to suspend the Constitution' in a time of peace, 'under the pretext of quelling riots which were occasioned by distress and starvation', and 'afterwards by his vote shielded those Ministers against the cries of those whom they had oppressed'. However imperfect Baillie might be, 'it will be impossible that he can act worse' than Protheroe.[81]

When the Independents proposed Baillie, Protheroe surprised everyone by withdrawing from the contest, only to be nominated by his friends anyway. Baillie then confused matters further by withdrawing to prevent 'a furious contest, inflamed by party zeal, and embittered by religious animosities'. The Independents were not willing to accept Baillie's withdrawal either, and they forged ahead with 'inflexible determination' to secure his return.[82] Baillie acceded to this determination and the election proceeded to its predictable conclusion with the two unusually reluctant Whig candidates. Davis topped the poll. Like Romilly, Baillie and the Independents lost to Protheroe by a substantial margin. A writer in Liverpool contemptuously dismissed Bristol as a town containing only fifty-two voters, that is the Corporation, but the strength of the White Lions did not eliminate popular participation. Though they owned one seat and influenced the other, the Whig interparty brawls over principle began the redefinition of Bristol politics.[83]

Bristol's 1820 contest produced less debate, fewer broadsides and pamphlets, less attention to issues, and a temporary restoration of Whig unity. Edward Protheroe, snr. refused to stand again when he discovered just before the dissolution that his brother Sir Henry Protheroe had secretly spent thousands of pounds on his behalf during the 1818 election. The Whigs turned to a new, generally appealing candidate in the person of Henry Bright, a West Indian merchant. Bright's interests in Jamaica mollified what might be termed the conservative Whig branch responsible for Protheroe's victories, but his stand on many other matters, notably religious

---

[80] *A Peep at the Commons* (London, 1820), 32.
[81] Walker, *Address to the Electors*, 9.
[82] Williams, 'Bristol in the General Elections of 1818 and 1820', 173–201.
[83] *Liverpool Poll Book* (Liverpool, 1818), 34, reprinting a letter in the local press signed by Junius.

toleration, appealed to the Independent Whigs. Nominated by a Methodist minister, John Rowe, Bright pledged himself to 'Liberty, both Civil and Religious', but initially avoided a more concrete statement which might antagonize the conservative faction. When Bright finally succumbed to the pressure of Davis's vehement anti-Catholicism and announced formally that he was 'not a friend to the Catholic cause', he did not seriously jeopardize his liberal support.[84] Few men of any political persuasion could safely advocate emancipation. Nor did Bright lose many Independents by refusing to promise to support the repeal Sidmouth's Six Acts.[85] The electorate read the details of the Cato Street conspiracy just long enough before the contest to see the Six Acts in a new light.

In fact, so broad was Bright's appeal that 1820 was not an election in any meaningful sense. Few Bristolians took seriously a Radical effort to choose James Evan Baillie, brother of the unsuccessful Hugh. Baillie then added to the farcical nature of the 'contest' by refusing to stand. The Radicals quickly recognized the futility of their position and may have realized the absurdity of their support of a slave-owner when they surrendered after only two days.[86] Thus the briefly restored Whig/Tory compromise was marred only by 111 voters who doubled for Bright and Baillie.[87] Four other electors cast simultaneous Davis and Baillie votes for reasons known only to themselves. While this pitifully small number rejected the old compact, Davis and Bright accumulated nearly 3,000 votes each, with plumpers contributing roughly a quarter of each of their totals.

[84] *Gazette*, 24 Feb. 1820; *Felix Farley's Bristol Journal*, 1 Mar. 1820.

[85] C. H. Walker, *Address to the Electors of Bristol Showing the Ineligibility of H. Bright to Represent Them* (Bristol, 1820); id., *A Second Address to the Electors of Bristol* (Bristol, 1820); id., *A Third Address to the Electors of Bristol* (Bristol, 1820).

[86] All of the parliamentary registers incorrectly identify the Radical candidate as Hugh Baillie, but the surviving manuscript poll book leaves no doubt that James Evan Baillie was the candidate. Oddly, the poll continued with only two candidates since Bright's supporters refused to let Davis top the poll. Bright outpolled Davis, and the embarrassed True Blues refused to chair Davis as a result. *Bristol Mercury*, 13 Mar. 1820; *Gazette*, 19, 24 Feb. 1820; *Observer*, 2, 9 Mar. 1820.

[87] The White Lion Club did not actively support Davis in 1820, partly because of his financial embarrassments at the time. Davis, counting upon a further delay of the resumption of specie payments, invested heavily in Government stock in 1818 and 1819. With the threatened return to gold, Davis's speculation backfired and he lost substantially. The White Lion recruited Philip Miles to stand, but Miles's poor health forced him to retire from the contest before a canvass. Without guidance from the White Lion, the True Blues lost much of their advantage, as Bright's topping the poll demonstrated. Bright placed first by attracting 767 plumpers to Davis's 689. Baillie's total was only 115 despite the report in some accounts of 127 votes.

Independent v. West Indian Whigs

The complex struggles of 1812 and 1818 had begun to redefine the term 'Whig' in Bristol. An issue of national concern completed the transition at elections beginning in 1826. Slavery clarified and solidified Whig differences as it took pride of place in the continuing dispute. The original Foxite Independents became further estranged from the more conservative West Indian merchant faction of the party, increasingly identified with slavery. Whig political rifts did not always revolve around slavery, but typically slavery played at or near the surface. The end of the slave trade had not proven to be particularly divisive despite the the general importance of both sugar and slaves in Bristol's economy. After 1807 men like John Cam Hobhouse's father could no longer turn a gross profit of more than £6,000 on a single, relatively small shipment of human cargo to the West Indies. The abolition of slavery itself, on the other hand, could hardly have been more divisive. Abolition threatened more than lost profits; it would destroy livelihoods, and the issue was taken up as much over economics as grand principles.[88] Burke may have been unduly harsh in saying of the Bristol merchant, 'He has no church but the Exchange; no Bible but his ledger; and no God but his gold.'[89] With many of them, however, slavery was purely business.

Slavery dominated the 1826 election. Printed subscription lists used to record contributors to the Independent election fund in 1826 heralded their candidate's opposition to slavery. By choosing Edward Protheroe, snr. as their candidate (without his knowledge or consent), however, the Independent Whigs tried to improve their competitiveness *vis-à-vis* the West Indians to whom they had lost twice. Since Protheroe had been returned twice by the other Whig faction, the Independents simultaneously clouded and clarified the issues. In the eyes of the Independents, Protheroe was far preferable to the West Indian slave-owner Bright. Protheroe had said virtually nothing in his previous election addresses about slavery, but could be counted at least as a 'hopeful' on the issue. Without Protheroe's personal co-operation, though, the Independents fought a losing battle from the beginning. It surprised no one that Davis and Bright retained their seats. Davis amassed nearly as many votes as his two

[88] R. E. Zegger, *John Cam Hobhouse* (Columbia, Mo., 1973), 34.
[89] Hunt, *Memoirs*, iii. 40.

Whig opponents combined, while Bright managed a comfortable second-place margin of more than 400 votes.[90] Only sixteen voters out of the more than 6,000 participating in the 1826 election doubled for the two Whigs who stood on opposite sides of the slavery issue.

This combustible issue also generated heat at the 1830 contest. The Independents' new candidate, Edward Protheroe, jnr., was not the tepid Whig his father had been. The younger Protheroe was a 'true' progressive Whig and was going to be a 'Whole Bill Reformer'. On the issue of slavery Protheroe took no half measures. A Member for Evesham since 1826, Protheroe had voted for Brougham's motion that the Commons 'take into consideration the most effectual means of mitigating the condition of the slave population, and finally of abolishing slavery altogether'.[91] Protheroe's initial letter to his supporters emphasized his 'determination' in supporting Brougham. Slavery actually sparked a riot during Protheroe's initial entry into Bristol in which twenty-six people were 'carried off as dead' to local infirmaries.[92] To replace Henry Bright, the West Indians chose James Evan Baillie, a slave-owner who was to receive almost £13,000 of the £20 million paid by the Government in compensation to slave-owners after abolition.[93] One of men nominating Baillie claimed: 'Slavery and Anti-Slavery is now the cry, instead of Whig and Tory.'[94]

Whig disunity found expression in the avoidance of party labels by both White Lions and West Indian Whigs during 1830's electioneering. Henry Bush's nomination of Davis appealed to all constituents, rich or poor, Whig or Tory, and argued that Davis's defence of trade and commerce benefited and would continue to benefit all Bristolians. Though no one could have not known that Davis was the White Lion candidate, Davis himself disclaimed party labels, using instead commerce and trade as the watchwords of his campaign. One of his

[90] The results of the 1826 election were: Davis 3,887; Bright 2,314; and Protheroe 1,874.

[91] In Sept. 1831 Protheroe almost fought a duel with Lt. C. Claxton, RN over Protheroe's open letter to Bristol's freemen castigating 'hired agents of the West India aristocracy'. At the last minute their seconds prevented shots being fired, but the pistols underscored the intensity of feelings about abolition. BRO, Hare MSS 8033/2; *Poll Book*, p. x.

[92] BRO, Hare MSS 8033/3.

[93] Ibid., 8033/22; Vincent, *McCalmont's Parliamentary Poll Book*, 87–9.

[94] Protheroe, jnr. kept the orange colour associated with his father's campaigns despite their political differences, but easily shed his father's Tory tinge. *The Bristol Poll book*, (Bristol, 1830), p. xiii.

election cards, while printed with blue ink and calling for true blue support, repeated Bush's theme: Davis was 'The Friend of All'. Another, also printed in blue portrayed Davis against the background of a ship streaming a banner marked 'TRADE'. Taking his cue from the White Lions, the Revd. Sir Abraham Elton nominated J. E. Baillie not 'as a Whig or as a Tory; . . . but . . . as an honest man, that noblest work of God'. Baillie invoked the memory of his predecessor, Henry Bright, but neither he nor Davis ever referred to party while taking advantage of intense partisan activity.[95]

After the uncontested Whig/Reform triumph of 1831 Whig harmony rapidly disappeared because the Independents abandoned Baillie over slavery the very next year. Baillie's principles and his slaves actually lent themselves more comfortably to a joint campaign with an anti-reformer like Vyvyan. Baillie appealed to those voters more accurately described as 'Conservative', a political appellation new to Bristol in 1832.[96] The Independent candidates Protheroe and John Williams, on the other hand, might have been better described as 'Liberal' than 'Whig'. Both represented that breed who had successfully demanded *'the Bill, the whole Bill, and nothing but the Bill'*.[97] The results of the contest afforded no comfort at all to Bristol's reformers. Despite the reformist Whigs giving Bristolians the option of casting both votes for Independents for the first time in twenty years by offering two candidates, the White Lion's influence over Bristol's second seat persisted. Baillie actually formally declined to stand twice in the months prior to the contest in 1832 and never left the Isle of Wight during the electioneering, but the White Lion forces decided early in the election to coalesce with Baillie's supporters in order to counter the joint 'Liberal' campaign.[98] The blending of Baillie's Pink and Blue colours with Vyvyan's True Blue

[95] *The Bristol Poll book*, (Bristol, 1830), pp. xii, xv.

[96] BRO, Rose Collection, news-cuttings note the acceptance of 'Liberal' by erstwhile Whigs and 'Conservative' by Tories in 1832. Latimer, *Annals*, 143, 203; *Monthly Repository*, Dec. 1831.

[97] Robert Seymour, *Four Specimens of the Political Publick*, 1 Aug. 1831. Stephens, Hawkins, and George (comp.), *Catalogue*, 16756, reproduced in H. T. Dickinson, *Caricatures and the Constitution, 1760–1832* (Cambridge, 1986), 324–5.

[98] CRO, Vyvyan MSS, DDV/BO/62/9–12. The Whigs withdrew Hobhouse's name at the end of the first day, leaving Baillie alone. The first broadsheet by the White Lion against Baillie did not appear until 3 Jan. 1835, attacking his support of the Triennial Bill, his inquiry into the pension list, and his opposition to the Corn Law. Hobhouse himself noted that Baillie's defeat was no loss to the Whig party. BL Add. MSS 61826, Hobhouse diary, 6 Jan. 1835.

worked just as well without Baillie's knowledge or consent. The White Lion retained Baillie's seat for him while regaining their own for Vyvyan. 'Conservatives' dominated Bristol's first reformed election as in the past. Bristol's nominally split delegation contained two MPs who were virtually indistinguishable politically. But in Bristol as elsewhere old terms die hard. The Independents failed to return a single candidate until the 1837 election of a champion of the secret ballot, F. H. F. Berkeley.

The very poor showing of Bristol's reformers in 1832 demoralized the Independents to such an extent that they failed to find acceptable candidates to stand in 1835. Part of the problem stemmed from finances. As the Tories put it late in 1834, 'the Destructives have no money'. Rather than permit the Tories, who now called themselves Conservatives, to take both seats by default, however, the Independents tried to recruit John Cam Hobhouse, who had just won a seat for Nottingham. Hobhouse had declined the honour once already, and he again refused to attend the contest and even refused to sit for Bristol instead of Nottingham if elected.[99] The Independents also turned to J. E. Baillie despite their determined opposition to his candidacy three years earlier. The abolition of slavery in 1833 had eliminated the major source of antagonism between the Whig factions, and the Independents could take some consolation from Baillie's more acceptable if mild views on several other crucial issues, including the Corn Law and triennial Parliaments. Their endeavour to elect an absent, already elected, completely unco-operative candidate, along with an erstwhile enemy, was doomed to defeat.

The White Lion had planned as late as autumn 1834 to mount yet another coalition to elect Baillie and Vyvyan. The Tories turned against Baillie only after his default selection by the Whigs.[100] Having lost their coalition partner, the White Lion for the first time in the century nominated a second candidate, P. J. Miles, and mounted a successful joint campaign. The White Lion was not pleased with Vyvyan's performance in the first reformed Parliament, and they supported his re-election reluctantly, complaining that he had been too taciturn in the House and had not helped obtain money

[99] Ibid., entries for 6–8 Jan. 1835. Hobhouse's father died in 1831. *Carpenter's Monthly Political Magazine*, Sept. 1831, 35.
[100] CRO, Vyvyan MSS, DDV/BO/62/1, 10.

for reconstructing the Custom House and Excise Office destroyed in the fire.[101] Reluctant support sufficed.

After the White Lion swept away the reunited but pathetically weak Whigs in 1835, two successive elections produced split delegations. A Tory candidate topped the poll in 1837 and 1841, but the White Lion could not elect their second candidate. Both elections involved identical candidates, and both (all three if 1847 is included) achieved identical results. P. W. S. Miles, an extremely prosperous merchant banker, stood with William Fripp, a equally wealthy retired soap manufacturer and sometime mayor of Bristol. The Whigs countered with F. H. F. Berkeley, a Liberal who favoured the ballot, shorter Parliaments, and the relaxation of the Corn Laws, but who was also the younger son of an earl.[102] With the White Lion as active as ever, Miles, who had just turned 21 and was at the time of the 1837 contest in the midst of his Grand Tour, gained his seat easily, and kept it in 1841. These election results returned Bristol to the eighteenth century *status quo*, though polls were required to achieve the split delegations reminiscent of an earlier time.

THE IMPACT OF REFORM: A QUANTITATIVE ASSESSMENT

Did the Reform Act mean nothing in Bristol? In point of fact, the striking similarities in Bristol politics before and after 1832 simply mask Reform's transformation of electoral behaviour. The White Lion Club may have fought election after election in the same way, large amounts of money may have been spent by Whigs and Tories at each contest, and elections may have yielded almost exactly the same results from year to year, but these continuities did not prevent substantial changes within the electorate. The Act's popular impact is apparent not through descriptive accounts of the electioneering process, but through systematic comparisons of the political choices of the voters. Changes in the voting behaviour of those already enfranchised and changes stemming from the alteration of Bristol's electorate through the exclusion of non-resident freemen voters and the addition of thousands of £10 householders can be discerned only

[101] BRO, Rose Collection, unfoliated, 1837–41.
[102] Berkeley was the fourth son of the fifth earl.

by recourse to quantitative analyses of poll books.[103] Missing poll books for 1826 and 1818 prevent some relevant analyses, and the manuscript poll book for the election of 1820 reveals far less that it ought.[104] Thus unreformed electoral behaviour in Bristol is sometimes invisible, and visible behaviour is occasionally more opaque than desirable. The voting evidence for elections after Reform, on the other hand, is comprehensive and complete, and voting behaviour in Bristol before, during, and after Reform can be examined profitably if conducted in the context of the idiosyncrasies of Bristol politics.

Summary statistics for Bristol elections indicate a change in the nature of voting behaviour in Bristol during the Reform era that was magnified by the passage of the Reform Act. Looking strictly at those voters who supported Whig or Tory candidates, Bristolians appear to have acquired a far more partisan orientation after 1830, and this enhanced orientation grew to complete domination soon after 1832. At the elections of 1812, 1820, and 1830, only a quarter to two-fifths of the electorate cast ballots exclusively for Whig or Tory candidates while the remainder split their support. The level of strict party voting rose markedly at Bristol's first reformed election when nearly half of the electorate voted exclusively for one party or the other. The presence of a single Tory candidate in 1832 renders this high level of strictly party voting particularly impressive, but the new level of partisanship evident in 1832 pales in comparison to levels attained at Bristol's three subsequent contests. Virtually nine of ten voters in 1835, 1837, and 1841 cast strictly party ballots.

The structure of these elections played some role in the decisions of the voters, just as structure had always influenced voting patterns. Examinations of eighteenth-century electoral behaviour have demonstrated the general unwillingness of voters to cast plumpers. Normally, far fewer partisan votes were cast in three-man elections (two candidates of one party versus a sole candidate of the other) than in four-candidate elections (at which each party nominated two candidates). At four-candidate contests all electors could cast partisan ballots without paying some political or economic price.

---

[103] *Parl. Deb.* 9 (17 Dec. 1831), 505. In 1850 55% of Bristol's dwellings were rated at less than £11. After 1835 only 20% of Bristol's householders held the franchise. G. Bush, *Bristol and its Municipal Government, 1820–1851* (Bristol, 1976), 211.

[104] Williams, 'Bristol in the General Elections of 1818 and 1820', 175 n. 3. Baillie's 1820 total was a mere 115 votes (Bristol Central Library, B4419).

TABLE 2.1. *Strictly Defined Party and Split-Voting in Bristol,*
1812–1841

Year	Strictly partisan votes (%)	Split votes (%)	No. of candidates
1812	41.9	58.1	4
1820	42.6	57.4	3
1830	23.2	76.8	4
1832	49.2	50.8	4
1835	93.0	7.0	4
1837	89.0	11.0	3
1841	87.0	13.4	3

Sources: Printed parliamentary poll books of 1812, 1830–41; manuscript poll book, 1820, Bristol Central Library, B4419.

Without two candidates from each party, many individual voters faced a complicated decision. The rule applied to Bristol elections, as indeed it applied to most English constituencies until the virtual elimination of two-member constituencies in 1885.

Bristol elections, however, were not as simple as that. The number of candidates listed in Table 2.1 often conceals more than it reveals. The 1812 election, for example, involved four candidates, but the four included an unopposed Tory, two battling Whigs, and an outsider who attracted a few votes from one of the Whig factions. Of the four-man Bristol elections reported in the table, the normal configuration of two versus two existed only in 1835. Genuinely radical candidates, however, such as Henry Hunt (1812) and James Acland (1830) resulted in parodies of four-man contests.[105] Nor did Bristol's unreformed three-man contests necessarily resemble the normal pattern; often one Tory and one conservative Whig stood against a more radical Whig before 1832. Counting partisan votes under these conditions demands flexibility.

Nevertheless, more than a mere structural explanation underlies the transformation of voting behaviour evident in Table 2.1. A striking shift to partisan voting appeared first at a four-man contest

[105] James Acland was, among other things, the editor, author, and publisher of Bristol's first daily, *The Bristolian*, 'a cheap paper of indifferent character'. He had just been released from gaol where he had served time for libel. BRO, Rose Collection, unfoliated.

(1832) and gained strength at the subsequent four-man election in 1835, but it continued unchecked at the two following three-man elections (1837 and 1841). The extremely high level of partisan voting that marked Bristol's 1837 and 1841 contests required a third or more of the electors to plump for solitary Whig candidates; that they did so unhesitatingly strongly suggests that the key to the change lay not in the availability of two candidates from each party, but in a new willingness to cast partisan votes even if partisanship demanded a plump. Ironically, structural idiosyncrasy marked many of Bristol's elections, but structure was largely irrelevant.

The summary statistics reported in Table 2.1, though strictly accurate, exaggerate the changes in voting habits. By examining votes only as they were related to the parliamentary parties, the table ignores Bristol's complicated and critically important local political considerations. A voter who doubled for R. H. Davis and Edward Protheroe, snr. in 1812 split his support between the parliamentary parties, but the nearly 50 per cent of the electorate who did so were not casting politically inconsistent votes. Nor were the 17 per cent of the voters who plumped for Sir Samuel Romilly that year behaving irrationally by casting a Whig plumper when there was another Whig candidate to whom they could have given their second votes. Far from it. Local considerations in combination with national issues virtually demanded either a double vote for Davis and Protheroe or a single vote for Romilly. Most Bristolians met that demand. Table 2.2 repeats the kind of examination reported in Table 2.1, but rather than defining votes strictly according to the parliamentary parties, it recognizes the emotional, tactical, and often formal link between the Tory White Lions and the West Indians Whigs. In this more locally sensitive comparison of Bristol elections, a shift in voting habits over the Reform era remains apparent, but appears both less dramatic and less uniform.

Almost half again as many Bristolians cast party ballots in 1832 as in 1830 whether or not West Indian Whigs are counted as Whigs or Tories. Voters had little difficulty distinguishing between the three different Whig candidates that year. The votes of White Lion parish leaders, identified by circular letter just after the election, reflected the real partisan divisions involved in Bristol's first reformed election. Tory party activists to a man cast doubles for Vyvyan and Baillie. Moreover, virtually all rank-and-file Tory voters (and nearly 46 per cent of all voters) followed suit and doubled for the solitary

TABLE 2.2. *Partisan Voting in Bristol: Recognizing Alliance of White Lion Tories and West Indian Whigs* (%)

Year	Partisan votes	Split votes	Unnecessary plumps*	Partisan plumps**
1812	82.4	13.2	4.3	17.4
1820	57.1	2.0	40.9	20.7
1830	58.1	35.5	6.1	16.6
1832	85.7	4.9	1.3	8.1
1835	86.4	7.0	6.5	NA
1837	86.9	11.0	2.1	37.3
1841	83.2	13.4	3.4	33.1

NA Not applicable.

* Unnecessary plumping means casting a single vote despite the presence of two candidates of the same party at a contest.

** Partisan plumping means casting a single vote because only one candidate stood for a particular party.

Sources: See Table 2.1.

White Lion candidate and the West Indian Baillie. So successful was the coalition of conservative forces that only 7 per cent of the voters plumped for Vyvyan despite his nominal stance as the sole White Lion candidate. Fewer than 5 per cent of Bristol's voters split their support in any fashion between the two sets of candidates, and only a handful cast plumpers unnecessarily for one candidate instead of doubling for one side or the other. The two reformist Whig candidates, Protheroe and Williams, stood so clearly apart from the West Indian Whig Baillie that Bristol's Independent Whigs toed the party line in 1832 and subsequently.

The increasing proportion of the electorate plumping for political reasons in 1837 and 1841 highlights the increase in partisanship that accompanied Reform. Plumping had not been unusual in Bristol's unreformed elections. Political motivations appear to have generated many of the hundreds of plumpers for Sir Samuel Romilly. Following Reform, however, partisan plumping reached and maintained impressive levels. A third or more of the electors in both 1837 and 1841 cast the plumpers required by the appearance of a single Whig candidate, resulting in his return at both elections. Offsetting the total of 137 Tories who plumped without cause, more than 2,400 Whigs plumped with good reason in 1837, and more than 2,900

Whigs did so four years later. Party feeling of this intensity developed with Reform.

Reform changed Bristol politics, but there had been many partisans in Bristol well before 1832. Expressions of political opinions by some of them reinforce this view. For many the debate over Reform may have only enhanced long-held and strongly felt political principles. Just after the 1832 election, for example, James Chanter told Sir Richard Vyvyan:

I have, ever since I became a thinking Man, advocated the political principles which I now hold. And the more I see: and the more I hear of adverse ones, the more I am satisfied in my conscience that I originally adopted those which are calculated to uphold the safety, the honour, and the Interest of our country.

By the 1832 election, Chanter had been wielding his franchise for twenty-five years, and he claimed that his political position had hardly changed over those years. He had been voting according to his conscience and expressing his strong partisan loyalty when he cast a double vote for Davis and Protheroe in 1812, just as he voted according to his principles by doubling for Vyvyan and Baillie in 1832. None of his votes measured up to the rigid standard the parliamentary parties demanded by the measurements in Table 2.1, but those failures did not in any way diminish their partisanship. In Chanter's experienced and well-informed opinion, Bristol's Tories simply supported 'a cause which *they* as well as *myself* believed to be for the welfare of their country'.[106] With men like Chanter in the electorate as early as 1812, it would be surprising if Table 2.2 failed to indicate partisan behaviour in Bristol across the entire span of these elections.

Charles Taylor, another man instrumental in Vyvyan's 1832 victory, told Sir Richard in a similar vein:

Whatever may have been our services, they were cheerfully given, and whatever the sacrifices of our time, they were willingly made in support of a cause endeared to us by early association and more mature conviction.

Preston Edgar repeated the sentiments of Chanter and Taylor when he assured Vyvyan that 'the Blue Party is that I have been from my earliest life firmly attached to [*sic*]'.[107] These men, and in their

---

[106] CRO, Vyvyan MSS, DDV/BO/61/21.   [107] Ibid., DDV/BO/61/23–6.

The Impact of Reform

opinion many of their fellows, had behaved in 1832 much as they had behaved before. Their partisanship stemmed from neither the agitation over Reform nor the Act itself.

With local politicians of this calibre in the Bristol electorate at the beginning of the century, with cross-sectional electoral evidence that Reform affected voting behaviour unmistakably, and with other indications that the changes that accompanied Reform may be somewhat misleading, a more robust measure of partisanship is required to assess electoral change. Cross-sectional comparisons are useful, but a diachronic perspective reveals much more clearly the relationship between Reform and partisanship in Bristol. Table 2.3 reveals that Chanter, Taylor, Edgar, and their peers notwithstanding, Reform altered the nature of electoral behaviour in Bristol. Measured either from the perspective of the parliamentary parties alone or from the more realistic perspective of the Tory/West Indian Whig alliance, the choices of Bristol's electors across elections indicate a changing political environment in the 1830s.

The political universe visible to Bristol electors in the 1820s and 1830s, revolving around the three major local factions and the two parliamentary parties, remained reasonably stable over the years between the end of the Napoleonic wars and the early reign of Queen Victoria. This stability determines the longitudinal measurements reported in Table 2.3. It is undoubtedly the case, however, that many of the issues of greatest concern in Bristol, notably Catholic emancipation, did not lend themselves to clear partisan divisions. To expect completely consistent voting, therefore, particularly before the emergence of Reform as a compelling issue, might seem unreasonable. Nevertheless, well before the referendum election of 1831 it was possible to make clear and consistent choices at Bristol elections on the basis of national and local issues. Unless an elector experienced some major personal political change, a vote for the White Lions at one election should have been followed by a vote for the White Lions at subsequent elections. Edgar's words and Chanter's votes indicate their adoption of a political colouring (Blue) early in life. Despite the complexities of Bristol politics, they remained Blue. Edgar's may not have been the 'rational man's' view, but his certainly was the political reality apparent in most modern electoral behaviour. Political consistency can be expected from most voters at most elections. Modern voters' political views often are dictated by their party allegiances rather than the reverse, and their

adherence to a party ribbon election after election is a given.[108] With
the parliamentary parties fairly well defined and the local varieties of
party very clearly distinguished, it is difficult to expect otherwise
from Bristol's electorate. Informed and interested voters, *ceteris
paribus*, should have voted consistently. Moreover, this analysis only
seeks evidence of stability or change in levels of political consistency
at the elections in question. The fact of a significant increase or
decline in the number of voters behaving consistently if measured by
partisan standards will reveal much about the impact of 1832.
Increasing consistency can best be interpreted as evidence that
Reform enhanced the politicization of the electorate and tended to
inculcate among voters modes of behaviour common to electorates in
advanced industrial societies. Decreasing consistency would suggest
the opposite.

Making sense of the votes of thousands of individuals across
elections requires statistical comparisons. It may be useful on
occasion to follow a single voter or group of voters from one election to
the next, but an assessment of the overall pattern necessitates a level of
abstraction that eschews the particular individual in favour of a
simultaneous look at all individuals. λ is a standard statistical measure
of association that compares distributions of nominal-level variables
such as votes. Varying between 0 and 1, it measures the proportional
reduction in error achieved in predicting a dependent variable by
knowing the values of independent variables. If every elector who
voted for the Whigs at the election of 1831 invariably followed that
Whig vote with another in 1832, or invariably voted Tory (or split)
after that initial Whig vote, λ would reach a perfect 1. Alternatively, if
a voter's choice at one election was unrelated to his choice at the
following election, λ would indicate this lack of a relationship by a
score of 0. Scores of less than 0.2 are not significant under most
conditions, while scores greater than 0.4 indicate a substantially
improved consistency on the part of the group being examined.[109]

But λ is not the only way to look simultaneously at massive
numbers of individuals over time. Several measures of association
are appropriate for assessments of voting behaviour across elections.
Modern elections circumscribe voting choice severely. Individual

---

[108] Studies of modern voters suggest that 'floating' voters (those who switch
parties) are as well informed and as politically involved as those who remain loyal to
one party. Speck, 'The Electorate in the First Age of Party', 51.
[109] H. M. Blalock, *Social Statistics* (New York, 1979), 310–15.

voters may have several candidates from whom to choose, and the number of candidates may vary widely, but each voter is given only one vote to cast for the single position to be filled, leading to votes that are definitionally nominal. In the circumstances of nineteenth-century elections, however, votes might be considered ordinal-level data. Indeed, perceiving these voting choices as ordinal arguably best reflects the political reality of a system using multiple votes. Each voter possessed two votes at parliamentary general elections, but laboured under no obligation to use both. By arbitrarily assigning positive and negative values to the two parties and weighting the number of votes actually cast, the realm of possibilities confronting each individual voter can be encompassed by five ordinal categories. Two votes for party A, which for this purpose is assigned a positive value, can be summarized by the score +2. A single vote for party A, for whatever reason, is counted as +1. A plump for party B is the reverse of a plump for A, or −1. A double vote for party B is given the score −2. Finally, one vote for party A (+1) cast simultaneously with one for party B (−1) results in a score of 0, the negative having cancelled the positive. This ordinal scale duplicates nicely the realities of the complicated voting world of both reformed and unreformed systems.

When using an ordinal scale, Kendall's τ_b best measures the relationship between the voting choices of individual electors at contiguous elections because in addition to providing an excellent measure of the strength of the association, τ_b provides a useful analytical bonus by indicating the nature of the relationship as well as its strength. Unlike other measurements of association that range between 0 and 1, τ_b varies on a finite scale between 0 and ±1, permitting a much more potentially revealing assessment of relationships. Whig votes inevitably following Whig votes coupled with exclusively Tory voting would yield τs and λs of +1. If double Tory votes invariably followed double Whig votes (and vice-versa), however, τ_b would much more closely duplicate reality by reaching its maximum negative score of −1. Positive τs mean the relationships being examined were direct: Whig votes followed Whig votes. Negative τs mean the relationships were inverted: Whig votes followed Tory votes. Using individual-level data, τs with absolute values in excess of 0.5 indicate extremely strong relationships.[110]

[110] In a two-seat, two-vote system τ_b is appropriate because comparisons generate tables with equal numbers of rows and columns. With rectangular cross-tabulations

TABLE 2.3. *Longitudinal Voting in Bristol, 1812–1841*

Election years	Strictly partisan		Local party alliances
	τ_b	λ(asymmetric)	τ_b
1812–20	0.35	0.09	0.05
1820–30	0.39	0.06	0.11
1830–2	0.29	0.17	0.11
1832–5	0.69*	0.61*	0.58*
1835–7	0.74*	0.57*	NA
1837–41	0.81*	0.67*	NA

* Statistically significant.
NA Not applicable; no West Indian Whig/Tory alliance.
Sources: See Table 2.1. These measures are applied using strict definitions of partisan and non-partisan voting; see discussion.

Table 2.3 compares voter consistency across elections using both τ_b and λ. The strength of relationships between the choices of voters from election to election is revealed by the absolute values of both measures, while the nature of these relationships is indicated by the positive or negative values of the reported τs. The exclusively positive figures in Table 2.3 make it clear that switching from party to party rarely occurred in Bristol. Those voting for a political party in one year did not shift *en masse* to the opposite party in a subsequent election. More importantly, though, the tendency of voters to repeat a partisan vote at successive elections increased enormously in the years after 1832. Reasonably large numbers of Bristolians voted consistently between 1820 and 1830 and again between 1830 and 1832, but political consistency became the norm between 1832 and 1835 and continued until the end of the period. The λs reported in Table 2.3 simply confirm the pattern of the τs. Though showing a slight improvement after 1830, not a difficult task given the minimal scores of earlier pairs of elections, the real change in Bristol coincided with the Reform Act.

At the same time, if the West Indian Whig/Tory alliance that existed in Bristol during the years prior to 1835 is taken into

(unequal rows and columns). τc is the more appropriate measure of association. Ibid. 439–46; B. D. Bowder and H. F. Weisberg, *An Introduction to Data Analysis* (San Francisco, 1980), 76.

consideration, the same general impression is conveyed (see column 3). Just as in the consideration of strictly partisan voting (column 1), τ_b shifts to a substantially higher, statistically significant, level only after 1832. The τs are positive at earlier elections, but the strength of the relationship was far weaker.

These figures generally reinforce the patterns revealed in Tables 2.1 and 2.2, but the circumstances of the general election of 1835 reveal the truly remarkable transformation that had taken place in Bristol after 1832. The West Indian Whigs accepted Hobhouse's candidacy, however brief, and the Independent Whigs accepted Baillie's candidacy, albeit with great reluctance. At long last Bristol's Whigs stood united, and the union held in the face of Hobhouse's withdrawal. What is surprising and important about this contest is the behaviour of the Whig voters revealed in Tables 2.3 and 2.1. The newly united Bristol Whigs maintained a solid front. The absence of slavery as an issue certainly helped their cause, but more than slavery accounts for the partisan loyalty and determination shown in this hopeless stand against the White Lion Club. As Table 2.1 indicated, 93 per cent of the electorate cast strictly party votes. More significantly, the λ of 0.61 and the τ_b of 0.69 achieved between the elections of 1832 and 1835 indicates that the bulk of those who voted Whig at the first reformed election continued to do so in 1835, just as they did in 1837 and 1841. The Independent Whig rank and file proved capable of making the shift to Baillie in 1835 despite their virtually united stand against him just three years earlier.

Unfortunately for Bristol's second White Lion candidate in 1837 and 1841, most of the 10 per cent of the splitters were householders who, rather than wasting one of their newly acquired votes, voted for the sole Liberal candidate and the leading White Lion candidate, leaving the second Conservative at the bottom of the poll each time. Bristol's freemen alone would have returned the two Tories. Bristol's householders alone almost certainly would have returned two Whigs if the party had offered two candidates. Under the circumstances, a split delegation seemed reasonable, but it was a split achieved in the presence of two united, powerful parties and an electorate now predominantly partisan. If too much splitting occurred among new Whig voters, it did not affect the party's fortunes since they had only one candidate to elect.

BRISTOL AND REFORM

Bristol's early nineteenth century local parties with essentially local concerns gave way grudgingly to local parties with some national concerns by the time Reform began to be considered seriously. After 1832, growing numbers of Bristol's Whigs and Tories did not need to qualify their partisanship. The abolition of slavery, which effectively eliminated much of the potential divisiveness of Bristol's two Whig factions, made that transition much easier. Bristol's electorate hardly needed to be politicized in 1832; they were already masters of the art of political debate. Nor did they need to be inducted into the mysteries of partisanship. They had mastered parties while fighting local battles. But Reform (and abolition) reduced a tripartite, idiosyncratic party system to a bipartisan nationally oriented system in a relatively short time. Bristol's existing party structure greatly facilitated the transition, but the debate over Reform and the alterations occasioned by Reform were the twin catalysts that effected the change.

3

Reform Resplendent: The Political Transformation of Maidstone and Colchester

IF Bristol stood near one extreme on the spectrum of popular responses to the Reform Bill in 1831, Maidstone and Colchester stood near the other. Reform generated very little visible anxiety in either town, much less riot. The residents of Maidstone were by no means apolitical. Quite the reverse; it was precisely because they were so politicized and so accustomed to political battles that a fight over an issue seemed less than extraordinary. Citizens of Colchester were far less developed politically in 1831 than their Maidstone counterparts, but they too were accustomed to elections, parties, and intense political debates in the years leading up to Reform. But while the inhabitants of these two towns failed to work themselves into a frenzied demand for Reform, voters in both places were powerfully affected by the agitation surrounding the Reform Bill and its actual passage. Reform, Act and era, transformed informed voters into nationally oriented partisans.

MAIDSTONE

Maidstone's voters had spent a good portion of the eighteenth century fighting for their survival. Time and again Maidstone's Corporation had tried to restrict the electorate for both parliamentary and municipal elections, and each time the electorate rallied successfully to its own defence, winning in the courts and at the hustings.[1] Having kept their open Corporation and their broadly

---

[1] J. A. Phillips, 'Electoral Polarization in the Reign of George III', in E. Hellmuth, (ed.)*The Transformation of Political Culture* (Oxford, 1990), 185–203.

interpreted freeman franchise, Maidstone arguably had little to gain by Reform. The £10 qualification threatened more than it offered. Support for Reform in Maidstone, therefore, involved abstract principles more than in many other constituencies.

Besides, Maidstone's inhabitants required much provocation before breaking the law. While Reform was emerging as a political issue, Maidstone suffered severely from the combined effects of a poor harvest and inclement weather. During the month of January nearly 5,000 loaves of bread had been distributed to the poor, and the crisis grew worse. By the end of February Maidstone's churchwardens (a single parish encompassed the town) had expended all the funds at their disposal. A hungry crowd of about seventy men, hearing that neither money nor bread was available for their relief, responded not by rioting but by demanding the names of any among Maidstone's ratepayers who were in arrears. Given a name, the crowd adjourned to the house of the culprit, where they demanded that he pay his rates immediately, backing up their request with the threat that 'they had knives, and if the money were not forthcoming, they would possess themselves of what the house afforded and divide it'.[2] Hardly able to refuse their request, the delinquent ratepayer offered a cheque, which the crowd rejected. He managed to have the cheque cashed, paid the men the money that he owed, and they departed peacefully. At no point did the mob demand anything other than what they perceived as legally theirs. The county of Kent spent more than £25,000 combating the problems, real and perceived, created by the incendiaries associated with the Swing riots, but Maidstone's destitute posed no threat.[3]

With Maidstone's poor reacting legalistically even to hunger, it is not surprising that Maidstone's voters chose not to riot over Reform.

[2] *Maidstone Gazette*, 23 Feb. 1830.
[3] Letters to Robert Peel (Home Secretary) and others indicate serious unrest. At the end of Oct. 1830 a body of more than 400 men were reported to be 'going about from house to house extorting money, destroying machines, and using threatening and seditious language'. Special constables were sworn in, but this episode required a detachment of cavalry to disperse. The Kent assizes sentenced a number of men to death or transportation for these and other actions in the surrounding countryside. Machine-breaking and barn-burnings throughout Kent and the Southern counties formed an unpleasant backdrop for violent episodes near Maidstone itself in 1830. Thirty-four cavalrymen were despatched to within four miles of Maidstone on 30 Oct. to disperse more than 400 potential rioters. The folder containing the Home Office reports for Kent measures approximately 6 inches compared to the more normal half an inch for other counties. Ibid. 7 Dec. 1830; E. Hobsbawm and G. Rude, *Captain Swing* (New York, 1968), 213; PRO, HO52/8/28, 214, 388.

They nevertheless expressed a keen, constant interest in the progress and ultimate success of the Reform Bill. The *Maidstone Gazette* addressed as early as February 1830 the issue of 'a General Reform of the whole system of government' in reporting the formation of the Birmingham Political Union. The editor of the *Gazette*, George Whiting, professed to 'tremble for the consequences' if the 'Duke of Wellington . . . is permitted to proceed in his present taciturn and imperturbable course'.[4] Maidstone first petitioned over Reform in that month after a county meeting attended by an estimated 7,000 people.[5] Another Maidstone Reform meeting gathered on Penenden Heath in October.[6] At this second meeting, placards demanded a reform of the Commons, universal male suffrage, the ballot, and annual or biennial Parliaments. Maistone's large contingent of paper-makers struck for a day in order to attend.[7] Thus Maidstone was well informed and actively interested, if non-violent, from the beginning. The town's coalition for Reform, which claimed to be non-partisan, was in fact anything but. Maidstone's Corporation (Tory) party opposed Reform; the town's anti-Corporation (Whig) party advocated Reform from the beginning.

The kind of sophisticated local political party structure that dominated politics in Bristol could also be found in Maidstone, a town with a population that remained under 13,000. In the years before Reform, this inconspicuous town possessed a clearly defined party structure and could reasonably claim to have adhered to the demands of partisanship since the middle of the eighteenth century.[8] Partisanship in Maidstone benefited from a unique unbroken string of contested elections beginning in the reign of Anne; only London came close to duplicating such a continuous sequence of electoral battles over parliamentary seats. Other Kentish boroughs contained relatively active electorates during these years, but the inevitability of contests in Maidstone is none the less remarkable.

---

[4] *Maidstone Gazette*, 2 Feb. 1830.   [5] Ibid. 16 Mar. 1830.

[6] Wells cites the placards as 'vote by ballot in 2 years', but according to the *Gazette*, the two years on the placards related to Parliament's duration, not the time-frame for the achievement of their demands. R. Wells, 'Rural Rebels in Southern England in the 1830s, in C. Emsley and J. Walvin (eds.), *Artisans, Peasants, and Proletarians* (London, 1985), 126, 134; *Maidstone Gazette*, 2, 16 Nov. 1830.

[7] PRO, HO40/27/2, 1 and 2 Nov. 1830, Letter to Phillipps. See also HO52/8/333, and HO52/10/550–66.

[8] Maidstone was one of only five towns in England that refused all information to the Municipal Corporation Commissioners.

In stark contrast to Bristol where a completely closed municipal corporation restricted popular political activity to parliamentary elections, Maidstone's partisanship developed in the presence of an extremely open and electorally active Corporation. Despite every effort by the mayor and aldermen during the middle years of the eighteenth century to close the Corporation, Maidstone's municipal government remained completely open. Maidstone's freemen obtained with their freedoms the right to elect the common council. Since the Corporation failed in its determined and protracted effort to remove this right from the freemen, elections to the council in Maidstone led to the relatively common Corporation/anti-Corporation party structure characteristic of eighteenth-century municipal battles.[9] While Bristol's closed Corporation had left little room for party activity except in the context of parliamentary elections, Maidstone's parties fought as fiercely over elections to the common council as they did in the less frequent contests to return Members to Parliament.

Over the course of the last decades of the eighteenth century, Maidstone's local parties adopted a national orientation.[10] At the general election of 1774 and at every successive election until the end of the century, virtually all the voters who cast anti-Corporation votes at Maidstone's municipal elections also cast anti-ministerial votes at parliamentary elections. At times the two parties achieved absolute solidarity and loyalty among Maidstone's electorate. The voters who supported the single Foxite candidate for Parliament in Maidstone at the general election of 1790 voted to a man for the anti-Corporation slate at the common council election the following year. Undaunted by their losses, the anti-Corporation/Whig party maintained a tightly disciplined share of the electorate that continued to play a very visible, and no less determined, role in the political life of Kent's county town. Their disciplined behaviour posed a genuine and constant threat to the dominance of the Corporation/Tory party. Both local and national elections reinforced the issues dividing Maidstone's electorate. The sorts of extraordinary exertions commonly associated with hard-fought general election campaigns, such as the mobilization of hundreds of non-resident freemen, marked

[9] See e.g. R. W. Greaves, *The Corporation of Leicester* (Leicester, 1939); id., 'Roman Catholic Relief and the Leicester Election of 1826', *Transactions of the Royal Historical Society*, 22 (1940). See also Webb and Webb, *English Local Government*.
[10] J. A. Phillips, 'Municipal Matters'.

these battles over mere council seats in Maidstone. The Corporation party defended its local hegemony more determinedly than it sought to elect MPs. While the challenges of the anti-Corporation party were usually unsuccessful, they provided tangible incentives for the Tories to maintain a vigorous party organization at all times. Party spirit reached such a peak in Maidstone before the turn of the nineteenth century that a contemporary observer noted that 'many neighbours would not traffic with those who were of opposite opinions'.[11]

The partisan orientation of Maidstone municipal politics under George III did not disappear under George IV. Local elections continued to be driven by partisan loyalties which hardly changed at all during the next three reigns. For example, the municipal election of 1828 to fill five common council seats pitted two slates, each with five candidates. The members of both the Corporation/Tory slate (headed by Francis Barham) and the anti-Corporation/Whig slate (headed by James Oliver) had cast strictly party ballots at the previous parliamentary election. Maidstone's voters greeted these two slates with rigid partisan voting. Of the 209 men appearing at the hustings on the first day, 199 (95.2 per cent) cast all their votes for one slate or the other. A compromise fashioned hastily when a very tight race threatened both parties with the loss of all five seats did not prevent the rest of the electorate from casting strictly partisan votes. The Tories withdrew two of their candidates when the Whigs withdrew three. After the compromise all remaining voters cast either three Tory or two Whig votes.[12] Thus Maidstone's parties were able to command absolute loyalty even when circumstances dictated genuinely bizarre varieties of voting behaviour. Not one elector, Tory or Whig, cast a vote for anyone other than the five men selected by the party compromise before the second day's poll began.

Voters exhibited roughly the same level of party loyalty (93 per cent) in the six-man common council election eleven years earlier.[13] This level of intense party loyalty had characterized Maidstone

---

[11] J. G. Jones, *Sketch of a Political Tour through Rochester, Chatham, Maidstone, and Gravesend* (London, 1796), 79.

[12] Three voters after the compromise cast failed the party test. Calculated from KAO, Md/AEb2/29, A Poll for the election of five Common Council Men, 23 May 1828.

[13] KAO, Md/AEb2/25, A Poll for the election of three Common Council Men, 28 Oct. 1817.

municipal elections for decades. It was as evident in the 1790s as in the 1820s, and could be found at virtually any election across these years. The Reform Act did not alter the electorate's response to local political battles. The common council election of 1835 evoked almost exactly the same level of party voting (94.4 per cent).[14] Measured cross-sectionally at least, the behaviour of Maidstone's voters at local elections left no room for improvement.

Parliamentary elections, on the other hand, did offer scope for partisan improvement, though the failings of many voters prior to 1830 may have stemmed in part from the vagueness of the parliamentary affiliations of some candidates. For example, neither John Wells nor George Longman fitted very easily into a party mould in 1818. Longman stood with A. W. Robarts, an unmistakable Whig, against Wells, but by 1826 the Whiggish *Maidstone Gazette* applauded much of Wells's behaviour in the Commons.[15] Similarly, in 1830 vagueness over issues clouded the returns. According to the *Gazette*, 'both parties employed nearly the same watchwords; both advocated the same principles, the difference being only in the degree of boldness with which they were propounded, and both incumbered themselves with the same pledges'. All three candidates in 1830 espoused reform of some kind, and Maidstone's voters may not have been able to distinguish 'reform' from 'something like reform'.[16] Early in 1830 many could espouse mild reforms, and neither of Maidstone's MPs was likely to support other than the mildest. Moreover, after Wellington's apostasy over Nonconformity and Catholics, 'few had the boldness to avow themselves the thick and thin supporters of the Wellington cabinet' because those who did 'were not only denied a patient hearing by their quondam constituents, but literally groaned and hissed into their resignations'.[17]

[14] KAO, Md/AEb2/30, A Poll for the election of two Common Council Men, 11 Apr. 1835.

[15] Neither the party affiliations nor the names of the candidates at Maidstone's elections of 1818, 1820, and 1826 are reported accurately in the standard lists of parliamentary election results. These uncertainties explain the discrepancies between the figures in Table 3.1 and those reported in J. A. Phillips, 'The Many Faces of Reform', *Parliamentary History*, 1 (1982), 123–4. That analysis counted Wells as a Whig, based upon his approval by the *Maidstone Gazette* (e.g. 16, 23 Feb. and 2 Mar. 1830). He appears, however, to have moved into a Whiggish stance relatively late in his parliamentary career. This analysis counts Wells as a Tory in 1818 and 1820 since he certainly began that way and seems to have held essentially the same position two years later.

[16] Ibid. 9, 23, Feb. 1830.

[17] Ibid. 24 Aug. 1830. See also J. A. Phillips, 'The Many Faces of Reform'.

By the spring of 1831 Tory propaganda had persuaded some of Maidstone's freemen to abandon Reform because of its attack on their 'birthrights', but the Whigs countered effectively by playing the royal card so much in evidence across England and by ensuring that the 1831 election would be a plebiscite over Reform. Since the Tory candidates would 'not swallow the Russell purge', they were rejected forthwith.[18] Maidstone's mildly reformist incumbent, Robarts, and a total stranger who was a much more ardent reformer captured fully three-quarters of the total vote. Yet in Maidstone, as in England generally, the obituaries eagerly written to mark the demise of the Tories after the Whig successes in 1831/2 proved premature. The victory of the Tory Wyndham Lewis in 1835 presaged the resurgence of the Tories in 1837 and 1841, when they took both seats. By 1841 it looked as if the Tories held as dominant a position in Maidstone parliamentary politics as they they had held for so long in the affairs of the Corporation. The Whig electoral successes of 1831/2 had proven to be nothing more than flashes in the pan.

The Tory resurgence is not really visible in the long-term trends reported in Table 3.1, but the diminishing split vote in Maidstone after 1830 meant that if both parties contested both seats, a sweep was more likely.

The level of split-voting fell in 1831 to a quarter of what it had been. The 1831 election uniquely involved four candidates, but electors were responding to more than the rare opportunity to cast party votes without penalty because they did not revert to split-voting when three-man elections resumed in 1832. After Reform fewer than 10 per cent of the voters split between the Blues and Purples, and by 1841 virtually every Maidstone elector supported one party exclusively. The solitary Whig candidates at later Maidstone elections did not prevent the virtual disappearance of splitters (1 per cent in 1841). At the same time the rather large number of voters willing to cast 'partisan' plumpers prior to Reform increased markedly in 1832 and 1835. Solitary Tory or Whig candidates attracted plumpers from a quarter to a third of the electorate between 1818 and 1830, but by 1835 nearly half of the electorate were willing to cast plumpers for the sole Whig candidate. The equally critical category of 'unnecessary' plumping also changed

[18] *A Poll for Members* (Maidstone, 1831), pp. v–vii; *Maidstone Gazette*, 19 Apr., 10 May 1831.

TABLE 3.1. *Split-Voting and Plumping (Partisan and Unnecessary) in Maidstone* (%)

Election year	1818	1820	1826	1830	1831	1832	1835	1837	1841
Split votes	7.7	20.9	23.8	22.3	5.9	8.7	7.1	9.6	1.0
Partisan plumps	28.2	24.5	32.3	28.1	4-man	38.9	48.2	35.9	31.8
Unnecessary plumps	—	2.7	34.0	33.5	3.2	1.3	6.6	2.0	0.8

Note: The figures reported in J. A. Phillips, 'The Many Faces of Reform,' assumed John Wells to be a Whig. Those figures simply present a more extreme version of the pattern strongly in evidence here. (See n. 15.)
Sources: Poll books.

abruptly at the election of 1831 when voters simply stopped behaving in this essentially non-partisan fashion. After casting non-partisan plumpers in large numbers in 1826 and 1830, voters abruptly adopted a more partisan line, a behavioural shift that reflected the heightened partisan spirit inspired by Reform. This injection of this new issue into the existing partisan structure in Maidstone helped push the uncommitted among the electorate into one camp or the other.[19]

The 1830 and 1831 elections permit a rare direct comparison that helps clarify the impact of the events of the intervening months. At the first of these contests, A. W. Robarts stood with Philip Rawlings against the solitary Tory, Henry Winchester. Very few voters (6 per cent) made the mistake of linking Rawlings and Winchester, but nearly a third of the electorate refused the dictates of party and voted for Robarts alone. More Whig voters plumped unnecessarily for Robarts than Tory voters plumped with reason for Winchester. Yet this sort of behaviour disappeared with the next election when Robarts stood with C. J. Barnett. This time splitting and non-partisan plumping vanished. More than a third of the electorate plumped for Robarts without reason in 1830; fewer than 1 per cent did so in 1831. A few more Tories blundered in this way; 2.6 per cent plumped unnecessarily for Winchester that year. Taken together, Whig and Tory unnecessary plumpers accounted for merely 3 per cent of the votes at Maidstone's last unreformed election.

Local political circumstances dictate caution in interpreting the strong trend evident in these cross-sectional comparisons. The dramatic shift at the election of 1831 seems genuine enough because the Reform Bill changed the milieu of political struggles in Maidstone. Notwithstanding Maidstone's familiarity with the demands of parties, the 1831 election occurred in a heavily charged atmosphere made all the more ominous by echoes of the Swing riots. At the same time, the figures for 1832 and 1835 must be viewed with some suspicion. At both of these elections an extremely wealthy Tory candidate stood alone and expended thousands of pounds to improve his chances. Wyndham Lewis's abortive effort in 1832 lessened neither his enthusiasm nor his determination to win a Maidstone seat. The abatement of Reform fever after 1832 also

---

[19] *Maidstone Gazette*, 16 Nov. 1830; PBO, HO52/8/33, HO52/10/550–66.

tended to improve the potential impact of a wide and heavy distribution of gold sovereigns. Lewis's third attempt in Maidstone in 1835 (he stood first in 1826) proved a charm. He topped the poll by a considerable margin with the assistance of nearly 500 plumping voters (a remarkable 48 per cent of the electorate) whose behaviour must be viewed with a degree of scepticism. Political principle may have driven some voters into Lewis's camp, but the suddenness of their decision to behave with such 'partisan' spirit after refusing to do so just three years earlier, raises the distinct possibility that the colour to which they responded was less Tory purple than Tory gold. After the close of the poll, the Whigs published a 'black list' naming thirty-seven voters whose registration the Whigs had defended against an attempted Tory block. These Blue voters had subsequently 'sold themselves to the Purples', who 'had been bribing in all directions throughout the night'.[20] But the Whigs accused only thirty-seven voters, and Lewis topped the poll by a margin of 131.

As early as 1826 Maidstone's voters were willing to plump for a solitary Whig candidate despite the unwillingness of Robarts to spend money on his election. Robarts had contested both previous elections (1818 and 1820), and while the electorate had grown accustomed to his face, they were not accustomed to supporting him exclusively. Nor were they comfortable with the idea of completely unremunerated support for candidates of either party. Still, Robarts won his seat in 1826. He was joined by another Whig candidate at four subsequent elections. Philip Rawlings's initial attempt in 1830 failed miserably. A smaller proportion (28 per cent) of the voters plumped for the sole Tory, Winchester, than had plumped for the lone Whig in 1826, but their numbers were sufficient to leave Rawlings in the dust.

Predictably, Maidstone's voters staged impressive demonstrations of their support of Reform in 1831 and 1832. After decades of Blues versus Purples at Maidstone elections, a segment of the freemen organized an anti-Reform party in 1831, the 'Inflexibles'. The example set by the Inflexibles was followed in 1832 by the creation of two Tory support groups, the Conservative Committee and the Constitution Club, which in turn fuelled a reaction during which

---

[20] This list of voters and their addresses, all of whom were craftsmen or labourers, condemned those who won their franchises 'through the exertions of the liberals and who have voted plumpers for the Tories'. *Maidstone Gazette*, 13 Jan. 1835.

many freemen joined either or both of Maidstone's two Whig/
Liberal clubs known as the Loyal True Blue Club and the Maidstone
Political Union.[21] Maidstone's voters were in one sense merely
incorporating the issue of Reform into the town's long-established
political division. Rather than addressing the specific issues involved,
the Whig *Gazette* simply accused the Constitution Club of adhering
to only two principles, 'bribery and corruption'. Nevertheless, the
Reform Bill heightened existing tensions and gave renewed focus to
the oppositionists in Maidstone.

Three years after Reform, one of Maidstone's MPs suggested that
the town's reformed electorate was 'if possible worse than the old'.
This perception was 'not simply the after-dinner conversation of two
cynical men of the world with a prejudice against the Reform Act
and all that it stood for', but rather a closely informed opinion about
the nature of the new political system.[22] The MP, none other than
Robarts, understood politics well enough to be returned yet again
twelve days after he disparaged his reformed constituency in 1835.
Robarts had 'grown grey in the service of Maidstone's voters' and
might have been expected to understand both them and the system.
Yet while he condemned voters for their corruption, they re-elected
him without the inducement of treating of any kind. The elimination
of all forms of Blue bribery at Maidstone elections may have
weakened the Liberal cause somewhat, particularly in the face of
what appears to have been wholesale attempted bribery on behalf of
Purple candidates, but Roberts's return twice without the least
support of remuneration raises doubts about his dismissal of
Reform's impact. Besides, while Robarts bemoaned their pecuniary
expectations, he simultaneously testified to an active, interested,
politically sophisticated electorate. If they looked upon some kind of
payment almost as a birthright, they were no less 'generally alive to
public affairs'. Robarts admitted that they 'look into the votes and
speeches of members' (an activity facilitated by the steady diet of
MPs' voting decisions reported in the *Maidstone Gazette*) and 'give
their opinions'.[23] As long as both parties offered payments for votes,
the apparent bribery arguably need not have affected voting choice
in any way. And the Blues were able to win even after they stopped
paying altogether.

---

[21] *Maidstone Gazette*, 19 Apr. 1831; 14 Aug., 20, 21 Nov., 4, 11, Sept., 4, 11 Dec. 1832.
[22] Gash, *Age of Peel*, 320, 125.   [23] Greville, *Memoirs*, iii. 138.

The behaviour of Maidstone's electorate as revealed in Table 3.1 indicates the danger of relying too heavily on anecdotal impressions of electoral behaviour, however well informed. Robarts's assessment of the effects of Reform in Maidstone were largely inaccurate. Maidstone's voters had behaved in a partisan manner for decades before Reform, and this level of partisanship actually increased during the two years preceding the passage of the Act. Bribery notwithstanding, the pattern of partisan behaviour unquestionably strengthened over the years following the election of 1830. Moreover, Maidstone's voters continued to plump for the sole Whig/ Reform candidate at the elections of 1837 and 1841 despite the noticeable absence of bribery on the part of the Blue party. The Blues' honesty after the loss of Robarts was only partly the result of principle; much of the absence of Whig bribery after 1835 stemmed from a general lack of funds. Finding any Blue candidate proved difficult after Robarts's 1837 withdrawal and his subsequent defeat at two by-elections in 1838. Finding a Whig candidate willing to do more than simply offer himself as an object of their support proved impossible. Consequently, the Blues found themselves out of office only six years after their overwhelming victory at the 1831 election. Gone more quickly than the Whigs could have imagined were the days when Robarts could jokingly refer 'to the late contest—or rather, to distinguish it more properly, the late farce'.[24]

Benjamin Disraeli astonished everyone except himself by winning a seat in Maidstone in 1837 along with another Conservative, Wyndham Lewis.[25] Disraeli actually owed his victory to Lewis, who had wrested one of Maidstone's two seats away from the Whigs through an expensive, hard-fought battle in 1835. The Whig incumbent, Robarts, appeared all but invincible after two decades in Parliament, and an enormous effort from Lewis had been required to defeat the second Whig. Initially, Maidstone's Tories had intended only to repeat their success by returning Lewis again in

[24] *Maidstone Gazette*, 10 May 1831. Disraeli was recruited as a Conservative candidate through the auspices of the Carlton Club. W. F. Monypenny and G. E. Buckle, *The Life of Benjamin Disraeli*, 6 vols. (London, 1910–20), i. 376–7.
[25] Disraeli's Conservative claims were far from untarnished. For a discussion of Disraeli's ill-fated effort to blend romantic Toryism with nostalgic Radicalism, see M. Girouard, *The Return to Camelot* (New Haven, Conn., 1981), 81. Disraeli called himself a Radical at High Wycombe in 1832 and again in 1835 since 'Toryism is worn out and I cannot condescend to be a Whig'. See also C. Driver, *Tory Radical: The Life of Richard Oastler* (Oxford, 1946) and B. Disraeli, *What Is He?* (London, 1833).

1837, but their early canvass on his behalf yielded such positive results that they asked the Carlton Club to send a second candidate. The new man, recommended highly by Lewis, or at least by Lewis's wife Mary Anne, fitted rather poorly into the Maidstone-Tory mould.[26] Even a subdued Disraeli topped anything in Maidstone's experience.[27] A contemporary observed:

> He was not popular with the mob. They offered him bacon, ham, etc., and repeatedly suggested that he was a Jew. . . . His appearance was very remarkable—long black hair in curls—and he was dressed in what appeared to be an extraordinary way, the extreme, it may be supposed, of fashion. Nothing like it had ever been seen in Maidstone before.[28]

Lady Salisbury may have characterized best the impression he created when she wrote that Disraeli was 'evidently very clever, but superlatively vulgar'.[29] Understandably, this unusual, not to say bizarre, candidate generated considerable incredulity and merriment in the Blue camp. Asking 'Who is Mr. B. D'Israeli?' the *Gazette* quickly launched a series of vicious attacks contending that if Disraeli were returned, 'the people of Maidstone would deservedly be considered the scum of the earth'.[30]

The Tories anticipated an easy campaign from the start; before Disraeli's recruitment, Lewis believed he could count upon '750 plumpers alone out of the 1400 votes'. If these Tory plumpers could be converted into Tory doubles, a walk-over seemed inevitable, and those conversions appeared likely. Disraeli reported: 'it seems to me that all the strength and property of the Boro' are on our side, and opposition to the Poor Law makes us popular with the multitude.' On 3 July Disraeli's canvass placed the Tory candidates more than 200 votes ahead of Robarts. Five days later Disraeli began to doubt that the Whigs would force a poll. All uncertainty ended when Robarts, in trouble financially and physically, resigned just before the prorogation on 17 June. As nomination day approached five days

[26] B. Disraeli, *Letters*, ii. 286, n. 6. Mary Anne Lewis's role in the selection of Disraeli is revealed by her acknowledgement even before Disraeli's initial return for Maidstone that 'They call him my Parliamentary Protegé.'

[27] O. F. Christie, *The Transition from Aristocracy 1832–1867* (London, 1927), 227.

[28] Sir John Hollams, *Jottings of an Old Solicitor* (London, 1906), 7–8, cited in B. Disraeli, *Letters*, ii. 284, n. 1.

[29] C. Oman (ed.), *The Gasgoyne Heiress* (London, 1968), 248, cited in B. Disraeli, *Letters*, ii. 281, n. 3.

[30] *Maidstone Gazette*, 11 July 1837. *Punch* continued to use this anti-Semitic spelling of Disraeli four years later (28 Aug. 1841).

later, Disraeli could happily claim to be the only new Tory candidate not facing opposition.[31]

Robarts's last-minute withdrawal forced the Blues to fight with a last-minute candidate, T. Perronet Thompson, ex-MP for Hull, editor of the *Westminster Review*, and Radical member of 'Mr. Hume's party' in the Commons.[32] Thompson had railed against the Corn Laws for more than a decade. His *Catechism on the Corn Laws*, published in 1826, attacked all protectionism; his *Exercises* portrayed protection as a form of robbery. As long as the Corn Laws protected the 'selfish monopolies' of landlords without reference to any 'natural' price, the resulting 'superfluity of price' kept rents unnaturally high and drove a wedge between landowners and the rest of society. In Thompson's outspoken view, the Corn Laws enslaved Englishmen. Thompson also advocated householder suffrage, the secret ballot, shortened Parliaments, and the disestablishment of the Church. It would have been difficult to find a more radical candidate. More moderate Whigs may have been less than enthusiastic about Thompson's candidacy, but all were happy to have anyone to stand so late in the day. And Disraeli seemed such a vulnerable target that the Blues hoped to prevent a joint Purple return. Maidstone's Radicals were 'absolutely rabid' for Thompson, and moderates stood by them without much prodding. The Radicals claimed to 'have actually procured the support of a majority of the electors without a single bribe or gift of a half-pint of porter'.[33] Their failure to make good those claims was painfully evident when Thompson fell 100 votes short of Disraeli, who in turn fell 100 votes short of Lewis. The Conservative party captured both Maidstone seats for the first time in the nineteenth century.

The fortunes of Maidstone's reformers deteriorated further after this stunning loss. The Conservatives won both seats again despite a string of political disasters that might have been expected to return the seats to the Whig fold. Wyndham Lewis died in 1838 and Disraeli deserted Maidstone for Shrewsbury. Lewis's replacement (who managed to win two by-elections in 1838) also deserted the town before 1841, leaving the Tories with two new, locally unknown candidates. But against the odds, the Tories substantially increased their majority. Disraeli had won the second seat in 1837 by just over

---

[31] B. Disraeli, *Letters*, ii. 277.
[32] L. G. Johnson, *The Man with Forty Crowns*.
[33] *Maidstone Gazette*, 18, 25 July 1837.

100 votes; George Dodd won it in 1841 by more than 300. The Tories also attracted more rigidly partisan voting. Ironically, after being used by the reformers against Disraeli in 1837, the Jewish issue worked to their disadvantage in 1841. Responding to the Whig candidate, David Salomons, the Tory *Maidstone Journal* announced, undoubtedly with some relish after the *Gazette*'s ridiculing of Disraeli, that 'the blues [Whigs] have found a man,—*at least a Jew!*' The Whigs' racist counter argued that a powerful 'under-current of Tory gold and corruption' running 'in a narrower and dirtier channel' than ever before threatened to pervert 'a set of the most dependent "white niggers" that ever showed their pale faces in Christendom'. They heralded Salomons as the 'Free Trade' candidate and tried to turn his religious background to their advantage by arguing that he stood firmly with those 'who differ from the established Church'.[34] The *Gazette* reported afterwards that 'upwards of a hundred decided Liberals, . . . seeing the little chance there was of a successful result, did not go to the poll'.[35] The Tory domination of Maidstone seemed complete only a few years after the Whig/Reform triumph. Yet despite this drastic decline in their fortunes, Maidstone's Whig voters proved extremely loyal. More than a third of the entire electorate plumped for the lone Whig in 1837 (providing almost 80 per cent of his total vote), and the same third ignored the last-minute addition of a Jewish candidate and plumped Whig again in 1841 (accounting for almost 90 per cent of Salomons's total support).[36] Such determined behaviour against all hope, particularly when the other side would pay well for one vote as well as two, suggests that Maidstone politics after the Reform era were not as they had been.

COLCHESTER

Colchester, though it shared far more of Bristol's municipal political characteristics than Maidstone's in the decades preceding Reform, lacked the highly developed party structures evident in the other towns. Colchester lacked Maidstone's political and economic vitality. A small and very sluggishly growing town that felt none of the effects

[34] *Maidstone Journal*, 29 June 1841.   [35] *Maidstone Gazette*, 6 July 1841.
[36] Ibid. 28 June 1841; *Maidstone Journal*, 29 June 1841.

of nascent industrialization, Colchester suffered from unemployment and underemployment.[37] As late as 1851, its largest water-powered mill employed only eight people. Colchester's largest brewery that year employed six. The economic consequences of relative economic failure during the reigns of the last Hanoverian kings were serious. Gas was not laid on for the town until 1836, and the long-delayed acquisition of gaslight did not dispel the persistent economic gloom stemming from the death of the wool trade in the later eighteenth century. Having lost by the end of the Napoleonic wars virtually all the economic strength gained over several hundred years from the production and sale of woollen cloth, some Colcestrians sought to ease the post-war slump by establishing two silk mills and several breweries. Others turned to the mass production of shoes. Unfortunately, nothing worked. During the early decades of the nineteenth century, Colchester's only reliable source of revenue came from retailing goods to the surrounding agrarian population. The number of retail shops in the town more than tripled during the years in which the population hardly grew at all. Bypassed by significant economic change, Colchester also found itself bypassed for a long time by the railroad; its first rail link to the world was completed only in 1843.

Somewhat surprisingly, these economic doldrums failed to generate serious political discord among Colchester's inhabitants, in the exercise of either their local or national franchises. In fact, precarious finances may have contributed to the quiescence of local politics. Many freemen in Colchester seem to have been more concerned to receive the 16 shillings to which each was entitled annually from the sale of their grazing rights to borough land than they were to tamper in the administration of the Corporation.[38] A few determined Radicals such as Chignall Wire fought the Corporation through suits in King's Bench, but even the Radicals saw little point in electoral battles.[39] During the relatively prosperous years of the mid eighteenth century, struggles between Corporation and anti-Corporation factions within the electorate were exacerbated by

[37] While urban England grew at a rate approaching 25 per cent per decade, Colchester grew at barely half that rate between 1811 and 1821 and improved only slightly to 16 per cent over the next ten years. Thomas Cromwell, *History of the Borough of Colchester*, 2 vols. (London, 1825), i. 179.

[38] Brown, *Colchester*, 38.

[39] The Corporation's income in 1823–4 stood at only £2,750, of which levies on Hythe River traffic generated £1,550.

religious discord.[40] After winning control in 1768, however, the Corporation consolidated its hold on the borough and its parliamentary seats, and maintained it for decades.

Colchester's Corporation fell about midway between Bristol's absolutely closed system and Maidstone's open, politicized, and participatory municipal structure.[41] Resident freemen were permitted a limited measure of participation since they had the right to choose replacements for the eighteen men who sat on the common council and to vote for the borough's recorder and its four headmen who selected most of the town's other officers. Surviving poll books demonstrate that the municipal voting rights of Colcestrians were honoured more in the breach than in the practice. Colchester's relative electoral inactivity in the selection of local offices stemmed more from the homogeneity of the town's political preferences than from any overt effort by the Corporation. Affected perhaps by their utter reliance on a stagnant, agrarian economy, a solid preponderance of Colcestrians espoused conservative principles. Rather than being divided into two relatively equal and extremely antagonistic political camps as in Maidstone, or into several decidedly unequal but no less vociferously hostile political camps as in Bristol, Colcestrians formed an ordinarily reliable core of support for Tory candidates, whether they stood for local or national office. On the whole, 'Conservative Colchester' was the antithesis of 'Radical Leicester'.

Elections to the common council in Colchester usually passed without incident and without a formal poll. The local Tory majority experienced a challenge to their authority only at parliamentary elections when non-resident freemen arrived in large numbers to cast ballots. They encountered no opposition in deciding the eighteen common council seats nominally open to a contest since only resident householders paying scot and lot held the municipal

[40] Support from the town's Dissenting element proved too fickle to be relied upon, leaving the opposition unable effectively to challenge the Anglican, Tory Corporation in local or national elections. Tierney accused the Dissenters of 'conduct I can give no other name than that of treachery' after his humiliating loss in 1790. *Chelmsford and Colchester Chronicle*, 4 June 1790. For a fuller discussion see Bradley, *Religion, Revolution*, 301.

[41] The Colchester Corporation included a mayor, 11 aldermen, 18 assistants, 18 common councilmen, a recorder, and a town clerk. The headmen, constables, and other local office-holders did not make up the 'Select Body' identified in the restored borough charter of 1763 (the previous one having been revoked for corruption in 1742). After another reformation in 1811, the town received a new charter in 1818. Cromwell, *History of Colchester*, passim.

franchise.[42] Municipal elections could provoke contests, and when a contest occurred, partisan considerations appear to have contributed significantly to the process, but ordinarily local men could not muster a serious challenge to the Tory hegemony. At the election for headmen in 1821, for example, the political principles of candidates in three of Colchester's four wards placed them in opposite camps, giving the voters a choice between Whigs and Tories. In a three-day contest involving three Whigs and a moderate against four staunch Tories, the Corporation swept the field. So content were townsmen generally with their one-party municipal government that many petitioned *against* municipal reform in 1835.[43] When the Municipal Corporations Act swept away the old Corporation, the resident electorate, now similar for municipal and parliamentary matters, altered their local arrangements only briefly and minimally. Except for 1836, Colchester's Tories controlled the new Corporation until nearly the end of the nineteenth century. Roland Thorne has correctly classified both Colchester and Maidstone as 'quite open', but Colchester's openness was far more limited than Maidstone's. Colchester's Corporation had no need to fight the municipal battles that provided such a fertile background for parliamentary elections in Maidstone.

Yet Colchester cannot be characterized as politically backward in the decades immediately preceding Reform. Rather the reverse is the impression conveyed by the political debates common to the town. The Tory majority among resident freemen did not at all hinder Colchester's keen awareness of political issues, not did it ensure complete political accord. At the parliamentary election of 1820, Colcestrians faced a contest between a Radical and two Tories, but the Tory candidates were not formally united. The Corporation wanted to avoid having Wildman's voice 'rendered useless and nugatory because the other Representative [Harvey] voted on the other side'. They prevailed upon the incumbent Tory, James Wildman, to agree in principle to a coalition with a candidate the Corporation hoped to acquire, General Rebow. The Corporation bribed Wildman with the assurance that he would be asked to spend

---

[42] Brown, *Colchester*, 37–43.
[43] *The Poll for the Election of Headmen* (Colchester, 1821). The Municipal Corporations Commission generated no report on Colchester. Webb and Webb, *English Local Government*, iii. 717. n. 2. All six aldermen elected in 1835 were Liberal, but even that year the 18 common council seats were split between the parties. No Liberal won a seat on the Corporation again until 1882. Speight, 'Colchester', 77.

no more than £1,000 in the contest. Otherwise, one member of the Corporation argued: 'what one *weaves*, another as studiously *unweaves*. What one *says*, the other as studiously rises to *unsay*.'[44] But General Rebow declined to stand, and Wildman found it impossible to coalesce with the last-minute substitute Tory candidate, Sir Henry Russell. Just returned from many years' service in India as a judge, Russell had few connections with Colchester. Thus Colchester possessed two Tory candidates but no Tory slate. Two independent Tory candidates, however, did not leave voters confused. Wildman was a firm supporter of the King's Ministers, and stood in the true-blue interest. Russell identified himself just as clearly and could not have been more unequivocally Tory.

During this contest Colcestrians revealed very sophisticated perceptions of party that reflected beliefs long held and widely shared. A handbill attacking the town's Corporation referred without hesitation to the 'Tory and Whig principles' represented in the town and decried the domination of the Corporation by those adhering to the former.[45] Speakers at hustings echoed this perception of party versus party. William Smith, who plumped for Wildman in 1818 and 1820, 'was attached to Mr Wildman on principle; and when he took up a man on principle, he never deserted him'.[46] Smith argued that Wildman 'supported the Ministers from conscience; he was not to be duped by popular applause, or awed by the dagger of an assassin'. At the other end of the political spectrum, Dixon Holmes, a Londoner, claimed to be 'firmly attached . . . to Mr Harvey for the principles he always professed—supporting the rights of the people, and never forgetting his parliamentary origin and creation'. Harvey, known as 'a Reformer' by friend and foe alike, had been outspoken in his views since his first Colchester election in 1812.[47] Years later, one man remembered Harvey's 'vigorous logic—terrible sarcasm—his honest and manly avowal of his principles and opinions', which resulted in his 'easy conquest over waverers'.[48] Later in the day, an unidentified person in the crowd attacked Francis Smythies, a Colchester notable, for saying

[44] *Poll for Members to Serve in Parliament* (Colchester, 1820), 20. For a virtually identical argument in Shrewsbury see Ch. 5.

[45] CLHL, E. COL. 1/324.26/16, Harvey Papers.

[46] See Ch. 2's discussion of the strong political opinions expressed by James Chanter and his fellow Bristol White Lions.

[47] CLHL, E. COL. 1/324.26/14, 16.

[48] R. Ainslie, *Discourse at the Death of Daniel Whittle Harvey* (London, 1863), 9.

that 'he had not made up his mind on politics' which the protester argued meant that 'therefore he was of no principle'.[49]

A variety of political clubs enhanced political awareness in Colchester as in Maidstone. The Loyal Association or Pitt Club or True Blue Club represented the same interests whatever name it happened to use in a given year, and several other conservatively oriented clubs assisted the True Blues during these years.[50] The reformist *Mercury* more than once pointed out the irony of a Pitt Club standing so fervently against Catholic emancipation, but this inconsistency troubled not the Blues.[51] They espoused the standard Tory line—anti-Catholic, anti-Reform, pro-Corn Law—without hesitation. Ancillary clubs typically shared the determined, virulently anti-Catholic Toryism of the parent Pittite organization. The True Blues asserted in 1830 that 'it is not a term of abuse to call a man an Ultra-Tory', but for the most part, they claimed not to be ultras.[52] Only the members of the Brunswick Club (1828) seem to have strayed over the line from Tory fervour into ultra-Toryism.

Colchester's Whigs countered with their own organizations. Their numerical weakness did not prevent concerted, persistent efforts to organize opposition. The Whig Hand-in-Hand Club could trace its origins to 1790. The pace of Whig club formation quickened in the reigns of the last two Hanoverian kings. A Loyal Independent Club emerged in 1821 to assist the London Burgesses Club that had been formed earlier to support the Radical, Harvey. The Cross-Keys Club, named after the Inn in which meetings occurred, appeared the next year. And recognizing the anti-Catholic feeling ubiquitous in the town, the Whigs formed the New Independent Club in 1830 for those who favoured reform except in this area. After all, the votes of anti-Catholic reformers probably outnumbered those who supported the fullest emancipation. The opponents of the Tories during the 1820s and 1830s mirrored the nation and encountered some of the same difficulties in reaching a consensus. Whigs and Radicals often made uneasy bedfellows, but their disagreements helped stoke political debates. Altogether, more than a score of political clubs kept issues alive in Colchester during and between elections.

[49] *Proceedings of the Late Election at Colchester* (Colchester, 1820), 30, 23, 32.
[50] Speight, 'Colchester', 165–95.
[51] CLHL, E. COL.1/324.26/DG29212,13; CLHL, 'Book of Colcheseter and Chelmsford Compiled by a Member of the Rebow Family', 45.
[52] *Essex Standard*, 10 Nov. 1837; Speight, 'Colchester', 169–70.

The keen political awareness expressed by these men did not prevent the time-honoured use of colours in lieu of specific party terminology to illustrate partisan feelings. Colours summarized political differences as effectively as other shorthands. The son of the third candidate in 1820, (Sir Henry Russell, a Ministerialist) described the situation in Colchester in a manner that revealed the clarity of local political perceptions. He explained that since his father intended to stand in the 'True-Blue interest', he the son

enquired the colour of the Blue party; it was then told me it was purple. From this, I hoisted the purple colours alone. Upon my entering the town, it was said, you have taken Sir Francis Burdett's colours, the very opposite of the principles you profess; *the colours of the Blues here are purple and white.*[53]

Chagrined by his mistake, Russell's camp immediately added white banners to their purple ones to rectify the erroneous impression that purple banners alone conveyed. Since his father faced a Radical of a Burdettite hue, he could hardly have done otherwise. Though he now flew the correct colours to advertise his father's support of the Ministry, the younger Russell's problems with colours were far from over. The other Tory candidate, James Wildman, objected to Russell's use of purple and white banners, claiming those colours as his own. Russell's son rejected Wildman's claim to the colours:

I think it an equal presumption of Mr Wildman to say they are his colours; they are the colours of the loyal and independent Blue interest of this Borough, and do not belong to this man or that man; they are the colours of the party and the principles that I come under, and which I will never flinch from professing.

The editorials that emerged in the newspapers serving Colchester in the 1820s helped to shape these clear visions of the nature of political conflict. The vicious attacks on the Liverpool and Wellington administrations by the *Kent and Essex Mercury* were countered by the determined Toryism of the *Colchester Gazette* until its sale to a Liberal Dissenter in 1829 forced the Tories to found a new party organ, the *Essex Standard*, to maintain the flow of 'purple' prose in support of True Blue issues after 1831.[54]

[53] *Proceedings of the late Election*, 18–21 (emphasis added).

[54] The local Tories rejected for some time the term 'Conservative' when efforts were made to adopt it in the 1830s. Speight, 'Colchester', 99. For a full account of the varieties of opinion represented by the newspapers circulating in Colchester see ibid. 190–210.

The sophistication of popular political perceptions in Colchester, coupled with the predominant conservatism of resident voters, renders somewhat surprising the persistent electoral success of the Radical reforming MP, Daniel Whittle Harvey.[55] During his fifth stand at Colchester in 1831, Harvey reminded the voters that they faced a referendum to decide 'whether our laws and liberties . . . shall be confided any longer to a vile and profligate Oligarchy, . . . or whether the Commons of England shall hereafter be, as the Constitution defines, a full and fair Representative of the People'.[56] These sentiments were far from rare across England that year, but Harvey had been making similar claims from the beginning of his tenure in Colchester. Despite his blemished record, Harvey was a dominant force; after losing twice, he topped the poll three times while winning a seat five times.[57] His success stemmed primarily from the influence of non-resident freemen voters, particularly the extremely large London contingent comprised of men far more liberal in their views than their local counterparts. But he also strove to make himself useful to his constituents of whatever political colouring, and 'on all questions truly local, he knew nothing of party'.[58] Harvey knew well the problem he faced, noting in 1831 that 'not twenty men in all of Essex favoured either universal suffrage or annual parliaments', two issues on which his support had been clear

[55] Harvey won the election for recorder of Colchester in 1813 by four votes, only to lose it after a scrutiny. Cromwell, *History of Colchester*, ii. 291. Harvey claimed to have been called to the Bar, but he was never called due to accusations of professional misconduct as a solicitor which included a conviction for fraud in 1814, an accusation of misappropriating £500 of a client's money, an accusation of purloining a document in a case in 1809, and a charge that he acted as solicitor for his father. Harvey was rejected by the benchers of the Inner Temple in 1819. A unanimous vote of 12 judges upheld the benchers' decision in 1822 despite Harvey's most determined efforts. CLHL, Rebow 'Book of Colchester', 45. (now in ERO). Harvey was exonerated in part in 1834 by Daniel O'Connell and a select parliamentary committee, but the Bar continued to refuse Harvey entry. 'Report of the Inns of Court Committee', *Parl. Pap.* 18 (1834), 327. CLHL, E. COL. 1/920, Report of Harvey's hearing before the Inner Temple, Feb. 1822. See also Ainslie, *Discourse*.

[56] CLHL, E. COL. 1/9579/49.

[57] Harvey lost the 1812 general election by 33 votes to Robert Thornton, who took the second seat with 737 votes. Davis topped the poll with 810. Harvey contested Davis's vacated seat in 1818, losing to Wildman by an extremely wide margin. He won the second seat at the general election later in 1818, with Wildman again topping the poll.

[58] Londoners voted Whig first, Radical second in 1820 and 1830. In 1830 186 Londoners voted for Mayhew, 159 for Harvey, and only 41 for Spottiswood. The next year, they responded positively to the Mayhew/Harvey coalition. Only 90 voted for Spottiswood, but 231 and 230 voted for Harvey and Mayhew respectively.

for some time.[59] Managing to persuade 'Conservative' Colchester to send him to Parliament took clever manœuvring, if not outright magic.

Harvey's willingness to compromise his principles when absolutely necessary greatly assisted his cause. The votes of liberal non-residents would not have been sufficient without local support. Much like John Galt, Harvey looked upon 'the free-trade doctrine, and the doctrine upon which . . . Catholic relief was founded, viz. that all mankind had natural rights in society, as truths of the same science, but as such liable to be regulated by expediency'.[60] However strongly he might feel personally, he recognized the necessity of placating conservatives on Catholics and corn. By acting strictly as a 'delegate' for Colchester on these two critical matters, Harvey voted against his principles without violating them. Harvey's consistent support of Catholics could not be squared with overwhelming anti-Catholic sentiments in Colchester, a borough where the public hangman had burned the Catholic Emancipation Bill in 1807 and where a well-attended meeting at the Castle Library petitioned both Houses of Parliament 'against any further concessions to the Roman Catholics' in 1819. Therefore, Harvey reluctantly promised in 1826 that he would never vote for the Catholics 'unless requested to do so by his constituents'.[61] The Corn Law posed a similar problem for Harvey, a determined free-trader, and he resolved it in the same fashion. He bowed to the agricultural interest, assuaging his guilt with the thought that free trade 'had to be gradually achieved'.[62]

Just as Daniel Whittle Harvey's Radicalism played the dominant role in Colchester's elections prior to 1832, Richard Sanderson's Conservatism dominated parliamentary politics in Colchester's reformed elections. Ironically, Sanderson entered the fray initially by replacing Sir G. H. Smyth, who in 1829 resigned his seat to protest against Catholic emancipation. Sanderson lost Smyth's

[59] Harvey summarized Colchester's political views for the House of Commons. *MoP* (15 Apr. 1831), 1442.

[60] J. Galt, *The Member: An Autobiography* (London, 1832), 101.

[61] CLHL, E. COL. 1/920, 1 May 1819. Harvey's Radicalism was reminiscent of John Fielden's. S. A. Weaver, *John Fielden and the Politics of Popular Radicalism* (Oxford, 1987). In the same breath Harvey could not resist tweaking the anti-Catholics by reminding them that their hero Pitt had favoured Catholic emancipation. Thus Wildman, having 'pledged himself to follow in the footsteps of Mr Pitt', might not be trusted to behave accordingly on the same issue. *Colchester Gazette*, 10 June 1826.

[62] Ibid.

erstwhile seat before the poll in 1830 when his electoral agent was caught openly bribing electors. With both Smyth and Sanderson out of the running, the Tories' relatively weak candidate, Andrew Spottiswood, won Colchester's second seat at the penultimate unreformed election even though he arrived in the borough to begin his campaign only on the morning that polling began.

The Tory spell of ill fortune continued when Spottiswood's easy victory fell apart immediately after the election; he was disqualified by his post as the King's printer. William Mayhew should have then taken the seat, but he neglected to petition for his return in place of Spottiswood.[63] He subsequently won the by-election against an absentee candidate sponsored by the Corporation with the sole intent of bankrupting Mayhew with the expense of back-to-back polls. Mayhew managed to survive the two trials in 1830 and also stood successfully in the regular election of 1831 when he repelled Richard Sanderson's effort to recover his seat. He offered again as a Whig candidate in 1832, but lost when Sanderson finally recovered his seat. Sanderson was joined by Smyth in 1835 to create a united Tory slate that dominated Colchester for years. A well-known anti-Catholic, Smyth had been active in Tory circles for decades and would have posed a serious challenge to the reformers under any circumstances.

The 1835 poll marked the end of the reformers in Colchester.[64] Having kept reforming interests alive in the face of overwhelming odds for years, Harvey finally encountered a canvass so dismal that he abandoned the borough. With his departure to the more welcoming arms of Southwark, the reforming interest in Colchester faced an impossible task. Neither Harvey nor the liberal London contingent could be replaced. The remarkable aspect of the 1835 election was not the failure of the Whigs to win a seat, but their ability to turn in a respectable performance. Their candidate Henry

---

[63] Ironically, this had happened before. Harvey was unseated in 1820 by petition and replaced without a contest by Henry Baring because Harvey's opponent Henry Russell failed to sign his election petition and thus lost his right to fill the vacant seat. Cromwell, *History of Colchester*, ii. 289. Colchester faced by-elections when Davis resigned in 1818, when Harvey lost his seat in 1820, when Smyth accepted the Chiltern Hundreds in 1829, and again in 1830 when Mayhew defeated Sir William Curtis.

[64] Even the Radicals deserted the reformers for the Tories. See N. C. Edsall, *The Anti–Poor Law Movement* (London, 1971), 77.

Tufnell fell only sixty votes short of Smyth and a seat. In 1837, however, the Whig margin of defeat more than doubled and their future looked bleak. Disillusioned by the widening gap, the reformers conceded the town in 1841.

Voting habits in Colchester, indicated by the figures in Table 3.2, pose a number of interpretational difficulties. The levels of partisan and unnecessary plumping indicate sudden, substantial increases in partisan behaviour at the election of 1831. Partisan plumping jumped from just over a quarter of the electorate in 1830 to more than 42 per cent in 1831. If, on the other hand, Daniel Whittle Harvey is considered, as he asked to be considered, as a separate and distinct candidate allied to neither Whigs nor Tories, a different image emerges. Plumps for Harvey accounted for more than 60 per cent of all the votes cast in his favour in 1830, and for nearly a third of all the votes that year. Another 15 per cent of the entire electorate plumped for the solitary Whig, William Mayhew. Table 3.2 counts these voters as unnecessary plumpers since their behaviour permitted the return of the Tory Andrew Spottiswood. These unnecessary plumpers could easily justify their votes as embodying the highest principles. Since Harvey 'could not be a Tory' and stated as categorically that 'a Whig he could not be', Radicals had nothing to choose between the Tory and Whig candidates; they may have perceived their plumpers for Harvey as 'necessary'. By the same token, moderate Whigs who supported Mayhew may not have seen a double including Harvey as a reasonable choice.

The plunge in the level of unnecessary plumping at the election of 1831 supports the argument that the narrowly partisan decisions of 1830 might have stemmed from an excess rather than a deficiency of partisan zeal. More than half the voters in 1830 cast plumpers for Harvey or Mayhew, yet when the two candidates united for the sake of Reform in 1831 virtually no one plumped for one or the other of them. Just over a dozen Whig or Radical plumpers in 1831 took the place of the 575 Radical or Whig plumps cast in 1830. Table 3.2 lends some support to Speight's argument that the 1831 election was the first 'distinct polarization of the electorate' in Colchester, but it does not really support his other contention that 'the habit of splitting did not cease until the very eve of Reform'. The level of split-voting declined substantially in 1831, but splitting continued to plague the elections of 1832 and 1835 at approximately the level of 1830. The number of splitters dropped again in 1837, but the

TABLE 3.2. *Split-Voting and Plumping (Partisan and Unnecessary) in Colchester* (%)

Election year	1818	1820	1826	1830	1831	1832	1835	1837	1841
Split votes	62.0*	30.5*	NC	15.7	5.0	19.5	15.4	7.3	NC
Partisan plumps	16.8	17.7*	NC	26.4	42.1	46.0	33.2	34.1	NC
Unnecessary plumps	25.0	47.8*	NC	52.8	1.4	19.8	2.7	2.0	NC

NC No contest.
* These figures record nominal (i.e. Tory/Radical or Tory/Whig) splits and assume that voters should have doubled Whig/Radical.
Sources: Poll books.

absence of a contest in 1841 renders any interpretation of these figures problematic.[65]

A cross-sectional assessment of Colchester, as of Maidstone, suggests that not just the Reform Act, but the Reform era affected voting behaviour. Levels of partisanship increased as much during the agitation for the Bill as after its passage. Unnecessary plumping and splitting in Maidstone's 1831 election dropped to a tiny fraction of what had been normal earlier. The same shift just before Reform was more pronounced still in Colchester. Nearly half the electorate cast unnecessary plumpers in 1820 and 1830; virtually no one did in 1831. At the same time, a third as many Colcestrians split that year as in the previous election. By the standard of 1820, only a sixth as many split their support between the parties. Yet at the same time, both towns were affected significantly by the Reform Act's redefinition of the electorate. With these measures of voting behaviour pointing simultaneously to the months of agitation over Reform and the Act itself, another perspective is necessary to gauge the relative impacts of Act and era.

THE REFORM ACT AND THE REFORM ERA

A longitudinal perspective helps distinguish the impact of the political agitation of 1830/1 from the effects of the Act in 1832. In both towns party divisions in the years before Reform 'had their immediate origin in the politics of the 1790s'. To a large extent, the Tories based their appeal on reaction, repression, and a rather new and particularly intense patriotism.[66] Harking back to the tradition of Charles James Fox, the Whigs championed peace, toleration, and liberty. Reform provided a new litmus test, but in many ways the new issues resembled older political divisions. Moreover, the overlapping of national party divisions in Maidstone and Colchester with Corporation/anti-Corporation animosities added to the clarity of electoral choice at all elections between 1818 and 1841. If occasionally murky when particular issues such as religion obscured

[65] Speight, 'Colchester', 115.
[66] Colley, 'The Apotheosis of George III'; ead., 'Whose Nation? Class and National Consciousness in Britain 1750–1830', *Past and Present*, 113 (1986), 97–117. F. O'Gorman, 'Party Politics', 67.

the points of the political compass, political choices were usually broadly clear. Maidstone's True Blues seemed to address the point when urging the voters in 1834 to 'Let not names mislead you. Whig, Liberal, Radical all have a Common Enemy— the determined Tory.'[67]

Under these circumstances, the consistent behaviour of voters such as Chignall Wire makes sense. Wire, a Colchester publisher, confectioner, and militant Radical, found 'liberty' an appealing concept when he voted for Daniel Whittle Harvey in 1818. He might have voted for the other moderate Whig candidate, Peter Wright, that year, but Harvey was the only candidate decidedly in favour of Reform, particularly of Parliament. Wire continued to vote for 'liberty' in subsequent elections; his political convictions remained steady. And since he perceived local struggles in parliamentary terms, Wire voted consistently. In 1820 and 1830 he continued to plump for Harvey, but in 1831 he recognized the Reform coalition and cast a double for Harvey and the other reformer, Mayhew. He continued as a reformer in 1832, but seems to have lost his confidence in Harvey because he plumped for Mayhew. He followed that Whig plump with two more in 1835 and 1837 as he voted for the solitary Reform candidate at each contest.

Edward Daniell, a Colchester lawyer, also counted himself a friend of liberty, and, like Wire, behaved with perfect political consistency in consecutive elections in Colchester. Daniell plumped for the moderate Whig, Peter Wright, in 1818, but switched to Harvey subsequently, voting for him at each contested election until Harvey withdrew in 1834. Daniell then plumped necessarily for the Whig candidate Tuffnell in 1835 and for Todd in 1837. Only his unnecessary plumper for Harvey in 1832 slightly blemished his otherwise pristine record of party voting. Wire also plumped unnecessarily in 1832, but for Mayhew. These two unnecessary Whig plumpers by otherwise devoted partisans reflect the tension caused by a small rift among the Whigs in Colchester in their most successful year. After Reform, more moderate Whigs preferred Harvey to Mayhew since Harvey's radicalism, formed in the teens, had mellowed. Harvey was a devoted reformer, to be sure, but Mayhew was the truly Radical candidate in 1832. Harvey had been overtaken by events. These votes aside, Chignall Wire and Edward

---

[67] *Maidstone Gazette*, 25 Nov. 1834.

Daniell each boasted perfectly consistent voting records; both returned to support Whig candidates election after election.

At the other end of the political spectrum from Chignall Wire stood Francis Tillet Abell. An alderman and sometime mayor of Colchester, Abell believed in the principles of the Tory party. A long-standing member of the Pitt Club, Abell helped form the ultra-Tory Brunswick Club in 1828. A man with little time for liberty and less time for Catholics, Abell should have supported Tory candidates as consistently as Wire voted for reformers. And he did. Abell plumped for Wildman in 1818, voted Wildman and Russell in 1820, plumped for Sanderson in 1830, 1831, and 1832, and happily doubled for the united Tory slate of Sanderson and Smyth in 1835 and 1837. The consistency of his principles matched the consistency of his party, and his behaviour followed suit. Wire and Daniell had nothing to teach Abell about consistent partisan voting.

Voters with similarly strong views and equally consistent voting records were far from rare in Maidstone and Colchester. Colcestrians could be found as early as 1820 voicing the strong and consistent political beliefs noted in the letters of a number of Bristolians a decade later. Just as a Bristolian could explain to Sir Richard Vyvyan that he had advocated 'the political principles which I now hold . . . ever since I became a thinking Man', a Colcestrian could explain to those assembled at the hustings in 1820 that 'when he took up a man [Mr Wildman] on principle, he never deserted him'. If a Bristolian could claim honestly that it was 'the Blue Party . . . that I have been from my earliest life firmly attached to', a Colcestrian could claim equally honestly to be attached to Mr Harvey, 'for the principles he *always* professed'.[68]

It was possible, of course, for voters to change their principles, their minds, their parties, or some combination of the three. Edward Daniell executed a perfectly partisan voting record between 1818 and 1837, but he switched from Wright in 1818 to Harvey in 1820. Just before the opening of the poll in 1820, Daniell found it necessary to admit publically 'that about three years ago, Mr Harvey and himself were almost personally opposed to each other. But it did not follow, Daniell argued, that because he disagreed with a man to-day, or last year, or the year before, he should continue in a state of enmity with him all his life; certainly not when the cause of

[68] *Proceedings of the Late Election*, 23; *Poll for Members to Serve in Parliament* (Colchester, 1820), 20.

disagreement was removed.' Daniell used the language of principle in explaining his reconciliation with Harvey. He attributed his conversion primarily to Harvey's parliamentary behaviour, noting that his former reservations had less to do with Harvey's expressed views than with Daniell's belief in the level of Harvey's conviction. Now that Harvey had quelled his misgivings by voting a consistent Whig line in the Commons, Daniell was in Harvey's camp and expected to 'continue so always'.[69]

Ordinarily, however, the relative clarity and longevity of local partisan structures (less clear and less long-lived in Colchester than in Maidstone), and the persistence and blending of issues perceived in the provinces to be important meant that a preference for a particular party at one election should have translated into a series of votes for that party at sequential elections. Table 3.3 demonstrates that electorates in both these towns often failed to behave consistently prior to Reform, but that conversely, most of the voters at reformed elections behaved exactly in accordance with this expectation.

Prior to 1832, many voters in Maidstone followed a roughly consistent pattern. Robert Allender cast Whig plumps in 1826 and in 1830. Joshua Aldridge, on the other hand, followed his split vote for Robarts and Wells with another split in 1830 when he coupled Rawlings with Robarts. And while Allender continued to vote Whig in 1831 and 1832, Aldridge, along with quite a few other freemen, switched to voting for Tory candidates exclusively. For the Maidstone electorate as a whole, Table 3.3 indicates moderately high voter consistency before 1832 when measured with λ, which tests the relationship between the voting choices of individual voters at two successive elections using a scale ranging between 0 (no relationship between one vote and the next) and 1 (absolute consistency).[70] λ reveals a persistent, though not strong (i.e. <0.4), pattern at Maidstone's unreformed elections; the political choices of many voters were related from election to election from the first pair examined. Nevertheless, Reform dramatically altered the nature of those relationships. After 1832, very strong (>0.75) voting consistency emerged and persisted. Tory votes followed Tory votes and Whig

---

[69] *Proceedings of the Late Election*, 9.

[70] λ (asymmetric) is the appropriate measure because the potential influence of one vote on the next works only chronologically. A vote in 1832 can hardly have affected a vote of 1831.

TABLE 3.3. *Electoral behaviour across Elections in Maidstone and Colchester: λ (Asymmetric)*

Election years	1818–20	1820–6	1826–30	1830–1	1831–2	1832–5	1835–7	1837–41
Maidstone	0.32	0.34	0.39	0.32	0.33	0.76	0.77	0.67
Colchester	0.24	NC	0.05	0.38	0.75	0.69	0.71	NC

NC No contest.
Sources: Poll books.

votes followed Whig votes much more frequently after Reform than before.

Colcestrians were far less consistent than their Maidstone counterparts in their voting choices at early nineteenth-century elections. They did not achieve the level of politically consistent behaviour found in Maidstone as early as 1818/20 until 1830/1. More to the point, a remarkable alteration occurred in Colchester between the next pair of elections. The shift to strong political consistency in Maidstone at the 1832/5 contests was felt in Colchester between 1831 and 1832. Once Colcestrians achieved this level of consistency, they maintained it. The drastic physical alteration of Colchester's electorate in 1832 did not result in a further improvement, but then little improvement could have been achieved. Consistency simply remained very high.

Measured with τ_b, which considers these votes as ordinal-level data by arbitrarily assigning positive and negative values to Tory and Whig votes ranging from $+2$ (for two Tory votes) to -2 (for two Whig votes), the pattern of choices is more revealing.[71] The top half of Table 3.4 demonstrates the strong tendency of Maidstone's electors to vote consistently for the same party before the passage of the Reform Act. It also throws into sharper contrast the sudden shift that occurred in Maidstone in 1832 and the more gradual shift that began in Colchester between 1830 and 1831, gained strength between 1831 and 1832, and culminated after the passage of Reform. In fact, Colchester exactly duplicated Maidstone's consistency score in 1830/1 and again in 1832/5. Between 1832 and 1835, virtually everyone in Maidstone voted consistently. Whig voters continued to vote for Whig candidates without being rewarded in any way for having done so. The same could be said of Colchester between 1831 and 1832. Both electorates demonstrated extraordinarily strong partisan consistency after the Reform Act, but Colchester began to move to that point earlier.

If the choices of these voters are related to Ministries instead of parties, their partisan loyalties are revealed more strikingly still.

---

[71] This scale conforms to the realities of the complicated voting choices present at these elections, reformed and unreformed, because it indicates the nature of relationships as well as their strength. Kendall's τ_b is the appropriate measure when the table created by the nominal variable comparisons contains an equal number of columns and rows. If the tabular comparison involves an unequal number, τ_c is the appropriate comparative statistic. W. Buchanan, 'Nominal and Ordinal Bivariate Statistics', *American Journal of Political Science*, 18 (1974), 625–46.

TABLE 3.4. *Electoral Behaviour across Elections in Maidstone and Colchester:* τ_b

Election years	1818–20	1820–6	1826–30	1830–1	1831–2	1832–5	1835–7	1837–41
Whig–Tory Scale								
Maidstone	0.69	0.57	0.62	0.54	0.51	0.81	0.86	0.75
Colchester	0.53	NC	0.30	0.54	0.73	0.81	0.82	NC
Government–Opposition Scale★								
Governments	T–T	T–T	T–T	T–W	W–W	W–T	T–W	W–W
Maidstone	0.69	0.57	0.62	−0.54	0.51	−0.81	−0.86	0.75
Colchester	0.53	NC	0.30	−0.54	0.73	−0.81	−0.82	NC

NC No contest. T Tory Government. W Whig Government.
Sources: Poll books.

After many years of Tory Governments, both Whigs and Tories formed administrations under William IV. John Galt argued that 'a Tory is but a Whig in office, and a Whig but a Tory in opposition, which makes it not difficult for a conscientious man to support the government'.[72] Behaviour of the Maidstone and Colchester electorates suggests the opposite. Lord Grey's Whig ministry of 1830 was succeeded by Sir Robert Peel's brief administration in 1834/5. Lord Melbourne restored the Whigs immediately following the general election of 1835. These ministerial shifts meant that at the general elections of 1831, 1835, and 1837, casting a partisan vote at two successive elections meant shifting one's position towards the Government itself. Robert Allender of Maidstone, who voted Whig in both 1830 and 1831, voted for the Opposition the first time and for the Government the second time. By using the polarities of Government and Opposition in place of Whig and Tory, the bottom half of Table 3.4 reflects the primacy of party at both reformed and unreformed elections in the towns. The negative scores for 1830/1, 1832/5, and 1835/7 show that these voters were loyal to parties, not administrations.

The slightly earlier political transformation of Colchester stemmed not from the lingering impact of local political considerations at parliamentary elections, but from their sudden disappearance in 1831. In 1831 for the first time Colcestrians faced a united, purely national slate in the persons of Harvey and Mayhew, and responded to this election, which Harvey called a 'referendum', by either supporting the Reform ticket or rejecting it. This new, strictly national orientation carried forward to the next election, and to subsequent elections. Having been asked to vote for candidates on the basis of their orientation towards national issues alone, Colcestrians responded positively. The scores in Table 3.4 show that they continued to respond in the same way after their introduction in 1831; their behaviour under the Reform Act reflects a fundamental politicization during the debate over the Reform Bill.

Maidstone voters, on the other hand, did not experience such a radical transformation of the terms of the campaign in 1831. Already highly politicized as a result of decades of elections in which national issues took the forefront and remained there during campaigns, voters approached 1831 in much the same spirit as before, and

---

[72] Galt, *The Member*, 7.

behaved in much the same fashion. The *Maidstone Gazette* waged a determined attack against the Duke of Wellington's Government in 1830, well before anyone could have anticipated the general election required by the death of George IV.[73] While the paper called for 'a General Reform of the whole system of government', it also called for an end to Tory rule.[74] The newspaper carried the voting records of Maidstone's MPs as well as those of virtually every other Kentish MP. So accustomed to partisan, issue-oriented politics was the *Maidstone Gazette* that, by 1830, it expressed surprise at the remarkable 'coincidence of opinion' prevailing at the general election that year. When the *Gazette* referred to each party 'faithfully adhering to the colour of its ribbon, and to the political sentiments which it was supposed to typify', and when it expected the electorate to judge whether their MPs' 'political creeds were *ex facie* distinct in their essential article', politics in Maidstone could hardly become more partisan.[75] However partisan the elections of the Reform era might have been, they could not have appeared very unusual in the context of elections that had been highly partisan for decades.

National political concerns had certainly appeared in both towns with sufficient clarity to permit strictly partisan voting along national lines in unreformed elections. Nevertheless, in both towns, vestiges of an earlier system were perpetuated both by voters who considered other matters in addition to national political issues when making their choices for MP and by voters who concerned themselves primarily with local issues. Measured by τ_b, the voters in Colchester and Maidstone (but Maidstone in particular) had demonstrated remarkably high levels of partisan loyalty across elections as early as 1820, but these levels ($> +0.5$) in both towns still indicated quite a few voters who switched their alliances from one election to the next.

Reform, Act and era, was unmistakably powerful in Bristol, Maidstone, and Colchester, but to what degree was this sort of impact felt in other boroughs? Reform's considerable impact might have been anticipated in Bristol, but the degree of change wrought in Maidstone and Colchester is more suprising. How did the demand for the Bill, the whole Bill, and nothing but the Bill and, as importantly, the granting of that demand, affect other provincial towns?

[73] *Maidstone Gazette*, 5 Jan. 1830.   [74] Ibid. 2 Feb. 1830.
[75] Ibid. 24 Aug. 1830.

4

Reform Act or Reform Era?:
Political Change in Shrewsbury
and Northampton

FEW nineteenth-century towns were more diverse physically, socially, or economically than Shrewsbury and Northampton, yet both towns reveal an important aspect of Reform in the boroughs. The behaviour of voters in Maidstone and Colchester raised the possibility that the agitation for Reform may have been more influential than the Act itself. Elections in Shrewsbury and Northampton demonstrate the politicizing effects of popular agitation during the months of debate, delay, and dismay leading up to Reform. The provisions of the Reform Act affected political behaviour in both towns, but the politicization stemming from the excitement of 1831 played an even greater role in altering their political fabric.

UNREFORMED ELECTIONS IN SHREWSBURY

Few Shrewsbury elections passed unpolled, and a serious consideration of current political issues by the electorate was not uncommon even before the Regency. Religion (notably virulent anti-Catholicism), reform, and popular rights vied with vestiges of patronage and corruption in determining the general elections of 1806 and 1807.[1] Similarly, debates over parliamentary reform, the suspension of

---

[1] Shrewsbury had been long concerned with the Catholic question. In 1812 Lord Berwick refused to approve of Henry Bennet's 'parliamentary conduct nor of his having taken up the pen in behalf of Catholic emancipation' because he had seen 'too much of papacy'. Nevertheless, Berwick permitted his tenants 'to follow their own consciences and judgements' since the issue was so sensitive. SLHL, Berwick MSS 6760/362, 363.

habeas corpus, taxation, economic retrenchment, the Catholic question, and Henry Brougham's plan for educating the poor marked the election of 1818.[2] Whig and Tory labels can be attached easily enough to candidates in most Shrewsbury elections. If the candidates usually distanced themselves from party terminology, their supporters often showed no such reticence.[3] One of Henry Bennet's nominators in 1818, Thurstan Cook, jnr., argued that Bennet's conduct could have received no higher praise than the 'high eulogium of Mr Tierney'. Cook pleaded that those like himself who had found themselves opposed to the election of Richard Lyster 'on political grounds' four years earlier had found their opposition justified. As Shrewsbury's MP, Lyster had committed a number of 'political sins and offences'. Those who supported Bennet should reject Lyster and thus 'throw off the odium and inconsistency which now attaches to Salopians for returning one Tory Member, and the other [Bennet] of the combined principles of Whiggism and reform'.[4] Unfortunately for Cook and his fellow Whigs, no other candidate emerged, and Shrewsbury's representation remained 'inconsistent'. Richard Lyster and Henry Bennet took their seats without a poll.

Within a year, however, Shrewsbury's electors had a chance to vote, and though the by-election of 1819 was heavily influenced by personality, neither party nor principle disappeared entirely. John Mytton, the rich, eccentric, 22-year-old, anti-administration, anti-Corporation candidate, was better known for his enthusiastic fox-hunting than his political principles.[5] Yet, *contra* Roland Thorne

---

[2] Some of the 1818 debate was idiosyncratic. Charles Bage attacked the administration for engaging in the vile French practice of espionage. Bennet had earned Shrewsbury's gratitude by opposing hired government spies, those 'most hideous, most venomous, most despicable' of God's creatures. Bennet was clearly a Whig; he wrote to Creevey on 20 July 1818 about 'our plan for a leader', i.e. Tierney. Thorne, *House of Commons*, i. 264; Edwards, *Parliamentary Elections*, 19; *The Late Elections*, 274.

[3] In 1806 the supporters of Henry G. Bennet (the younger son of the Earl of Tankerville, a moderate Grenvillite, and a supporter of the administration) somewhat disingenuously accused his Burdettite opponent Thomas Jones of advocating 'Catholic claims', since Jones had written a pamphlet entitled *The Protestant Ascendancy in Ireland*. SLHL, Dq45/acc2228/unfoliated; *Salopian Journal*, 19 Nov. 1806.

[4] *The Late Elections*, 276–7.

[5] While still a child, Mytton inherited an annual income estimated to exceed £60,000. His antics included riding bears bareback in his drawing-room and duck-hunting in the dark in his nightshirt. His only competition as the most eccentric Shropshire Member came from J. C. Pelham, who tried for years to inaugurate a

who found 'nothing to choose between [the] politics' of Mytton and his opponent Panton Corbett, the former occupied a political position quite distinct from the latter. Corbett, the Corporation candidate, was cut from the same Conservative cloth as ex-MP Richard Lyster.[6] Corbett claimed to stand 'without any private or party views', but his political colouration was clear enough to anyone who cared to think politically in 1819; his support of the administration in the Parliaments of 1820 and 1826 can have surprised no one. Thus Mytton's candidacy did not completely eliminate either party or issues, though many voters may have cared too much about the financial rewards of voting in 1819. While Corbett actively if disingenuously disclaimed party ties, Mytton's much deeper pocket seemed more likely to harm Corbett more than his political views. William Eddowes condemned Mytton's attempted subversion of 'the most numerous and most worthless class of electors' with gold, accusing him of buying 200 votes.[7]

The general election of 1820 also passed unpolled. John Mytton discovered an incompatibility between 'a proper and punctual attention' to Shrewsbury's interests and his 'present pursuits', notably horse-racing.[8] His lavish expenditure in 1819, coupled with betting losses at the track, had proven fatal to his already strained finances. His decision to stand down before fleeing the country to avoid his creditors left a seat free for his erstwhile opponent Panton Corbett. Initially, Corbett and Bennet appeared certain to retain their seats in 1826 without a poll as well, but Bennet withdrew at the last moment after 'vile reports' concerning his personal life forced him to follow Mytton into exile, from which he, unlike the latter, never returned.[9] In Bennet's place, the Whigs nominated moderate

peripatetic Parliament that would sit in all the principal towns of the kingdom in rotation. Mytton fled to the Continent, returning to England only to die of delirium tremens while in the Fleet prison for debt. D. Sutherland, *The Mad Hatters* (London, 1987); W. H. Apperley (Nimrod), *The Life of John Mytton* (London, 1893), 93–7. See also Sir B. Burke, *A Second Series of Vicissitudes of Families* (London, 1860), 112–25.

[6] Thorne, *House of Commons*, i. 339; H. T. Weyman, 'Shrewsbury Members of Parliament', *Transactions of the Shropshire Archaeological Society*, 4th ser., 12 (1929–30), 118–9, 248–9.

[7] With two such candidates, many electors declined to vote. *Correct Alphabetical List of the Burgesses* (Shrewsbury, 1819), pp. iii, iv; *Shrewsbury Chronicle*, 28 May 1819; Edwards, *Parliamentary Elections*, 21. SLHL, Dq45/m/25, 22 May 1819.

[8] *Shrewsbury Chronicle*, 25 Feb. 1820.

[9] SLHL, Dq45/2228/unfoliated. *A Peep at the Commons* in 1820 noted Bennet's relationship to Lord Tankerville and the presence of his elder brother in the

barrister Robert A. Slaney. Still no contest threatened until the last-minute entrance of a third candidate, Thomas Boycott.[10] Boycott, a *'Thorough* friend to our Protestant Constitution as by Law established', revived the Catholic issue, and in doing so created a virtual referendum that measured each candidate's devotion to Protestantism. The *Chronicle* defended Slaney and Corbett as equally good sons of the Church, who 'would not condescend to raise the cry, "No Popery"' and attacked Boycott for failing to distinguish between 'the patronizing of the Catholic religion and the adopting of cautious measures for conciliating Ireland—for converting exasperated foes into cordial friends'.[11] If all Ireland's friends were England's foes, then they stood in good company with Pitt, Fox, and Burke.[12]

Boycott's effort to ride anti-Catholicism into Parliament failed, but his candidacy illustrated the backwardness of Shrewsbury politics.[13] Rather than standing together with Corbett, who shared his basic political complexion, Boycott stood alone and acted as if the election concerned only Slaney and himself. And Corbett's seat was never in doubt. The failure of the two Tory candidates to present a united front, coupled with Slaney's insistence that he stood as an

Commons, but also believed that Shrewsbury could not be controlled by patrons (p. 15).

[10] Slaney claimed 'Independent but Moderate Principles, unfettered by Party engagement'. *Shrewsbury Chronicle*, 21 Apr. 1826. Robert Aglionby Slaney (1791–1862), author of *British Birds*, sat for Shrewsbury, with occasional absences, from 1826 to his death in 1862. BL Add. MSS. 40403, 40310, 40491. Also Birmingham University Library, Slaney MSS 9/v/2.1–5; SLHL, Morris Eyton Collection, MSS 1–9; P. Richards, 'R. A. Slaney, the Industrial Town, and Early Victorian Social Policy', *Social History* 4 (1979).

[11] One reader demanded more, arguing in a letter to the editor that 'the thinking and reading portion of the inhabitants of Shrewsbury should demand that Boycott answer the arguments recently published in 'A Letter by the Reverend Sydney Smith' relating to Ireland. *Shrewsbury Chronicle*, 2, 9 June 1826.

[12] Corbett finally condescended to a bit of Catholic-bashing as he reassured those at the hustings that he had neither the remotest inclination towards Catholicism nor 'the slightest intention of giving political power to the members of that communion'. Edwards, *Parliamentary Elections*, 23.

[13] Boycott's total actually exceeded Slaney's by one vote on the evening of the fourth day of the poll, but at that point Boycott's support was exhausted while Slaney's was not. Recognizing defeat despite his single-vote advantage on the poll book, Boycott relinquished the contest. The poll opened for only the morning of the fifth day and closed with Slaney well clear in second place. The *Chronicle* reported a conversation in which the mayor asked for any additional Boycott votes. He was answered by William Hazeldine who said: 'I believe they have all done, Sir. Somebody thought my gray horse was coming to poll for Mr Boycott, so they have changed his colour by painting him green for Mr Slaney.' *Shrewsbury Chronicle*, 16 June 1826.

'independent, unshackled' candidate, left Shrewsbury by default without a genuinely partisan election. The joint stand of Disraeli and Tomline against Parry and Temple in 1841 was, in fact, the first Shrewsbury election at which candidates shared colours. Before the light-blue-and-white banners of the Conservatives together flew against the yellow-and-green of the two Whigs, each candidate had been careful not to duplicate banners of his fellows, whether friend or foe.[14] Party development in Shrewsbury lagged far behind Bristol, Maidstone, or Colchester.[15]

Shrewsbury does not lend itself readily to the kind of broad cross-sectional comparisons reported in Table 4.1. Too many idiosyncrasies demand explanation, and unpolled elections obscure matters further. Nevertheless, electoral behaviour in both 1826 and 1830 reflected the partisan deficiencies evident in the candidates. In 1826 nearly 60 per cent of Shrewsbury's electors split their votes (most of them Slaney and Corbett), or plumped for non-partisan reasons. Virtually no one cast a plump for the lone Whig, but Slaney's firm denial of party ties eliminated much of the electorate's incentive to waste a vote. Nor had conditions changed much in 1830. Again, two Tory candidates stood separately along with a single Whig, Slaney. Again, both Tories and Slaney eschewed the party labels they so clearly warranted. Again, a huge number (just over half) of the voters cast non-partisan votes by splitting or plumping unnecessarily. As O'Gorman aptly noted, much 'middle-ground' voting persisted in Shrewsbury in the year before Reform became an issue.[16]

As in 1826, religion took pride of place in Shrewsbury's 1830 election debates. Corbett's anti-Catholic rhetoric in 1826 returned to haunt him because he had voted for Catholic emancipation. He tried to explain his votes as necessary by pointing to Wellington's strong

[14] In 1826 Boycott's white and blue stood out against Slaney's green, which in turn could hardly be confused with Corbett's orange-and-purple. At the 1835 election one Conservative (Hanmer) flew dark-blue-and-white banners while his fellow Conservative at the election, but not 'on the ticket' (Pelham) flew sky-blue ones. Weyman, 'Shrewsbury Members', *passim.*

[15] Slaney's appeal may have stemmed more directly from his association with the Shrewsbury races than from his timid appeal to 'the Protestant Bible', the 'promotion of education among the poorer classes', and the 'amelioration of the condition of poor men'. Edwards, *Parliamentary Elections*, 24; J. F. A. Mason, 'Parlimentary Representation in Shrewsbury', in G. C. Baugh (ed.) *VCH Shropshire*, iii (London, 1979), 327.

[16] *Voters*, 378–81. Intense partisanship showed clearly across elections. Between 1830 and 1831 approximately 90% of Shrewsbury's partisan voters remained loyal to their party. See Table 4.3.

TABLE 4.1. *Split-Voting and Plumping in Shrewsbury* (%)

Election year	1818	1820	1826	1830	1831	1832	1835	1837	1841
Split-votes	NC	NC	55.1	44.5	15.8	31.5	20.6	11.0	2.9
Partisan plumps	NC	NC	2.2	13.3	4-man	28.1	28.8	4-man	4-man
Unnecessary plumps	NC	NC	4.6	5.6	9.3	1.3	2.3	3.0	0.9

NC No contest.
4-man Four candidates; politically motivated plumping not required.
Sources: Poll books.

support and stressing the bill's easy passage. He also reminded voters of his refusal to be a mere delegate, and his scrupulous avoidance of a pledge on the Catholic question. In this instance, he argued that his personal desires came second to the demands of the country's welfare and the Duke of Wellington's wishes. Unimpressed with his defence and the amount of money he was willing to spend, Corbett's former supporters deserted him in droves. He refused to stoop to outright bribery to appease them. A bit of election doggerel of the racing variety noted:

> Says Corbett to Salop
> Pray why should I gallop?
> My nag shall walk over the course.
> Says Salop, they've won it,
> And you could have done it
> By clapping gold spurs to your horse.[17]

More than 600 voters had promised Corbett their votes during his personal canvass, yet his total fell 160 short of that number, leaving him a distant third to Slaney.[18] Slaney's bill repealing the beer tax and his efforts to reform the Poor Law had boosted his popularity. Slaney also mentioned Reform during the election, but could hardly have frightened many Tories with his call for 'practical and moderate reform, not hasty and violent'.[19] The other victor in 1830, who assumed the leadership of Shrewsbury's Tories, had just returned from the residency of Nagpur. Richard Jenkins expressed his Toryism in the traditional promise to support 'Our Glorious Constitution in Church and State', but said little else.[20] He was accused of being a 'Tool of Tools', of using Shrewsbury as a diversion while he awaited a better position in India, of opposing free trade because of India, and of advocating slavery, again because of India, but none of these objections prevented his return.

Shrewsbury's final unreformed election presented a different profile. After some years of toying with parties but voting as if they did not exist, Shrewsbury's electorate finally took parties seriously.

[17] SLHL, DA45/1170/unfoliated.
[18] *Salopian Journal*, 4 Aug. 1830. Of the 607 votes promised to Corbett, only 58 failed to keep their promise by not voting; 167 actually voted against him. Three men tendered votes for him without success, and another 61 voters who had not been part of the canvass cast ballots for Corbett.
[19] *Shrewsbury Chronicle*, 6 Aug. 1830.
[20] F. A. Hagan, 'Richard Jenkins and the Residency of Nagpur', Ph.D. (California, 1960). *Shrewsbury Chronicle*, 6 Aug. 1830.

Before townsmen had an inkling that another electoral opportunity was in the offing, their agitation over Russell's Reform Bill led to a call for a public meeting that added Shrewsbury to the ranks of towns petitioning Parliament for Reform. More than 1,000 men signed the demand 'in the short space of two days, and, had more time been allowed, it would have received a further addition of signatures'.[21] If the elections of 1826 and 1830 tended to focus on one issue, the 1831 contest in Shrewsbury, as in many constituencies, was a pure referendum. No issue but Russell's Reform was raised aside from one minor complaint about 'stranger' candidates. Nor would any other issue have found an ear if it had been broached. As the Shrewsbury reformers put it: 'Those who are not with the people are against them. The cry now is "The Bill—the whole Bill—and nothing but the Bill."'[22] Shrewsbury's Tories could not divert attention to other matters such as religion and agriculture. They warned that the Reform Bill was 'a delusion', opening the door to 'Demagogues' who would repeal the Corn Laws, and eventually 'upset the Established Church and set religion at defiance'.[23] In this fevered environment the Whigs were desperate to prevent Shrewbury's remaining 'a nonentity, a cypher in the representation of the people, which it has hitherto been in consequence of sending one member to support the cause of Reform . . . and the other who . . . votes against him'. To this end, they recruited a reforming Nonconformist candidate from outside Shrewsbury, Richard Potter of Lancashire, to stand with Slaney.[24] The Tories responded with their own full slate, their incumbent, Jenkins, and Thomas Boycott.[25]

---

[21] The petition included those of high and low political status. In addition to William Hazeldine, Henry Benyon, W. P. Scoltock, and William Clement, all leaders, it included P. Horsman, a flax spinner, John Howell, a shoemaker, and many others further down the socio-economic scale. Slaney presented the petition, and Jenkins, while he dissented, professed to being 'not altogether an anti-reformer'. SLHL, Dq45/6/12 Mar. 1831; *MoP* (21 Mar. 1831), 1033–4.

[22] SLHL, DA45/1170/Broadside of 29 Apr. 1831.

[23] SLHL, Dq45/6/ND, Broadsheet entitled 'The Reform Bill and Delusion'.

[24] W. P. Scoltock seconded Potter's nomination. Edwards, *Parliamentary Elections*, 27.

[25] The Whigs pressed ahead with Potter even though the death of his sister prevented his personal participation in the election. Richard Potter (1778–1842), an ancestor of Sir Stafford Cripps, left nothing useful in his papers except a record of the weather and his loyal chapel attendance. London School of Economics, Potter MSS, vol. 6, 6 June 1830, and vols. 3–13*b*, *passim*.

The county election, the first in Shropshire in more than a century, helped inundate Shrewsbury with placards and broadsides, some of them brought from London, heralding Reform. Frequently the messages in these scores of different posters neglected to mention the candidates themselves. A poster for the borough election was indistinguishable from one for the county election;[26] the only message was Reform, and a royally sponsored Reform at that. Potter painted the Reform Bill as the perfect blend of the King's wishes and 'the people's will' and reminded the electorate that his 'political principles are not of late formation, I was a Reformer when Reform was unfashionable.'[27]

While many placards ignored candidates in favour of issues, an advertisement for 'Russell's Purge', 'a sovereign remedy for Aristocratic stomachs, or Placemen and Pensioners given to sitting without exercise, for stomachs gorged to satiety with luxuries created by overstrained taxation and the sweat of the Peasant's brow' appealed simultaneously for votes for Slaney, who stood for Shrewsbury, and Mytton, who stood for Shropshire.[28] Reform overrode ordinary political boundaries, but at the same time the poster included only the two local Whig candidates in its appeal. Slaney's running mate, an outsider, was not mentioned, nor was Mytton's partner in the county election, another outsider. This blending of local men with a national issue suggested that Salopians might not 'want radicals from Lancashire [a reference to Richard Potter] to teach them loyalty', as Shrewsbury's Conservatives claimed.[29]

The full party slates in 1831 significantly altered the structural circumstances of the election and may have accounted for some of the dramatic improvement in partisanship evident in Table 4.1. Partisan voting declined in 1832 when Shrewsbury reverted to a three-man contest the next year, and even in 1835 the level of partisanship reached in 1831 could not be duplicated. In fact, Shrewsbury voters did not again achieve 1831's low level of split-

[26] R. Porter, *English Society in the Eighteenth Century* (Harmondsworth, 1982), 126, calls attention to the gap. SLHL, DA45/1170/several undated 1831 posters from London.
[27] SLHL, DA45/1170/28 Apr. 1831; *MoP* (23 June) 97, (4 July 1831), 296.
[28] SLHL, DA45/1170/3 Apr. 1831.
[29] William Lloyd, the other Whig candidate for Shropshire, also had few local ties and was ignored along with Potter. The Whigs appealed, therefore, to party, Reform, and local connections by pairing Mytton and Slaney in their propaganda.

voting until the next four-man contest in 1837. The increased partisanship may also have owed something to the abbreviated contest. After a single afternoon's polling that recorded the votes of only 303 men, Slaney and Jenkins stood so far ahead of the other two candidates that Boycott (the second Tory) and Potter (the second Whig) withdrew to permit the return of Slaney and Jenkins for the second time. The 300 who managed to vote may not have been representative of the entire electorate, though their conjoint performance was hardly exclusively partisan. A quarter of these voters still failed the party test by splitting (15 per cent) or plumping unnecessarily (10 per cent). Virtually all the plumpers ignored the presence of the second Whig and plumped for the incumbent Slaney. A very few plumped for the other incumbent, Jenkins. Neither of the outsiders, Potter and Boycott, attracted a single plumper. Old habits die hard. Shrewsbury remained a cipher, as W. P. Scoltock had feared, because Slaney and Jenkins rode their plumpers and splitters to Parliament.[30] Even so, the pronounced shift in 1831 cannot be attributed entirely to either the presence of four candidates or the abbreviated poll. Shrewsbury's electorate responded to Reform, as split-voting dropped in less than twelve months from more than 42 per cent of the entire electorate to less than 16 per cent.

REFORMED ELECTIONS IN SHREWSBURY

The notable increase in partisan behaviour between the elections of 1830 and 1831 did not prevent further substantial improvement in 1832. Though split-voting increased sharply, the figures in Table 4.1 suggest generally that Reform accomplished more than a mere change in the size and composition of Shrewsbury's electorate. In reformed Shrewsbury the proportion of the electorate willing to cast partisan plumps jumped from the negligible 2 per cent in 1826 and 13 per cent in 1830 to more than 30 per cent in 1832. What is more, Slaney was the recipient of the plumpers each time; voters responded to virtually identical circumstances in an entirely new way. The eradication of non-partisan plumping also points to the

[30] SLHL, DA45/1170/unfoliated.

impact of Reform. At the elections of 1832 and 1835 very few men cast plumpers needlessly. Clearer differences separate the four-man contest of 1831 from the two reformed four-man contests of 1837 and 1841. Almost 10 per cent of the voters plumped in the face of full slates of candidates in 1831. Very few behaved in such a politically indefensible manner in 1837; almost no one did in 1841.

Shrewsbury's first reformed contest was also procedurally different, as it was taken by ward in six polling-booths rather than at the hustings set up traditionally under the market house. The new polling-booths, coupled with the new electoral register, permitted more than 1,300 votes to be cast in just five hours. Without multiple booths, no more than three or four hundred men could have voted in five hours under the best circumstances. Voting procedure aside, however, 1832 resembled earlier elections. The two Conservative candidates, Sir John Hanmer and John Cressett Pelham, used typically unreformed tactics and mounted separate campaigns that addressed fewer issues and party questions than its predecessor.[31] Hanmer raised one potentially popular issue by pointing out his earnest support of the anti-slavery movement, but otherwise he stressed only the need for monetary reform.[32] Slaney, the solitary Whig, also raised few issues as he contented himself with Reform accomplished. Many voters appear to have held political views more advanced than Slaney's, but those who were preparing to celebrate a 'Reform Festival', complete with bells, cannon, trumpeters, and processions, supported him by default.

Such tepid electioneering helps explain the more than 30 per cent of the voters who split their support, two-thirds of them voting for Slaney and Pelham. Nevertheless, almost a third of the electorate cast partisan plumpers for Slaney, and virtually no one plumped for one of the Tories unnecessarily. Thus more than two-thirds of the electorate cast partisan ballots even without the atmosphere of a referendum to spur them on. This represented a decline from the 83 per cent who cast partisan votes in 1831, but at the same time voters did not revert to the non-partisan patterns of 1826 and 1830.

Partisanship increased in 1835 despite the continuing Tory inability to mount a joint ticket. J. C. Pelham's nominator at the hustings persisted in portraying Pelham 'as a man independent of all

---

[31] Hanmer, only 23 years old in 1832, was third baronet, later to become first Baron Hanmer as a Liberal. B. Disraeli, *Letters*, ii. 618.
[32] Edwards, *Parliamentary Elections*, 30–2.

parties', but 'who would take a liberal view of all measures'.[33] Slaney countered by urging electors 'not to be deceived by Tory candidates in the guise of Reformers', but even without a joint Tory campaign, electors had no difficulty in discerning the parties of all concerned. Nearly 50 per cent doubled for the two independent Tories in 1835, leading to a Tory sweep at the polls. Slaney made an easy target against whom the Tory rank and file could rally in the absence of strong party leadership. Responsible in part for the horrors of both Catholic emancipation and Reform, Slaney now called for additional relief for Nonconformists, appeared to attack the Church by demanding the abolition of pluralities, and attacked England's existing municipal corporations. By calling for more change, Slaney raised the worst Tory fears. With united feelings in the place of united candidates, the Tories ousted Slaney by a relatively close margin of about fifty votes out of 1,250.

Major political debates and extremely active parties finally reappeared at Shrewsbury's third reformed election in 1837. Both parties fielded two candidates, and in the face of a determined Whig effort to return two Members on a 'United Reform' ticket, the Tories at last mounted a reluctant joint effort, bringing Richard Jenkins out of retirement to stand with the Tory incumbent, J. C. Pelham. Both Jenkins and Pelham continued to tout their 'independence'. Neither man ever referred to the other or to party. But Conservative voters knew that both Jenkins and Pelham opposed 'violent men who are trying to effect the destruction of the established church and the ruin of the constitution'.[34] And unlike their candidates, the Tory party displayed an enthusiasm hitherto unseen. They blanketed the town with attacks aimed at all Whigs and fervently urged a joint Tory return.

The Tories focused so intensely on the new Poor Law that the 1837 election took on some of the qualities of a referendum. The Poor Law had not seemed important in 1835, but by July 1837, no one could be mistaken about the nature of the new law. The Tories could not have hoped for better fuel for their fires. Posters

---

[33] Pelham was considered a 'less extreme Tory' in 1831 when he stood for the county. He sat for Lewes between 1796 and 1802. Mason, 'Parliamentary Representation', iii. 263; Edwards, *Parliamentary Elections*, 33.

[34] Crosby, *Parliamentary Record* incorrectly reported G. H. Dashwood as the candidate for Shrewsbury in 1837 instead of the actual candidate, Francis Dashwood. SRO, Shrewsbury MSS 1060/454/fo. 111. Sir John Hanmer, the other Tory incumbent, withdrew well before the election. Edwards, *Parliamentary History*, 35.

addressing the 'WORKING CLASSES' explained that the election might be their last opportunity of lifting up their voices against the 'heart-rending POOR LAW ACT'. 'Remember', one explained, 'Old Age will approach—and that you are liable to Sickness and Sorrow.' It predicted that townsmen would remember the year 1837 'when Mr Pelham and Mr Jenkins so humanely came forward to save you from the precipice towards which the Whigs are attempting to drive you'.[35] One broadsheet simply printed a comparison of the old and new dietary plan in a Poor Law Union headed by the Whig Duke of Richmond. Not only was the quantity reduced by 52 ounces per week per person, but the new plan substituted 4 pints of broth for 12 ounces of 'good table beer'. The placard then asked incredulously, 'does such a law in reality exist in our once happy England?'[36] Another referred to the 'Bastille Unions' imposed by the Act and yet another asked: 'Could you endure incarceration in a WORK-HOUSE PRISON!' It also suggested that Slaney, who took such pride in voting against slavery, should remember that 'charity ought to begin at home'.[37]

The resurgence of anti-Catholicism saved 1837 from becoming exclusively eleemosynary. Religious fires burned almost as brightly as during the debate over emancipation. Richard Jenkins resumed the theme he had raised in 1831 and warned somewhat confusedly that the Whigs would sacrifice Christianity 'to the Jews', and would erect 'a Popish ascendancy . . . on the ruins of the Protestant faith'.[38] Papists were 'on the loose', Protestants were being murdered in Ireland, and the 'O'Connellite' Whigs toadied to Catholic demands by granting £9,000 p.a. to a 'Roman Catholic College [Maynooth] which is the Nurse of Popery, the Curse of Ireland'.[39] To stamp out such pernicious evil, all good Protestants were obliged to 'stifle the Demon of Superstition, Idolatry, and Democracy by returning men who . . . unite under the cry of NO POPERY!' Another placard urged voters to fight 'the Demon of Democracy and Papal Tyranny', and crush the 'bloodthirsty radicalism' of the Whig candidates.[40]

[35] SLHL, DA45/1170/18 July 1837.   [36] SLHL, DA45/1170/ND.
[37] SLHL, D/Dq45/6/m/56.
[38] SLHL, Dq45/6/2 Jan. 1834. As Evans has noted, 'Church affairs became the central pillar of the Tory revival' of 1834–5. E. J. Evans, *The Forging of the Modern State* (London, 1983), 245.
[39] SLHL, DA45/1170/18 July 1837.
[40] SLHL, DA45/1170/17 July 1837.

The Tories summed up the election's revolution around the Poor Law and the Church effectively by asking:

> Are you prepared to starve the Poor!
> to destroy the Church!
> to degrade the Crown!
> and to overthrow the altars of the Protestant Faith!
> if so, vote for
> SLANEY, DASHWOOD, and the DESTRUCTIVES—
> if not—PELHAM AND JENKINS FOREVER![41]

This new level of Tory party activity, the continued efforts of the Whigs, the four-man structure of the contest, and the double dose of municipal and parliamentary propaganda led to the highest level of partisan behaviour in Shrewsbury's history. Nearly 90 per cent of the electorate cast partisan ballots. Predictably, most of the handful who split their votes did so by trying to recreate Shrewsbury's representation of 1830–1, but their votes for Slaney and Jenkins appear to have been motivated by considerations that had almost disappeared from this Shropshire town. Virtually no one plumped because there was no need to do so. The few who did were overwhelmingly Slaney supporters who may have distrusted Dashwood's lack of connections in the town. The Tories had ridiculed the Radicals for failing to procure 'even one single Salopian to join their old favourite Hack', Slaney, and predicted that Dashwood would prove to be a second 'Potter's job'.[42] They were right. Dashwood finished a distant fourth in an otherwise close race in which only three votes separated the victors Jenkins and Slaney. The Whigs succeeded in giving Slaney back his seat, but never came close to returning both reformers. The new Tory determination came closer to success; Pelham stood only 40 votes behind Slaney. Shrewsbury again became a 'cypher'.

Benjamin Disraeli jettisoned Maidstone for Shrewsbury in 1841 because of financial embarrassments that persisted for years after the turbulent contests that had provided his entry into the Commons. Often only luck had permitted him to stay a step ahead of his creditors.[43] Besides, Maidstone's Radicals were too strongly en-

---

[41] SLHL, Dq45/6/unfoliated/15 July 1837.

[42] SLHL, DA45/1170/17 July 1837. 7% split for Slaney and Jenkins; nearly 4% split for Slaney and Pelham; 2% plumped for Slaney.

[43] Monypenny and Buckle, *Life of Disraeli*, i. 113; B. Disraeli, *Letters*, ii. 256; iii. 77 n. 1; 337 n. 6. On 23 Apr. 1837 Disraeli asked William Pyne: 'Can I remain here for one week with safety and propriety?' See also J. A. Phillips, 'Municipal Matters'.

trenched and too determined in their support of popular principles for his taste, and the unexpected death of his Maidstone colleague Wyndham Lewis, whose gold had buttressed Maidstone's Conservatives since 1835, effectively severed Disraeli's link to the town. Not content merely to wear the watch-chains Lewis bequeathed him, Disraeli took Lewis's widow, and with her a portion of his considerable fortune.[44] George Tomline, also vacating a troublesome constituency, Sudbury, joined Disraeli. Shrewsbury may have 'never had a good name for purity of elections', but it hardly compared to the 'low grade of political ethics' that had rendered Sudbury 'notorious'.[45] Disraeli and Tomline could see that while so many towns had been swept into the arms of the Whig party by fervour for 'the Bill, the whole Bill, and nothing but the Bill', Shrewsbury had continued to return one Tory and one Whig.

Opposition from two Whig candidates in 1841 forced the joint Tory campaign into 'the most strenuous exertions' in the face of 'party spirit [that] ran very high'.[46] Tomline attacked the 'Whig' Poor Law and proclaimed his 'unalterable opinion and duty to protect the interests of the poor man'. He also expressed outrage at Whig efforts to 'sell factory children to Millowners' and the Whig refusal to restrict child labour in the mills to ten hours. The Whig Government, having 'passed . . . the VILE NEW POOR LAW BILL', should be removed.[47] The Tories also asked the question that the Whigs may have dreaded most in 1841: 'Who transported the Dorchester labourers?' Free pardons had been granted to the Tolpuddle martyrs in 1836, but pardons did not erase the stain.[48] George Loveless, perhaps the most famous of the martyrs, entitled his pamphlet describing the experiences of the Dorchester labourers *The Victims of Whiggery*. The transportation of six Dorchester farm labourers for swearing or administering oaths in defiance of 57 George III, c. 19 reinforced the image created by the harshness of the 'less eligibility' provision of the new Poor Law. Tomline and Disraeli also continued to beat the Protestant drum more than a decade after Catholic emancipation. A vote for 'true Protestant

[44] B. Disraeli, *Letters*, iii. 58.
[45] Monypenny and Buckle, *Life of Disraeli*, 113; Seymour, *Electoral Reform*, 174.
[46] William Wybergh How led the Shrewsbury Tory party. SLHL, DA45/1170/ unfoliated, 8 June (3), 12 June 1841.
[47] SLHL, DA45/1170/ND, placard from Conservative Office, Wyle Cop.
[48] J. Marlow, *The Tolpuddle Martyrs* (London, 1985), 63–5; see also G. Loveless, *The Victims of Whiggery* (London, 1837).

Conservatives' would help defeat 'Jesuits and Infidels, . . . Chartists and Socialists' who were 'banded together with revolutionary design'.[49] The Tories also argued that Whig desire to repeal the Corn Law was a low trick intended to reduce agricultural wages, destroy England's general prosperity, and maximize the ill effects of the new Poor Law.

For their part, the Whig candidates played down their advocacy of Corn Law repeal, ignored the religious question, and focused their energies on an *ad hominem* attack aimed at Disraeli.[50] Disraeli's marriage in 1839 to Wyndham Lewis's widow had not eliminated his financial distress; the Whigs insinuated that he needed a seat in the Commons primarily to avoid prison over judgments against him of more than £22,000 in just the previous three years. Facing massive debts and borrowing to meet his immediate needs at interest rates of up to 40 per cent, Disraeli responded with 'the big lie'.[51] One of Disraeli's election posters of 25 June asserted that 'there is not a single shilling on the list of judgments, thus paraded, which has not been completely satisfied'. He also responded to this *ad hominem* attack, 'unprecedented for its malignity and its meanness', by emblazoning his banners for the first time with his family crest, the castle of Castile with the legend 'forti nihil difficile'. Whig propagandists translated the legend for Shrewsbury's voters as: 'the impudence of some men sticks at nothing.'[52]

Shrewsbury could not boast a Conservative party organization as venerable and powerful as Bristol's White Lion, but the Conservative Office in Wyle Cop orchestrated the 1841 election with considerable skill. Voting fell 'along party lines', and Tomline and Disraeli managed a comfortable majority.[53] But Disraeli saw it differently.

[49] SLHL, DA45/1170/ND, Address to the Electors of Shrewsbury.

[50] Temple denied Disraeli's charge and countered that Shrewsbury's mayor John Loxdale had given Temple his first brief. Temple and the Whigs may have been more successful, and certainly might have generated more enthusiasm with references to the Shrewsbury races.

[51] 'Big' lies in the 19th cent. could be dangerous. William Yardley challenged Disraeli to a duel since Disraeli's flat denial of his allegations about Disraeli's debt was tantamount to calling Yardley a liar. Only the personal intervention of Shrewsbury's mayor John Loxdale prevented shots from being fired. Disraeli also expected to fight a duel with a man named Austen, the counsel for a number of petitioners against him, in Maidstone in 1837. He told Mary Ann Lewis: 'Anything is better than submitting to an insult.' *Letters*, iii. 61.

[52] Bodleian Library, John Johnson Collection of Printed Ephemera, Elections, Box 6, unfoliated.

[53] Mason, 'Parliamentary Representation, iii. 327.

Victory was his own achievement. As he told his sister: 'They did against me, and said against me, and wrote against me all they could find or invent, but I licked them.'[54] For the second time since the Reform Act, Shrewsbury sent a Tory delegation to Parliament.

ELECTIONS IN NORTHAMPTON

Reform affected Northampton as much as Shrewsbury, and critical changes also began before 1832. As shown in Table 4.2, Northampton's split-voters, normally a large component of the unreformed electorate, began to disappear with the general election of 1831. The proportion of splitters at this last unreformed contest fell to a mere 15 per cent from the 43 per cent recorded just a year earlier, and splitting continued at a substantially reduced rate for the remainder of the period. The overall pattern in Northampton was much the same as in Shrewsbury (and Colchester). A concomitant rise in the number of partisan plumps cast at Northampton's usual three-man contests strongly supports the impression conveyed by the decline in splitting, as do the consistently miniscule numbers of unnecessary plumpers cast after 1831.

Northampton was a shoemaking town much smaller than Shrewsbury at the beginning of the century. Tremendous growth in the early decades of the century, particularly after the building of a link to the Grand Union Canal in 1815, allowed it to surpass Shrewsbury with a population topping 21,000 in 1841. A period of relative prosperity accompanied this growth, but few crumbs trickled down to the level at which many people eked out their existences. As Parliament and the nation debated the Reform Bill, many Northamptoners could have found little time to ponder anything other than the source of their next meal. Almost a third of the population lived 'beneath the line of subsistence'.[55] Those who found employment in the expanding shoemaking establishments suffered particularly. A rapidly growing market for shoes produced employment for many but wealth for few. Under the best circumstances shoemaking provided a meagre living. The shoemaking process did not lend itself to mechanization, and severe competition forced manufacturers to

[54] *Letters*, iii. 347, Disraeli to Sarah Disraeli, 7 July 1841.
[55] J. Foster, *Class Struggle and the Industrial Revolution* (London, 1974), 33–4.

TABLE 4.2. *Split-Voting and Plumping in Northampton* (%)

Election year	1818	1820	1826	1830	1831	1832	1835	1837	1841
Split-votes	21.2	40.9	36.4	43.0	15.3	12.3	12.0	7.6	11.3*
Partisan plumps	33.8	4.7	11.0	28.8	4-man	4-man	42.6	40.1	4-man
Unnecessary plumps	3.8	34.8	4.1	4.7	25.6	2.3	1.9	0.9	1.1

4-man Four candidates; politically motivated plumping not required.
* Splits for McDouall (Chartist) and Willoughby (Conservative) are counted here as Conservative votes because of the overt alliance of the two candidates against the Whigs.
Sources: Poll books.

preserve their profits through not increased production but reductions in wages. Subsistence wages had become the norm by the Reform era and Northampton soon 'became a by-word in the trade for shoddy work and sweat-shop conditions'.[56] At the time of Northampton's first polled nineteenth-century election in 1818, roughly a quarter of all families owed their living to shoemaking. The proportion had risen to nearly half by 1841. In a town so dominated by a single industry, conditions among shoemakers determined to a great extent the nature of the local economy.

Northamptoners could hardly have found Lord John Russell's Bill exciting except in the abstract. A single-industry town with a depressed economy might have been expected to produce only a handful of voters, but Northampton's residents enjoyed England's most egalitarian franchise; only Northampton and eleven other boroughs permitted every male inhabitant not in receipt of poor relief to vote in parliamentary elections. This notorious potwalloper franchise included anyone, even mere lodgers, with 'sole dominion of a room with a fireplace in it'.[57] Unlike the other householder boroughs, most of which contained very few voters, Northampton's impoverished but burgeoning population produced almost 1,300 voters in 1818 and nearly 2,600 in 1831. Reform actually stifled electoral growth. Prior to Reform, the number of voters kept pace with the number of residents. Very few Northamptoners, on the other hand, could have ever hoped to qualify for the franchise after Reform; £10 dwellings in Northampton were far beyond the means of most residents.[58] The Tories called attention to this by asking in 1831: 'What! will you cut your own throats because Lord Althorp offers to provide a razor gratis?'[59] Enough ancient-right voters remained after 1832 to keep the electorate near 2,000 a full decade after Reform, but the £10 qualification meant a steadily shrinking electorate over the middle years of the century.

Like Shrewsbury, Northampton had been aware of some political issues in the later eighteenth century, including the Fox–North

---

[56] Foster, *Class Struggle*, 86.

[57] Seymour, *Electoral Reform*, 26. Northampton was the only large borough with a potwalloper franchise. Cirencester and Taunton each contained a fair number of voters, but all the other potwalloper boroughs were tiny.

[58] Oddly, however, *The Companion to the Newspapers* listed 1,087 £10 houses in Northampton in 1834, while Maidstone contained 1,417 and Shrewsbury 1,651 (pp. 186–7).

[59] Northampton Public Library, 1/1831, Broadside, 12 Mar. 1831.

dispute and the French Revolution of 1789. Edward Bouverie had hammered his personal following into a party organization before his death in 1810, and that party adapted itself to new circumstances rather quickly.[60] Nevertheless, partisan politics did not immediately accompany the resumption of contested elections in 1818. Northampton resisted partisan, issue-oriented elections. If Shrewsbury's voters only grudgingly recognized the exigencies of party and resisted campaigns predicated upon national issues, Northampton's voters clung more determinedly to an older political reality. Voting along partisan lines in the later eighteenth century had required considerable pressure from local leaders, and in the absence of effective leaders after the death of Bouverie, voters tended to ignore the parliamentary parties.

Confusing the picture of unreformed Northampton politics is the somewhat misleading incidence of partisan plumping in 1818, when just over a third of the electorate plumped for Sir George Robinson. While Robinson's decided Whiggery attracted some plumpers from partisans who responded to the issues that he raised, many voters cast plumpers simply in reaction against patronage and corruption, both of which the other candidates represented.[61] Northampton's Whigs made as basic an appeal as possible. Four men paraded an enormous loaf of bread through town decorated with green and yellow ribbons (Robinson's colours) and a large banner announcing 'No Corn Bill'.[62] Basic appeals notwithstanding, Robinson's Tory opponents won.[63]

The four solid months of expensive treating and bribery on both sides prior to the three-week-long poll had little connection with political principles. 'Riotous and disgraceful' events during the

[60] D. Gray, *Spencer Perceval* (Manchester, 1963), 28–33, 100. Unfortunately, all references to Northampton in Greville's manuscript diary were cut out before the editors obtained possession of it. Greville, *Memoirs*, iii. 62.

[61] Employee coercion by politically aware owners of shoemaking establishments may have accounted for some of the changes in Northampton despite unfavourable local conditions, but Northampton's electorate was not composed entirely of politically or economically susceptible shoemakers. Besides, an extraordinary number of issues appeared in the press, including 'the seizure of Ecclesiastical property' and 'the establishment of popery in Ireland'. NtRO, Gotch MSS 345.

[62] Ibid. 940, J. D. Gotch to his mother, 13 Feb. 1818. The polling did not take place until 16 June 1818.

[63] The Tory candidates were the Marquis of Northampton's son, Earl Compton, and Sir Edward Kerrison. They won by a mere 27 votes of almost 1,300 cast. One summary suggests that Earl Compton's return was unchallenged, the fight was restricted to Kerrison v. Robinson. *The Late Elections*, 244–5.

polling forced the mayor to read the Riot Act twice. The lingering political influence of the Compton family (earls of Northampton) confused the picture further. Northampton had in the past proven ruinously expensive to potential patrons. The infamous 'election of the three Earls' in 1768 bankrupted Earl Halifax, virtually bankrupted Earl Northampton, and damaged Earl Spencer's finances sufficiently to force the withdrawal of the Spencers from active participation in the politics of the borough. Only the Comptons had recovered their footing sufficiently to become active again before the end of the century. Their influence helped maintain twenty-two years of electoral quiescence after 1796 and determined some votes in 1818. But if patronage tainted some votes, it did not decide Northampton elections.[64]

Following the unusual 1818 election, partisan voting fell to extremely low levels in 1820, when Sir George Robinson and W. L. Maberly easily unseated Lord Compton.[65] The sole Tory, Lord Compton, insisted that he was 'entirely unconnected with any other candidate', but so did the Whig Maberly. Rather than asking for plumpers, Compton instead openly solicited second votes only since 'the supporters of neither of those Gentlemen who are seeking the same honour will deem me the enemy of their respective Friend'.[66] His hope was misplaced. After four days Compton felt that 'all Hope of ultimate success is now at an end', and he was right.[67]

Non-partisan patterns continued to dominate the electorate in 1826, but party in its local manifestation played a larger role. Northampton's closed and notoriously corrupt Corporation used £1,000 to help finance the campaign of Sir Robert Gunning, a Tory.[68] Nevertheless, a single Tory could not induce more than a

[64] J. A. Phillips, *Electoral Behaviour*, 82–3, 114–72. Spencer Joshua Alwyne Compton succeeded in 1828 as ninth earl of Northampton, eventually to become first Marquis. Northampton petitioned for peace in 1812, and engaged in enough other political behaviour to indicate the survival of some sense of party there. J. E. Cookson, *The Friends of Peace: Anti-War Liberalism in England, 1793–1815* (Cambridge, 1982), 247–9.

[65] Improving substantially upon his father's successful bid for a Northampton seat in the Parliament of 1774, his son and namesake won seats at the four subsequent elections before ill health forced his resignation from the last unreformed Parliament. *Northampton Free Press*, 1 Dec. 1832.

[66] *Northampton Mercury*, 4 Mar. 1820.

[67] When Compton announced his pessimism he trailed Maberly by 136. He eventually lost to Maberly by 160 votes. Ibid. 11 Mar. 1820.

[68] *Parl. Pap.*, 25 (1835), 1965–81; J. C. Cox and C. A. Markham (eds.), *The Records of the Borough of Northampton*, 2 vols. (Northampton, 1898), ii. 511–12.

handful of voters to cast plumpers, nor could the reason for plumpers have been very clear since each candidate scrupulously avoided party labels. But Gunning admitted his inclination 'to support the Measures of His Majesty's Government', and he and Robinson represented the extremes of the spectrum. A double for them should have appeared absurd to any politically aware voter.[69] Robinson had presented a petition in Parliament in favour of Catholic emancipation while Gunning 'felt it his Duty to strenuously oppose any further Concessions' since he saw 'the admission of Roman Catholics to Office and to Power as likely to lead to the most injurious Consequences'.[70] But many electors chose to ignore these glaring differences. More than a third of all voters coupled Gunning with Robinson or the other Whig, an insufficient number to return him to Parliament, but quite enough to illustrate the limitations on partisanship in unreformed Northampton.

Party labels followed the 1827 establishment of a Whig Club in Northampton to counter the Tory King and Constitution Club.[71] These two clubs began to push voters into the ranks of the politically aware.[72] The difficulties they encountered in these efforts were illustrated by the continuation of non-partisan voting habits in 1830. More voters split their support (43 per cent) than four years earlier. The single Tory candidate in 1830, however, attracted plumpers that accounted for almost 29 per cent of the total vote, the first time since 1818 that the electorate had been willing to acknowledge a solitary candidate. Sir Robert Gunning's plumps actually gave him Northampton's second seat in 1830, however briefly. These Tory plumps were all the more impressive because Gunning flatly refused to expend his own money in purchasing a seat.[73]

[69] Forrester, *Northamptonshire County Elections*, 124.

[70] *Northampton Mercury*, 2 June 1826.

[71] V. A. Hatley, 'Some Aspects of Northampton's History, 1815–51', *Northamptonshire Past and Present*, 3 (1965), 249; *Northampton Mercury*, 6, 13, 20, 27 June, 4 July 1818; NtRO, Gotch MSS 337–41.

[72] Club activity expanded in 1831/2, partly in response to a partisan press, better publicity, the clarification of political principles, and the intensification of partisan feelings. By the end of 1831 the Constitutional Union Society met monthly as did the Northampton Political Union by the early months of 1832. The more successful Tory Oak Club began to be regularly active soon afterwards.

[73] The scandal of the £1,000 paid to Gunning by the Corporation illustrated his attitude towards election expenses. The Corporation became involved in an expensive King's Bench suit over the expenditure. The Whigs celebrated the royal assent to the Corporate Fund Bill in July 1832 which eliminated the possibility of any similar

In plumping massively for Gunning, Northampton's Tories had come a long way in four years. Unfortunately, their loyalty to Gunning went rather deeper than it should have. Almost a quarter of them ignored the appearance of a second Tory candidate in 1831 and plumped for Gunning again. Gunning's candidacy accounted for all but 12 of the 679 plumpers cast by the entire electorate in 1831. The high overall total of unnecessary plumping (25.6 per cent) in 1831, then, reflects the Tories alone. The Whigs supported both of their candidates, but the Tories, having mastered the art of plumping, needed to learn when it was appropriate. At this final election under the old order, Gunning (and his fellow Tory James Lyon) had to face a Whig campaign that raised issues clearly and cleverly. A song written for the occasion asked:

> Who would be a heartless slave
> Eat the portion of a knave
> Dance o'er Civil Freedom's grave,
> and trample thereupon?

Not the supporters of Smith and Robinson, of course, who shunned such disgrace. The Whigs were:

> Men who loved their country's cause,
> EQUAL RIGHTS AND EQUAL LAWS.[74]

The Conservatives also suffered from the identification of the King with Reform. In 1830 R. Vernon Smith had argued that reformers were friends of the people, but by 1831 he could argue they were friends of *the King* and the people. The invocation of the royal will inevitably placed the Tories on the defensive. How could the Corporation, for example, those 'late stickling advocates of the inherent principle of the divine right of kings who erst maintained that "Kings could do no wrong"' now carp about a Reform Bill advocated by the King himself?[75] Gunning had hedged his stand in 1830, but now opposed Reform. He tried to pass himself off as a 'moderate' reformer on occasion, but newspaper reports exposed his voting record. Reform was no longer theoretical, and Gunning had voted against it in every division prior to the election.[76] He

---

payments as the end to 'the curse and misrule of Tory adminstration'. *Northampton Free Press*, 4 Aug. 1832.

[74] NtRO, Gotch MSS 1234.
[75] *Northampton Free Press*, 24 Mar. 1832.   [76] Ibid. 26 Apr., 3 May 1831.

countered by portraying Reform as an unconstitutional attack on prescriptive and chartered rights. He also played the Catholic card by stressing the potential increase in the number of Roman Catholics and anti-Unionists in Parliament. Riding the wave of Reform, the Whigs also benefited from Sir George Robinson's long experience. He had become a regular feature of Northampton politics and seemed destined to remain so had not ill health removed him unexpectedly.[77] Pulling out all the stops, the Whig party managed to entice Edward Bouverie, son of the creator of the party, to canvass personally for Robinson and Smith. A joint campaign for Reform resulted in party votes and their joint return.

The emergence of a highly partisan press assisted the development of partisan behaviour in Northampton, as it did in so many other towns. Competition for the *Northampton Mercury* generated not just more newsprint, but partisan diatribes that intensified political battles, however much they may have been intended primarily to increase circulation. The editors of the *Northampton Free Press*, organized in 1831 to bolster Northampton's Reform spirit, delighted in taunting the editors of the staid *Mercury*, the paper that clung most persistently to an eighteenth-century standard of shallow, apolitical if mildly conservative, reporting.[78] The *Free Press* called for a reform of the Corporations before the *Mercury* supported parliamentary reform.[79] Another paper, the *Northampton Herald*, was instituted in 1832 in response to the disastrous county election and the appearance of the *Free Press*. The *Herald*, never pretending to be objective, boasted:

> If Rebellion's hideous form appears
> Mid orphans wailing and loving widow's tears,
> The 'Herald' will stand forth a fearless guide,
> Both proud and worthy of the Tory side.[80]

---

[77] Robinson resigned in Dec. 1831 and died in 1833. Smith actually improved upon Robinson's record of five victories. He too sat until his retirement from politics.

[78] The *Mercury* finally advocated Reform belatedly in Apr. 1832. See J. Black, *The English Press in the Eighteenth Century* (London, 1987).

[79] As the *Free Press* quickly pointed out (28 Apr. 1832). The *Maidstone Gazette* e.g. became heavily partisan by Jan. 1830.

[80] *Northampton Free Press*, 24 Dec. 1831; *Northampton Herald*, 12 Nov. 1831. Priced at 7*d.* and never particularly successful partly because of its price, the *Free Press* became the *Northampton and Leamington Free Press* in July 1833, and the *Northampton and Wellingborough Free Press* in Aug. 1834, before folding at the end of that year.

The *Free Press* tended to agree, though from a different perspective, noting:

though the Devil may be the father of lies, he has lost a good deal of credit by the improvement made since upon his invention by the *Northampton Herald*.[81]

Northampton also benefited in 1831 from a county election, the first since 1806, which in turn was the first since 1705. Thus Northampton's last unreformed election involved a double dose of propaganda.

While a relatively high level of apparently partisan plumping marked the 1818 election, there was, as Table 4.2 reveals, a striking departure from the general pattern of unreformed elections at reformed elections involving three candidates. More than 40 per cent of the reformed electorate plumped when necessary in 1835 and 1837, and the decline to almost 30 per cent in 1841 stemmed not from a decline in the number of Tories capable of plumping, but from their willingness to couple their single Tory vote with one for a Chartist candidate when asked to do so by the local Tory party. The inability to attract plumpers, which had marred Tory efforts prior to 1832, ceased to be an obstacle after Reform. Strikingly, this change occurred despite minimal changes in Northampton's electorate. Inhabitant householders whose franchises predated the Act comprised the majority of the reformed electorate. Thus the reformed electorate was the unreformed electorate for all intents and purposes. Many of the men who would not plump for partisan reasons prior to Reform behaved differently in the substantially altered political climate of the 1830s.

Partisan activity had gathered a full head of steam by 1832, and the Whigs who had flown banners for 'REFORM, RETRENCHMENT, and PEACE' in January 1832 pressed the pace in the months to follow. Whigs co-ordinated county and borough efforts. Lord Milton (Fitzwilliam's son) canvassed for Smith in 1832 and vice-versa.[82] Smith and William Hanbury, the other Whig candidate for North Northamptonshire, communicated regularly and planned strategy jointly.[83] For their part, the Tories were animated by antagonism

[81] *Northampton Free Press*, 26 May 1832.
[82] NtRO, Gotch MSS 363–8. For an account of the role of the Spencer family in the politics of this era see E. A. Wasson, *Whig Renaissance: Lord Althorp and the Whig Party* (New York, 1987), *passim*.
[83] NtRO, Gotch MSS 320–1.

towards Reform and anxiety about resounding Whig victories. They feared that predictions of their demise might be all too true, and acted accordingly. Their activity, in turn, spurred the Whigs to greater efforts, particularly in that critical new arena, voter registration. Both parties attempted to enrol every supporter in the months following the opening of the registers in September 1832. Acrimony intensified in the months immediately before and after Reform. The *Free Press* assaulted the *Herald* at every opportunity, and on virtually every level, high and low. The Whigs engaged in principled, petty, lucid, opaque, and *ad hominem* attacks on their enemies as the mood struck them.[84]

After such strenuous and prolonged political activity, both parties took steps to ensure that the actual poll in 1832 would not be anti-climactic. The reformers underscored the implications of their victory by flying the French tricolour, to the outrage of the Conservative press.[85] Yet, despite Reform fever, the Whigs failed to duplicate their sweep of the previous year, and Northampton returned a split representation. The second Whig, Bainbridge, 'a sort of Wholesale Dealer of the Liberal line', trailed the leading Tory by nearly 100 votes because more than one in ten split their votes and most of those coupled one of the Tories with Northampton's incumbent Whig, R. Vernon Smith.[86] That Smith, a Baptist and decided liberal, was the splitters' choice reflected the continuing role of local connections. Smith's politics appear to have counted for less among a few voters than the link he forged with the town.

Most of the determined non-partisans who coupled the unlikely pair of candidates in 1832 (about 12 per cent of the total), continued to do so in 1835, helping ensure another split delegation. With Reform as fact rather than mere potential, the issues may have appeared less pressing. The repayment of the £5 million Russian-Dutch loan, advocated by Smith and opposed by Ross, exercised the imagination rather less than the previous debate over the Constitution. Smith and Ross were returned again without much direct attention to political issues. The election focused most on parties because party now served as a convenient shorthand for the issues against the

---

[84] These included the charge that a 'Charles-street Conservative' conducted the political activities of the *Herald* and that the titular editor Smithson acted only as a front for the real editor, 'a certain notorious political clergyman resident in the county'. *Northampton Free Press*, 7 Jan. 1832.

[85] *Northampton Herald*, 15 Dec. 1832.   [86] Ibid. 1 Dec. 1831.

powerful backdrop provided by Reform. On 7 January J. C. Hobhouse arrived at Northampton to see Smith and Ross simultaneously addressing the electorate from two different windows. The Whig half of the crowd wanted to remove the horses from Hobhouse's coach and draw him around the town in celebration of the Reform Act.[87] Hobhouse barely managed to dissuade them. After so many years of lacklustre behaviour on the part of the local parties, party itself had been transformed into the most important issue in Northampton. And most heeded the call, though about the same small proportion (12 per cent) continued to ignore it.

The use of party in place of issues reflected in part the division among the Whigs between those who were satisfied with Reform and those who wished for more. Until the Whig party was able to reconcile this split, which it began to do by adopting the term 'Liberal', issues were too dangerous. After 1835, however, the party attempted to appeal to both factions by having one candidate represent the left and right wings of the party. The Tories had no such problems, but usually had only one candidate. Once the Whigs resolved their dilemma, issues could move to the fore, as they might have done anyway from the combined weight of more interesting topics and the opening of Northampton's Corporation to popular participation. Whatever the reasons, issues inundated the Northampton electorate in 1837. The Poor Law prompted reams of vituperative prose from Northampton's Tories. They mounted such a vicious attack that the Whiggish *Mercury* focused much of its effort during the campaign on damage control, at times resorting to absurd parodies of the Tory attacks for lack of a better alternative.[88] The *Mercury* faced an uphill battle in trying to brand the new Poor Law as Tory, but at the very least the *Mercury* wanted to prevent Raikes Currie, R. V. Smith, and the entire Liberal party from being branded as enemies of the poor.

Party itself also persisted as an issue. By 1837 Northampton's Tories had fully absorbed the meaning of the precipitous decline in splitting and the disappearance of non-partisan plumping. The Tories now expected most voters to cast partisan votes, which hindered their chances enormously since they were undoubtedly Northampton's minority party. Registration made that clear and

[87] BL, Add. MSS 61826, 7 Jan. 1835. Also NtRO, Northampton Borough Records, Election Papers 1834–5, Y2/4975–86.
[88] *Northampton Mercury*, 22 July 1841.

promised no reversal in the immediate future. Giving up all hope of both seats, the Tories had counted on enough splitters to give their single candidate a chance against two Whigs, but unless splitting continued at the levels of 1832 and 1835, their cause was lost. R. Vernon Smith's coat-tails had not yet proven long enough to accomplish a joint Whig return, but greater discipline among his supporters would be fatal to the Tory cause. Understandably, the Tories tried to drive a wedge between Smith and his colleague Raikes Currie.

The Tory press stressed the not inconsiderable differences between the Whig candidates, and argued that support for Smith should not mean support for Currie. Smith, by far the more moderate of the pair, supported the Corn Laws, game laws, and, as the Tories put it, 'the aristocracy'. Currie opposed them all. Smith had expressed his contentment with Reform and opposed further reforms, specifically the ballot, triennial Parliaments, and ironically, householder suffrage. In sharp contrast, Currie believed that 1832 was only the beginning; he supported more change of the most radical kind. Smith favoured the maintenance of the Established Church in Ireland and tithes in both England and Ireland. Currie opposed both. Smith had voted to keep the Bishops in the House of Lords; Currie wished to expel them. The only important area of agreement between the candidates was their joint support of the infamous Poor Law.[89] The lesson was obvious, the Tories thought. Northampton's more reasonable voters should couple a vote for the moderate Whig, Smith, with one for the moderate Tory, Ross, and return again a delegation split nominally but united ideologically. Unlike a Smith/Ross return, a joint Whig delegation would be a true split.

Northampton's Whig voters thought otherwise. The 1837 election may have come as a surprise, but the Whigs were relatively well prepared. Besides, as the Tories feared, partisan voting had not just become the norm, it had become sufficiently ingrained in a very short time to withstand a direct assault. The trend that emerged in 1831 continued; for the first time in the nineteenth century fewer than 10 per cent of the voters split their votes. The very real

---

[89] *Northampton Herald*, 8, 15 July 1841. Smith claimed credit for having helped to pass the Municipal Corporations Act, but unlike Shrewsbury, the Northamptoners focused very little attention on the Act even though it transformed local politics in Northampton every bit as much as in Shrewsbury.

differences between the Whig candidates mattered to few. More than 51 per cent of the electorate cast a Whig double vote, another 41 per cent cast a necessary Tory plump. A mere 8 per cent split, most of them coupling Smith and Ross. Far too few split to prevent Northampton's first joint Whig return since 1831.

Having failed to divide Whig voters, and facing two incumbent Whigs in 1841, Northampton's Conservative party attempted to recruit two Tory candidates united behind the Corn Laws, which the Tories intended to retain at all cost, and against the Poor Law, which they assailed at every opportunity. Tory efforts to recruit George Payne as a partner for Sir Henry Willoughby failed, leaving the Conservatives to fall back on an unusual expedient. Lacking a second Conservative candidate, they mounted an effort to capture both seats by linking their candidate with Dr P. M. McDouall, a Chartist. Tories and Chartists could unite easily enough in a chorus of denunciation of the Poor Law, and the matter of the Corn Laws could be set aside. Willoughby did not hide his enthusiasm for the Corn Laws while one of the Whigs, Currie, trumpeted his determination to eliminate all such protective measures in the cause of 'regular employment, better wages, and diminished toil'. But the Chartist demands were, after all, strictly political.[90] As far as McDouall was concerned, the economic question could be settled after the constitutional alterations that he demanded. Northampton still contained many working-class voters. McDouall 'addressed the working classes . . . in powerful language', explaining the 'misgovernment' under which the country laboured, and 'urging them to support an honest Tory in preference to a dishonest Whig'. He was not alone in these sentiments. A letter-writer denouncing Smith signed himself 'an out and out Chartist and no less uncompromising foe to Whiggery'.[91]

Willoughby was willing to sacrifice principle to practicality, but neither of the 'Tory' candidates should have worried about the strangeness of his bedfellow. McDouall's appeal attracted fewer than 200 voters, almost all of whom he shared with Willoughby. The most noticeable result of the Tory/Chartist appeal was the decline in

[90] Gotch noted that his doubts about the success of the Whigs in 1841 'arose solely from the avowed intention of the Chartists to unite with the Tories, the disastrous result of which union was shown at Nottingham'. NtRO, Gotch MSS 639, Gotch to R. V. Smith, 10 June 1841; *Northampton Herald*, 19, 29 May, 19 June 1841.

[91] Ibid. 26 June 1841.

necessary Tory plumps as some voters who would have voted for Willoughby alone added McDouall as their second choice. Not a single voter coupled the 'half-hog radical' Smith with the Chartist McDouall. Four times as many linked McDouall with Willoughby than joined McDouall with the 'whole-hog radical' Currie.[92] McDouall's presence did not confuse the election. Other than Tories who joined his name to Willoughby's, only a few voters split their votes between inappropriate candidates.

THE REFORM ACT OR THE REFORM ERA?

Static assessments of voting patterns in Shrewsbury and North-ampton leave few doubts about the powerful impact of Reform in both towns. These cross-sectional evaluations suggest that the critical behavioural shift did not follow Reform, but occurred during the politicization that accompanied the widespread agitation for the Reform Bill. Shifting from synchronic to diachronic statistical analyses, Table 4.3 also suggests that the era, not the Act, played the crucial role. Reform occasioned further increases in levels of partisan loyalty in both towns, but the striking transformation from the unreformed pattern was already visible in 1831.

Just two weeks before the first reports of 'Another Revolution in France' at the end of July 1830, a letter to the *Shrewsbury Chronicle* noted with some relief the end of a threatening era that had lasted forty years. The writer believed that the defeat of the extremists, whether Radicals, papists, or Whigs, meant that after so much turmoil the 'country is more tranquil than it has ever been in the memory of man'. A week later another writer noted the quiet surrounding the approaching election. Only one indecorous incident had blemished the electioneering at that point.[93] How rapidly this climate changed as the quiescence of the summer of 1830 gave way to the tumoil of 1831. Table 4.3 illustrates that transformation as partisan loyalty took on a new meaning in Shrewsbury and

---

[92] *Northampton Herald*, 22 July 1841.

[93] The only hitch after the election developed when the Tories refused to chair their candidate Richard Jenkins with the Whig victor R. A. Slaney. Otherwise, the 'contest was carried on peaceably with no great deal of bitterness'. *Shrewsbury Chronicle*, 16, 23, 30 July, 6 Aug. 1830.

TABLE 4.3. *Electoral Behaviour across Elections in Shrewsbury and Northampton:* λ *(Asymmetric) and* τ_b

Election years	1818–20	1820–6	1826–30	1830–1	1831–2	1832–5	1835–7	1837–41
				λ (Asymmetric)				
Shrewsbury	NC	0.00*	0.33	0.52	0.53	0.53	0.58	0.56
Northampton	0.41	0.33	0.17	0.42	0.64	0.75	0.70	0.76
				τ_b				
Shrewsbury	NC	0.03*	0.42	0.53	0.71	0.62	0.66	0.69
Northampton	0.51	0.49	0.48	0.65	0.74	0.83	0.83	0.81

NC No contest.
* Comparison of 1819 and 1826 in Shrewsbury.

Northampton between the elections of 1830 and 1831. Two problems hinder the identification of an absolutely certain pattern at these elections. The relatively high incidence of voter loyalty in Northampton in 1818 and 1820, explained largely by the personal appeal of Sir George Robinson, obscures the overall pattern less than the uncontested Shrewsbury elections of 1818 and 1820. Too few data points prevent the construction of a trend line, and beginning Shrewsbury's analysis with 1826–30 is hardly optimal. The Shrewsbury by-election of 1819 provides a poor substitute for the unpolled election of 1818, involving as it did only two candidates and circumstances that must be considered *sui generis*.

Despite these impediments, Table 4.3 seems clear enough in the main. As Reform began to dominate Shrewsbury's elections in 1831, the electorate responded with a new degree of partisan loyalty that is visible when following the voters from the election of 1830 to 1831 with λ (0.52). The persistence of splitting in Shrewsbury prevented this new degree of inter-election party loyalty from reaching the levels achieved in Maidstone, Colchester, or Northampton, but most voters even in Shrewsbury had fallen into the common mould of a party vote followed by another vote for the same party at all subsequent elections. Substantial numbers of voters, won by Reform to the view that they were either Whigs or Tories, behaved accordingly as their town experienced parliamentary and municipal reform. They continued to behave in 1841 much as they had behaved in 1831.

Northampton's voters also responded to partisan appeals as the Reform Bill was introduced, even though the town sorely lacked the party structure so important in towns like Bristol and Maidstone. Unlike Shrewsbury, however, the change that began with the election of 1831 continued at the next two elections. Voters in Northampton were significantly more likely to remain loyal to a party between 1831 and 1832 than between 1830 and 1831 ($\lambda = 0.64$). And Northampton's reformed electorate proved themselves capable of even greater inter-election loyalty. Between the first pair of reformed elections and the last, most Northampton electors followed one exclusively party vote with another for the same party as indicated by consistent λs above 0.70. Party loyalty in Northampton exceeded that found in Shrewsbury.

A corroborative, if slightly different, pattern emerges in an examination of the same voting choices using scaled votes and the ordinal comparisons provided by τ_b. The impact of Reform on the partisan loyalty of individual voters should not be dismissed, particularly in Northampton, but the transformation undoubtedly began at the elections during which 'Reform' was just a word. When relative levels of party support are distinguished by τ_b, Shrewsbury's voters, like Northampton's, achieved a very impressive level of partisan loyalty (>0.5) between the elections of 1830 and 1831 as Reform was debated endlessly, demonstrated greater loyalty between the the elections of 1831 and 1832 (>0.7), and maintained those lock-step voting patterns or something very similar at each subsequent election in the period. At the same time, τ_b makes it clear that Northampton's voters were affected more by the Reform Act itself, achieving a truly remarkable score of 0.83 at the first three reformed elections, indicating virtually perfect and perfectly loyal party voting in Northampton. Hardly anyone voted in other than a partisan, and consistently partisan fashion across elections just after the Reform Act.

Reform, Act and era, affected electoral behaviour dramatically in the five boroughs analysed thus far. Were England's boroughs generally affected by Reform? The simple answer is no, but the reasons for the failure of Reform to affect some towns are enormously varied and are instructive about the nature of English electoral behaviour, reformed and unreformed. In some boroughs, Reform failed to stimulate the kind of partisanship found in Shrewsbury and Northampton because it already existed. Voters in Lewes and Great Yarmouth, for example, needed no additional partisan stimulus. Politics in those two boroughs revolved around parties well before Reform became a serious possibility, as the next chapter demonstrates.

PART III
THE LIMITATIONS OF
REFORM

5

Reform Redundant:
Political Continuity in Lewes and Great Yarmouth

THOUGH Reform proved to be a tonic potent enough to alter electoral behaviour substantially in many boroughs, its potency was not evident in all towns. Reform failed to affect politics in Lewes and Great Yarmouth. Reform's inutility in these two towns, however, stemmed not from its ineffectiveness but from its redundancy. Political struggles from the later eighteenth century onward had produced antagonistic, extremely well-defined camps that warred under the banners of local/parliamentary political parties in these boroughs. Divisions were too rigidly fixed before 1832 for Reform to have had much of an impact. Reformers could fan the flames of partisanship in places like Shrewsbury, but they were preaching to the converted in Lewes and Great Yarmouth where voters were already partisans. Paradoxically, in both word and deed, Lewes gave every appearance of having been very much affected by Reform. Voters in Lewes appeared to respond to the powerful reforming spirit sweeping the country. A closer examination reveals the truth. Already rigidly if idiosyncratically partisan, Lewes felt 1832 only superficially. Conversely, the behaviour of Yarmouth's voters did not require painstaking interpretation. Voters there were unmistakably partisan more than a decade in advance of Reform.

IDIOSYNCRATIC PARTISAN BEHAVIOUR IN LEWES

During the later years of the eighteenth century Lewes, like Maidstone, customarily returned a split delegation to Parliament. A formal 'Coalition' representing opposite ends of the political spectrum expired just before the election of 1802, but Lewes continued to return split delegations until the Tories unified the town by narrowly winning the by-election of 1816 and handily winning both seats in 1818. The Tories repeated their *coup* in 1820, but Lewes then reverted to its customary split representation in 1826 and 1830. This long tradition, which in the early nineteenth century reflected the relative parity of the parties in Lewes rather than the formal political compromise of the later eighteenth century, ended abruptly in 1831.

During these years, townsmen in Lewes exhibited a widespread and rather sophisticated political awareness. They shared an apparently genuine loyalty to the throne mixed with an equally determined belief that 'the Rights and Privileges of the People should be inviolable'. A town meeting held on 8 September 1830 sent a congratulatory address to William IV on his accession to the throne, yet only two days later the same men sent an address of congratulations to the 'Brave Citizens' of Paris whose 'late Glorious Struggle in support of their Rights' deserved 'sincere and heartfelt congratulations'. Lewes hailed the 'Glorious Revolution' carried out by the 'Brave Citizens' of Paris 'in opposition to the Ordinance of their late imbecile Ruler'.[1] These addresses were part of a long series of missives from Lewes to the wider political world. Ten years earlier, for example, Lewes's burgesses demanded that their MPs support Queen Caroline 'against every unconstitutional Measure that may be taken against her'. They formally thanked London's MP, alderman Matthew Wood, for his spirited defence of Caroline against the 'wicked machinations of an unprincipled faction' formed against her. They congratulated Caroline the next year on the 'abandonment of those disgraceful proceedings' against her, and sent the King yet another note of support for Caroline.

The tone of their 'loyal' addresses to George IV made evident the seriousness with which they took their opinions and with which they expected others to take them, even the King. In the second address of 1821 they admitted that the Constitution gave George the 'unrestricted power' of choosing his counsellors, but they reminded him that it also gave the residents of Lewes the right to submit 'their sense of the manner in which the Constitution is administered'. Though it might 'excite the most painful emotions in your Majesty's bosom', these men saw no alternative to a 'just and faithful recital of

[1] V. Smith (ed.), *Town Book of Lewes*, 244, 279–81.

the grievances' that had given them 'too much reason to complain', from 'lavish expenditure' in war to 'deep and various evils' of peace, including arbitrary penal exactments and the open or secret persecution of all opponents. They attacked the Government for employing spies and decried the 'spiritual division' engendered by these evils. They virtually demanded the fixing of a day for the royal coronation and implored the King to dismiss his Ministers.

Not that this harsh declaration of dissatisfaction impeded Lewes's celebration of George IV's coronation. On that day a flourish of trumpets, the playing of the national anthem, four times four, and countless huzzas and exclamations of 'God save the King' were followed by a procession, complete with band, through the town. So popular were the opening ceremonies that they were repeated. As the King's health was drunk, no group could have presented a more loyal, contented appearance than the celebrants. Nor did any other grumblings about Caroline mar the town's peace after her premature death resolved the issue that had catalysed this hostility. But if political disquiet in Lewes subsided, the burgesses held fast to their belief in the appropriateness and importance of expressing their political views.[2]

The town's ordinary loyal addresses to William IV were transformed into ecstatic encomiums in 1830 by the discovery that the King and Queen Adelaide intended to pay the town its first royal visit in 600 years at the end of October. The celebration on the King's arrival rivalled any spectacle seen in Lewes. A public subscription for the event raised nearly £100, flags were borrowed from HMS *Hyperion* to decorate the streets, the town's fifteen Friendly Societies arrayed themselves and their banners along the King's route.[3] Soon after these joyous celebrations, however, petitions resumed their political focus as Reform quickly became the town's obsession. The motivating factor in Lewes originally may have been general dissatisfaction and fear brought on by economic hardship. Bad weather and a poor harvest in autumn 1830 had

---

[2] Slavery provoked Lewes's next petition. Lewes urged Parliament fully to effect the 1823 Commons resolution for ameliorating the condition of the slave population in the West Indies. The colonial legislature's rejection of the King's 'earnest recommendations' could not be tolerated. Slavery was an 'infringment on all divine and human rights', evoked abhorrence, and Lewes urged the prosecution of the matter to a successful conclusion regardless of the opposition encountered.

[3] The town purchased a massive silver cup and cover at a cost of more than £55 to commemorate the day.

been keenly felt, and the 'Incendiary Spirit, originating in the want of Employment for, and the low rates of Wages given to, Agricultural Labourers' that appeared first in Kent finally struck Lewes with the burning of a barn, two haystacks, and a lodge near St John Southover church during the night of 18 November 1830.[4] These fires resulted in a volunteer group of night-watchmen until the spring.[5] More than 400 men enrolled for the patrols; nightly shifts comprised of thirty-two men overseen by a captain divided Lewes into quadrants and patrolled in pairs between 10 p.m. and 5 a.m.

The night watch often left something to be desired. Volunteers either failed to report or found that they could not be bothered to complete their shifts. When they did bother to appear, their nightly reports (on printed forms) seldom indicated anything other than an impressive standard of literacy among the men. It probably was just as well that the watch escaped a real crisis. In commenting on Richard Brown's absence from his post the previous evening without leave, a watch leader expressed little concern since, as he put it, 'an old woman would answer rather better' to the demands of protecting the town.[6] He filed the report only as a formality. Brown may have been an extreme case, but he was not unique. Understandably, the presence of the watch received a very mixed reception from the populace. Perhaps some residents felt safer as a result of these men taking the names of two strangers 'passing on to Brighton' and the like, but many were not favourably impressed. Watchmen were occasionally 'grossly insulted' by other citizens as they followed their rounds.[7]

Probably coincidentally, Lewes experienced no further 'outrages', but other incidents kept the town in a state of alarm during the remainder of the year. Magistrates arrested two strangers for circulating handbills. More ominously, two local men, Robert Tankard and Melchisedec Jones, were taken into custody for entertaining a group of foreign journeymen tailors, 'a class of persons who we have private information are very active in promoting discontent and tumult'. While Tankard and Jones did

---

[4] PRO, HO52/10/584, letter from Kell & Son, clerks to Lewes magistrates, to Home Office, 19 Nov. 1830. Brighton also set up a special constable patrol and divided the town into watch sections. See 3 Jan. 1831 report, HO52/10/345.

[5] The brief attempt at a night patrol in Lewes during the winter of 1822 received no comment by the men establishing the patrol in 1830. V. Smith (ed.), *Town Book of Lewes*, 244, 279–81.

[6] ESRO, LEW/C7/5.   [7] ESRO, LEW/C7/34.

nothing specifically illegal, their behaviour fanned local unease. At the end of the year, Lewes's MP, Sir John Shelley, forwarded a grand jury report to the Home Secretary recommending Private William Moneypenney of the 3rd Dragoons for bringing to justice a man engaged in denouncing the Government.[8] Whatever the successes or failures of the night watch, it was in this climate of fear that the new spate of petitioning from Lewes emerged.

Lewes's petitions for Reform demonstrated a complex admixture of loyalty to the Crown and unhappiness with the Government reminiscent of the Queen Caroline affair. The petitions also revealed economic as well as political concerns. The first, submitted to both Commons and Lords in advance of Lord John Russell's introduction of the Bill, argued that 'the great distress at present existing among all the productive Classes of the community may in great manner be attributed to the corrupt state of the Representation'. While disclaiming any desire to embarrass the current Ministry by expressing 'particular opinions' or by trying 'to dictate . . . the minor details of Reform', the petitioners had fairly specific ideas as to its nature and its consequences. They believed short Parliaments and the secret ballot essential, along with 'an unsparing abolition of all useless place and unmerited pensions', a general revision of taxes and the Criminal Code, and the repeal of game laws. Reform would result in the abolition of (1) the tithe laws, (2) taxes on knowledge, and (3) the Corn Laws which pauperized the great body of working people. Specifics aside, Lewes demanded that 'the Elective Franchise should be so greatly extended as that the Commons' House should Represent the Rights of the many, and not the Interests of the few.'[9]

A very optimistic town meeting on 11 March 1831 drew up Lewes's second Reform petition, now addressed to William IV. Reform was in the air and on everyone's lips. After going through a long list of obvious passwords like 'Brighton', 'Sussex', and 'Careful', along with less obvious ones like 'End of all war forever', the night patrol chose 'Reform' as the password for the night of 3 March 1831.[10] Eight days later, claiming to have read Russell's entire Bill, the petitioners expected Reform to eliminate the 'system of virtual Representation' which had long since 'been found totally

---

[8] PRO, HO52/10/589–607.

[9] The first petition was signed by 263 men on 26 Jan. 1831. V. Smith (ed.), *Town Book of Lewes*, 281–92.

[10] ESRO, LEW/C7/4, 3 Mar. 1831.

inadequate to the wants and wishes and interests of all classes'. The threatened dissolution of Parliament after the narrow victory on the Reform Bill's second reading prompted a third petition demanding the dissolution of a 'Parliament which has forfeited the Confidence of the Country' by 'virtually' defeating the Bill and 'neutralizing the kind and Paternal intentions' of the King. The fourth exercise of Lewes's 'undoubted right of Petition' refuted allegations in the press that the people had grown 'indifferent' to the fate of the Bill. It warned the Lords that they were about to 'embark in a doubtful and dangerous course of politics' if they opposed 'the just wishes of the Crown, and to the rightful interests of the people'. Lewes wanted the Lords to pass the Bill 'without any unnecessary delay' to avoid 'endangering the peace of the country'.

The dismissal of Grey in May 1832 led to outrage and near hysteria. Meeting the day after but without knowledge of Grey's recall, Lewes warned the King not to appoint 'any Government formed in Opposition to the immediate and successful progress of that great Measure of Reform' lest 'the Sorrow of the Nation shall sink into despair, and indignation at Usurped Authority be converted into lawful resistance to its commands'. Prior to May, they had seen the King as their ally; now that the King's actions revealed his true colours, Lewes wanted the Bill even if he did not. Their simultaneous petition to the Commons sounded equally desperate. Great anxiety prompted their decision to insert the proceedings of their meeting into five newspapers including the *Morning Chronicle* rather than limiting their voice to their traditional outlet, the *Sussex Advertiser*.[11]

The opinions expressed in Lewes's petitions were reflected in Lewes politics. Reform prevented Sir John Shelley, incumbent Tory Member for Lewes, from successfully defending his seat of the previous fifteen years because 'feeling was practically unanimous against him'.[12] Such persistent and vocal popular support for Reform left the Tories on the sidelines in 1831 and 1832.[13] Lewes's political predisposition over these years raised locally the question that many had asked nationally: could the Tories survive as a political force in the face of such widespread contempt? But the fortunes of Lewes's Tories followed their fate nationally. Though

[11] V. Smith (ed.), *Town Book of Lewes*, 291.

[12] *Northampton Free Press*, 9 June 1832.

[13] ESRO, Shiffner MSS 2998; V. Smith (ed.), *Town Book of Lewes*, 227–38, 267.

they nominated only one candidate in 1835 and failed to achieve his return, Lewes's Tories still wielded political power after 1832. Their candidate lost by fewer than twenty-five votes out of more than 700 cast in 1835. Far from a permanently 'contemptible minority', they recaptured a seat at a by-election in 1837.[14] The general election six months later maintained the equilibrium which had been restored at the by-election. A Whig candidate topped the poll, but the Tories narrowly won Lewes's second seat. And the election of 1841 demonstrated that the restored parity of the two parties was not a temporary phenomenon. More than 800 voters participated, yet a mere 4 votes separated the top three candidates and fewer than twenty-five votes stood between the top and bottom of the poll. The Whigs won both seats in 1841, but by a less than comfortable majority of 2 votes. They had very little opportunity to celebrate their recapture of the second seat because the Tories immediately petitioned against the return, alleging bribery and corruption. Their effort, which could easily have jeopardized both Whigs seats, was forestalled by a negotiated settlement just as the case was about to be heard by a Commons committee. Summers Harford, who headed the poll, retired in favour of Fitzroy, thus continuing Lewes's split delegation.[15]

ELECTIONS IN LEWES

Although unincorporated until after 1832, Lewes had returned two MPs since virtually the inception of parliament itself.[16] Untouched by Schedules A and B of the Reform Act, Lewes continued to return two MPs to reformed Parliaments. Unpolled elections in Lewes obscure matters that are complicated further by the prevalence of three-man contests at early elections. Unreformed elections rarely involved two full slates of candidates, and the aversion to casting

[14] Buller, 'Bribery and Intimidation at Elections', 485.
[15] Kemp accepted the stewardship of the Chiltern Hundreds for the second time in Apr. 1837. The election to choose his successor pitted Henry Fitzroy (Tory) against John Easthope (Whig). Fitzroy won by 26 votes. Crosby, *Parliamentary Record*, 214; Hills, *Parliamentary History of Lewes*, 37–8.
[16] 'Lewes Election, 1818', *Sussex Notes and Queries*, 12 (1949), 132–5. See also T. W. Horsfield, *History, Antiquities, and Topography of the County of Sussex* (Lewes, 1835).

plumpers common among the town's voters camouflages the nature of unreformed politics in Lewes. Three-man contests, usually pitting two Whigs against a single Tory, asked more of Lewes's Tories than they were willing to give. Splitting their support might have jeopardized their lone candidate's chances of success, but Tories refused to plump.

Within these restrictions, the incidence of plumping and splitting at Lewes's six contested elections presented in Table 5.1 appears to support the notion that the Reform era transformed electoral behaviour in Lewes much as it altered behaviour in Bristol, Maidstone, and elsewhere. At the same time, as early as 1818 some voters exhibited signs of political sophistication which might well have been expected because of Lewes's history of strong local parties and unmistakable interest in national political issues.[17] The 1818 election provoked a strong partisan response even though a well-known but twice-defeated Whig candidate withdrew at the very last moment, forcing the Whigs to recruit a candidate from London.[18] Fewer than 5 per cent of Lewes's voters split their support between the parties under these adverse circumstances, and more than a quarter of all voters disregarded the last-minute arrival of the Whig candidate and plumped for him anyway. The Whig candidate lost, but his very candidacy proved the existence of a determined and capable Whig party in Lewes.[19]

Measured by standard summary statistics, however, this overtly partisan behaviour did not appear at other unreformed Lewes elections. The figures in Table 5.1 suggest that the elections of 1826 and 1830 concerned personalities rather than parties. Roughly half of the electorate split each time and virtually no one cast partisan plumps. Amid a flurry of advertising and traditional electioneering in 1826, Alexander Donovan prepared to present a united Whig front by standing with T. R. Kemp.[20] One Tory incumbent, Sir George Shiffner, chose to withdraw, leaving the other incumbent

---

[17] Hills, *Parliamentary History of Lewes*, 35–40.

[18] ESRO, Shiffner MSS 305; V. Smith (ed.), *Town Book of Lewes*, 221.

[19] ESRO, Shiffner MSS 170. These tables include the entire Lewes electorate at each election between 1818 and 1841. The relatively small size of the town permitted the use of all voters. For the nominal record linkage techniques employed to construct the database used in the analysis see J. A. Phillips, 'Poll Books and English Electoral Behaviour', in J. Sims (ed.), *A Handlist of British Parliamentary Poll Books* (Leicester, 1984).

[20] *Sussex Advertiser*, 10 Oct. 1825; 15 May 1826.

TABLE 5.1. *Summary Statistics: Lewes Elections, 1818–1841* (%)

Election year	1818	1820	1826	1830	1831	1832	1835	1837	1841
Split votes	4.2	NC	49.3	52.9	NC	NC	26.4	5.0	2.9
Partisan plumps	26.2	NC	1.3	6.3	NC	NC	24.1	NA	NA
Uncertainty coefficient	—	—	0.31	0.41	NC	NC	0.27	0.51	0.54

NC No contest. NA Not applicable (4 candidates).
Sources: Poll books.

Tory, Sir John Shelley, to stand alone. Kemp, recognizing Shelley's popularity, rejected his fellow Whig Donovan, formally denounced all 'Coalitions' (the name used by Lewes's late eighteenth-century local party), and stood alone. For his part, Shelley denied any national party ties and offered himself 'without regard to party'.[21] Under these circumstances, the return of a split parliamentary delegation was virtually assured. The election of 1830 repeated the events of 1826, except that Donovan knew the second time around that he would be canvassing alone. With massive splitting (52.9 per cent), Kemp and Shelley left Donovan 100 votes behind.

Two unpolled elections followed the non-partisan elections of 1826 and 1830, but the lack of polls in 1831 and 1832 stemmed not from lack of interest in Reform, but from the pervasiveness of Reform fever. Lewes's electorate, seething alternately with hope and fear as the Reform Bill was proposed and defeated, returned Whigs enthusiastically in both years. Their fervour actually generated a new political organization when a Political Union augmented Lewes's existing political clubs. Lewes voters had wanted 'the Bill, the whole Bill, and nothing but the Bill', and once they had it, its opponents would have wasted time and money in contesting a seat.

Voters greeted the resumption of contested elections in 1835 with a display of partisan behaviour not evident in 1826 or 1830.[22] A quarter of the electorate still split their votes in 1835, but a quarter represented a sharp decline from the half of just five years earlier. Split-voting dropped to a mere 3 per cent by 1841, the same tiny portion of the electorate reserved for partisan plumpers in 1826. Moreover, another quarter of the electorate cast partisan plumpers for the solitary Tory candidate, a fourfold increase from the level of 1830 (see Table 5.1). The willingness of Lewes's electorate to plump for partisan reasons cannot be tested further; four-man elections in 1837 and 1841 eliminated the need for partisan plumping. Nor does the incidence of unnecessary plumping clarify much because voters in Lewes simply did not cast plumpers without a very good reason and did not like doing it even then. Only nine men plumped unnecessarily in 1818, while eight voters cast equally inexplicable plumps in 1835. Therefore, splitters notwithstanding, the 1835

[21] ESRO, Shiffner MSS 826; *Sussex Advertiser*, 5 June 1826; V. Smith (ed.), *Town Book of Lewes*, 267. See also Zimmeck, 'Chartered Rights', 49–67.

[22] A Liberal 'Bundle of Sticks', and Conservative 'Constitutional Pruning Society' emerged in Lewes during the 1830s. *Parl. Pap* 7 (1835), 400–19.

election demonstrated a new level of partisanship that developed during the Reform era, one that increased at Lewes's two subsequent elections.

Conversely, another standard index, the 'uncertainty coefficient', only mildly supports the image of 'improving' partisanship among Lewes's electors after 1835. The 'uncertainty coefficient' measures the degree of improvement (on a scale of 0 to ±1) in predicting an elector's choice of parties contributed by knowledge of his previous vote. If, for example, knowing that a voter cast a Whig vote in 1835 invariably permitted an accurate prediction that the same voter would cast a Whig vote in 1837, the uncertainty coefficient would reach a perfect +1. Conversely, if knowing that a voter supported the Whigs in 1837 always permitted an accurate prediction of a Tory vote in 1841, the coefficient would reach a perfect −1. A score of 0 indicates the complete inutility of knowledge of an elector's previous vote in predicting a subsequent vote. On this scale, Lewes's voters showed a weak tendency to repeat a partisan vote in 1826 (+0.31) if they voted in 1818. Their votes were significantly more predictable in 1830 (+0.41), but then fell to only +0.27 in 1835 (after the gap of five years without a contested election). After 1835, though, voters demonstrated pronounced inter-election partisan loyalties, reflected at the contests of 1837 and 1841 by scores in excess of +0.51. Summary statistics are problematic at best, but the uncertainty coefficient corroborates the simple percentages reported in Table 5.1 and suggests that Reform affected electoral behaviour in Lewes.

Conversely, the willingness of voters in Lewes to plump necessarily in 1818, the absence of split-voting that year, and the relatively strong uncertainty coefficient scores for 1826 and 1830 suggest that strong political divisions may have affected Lewes well in advance of Reform. The decline in split-voting to extremely low levels in 1837 and 1841 (<5 per cent) also occurred at elections with two Tories standing against two Whigs. Thus the declines were achieved under circumstances that tested partisanship less severely.[23] Moreover, a fairly high proportion of Lewes's voters split their votes after Reform as well. These deviations raise the possibility that voters actually behaved in a heavily partisan but idiosyncratic manner in

---

[23] See C. E. Brent, 'The Immmediate Impact of the Second Reform Act on a Southern County Town', *Southern History*, 2 (1980), 129–78. Brent includes the voting distribution for 1841 but saw 1847 as a more important, 'realigning' election. Almost all Lewes voters continued to cast strictly partisan votes during the 1840s.

the years prior to Reform, and they continued to vote in a heavily partisan though less idiosyncratic fashion after Reform. Far more than in other boroughs, summary statistics fail to capture the nature of electoral behaviour in Lewes; summaries obscure more than they clarify. The figures in Table 5.1 do not, in fact, accurately reflect the nature of partisanship in Lewes.

The oddity of the 1818 contest provides the key to understanding voting behaviour in Lewes prior to Reform. The Whigs lost their principal candidate with Thomas Kemp's resignation in 1816, and they lost their second candidate, James Scarlett, on the very eve of the 1818 poll. Scarlett refused to suffer certain defeat at the hands of the two powerful, local, incumbent Tories, Sir John Shelley and George (soon Sir George) Shiffner. Showing considerable resource-fulness in the face of this sudden abandonment, the Whigs recruited Lord Erskine's son Thomas from London. Erskine had no chance from the beginning. A stranger arriving in town one hour before the commencement of the poll and standing against two popular local candidates could not win. Nevertheless, Erskine managed a solid start. Following his nomination by one of Lewes's living institutions, Sir Henry Blackman, Erskine actually won the show of hands with Shelley. Not deterred by this display of Whig strength, the Tories demanded a poll. Erskine's success exceeded most expectations; he managed a respectable 93 votes on the first day to Shelley's 125 and Shiffner's 115. But midway through the second day, with his deficit widening, Erskine withdrew.[24] Shelley and Shiffner received 255 double votes to Erskine's 99 plumpers. After Erskine's withdrawal, a candidate hastily recruited for the purposes of a petition received another twenty-seven plumpers. Thus nearly 400 electors cast strictly partisan votes while only thirteen split and fewer than ten plumped unnecessarily. It would have been extremely difficult to improve upon this level of strictly partisan behaviour. The failure of the Whigs notwithstanding, Lewes could hardly have been more sharply divided in 1818.

---

[24] The Whigs immediately proposed a second candidate, Henry Baring, and procured 27 token votes for him in the hope that they might win with a parliamentary election petition what they could not win at the hustings. Their petition was never filed, as they fell into some disarray after the defeat. Erskine intended to join in the petition against the return, alleging bribery, but his father dissuaded him from pursuing the petition. Erskine was the youngest (fourth) son of Thomas, first Baron Erskine. Educated at Trinity College, Cambridge and Lincoln's Inn, he became a KC in 1827 and chief judge of the Bankruptcy Court in 1840.

This notable demonstration of partisanship in 1818 ended as abruptly as it began, if levels of splitting and partisan plumping in 1826 are any indication. After a particularly dismal canvass in 1820, the Whigs chose dignity over humiliation, and the Tory incumbents were not troubled with a poll. When polls resumed in 1826 and 1830, Lewes elections still involved three candidates, but at these contests a single Tory stood against two Whigs. Under these circumstances, only a handful of voters were willing to cast the plumpers necessary to support the Tory candidate. Instead, nearly half of all voters split their support between the solitary Tory and one of the two Whig candidates both times (see Table 5.1). This apparently non-partisan behaviour would seem to more than offset the partisan performances turned in at the election of 1818 and raises the possibility that 1818 was an aberration. But appearances can deceive.

In point of fact, the voting choices of Lewes's electors were as partisan and politically 'rational' in 1826 and 1830 as they had been in 1818. The electorate failed the test of partisanship when subjected to the summary measurements reported in Table 5.1, but their failure to meet the assumptions underlying the tests masked behaviour that actually was rigidly partisan. The shift from three-man to four-man contests in 1837 and 1841 further confused matters. Summary statistics are simply not the most appropriate measures of electoral behaviour in Lewes because Tories absolutely refused to plump before and after Reform. The rise in the levels of straight party voting reported in Table 5.1 merely reflected a structural shift to four-man contests that allowed Tories to cast straight party doubles rather than any real change in partisanship. In short, the summary statistics reported in Table 5.1 indicate a change in partisanship which never occurred.

Qualitative evidence from these elections does little to alleviate the confusion. Whig disunity at the two elections immediately before Reform and the limited perspective of raw voting figures appeared to lay the blame for the partisan failure in Lewes at the feet of the Whigs. When Sir George Shiffner withdrew on the eve of the poll in 1826 because of his failing health, the Tories backed only their incumbent Sir John Shelley. They continued to support Shelley alone in 1830, both times against two Whig candidates who refused to stand together. The local Whig incumbent T. R. Kemp twice rejected the efforts of Londoner Alexander Donovan to form a coalition. Kemp's was the more traditional Whiggism, and Donovan's the newer, more extreme reformist view. Kemp insisted on mounting a completely separate effort. Both times Kemp headed the poll easily while Donovan lost his bid for the second seat, the first time by a relatively narrow margin of twenty-five votes and the second time by almost a hundred. Donovan's loss stemmed from the decision of virtually half of all Lewes voters to split their votes between Kemp and the sole Tory, Shelley. Surely then, this result stemmed from the failure of the Whigs to hold fast under such adverse circumstances. As one commentator noted, it was obvious that 'Kemp's supporters ratted, remained neutral, or voted for Shelley', permitting the Tories to capture a seat.[25] Only a close analysis of the votes of individual Whigs and Tories in Lewes reveals the flaw in this perfectly plausible but completely erroneous conclusion. Tories, not Whigs, split their votes in 1826 and 1830.

TABLE 5.2. *Consistent Straight Party Voting among Lewes Electors who Initially Cast a Whig Vote*

Original voting year	% voting Whig in				
	1826	1830	1835	1837	1841
1818	92	81	88	82	83
1826		77	87	84	80
1830			94	89	81
1835				90	88
1837					93

As revealed by the figures in Table 5.2, Whigs could hardly have evinced greater loyalty. Nine out of ten of those voting for the solitary Whig candidate in 1818 voted for both Whig candidates in 1826. Neither the potentially confusing uncontested election in 1820 nor the eight-year gap between the two polls diminished the loyalty of Whig voters. Indeed, this cohort of Whig voters who supported Erskine in 1818 persisted in their Whiggish behaviour in all subsequent elections. More than 80 per cent of the 1818 cohort cast Whig votes at every election in which they participated up to and including 1841. In fact every Whig cohort voted remarkably

---

[25] Zimmeck, 'Chartered Rights', 49–67.

consistently between 1818 and 1841. The 1826 voter cohort (i.e. those voters first recorded in the poll book of 1826) demonstrated slightly less cohesion than the norm at the general election of 1830 (only 77 per cent), but all in all, Whig voters were outstandingly tenacious in their support for any and all candidates offered by the Whig party over the entire period.

Another aspect of Whig voting, not evident in Table 5.2, is also revealing. Not a single Whig voter in the cohorts of 1818 or 1826 followed his Whig vote with a strictly Tory vote at the next election, and these men almost never voted strictly Tory at any subsequent election. The largest defection from the ranks of the Whig cohort of 1818 occurred in 1837 when a grand total of six men deserted their fellow Whigs and voted Tory. Almost invariably, if one of these men failed to follow a strictly partisan Whig vote with another, he split between the parties. Each Whig cohort followed this pattern. No more than twelve members of the 1830 cohort, for example, ever cast a straight Tory vote. The twenty-one (of 272) Whigs in the 1835 cohort who switched to the Tories in 1837 constituted the largest group of defectors by far, and they accounted for less than 8 per cent of their cohort. In short, men who voted Whig initially remained Whig for as long as they remained in the electorate. Perhaps most importantly, Reform did not affect Whig loyalty, even for those who entered the electorate after 1832.

Not so the Tories. A comparable examination of consistent Tory voting by cohorts over these elections reveals what appears to be a miserable record indeed (see Table 5.3). Only 6 per cent of the men who cast Tory double votes in 1818 maintained their initial Toryism with another strictly Tory vote in 1826. Their loyalty proved to be

TABLE 5.3. *Consistent Straight Party Voting among Lewes Electors who Initially Cast a Tory Vote*

Original voting year	% voting Tory in				
	1826	1830	1835	1837	1841
1818	6	8	44	71	73
1826		50	88	100	80
1830			79	95	100
1835				94	92
1837					90

no greater at the next general election. Only 8 per cent of those who had voted for the two Tories in 1818 cast a necessary Tory plumper in 1830. Tory loyalty remained unimpressive even after Reform. Less than half of the 1818 Tories plumped for the Tory candidate in 1835. These men from the initial cohort finally reversed this trend in 1837. Their partisan behaviour at the last two elections in the series improved dramatically, but at their best Tories were unable to match the worst performance of their fellows in the Whig cohort of 1818.

Rather than the uniformity across cohorts and across elections shown by the Whigs, Tory cohorts differed widely among themselves as well as across elections. Exactly half of the 1826 Tory cohort voted Tory in 1830, and their willingness to remain true to their original party began to rival and then surpass the Whigs at subsequent elections. They achieved unanimity in 1837; each returning Tory voted strictly Tory again. The 1830 Tory cohort also managed to achieve unanimity at a subsequent election (1841), a feat never achieved by the Whigs of any cohort. Overall, Tory partisan behaviour cannot be distinguished from that of their Whig counterparts at reformed elections. After an extremely poor beginning, the Tories appeared to experience a revival of loyalties which accounted for the revived Tory fortunes at Lewes elections in the post-Reform era.

An examination of split-voting among Tory voters reveals virtually the same pattern but is worth considering because it reveals the cohesion of the Tories prior to Reform, a cohesion no less powerful for its idiosyncrasy. Eighty-five per cent of the splitters in 1818 split again in 1826 and continued to split in 1830 (see Table 5.4). But at the first poll following Reform most of the 1818 splitters returned to the strictly Tory fold. Less than a third (29 per cent) split in 1835, and only a handful of the members of the 1818 cohort split at the next two elections. Half of the 1826 cohort continued to split their votes in 1830; the other half cast the plumpers required for a strictly Tory vote. Not a single splitter from the 1826 cohort switched parties entirely. Indeed, except for a handful of defectors from the 1818 cohort, these splitters were as unwilling to vote Whig as the Whigs were unwilling to vote Tory.[26] Only one splitter from the 1830 cohort switched to the Whigs in 1835, and the numbers switching from any cohort at any election were extremely small. An average of less than 5 per cent of these men transferred their party

[26] A complete count of Lewes switchers is impressive in the sense that virtually no one switched. *See table opposite.*

TABLE 5.4. *Splitters: Lewes*

Original voting year	% splitting in				
	1826	1830	1835	1837	1841
1818	85	86	29	7	2
1826		50	13	0	20
1830			16	0	0
1835				0	2
1837					3

allegiance between any two elections. With the one explicable exception, the highest level of switching remained under 9 per cent (compared to 8 per cent for the Whigs).

After Reform, very few of Lewes's voters split their support. As Tables 5.1 and 5.2 demonstrated, most voters cast a party vote at one election and followed it with another. Approximately 94 per cent of those who voted Tory initially in 1835 followed their partisan vote with another for the Tories in 1837; not a single one of this group split at the second contest. A negligible 2 per cent split in 1841.

Splitting actually provides the key to understanding Tory voting in Lewes. Before 1832 splitters were actually Tories voting under duress. The apparently non-partisan voting, which confused the pattern displayed in Table 5.1 can be attributed almost exclusively to the Tories. More importantly, given their idiosyncratic rules, these Tory splitters were almost as rigidly partisan as the Whigs; they simply refused to discard their second vote, both before and after 1832. The voters who quite happily cast Tory doubles in 1818 would not cast Tory plumps in 1826 or 1830. Less than half of them were

Party Switchers: Lewes (actual numbers)

	Tories to Whigs					Whigs to Tories				
	1826	1830	1835	1837	1841	1826	1830	1835	1837	1841
1818	10	6	18	14	11	0	0	2	6	5
1826		0	0	0	1		0	4	16	18
1830			1	1	0			3	12	19
1835				8	6				21	26
1837					18					14

willing to plump as late as 1835. Instead, these voters almost invariably joined their Tory vote with one for the moderate local Whig (Kemp in 1826 and 1830). The second Whig lost in 1826 and 1830 not because of Whig splitting, but because Tory splitters almost unanimously doubled for Shelley and Kemp. Similarly, in 1835, the Tories who refused to plump chose almost to a man (there were only three exceptions) to vote for the more thoroughly respectable, locally connected, and moderate Whig Sir Charles Blunt, Bt. Tory voters jeopardized their own candidate's chances by refusing to plump, and actually cost their candidate his seat in 1835, but in both earlier elections, uniform Tory support for one Whig led to lopsided election returns that placed the Tory candidate in the middle of the field. Though less loyal in the sense that they would vote for a local Whig if they had no choice other than a plumper, Tories were no less distinguishable as a group. The Tories might not have been willing to cast plumpers, but neither were they willing to change their primary political allegiance. They rarely defected, and the few defectors in the 1818 cohort shifted parties permanently. Members of other Tory cohorts voted with each other time after time.

Partisanship preceded Reform. The structure of unreformed elections masked the partisan solidarity of the Tories, but when unmasked, its strength matched the more easily discerned Whig solidarity. Thus the structure of elections held the key to Tory behaviour as measured via summary statistics. When given an opportunity to do so without suffering the penalty of discarding a vote, Tories and Whigs toed the party line both before and after 1832. When asked to make what they perceived as an unreasonable sacrifice, the Tories refused and voted for a local Whig along with the choice of their party. This behaviour did not lessen their solidarity, nor did it prevent their immediate return to the party fold when an opportunity to do so presented itself with the full Tory slate of 1837. Had Lewes experienced a series of four-man contests in place of the three-cornered elections so common during this period, Tory loyalty almost certainly would have matched the extremely high level achieved by the Whigs who benefited from their invariably full slates. By equating the particular form of the Tory split vote (e.g. the Tory candidate coupled with the local Whig) with the standard Whig double vote when only three candidates stood for election in Lewes, Table 5.5 illustrates the consistency of the political choices of all voters at all elections in Lewes.

TABLE 5.5. *Overall Voting Consistency: All Lewes Voters* (τ_b)

Original voting year	Subsequent voting year				
	1826	1830	1835	1837	1841
1818	0.734	0.688	0.508	0.513	0.543
1826		0.728	0.588	0.593	0.556
1830			0.610	0.589	0.528
1835				0.751	0.698
1837					0.826

The relationship between voting choices at all Lewes elections between 1818 and 1841 measured by τ_b was uniformly and strongly positive. Most voters behaved in a very predictable manner, casting identical party votes at election after election. The lowest τ for any of the voter cohorts at adjacent elections was a very strong +0.61 between 1830 and 1835. At all other adjacent election pairs, Tory and Whig voters achieved a truly remarkable degree of partisan consistency demonstrated by scores in excess of +0.7. At the same time, the level of consistency in the Lewes electorate cannot be said to have increased over time. The 1818 voter cohort behaved in 1826 much as the 1826 cohort behaved in 1830, or as the 1835 cohort behaved in 1837. The number of years between adjacent elections made little difference, nor did the existence of uncontested elections that frequently separate otherwise adjacent elections. The behaviour of the 1830 cohort in 1835 might have been affected somewhat by the two uncontested elections in Lewes between their first and second recorded votes, but in this most extreme instance they voted consistently.

The behaviour of each voter cohort also remained consistent over the entire range of elections. Tory voters in 1818 were still casting Tory votes in 1841, while Whig voters from the first election returned to support Whig candidates. Despite their consistency, Lewes's pre-Reform cohorts were affected to some degree by either the Reform Bill or the Reform era. The five-year gap separating the elections of 1830 and 1835 cannot adequately explain the relatively inconsistent behaviour of the 1818 cohort at that election. Their 1835 score which only barely exceeded +0.5 was followed by comparable behaviour in 1837 (+0.51) and in 1841 (+0.54). Put another way, more than a few members of the 1818 cohort changed parties permanently after 1830. Most of those who changed parties were Tories; very few Whigs shifted in the other direction. Their aggregate numbers, however, were sufficient to depress the scores for the 1818 cohort in later elections. The same is true of the 1826 and 1830 cohorts, but in all three instances, the least consistent behaviour was remarkably consistent.

Voters in Lewes were not unique. Well in advance of the Reform, some other constituencies were so rigidly partisan that increases were virtually impossible. Great Yarmouth, whose voters' reputations suffered from much negative publicity in the nineteenth century, was such a constituency. And if summary statistics served Lewes badly by concealing the rigidly partisan nature of Lewes's electorate, summary statistics are superfluous to a study of voting in Great Yarmouth.

STRAIGHTFORWARD, CONSISTENT PARTISANSHIP IN GREAT YARMOUTH

While three-man contests confused and obscured the measurement of partisanship in Lewes, a series of four-man contests in Great Yarmouth permit the unobstructed perception of a remarkable degree of partisanship that long preceded Reform.[27] Party divisions in Lewes are invisible in the summary figures presented in Table 5.1, but the voters of Great Yarmouth were so rigidly divided along party lines by 1818 that there is no need to construct a comparable table to reflect their voting patterns.[28] A standard tabular presentation of voting in Yarmouth would contain little more than a series of dashes indicating the absence of voters who cast other than straight party votes. Virtually no one in Great Yarmouth split his votes between the two parties. No one plumped unnecessarily. And when

[27] Election material for Yarmouth elections survives in considerable detail as a result of the substantial accumulations of Dawson Turner, Whig party activist in Yarmouth. BL, N. TAB 2012/6/vols. 1–10.

[28] Some degree of patronage had been wielded in Yarmouth early in the 19th cent. by the Harbords, Townshends, and Walpoles, but all interest in the borough had been extinguished by 1818. C. J. Palmer, *History of Great Yarmouth* (Great Yarmouth, 1856), 234. See also B. D. Hayes, 'Politics in Norfolk', Ph.D. (Cambridge, 1958). Only *A Peep at the Commons* suggests a continuing Townshend influence and the importance of Government money which amounted to perhaps £10,000.

called upon to cast plumps for partisan reasons, voters responded readily enough before and after 1832.

Voters in Great Yarmouth were as partisan in 1818 as they were in 1835. In fact, at every election over these years, before or after Reform, they were partisan almost to a man. In 1818, of the nearly 1,500 voters returning the Whigs T. W. Anson and C. E. Rumbold, a total of only fifty (3.4 per cent) split their votes.[29] Another twenty-one (1.4 per cent) ignored the dictates of party and cast a plumper, most of them for the Tory incumbent William Loftus. More remarkably, this exhibition of rigidly partisan voting, which would have made virtually any party organization in any other constituency in nineteenth-century England proud, was the worst performance turned in by Yarmouth's voters at any election, reformed or unreformed. Yarmouth voters approached their 1818 performance (4.8 per cent non-straight party votes) only one other time at the elections examined here; almost 4.4 per cent of the voters failed to cast perfect party votes in 1832 when thirty-two freemen and thirty freeholders split their votes while seven others plumped unnecessarily. At all other elections, even fewer voters deviated. Yarmouth eventually achieved near perfection. A total of fifteen men cast other than straight, full party votes in 1820. Six years later, despite the greater demands on partisanship imposed by a three-man election, only nine voters failed to cast perfect party votes. More than a quarter of the electorate plumped for the sole Tory candidate Sir E. H. Lacon, but a quarter of an electorate is not enough to win an election. With no splits to augment his vote total, Lacon was left a distant third on the poll.

This intense partisanship was achieved by Yarmouth's parties through strenuous efforts in a variety of areas. They played an active role in elections from the early years of the century. The Blues (Whigs) actively debated issues long before Reform became an issue, although Reform itself emerged early in East Anglia. The *Norwich Mercury* campaigned for Reform from before the general election of 1826, as the editors hastened to point out in an effusion of self-congratulation when the issue emerged in 1830.[30] Yarmouth's Tories

---

[29] Anson won the seat in 1818 only to succeed as second Viscount Anson six weeks later. He was replaced by his brother George, a veteran of Waterloo and just turned 21, who stood for election at the next five contests, winning a seat the first four times. The Anson brothers were grandsons of Thomas Coke of Holkham.

[30] Dickinson, *Caricatures*, 332. Reproduction of Seymour's cartoon of 21 Apr. 1832 from Stephens, Hawkins, and George (comp.) *Catalogue*, 16995.

were equally active, led by members of the Corporation who quietly submitted a loyal address to George IV during the Caroline affair without a public meeting since 'clamour and tumult are apt to prevail at such gatherings' because of the all too successful efforts of those who 'delude the ignorant and promote discontent among the people'.[31] The Corporation might well have been worried about discontent, but their party's organization seemed sound enough. They managed the election of 1826 with neither the consent nor the knowledge of their candidate.

Having approached absolute partisan perfection for three successive elections, Yarmouth's parties very nearly achieved it in 1830. The strong Blue (Whig) slate was not matched by the Reds (Tories). Neither of the Red candidates, West Indian merchant Andrew Colvile and barrister Henry Bliss, had close ties to Yarmouth, and neither cut much of a figure during the canvass. Yet not one voter out of 1,702 split between the parties. Only four unnecessary plumpers prevented a perfectly partisan vote; a single voter plumped for Anson, and three men cast plumpers for T. E. Campbell. Anson and Rumbold topped the poll for the fourth time with 945 double votes, and the two Tories shared 751 doubles. In 1831 the number of non-partisans or imperfect partisans nearly doubled as seven voters (six plumpers and a solitary splitter) failed the party test.

Great Yarmouth's parties spared no efforts in achieving this noteworthy result in 1831. Having raised a substantial war chest to finance massive printing efforts, most of it carried out by the print shop of John Barnes, the True Blues had blanketed the town with flyers, large and small, coloured and black-and-white, calling for Reform.[32] Most of these broadsides eschewed substance for the image of Reform. The Blues seemed content to focus on the quantity of placards, letting Reform sell itself. Their own convictions may have lulled them into underestimating the difficulty the Bill would encounter, particularly in light of a local Tory campaign that appeared destined for defeat despite an equally expensive and extensive publishing effort by the Reds, who spared neither ink nor

[31] NRO, D53/3, Broadside, 11 Dec. 1820.
[32] They raised nearly £2,400 in Apr. 1831 and another £1,700 the next month. Placards, broadsides, and banners ranged from relatively small notices of between 6 and 12 inches to posters more than 3 feet in length. One hundred and forty individuals contributed amounts ranging from the £100 donations of men such as Thomas Clowes and John Brightwen down to John Milton's half-crown. The total amounted to £2,374 12s. 5d.

paper besmirching Reform. The Reds seized upon any available issue, including the amount of money flowing from Government coffers into the pockets of the extended Grey family. Beginning with Lord Grey's £12,500 salary and ending with very small sums paid to several cousins, the Greys received more than £170,000, or, as the Reds pointed out, enough to support 3,300 families at £50 per annum. But Red efforts were overwhelmed by Reform fever, particularly since earlier unreformed elections suggested that the Whigs enjoyed a solid majority among the electors.

Reform simply could not have increased partisanship in Great Yarmouth. On the contrary, despite an extensive propaganda campaign, partisanship declined slightly at Yarmouth's first reformed election as voters cast more non-partisan votes than at any point since 1818. If the levels of vehemence with which partisan loyalties were expressed during the canvassing from October to December, canvassing so complete that Anson and Rumbold claimed to have met 1,650 of Yarmouth's 1,680 qualified electors personally, were an accurate guide, the partisan exclusivity exhibited by the electorate in 1831 would have been expected to continue in 1832. In September the Reds threatened that 'all spies discovered at [their] meetings will be TARRED AND FEATHERED—AND NO MISTAKE!' And partisanship did continue at an extraordinarily high level. A total of only sixty-nine men out of 1,555 total voters failed to cast party ballots in 1832, a relatively large number only in comparison to the tiny handful of non-partisans in the four previous elections. Thirty-six ancient-right voters failed the party test in 1832, of whom thirty-two actually split their votes. At the same time, thirty-three householders made their electoral debuts as non-partisans. The demands of a three-man election did not trouble the bulk of the electorate.

With Reform accomplished, the Tories raised a number of new issues including the 'Benthamite expedient' of consigning paupers to the dissecting-table. The issue had aroused both Tory paternalism and Radical indignation from its inception in 1829. Richard Oastler and Henry Hunt were uncomfortably allied against it, and when the measure appeared poised for success in 1832, many ordinary men and women joined in an outcry that turned into riots in towns from Aberdeen to Hereford. Francis Place and the moderates in the National Political Union may have been willing to support War-burton's Bill in 1832, but more critically, the National Union of Working Classes, which had an active chapter in Yarmouth,

vehemently opposed it.[33] Andrew Colvile raised the cry 'No
Anatomy Bill' in November 1832 (the bill had become law more than
three months earlier). The Red press quickly picked up the cry, and
William Meggy's print shop lent itself to the cause with vigour.
Branding the Blues as 'dissectors', but afraid that the delivery of the
bodies of paupers for dissection would not evoke enough sympathy
among those actually enfranchised in Yarmouth, the Reds latched on
to the more locally gripping point that the bodies of shipwrecked
sailors also were to be included in those subject to the vivisectionists'
scalpel. No seafaring town could countenance such actions. The
Reds also railed against free trade (an important issue in a town
engaged so heavily in trade), and against the flag used by some of the
Blues during the procession of Anson and Rumbold into town.
Spurred on more by enthusiasm than political wisdom, some
reformers hoisted a tricolour. The Blues defended the flag as
infinitely preferable to the 'Bloody Red Flag of the Turks', but their
action gave the Reds a chance to issue broadsides quoting Nelson's
words that where a tricolour appeared the country's enemies could
be found. George Manby, a Yarmouth barracks master, claimed that
he would not honour his pledge to vote for Anson and Rumbold
because of the insult to all implied by their use of the 'FLAG denotive
of REVOLUTION'.[34]

The Yarmouth Corporation also emerged for the first time as a
political issue in 1832. Everyone knew that a Red candidate was a
Corporation candidate, but in 1832 Colvile tried to sever the
connection by rejecting his 'Corporation' label. The Blues agreed
that Colvile knew virtually nothing about Yarmouth, but however
gullible he might be, his unsuccessful stand just the year before, his
pecuniary guarantees from the Corporation, the canvasses on his
behalf by members of the Corporation, and their particular anxiety
to elect him in order to defend themselves against Reform,
unmistakably tarred Colvile with the corporate brush. The Blues
also accused him of advocating slavery, a charge which Colvile, a

---

[33] R. Richardson, *Death, Dissection, and the Destitute* (London, 1988), 147–154;
BL N. TAB 2012/6/1/11 Aug. 1830; Colman Local History Library, F. D. Palmer,
Yarmouth Notes (Great Yarmouth, 1889), clippings of *Norwich Mercury*, 15 Apr., 9
Dec. 1830.
[34] Manby, a rare Tory voter in 1830, proved to be one of the rarest of voting species
in Yarmouth, a waverer. He switched parties and voted for Anson and Rumbold in
1831, only to switch back with a plumper for Colvile in 1832. BL, N. TAB 2012/6/9
Nov.; 3, 10 Dec. 1832.

West Indian sugar planter and merchant who owned more than 800 slaves, was hard-pressed to deny. Yarmouth had already hosted a number of anti-slavery meetings, and the agitation was building to the peak reached the next year. Colvile also benefited personally from the sugar subsidy that cost the nation more than £3 million, proving, the Blues argued, that free trade would be beneficial in economic as well as humanitarian ways. In an impressive display of party solidarity under adverse circumstances, the Tories loyally stood by their lone candidate in the new political order and put up a good fight. Drawing virtually all his support from Tory voters who unflinchingly discarded their second votes, Colvile won 45 per cent of the electorate and finished fewer than seventy-five votes behind the two reformers.

Measured strictly cross-sectionally, Yarmouth voting behaviour after 1832 simply continued the extremely strong pattern set during the previous fifteen years. Virtually all electors at all remaining elections cast purely party votes. At each of the three contests after 1832, five voters cast unnecessary plumpers and between eight and twelve split their votes.[35] With approximately 1,500 voters turning out at each contest, the handful of voters who strayed from partisanship accounted for less than 1 per cent of the total each time. Yarmouth's party leaders are unlikely to have been unhappy with the electorate's 99 per cent compliance rate. Unlike so many other constituencies, the double vote in Yarmouth did not prove to be a partisan stumbling-block.

Oddly, Yarmouth's municipal politics do not help explain the town's notable partisan exclusivity. Yarmouth's nearly unanimous partisan behaviour was achieved and maintained exclusively at parliamentary elections; before the passage of the Municipal Corporations Act, the town permitted no others. Yarmouth's thirty-six common councilmen were selected for life from among the freemen of the town at a meeting attended only by a majority of the members of the Corporation. The Corporation alone chose the

---

[35] Such tiny but persistent numbers of non-partisans raises the suspicion that the same individuals could be found on each poll book behaving in the same way. However, the non-partisan voters at each of these elections were not the same individuals repeating their non-party performance at each election. John Goodwin, a caulker, split in 1835 as well as 1837, and Henry Kettle, a shipwright, plumped unnecessarily for the Tory candidate Thomas Baring in 1837 and 1841, but the remainder of the splitters and plumpers behaved in a non-partisan fashion at only one election.

town's eighteen aldermen, also selected for life, from the ranks of the councilmen. One of the aldermen was chosen to serve annually as mayor. The Corporation filled all other town offices without any participation from the burgesses.[36] This recruitment into the Corporation by 'co-optation' effectively eliminated popular participation in local government and prevented the development of the sort of locally oriented partisan infrastructure so important in the development of partisan behaviour in places like Bristol and Maidstone. And Yarmouth's townsmen seem to have been content with this closed system until it was struck down by Parliament.

The issue of corporate reform emerged during the electioneering prior to the 1832 election, as the Blues entered the next phase of Radicalism and demanded the abolition of slavery, the reduction of taxes, and 'equal laws and equal rights'. Their demands for change prior to 1832 paled in comparison to post-Reform expectations. Issues at elections were profuse and sometimes profound. The electorate responded accordingly. At successive reformed elections issues such as triennial Parliaments, further suffrage extensions, and the ballot attracted attention. Short-lived enthusiasms such as Yarmouth's opposition to the Irish Coercion Bill contended with issues of greater durability, most notably the Corn Law. Anson and Rumbold had long championed free trade, but the focus of the free traders shifted to corn in the years following Reform, particularly after municipal reform. The introduction of a wide range of issues, including the penny post, excited discussion among Yarmouth's voters and not infrequently provoked formal responses from the citizenry. Whatever debates might have raged among the intelligensia about the role of MPs, Yarmouth's Whig representatives to Parliament were left under no illusion about their roles; they were required to pledge their support for major issues such as the ballot.[37]

By 1838 George Stewart could express the rather sophisticated opinion that William Wilshere could count on many votes from those who 'were far from being of Colonel [T. P. T.] Thompson's radical opinions, but all of whom were most determined to oppose

---

[36] NRO, Y/C19/31, Corporation Assembly Minute Book, 29 Jan. 1833, response to S. M. Phillipps's request for a description of the Corporation. Despite the town's compliance, the town was not included in the Municipal Corporations Report because T. J. Hogg failed to file a completed report. Webb and Webb, *English Local Government*, iii. 717 n. 2.

[37] *Norwich Mercury*, 14, 21 Feb. 1839.

Mr Baring'.[38] Party loyalty was such that a meeting of the Blue party in July 1838 agreed to support Thompson in lieu of Wilshere, though only if Thompson was clearly perceived to be 'not gaining a permanent seat but merely keeping the seat warm for' Wilshere.[39] But rather than resorting to this strategy, Wilshere actually stood again after the Blues resolved that he should be re-elected 'free of any expense whatever' since he had been forced from his seat unfairly. The normal Red attacks on the 'Bastile Workhouses', for which they blamed the Whigs unceasingly, failed to have the necessary impact. Nor did the Reds gain much ground by following a new and quite different tack. They accused the Blues of attempting through Wilshere's re-election to 'deter for the future any Conservative candidate from offering themselves' and to turn Yarmouth into a close Whig/Radical borough, a strange argument indeed from a party that had so recently fought tooth and nail to preserve Yarmouth as a close Tory borough. Wilshere easily won back his seat.[40]

Table 5.6 demonstrates diachronically what the absence of cross-sectional comparisons of Yarmouth's voters demonstrated synchronically; 1832 had little effect on the town. Reform fever is visible in the τ of 0.81 in 1831/2, and the Municipal Corporations Act which dramatically altered the nature of Yarmouth's local government may have enhanced long-term party loyalty somewhat, but the higher scores apparent after 1835 pale in comparison to the remarkably consistent partisan performances turned in by Yarmouth from early in the century.

'FUNCTIONAL' CORRUPTION IN YARMOUTH

With elections that appear to have been extremely issue-oriented and voting that appears to have been determined by parties, the ubiquitous charges of corruption levelled against Yarmouth over the years might appear unwarranted. They were not. Yarmouth voters richly deserved the frequent condemnations delivered from friend and foe alike. The town was quite unmistakably and thoroughly corrupt. Corruption was 'countenanced without compunction', and

[38] HRO, Wilshere MSS, D/EX 14/3/11, 8 June 1838.
[39] Ibid., D/EX 14/3/13–15.   [40] BL, N. TAB 2012/6/17–23 Aug. 1838.

TABLE 5.6. *Electoral Behaviour across Elections in Great Yarmouth: λ (Asymmetric) and τ_b*

Election years	1818–20	1820–6	1826–30	1830–1	1831–2	1832–5	1835–7	1837–41
λ	0.69	0.60	0.53	0.76	0.62	0.69	0.82	0.82
τ	0.66	0.66	0.67	0.81	0.67	0.71	0.79	0.82

Both τ and λ illustrate a town filled with loyal partisans from 1818 onward.

printed defences of bribery as 'ancient custom' and 'privilege' were circulated widely on occasion lest anyone feel too abashed to accept payment for votes.[41] Yet Yarmouth's all too evident corruption actually illustrated the relative insignificance of corruption under certain circumstances.

C. E. Rumbold's expenses for the 1818 election had fallen only 4 pence short of £11,000. He was dunned by everyone for everything. His agents claimed to have paid out £1,203 to resident voters, another £786 to those from Norwich and the country, and another £2,180 to voters from outside the country, including London. They asked him for another £1,724 to cover tavern bills, £188 for carriages and conveyances, £860 for cockades and colours, £724 for the purchase of freedoms for his supporters, £182 for printing, and a host of other smaller charges down to £50 for a subscription to the Yarmouth races and £98 15s. for music and ringers. Rumbold complained to his mother that his opponents Loftus and Lacon kept the poll open 'without a hope of success', but with so much money flowing into their pockets, election officials may have been responsible for the delay in closing the poll. Who would hasten to turn off a tap pouring out gold?[42] Yet as this torrent of gold descended upon Yarmouth, the rules about its distribution seem to have been strictly honoured. Every voter received his fair share, but no voter received a penny more or less than his fair share, 2 guineas.

A report from Norwich following the Tory victory at the 1837 general election acknowledged 'the most extensive and wicked system of bribery on both sides', noting that the 'Tories gave £1000 for 10 votes on the last day'.[43] The Gurney forces alone reportedly raised £30,000 for the election of Richard Gurney in 1818.[44] It was exactly this sort of admittedly expensive but potentially much more effective bribery that seems to have been entirely absent in Great Yarmouth. Quite the reverse, Yarmouth's bribery was restricted by custom to 2 guineas per voter and fees for services to everyone and anyone who could find a way to serve. In the Whig defeat of 1835 the

---

[41] *Parl. Debs.* 49. 1342–6; 98. 599.

[42] NRO, Rumbold MSS, L14/3–4. Kept with exceeding care, the total was adjusted after being drawn up initially to correct a £2 16s. error, leaving a grand total of £10,997 3s. 8d.

[43] Friends Library, London, Gurney MSS, E. J. Addington Extracts, L002.3/13291, 69, Samuel Gurney to Joseph Gurney, 19 Aug. 1837.

[44] K. Cave (ed.), *Diary of Joseph Farington*, 16 vols. (New Haven, Conn., 1984), xv. 5230, 23 June 1818.

Blues levelled charges of 'the most gross and unblushing bribery' by the Tories, but only two specific allegations were made. Instead of the customary 2 guineas, a voter named Boyce supposedly received 4 sovereigns. Another named Stevenson was given £2 10*s*. The Whigs claimed that Stevenson was so offended by the underhanded Tory bribery that he brought the money to a Blue booth and polled for Anson and Rumbold after collecting his 'legitimate' 2 guineas from the Whigs.[45]

In the electioneering preceding the election of 1837 John Brightwen told Rumbold that his original estimate of expenses was too low since 'the payment of two guineas to the Freemen was not contemplated'. And upon taking that into account, the 'prevailing opinion is that for £2,500 to £3,000 two Liberal candidates might be returned'. The Liberals would 'have no chance of carrying our point', unless they were willing 'to deal liberally (even lavishly) with the *worthy and independent*'.[46] For his part, George Stewart feared for the chances of T. P. T. Thompson who was planning to stand for Yarmouth in 1838 in Wilshere's place 'to keep the seat warm for him' if Wilshere could not stand himself, because Thompson resisted the idea 'that two guineas must be fair' and was 'too strongly of opinion [*sic*] that they [the freemen] are to be gained over by argument'.[47] Writing to William Wilshere some months later in 1838 after the latter had decided to stand personally at the 1838 by-election, John Clowes assured him that the town supported his claims over those of the defeated Tory Thomas Baring, but admitted that 'nothing can be done before the Two Guineas are paid'. The second victory 'might be worked for £2,000 or £2,500', but without the money the return of a 'Liberal candidate' could not be effected, whatever the principles of the majority of the electorate.[48] John Bayly reported to Wilshere in 1841 that 'Mr Smith called to say that 3 of the remaining 7 [freemen] had promised him to vote blue, he guaranteeing their 2 guineas on the Sunday preceeding the polling'. Bayly recommended that Wilshere pay the money; what else could he do in the face of voters 'swearing that if they were not to be paid they would never vote blue again'? Virtually every man asked for and expected the money. 'In fact, they were asked by a

[45] *Norwich Mercury*, 8 Jan. 1835.
[46] NRO, Rumbold MSS, L14/28, 24 Dec. 1836.
[47] HRO, Wilshere MSS, D/EX 14/3/12, 1 July 1838.
[48] Ibid., D/EX 14/3/33, 9 Oct. 1838.

Member of the Council whether they had received *their* election money?' Given such wholesale and completely above-board bribery, Bayly suggested that after paying the money this time, Wilshere should refuse in the future. 'Whenever an election again occurs, resist—open not a hotel, appoint not a chairman, or colour man— have no committee rooms—and give all to understand that if they spend any money they will not be repaid.' Why Bayly felt that Yarmouth voters would be any more amenable to not receiving their 2 guineas in the future than they were in 1841 is not clear, nor does it seem to have been likely. But by arguing this way, at least Bayly would collect the funds so immediately necessary to Whig fortunes and to his own well-being. He could worry about the next election, and the need to persuade Wilshere yet again to part with his gold, when it happened.[49]

What the two parties in Yarmouth never seem to have realized is that wholesale bribery is ineffective bribery, in fact, more than merely ineffective: wholesale bribery of the sort carried on at Yarmouth elections before and after Reform was almost entirely meaningless. The House of Commons committee chaired by Lord Francis Egerton which investigated allegations about Yarmouth corruption more than a decade after Reform did not hesitate to condemn electioneering in Yarmouth as patently illegal, but at the same time recognized the absurdity of identical bribes given to all and sundry. The committee concluded that bribery of the Yarmouth variety hardly deserved to be called bribery. Bribery so egregious could hardly have been less efficacious. It was almost wholesome. Since 'it had been an invariable practice to pay two guineas to each voter who applied for it, *and on each side of the question, whether the candidate won or lost*', elections in Yarmouth were expensive for the candidates but the political integrity of the elector remained unimpaired.[50] An elector's freedom of action and freedom of choice survived such bribery unscathed. Indeed, John Bayly recognized the inefficacy of bribery in reporting the state of the electorate to William Wilshere in 1841. He noted, having been over the register 'name by name', that the Whigs would win by '60 at least, if the Tories do not use *much* gold; and by 30 at least if they do so'.[51] Thus even if the Tories scrapped the standard formula of 2 guineas for exclusive Tory voting, which was countered by the Whigs' identical

[49] Ibid., D/EX 14/3/62, 28 Dec. 1841.   [50] Palmer, *History*, 237.
[51] HRO, Wilshere MSS, D/EX 14/3/52, 20 Feb. 1841.

offer, only a handful of Yarmouth's approximately 1,500 voters were thought to be susceptible.

Ironically, this kind of wholesale but completely equitable bribery seems to have affected the electoral process only by effectively countering the otherwise substantial obstacle to partisanship posed by the electorate's possession of the double vote. Bribery in Yarmouth actually assisted the political process by ensuring partisan voting. It did not matter which party a Yarmouth voter supported, since he could collect an identical fee from either side, but it did matter that he supported one side or the other. Neither party would offer more or less than the traditional fee. Yet while either party would reward a supporter with the standard 2-guinea fee, neither would prorate the fee for less than full support, a relatively common practice in many other constituencies where corruption flourished. A partisan plumper was guaranteed his 2 guineas despite his use of only one vote, *and* he could not increase the amount he stood to gain by offering both of his votes to the other side. As long as a voter cast a party vote, he could pocket his gold without demur. A splitter, on the other hand, could not collect 1 guinea from each side. A vote for either party was well rewarded; a vote for both parties carried no reward at all. With splitting saddled with such a severe economic disincentive, the voters could be expected to respond accordingly. And they did; virtually no one cast a split vote at any of these elections, unreformed or reformed. The truly remarkable partisan behaviour recorded at Yarmouth elections between 1818 and 1841, therefore, stemmed largely from wholesale bribery that, paradoxically, had no impact whatsoever on either the political principles of individual electors or the overall partisan division of the town except for the possibility that it strengthened both. Individuals accustomed to voting for one party or the other were more likely to develop partisan sensibilities than voters in towns where splitting and unnecessary plumping were common. By the same token, voters who invariably cast party ballots would certainly have been able to identify more readily with a particular party over time *if* they chose one over the other repeatedly. Nothing in the system itself encouraged consistent party voting, but for those who did support a particular party over time, for whatever reason, the system's additional encouragement to cast strictly partisan ballots might well have helped engender a form of partisan identification.

Moreover, from very early in the nineteenth century, Yarmouth voters attended closely to issues and debate. A letter to C. E. Rumbold from Dawson Turner marking the first anniversary of Rumbold's second return for the borough indicates attitudes antithetical to bribery. Turner admitted that Rumbold's initial victory stemmed 'more from an outburst of popular feeling and the demerits of another, more from any merits of your [Rumbold's] own'. In 1818 'only a vague idea prevailed with regard to your [Rumbold's] political principles', but by 1821 this lack of knowledge had been rectified.[52] And bribery was as common after Reform as it had been ubiquitous before.[53] Accounts for the election of 1832 reveal a complete obliviousness to the patent illegality of much of what passed for ordinary electioneering. For example, Samuel Tolver wrote to Adam Taylor complaining that the Blue party, and especially their agent Thomas Clowes, were 'behaving very shabbily and with much want of faith' in 'questioning the different items of the account'. He threatened a lawsuit to force the full payment of the account. Taylor wrote back to remind Tolver to be careful of the restrictions of 2 William IV, c. 45, section 71, adding 'you are no doubt quite aware of the penalties in *other* Acts of Parliament imposing on Sheriffs receiving fees'.[54] Tolver thanked Taylor for the reminder, but expressed his determination to collect the money owed. He claimed to be more than £10 out of pocket personally.

REFORM AMONG PARTISANS

Norman Gash dismissed Lewes as 'rotten to the core'.[55] Most accounts assess Great Yarmouth in equivalently negative language. Yet neither borough deserves such condemnation. Neither Lewes nor Great Yarmouth experienced any genuine alteration at the hands of Lord John Russell and company in 1832 because political developments in both towns since the later eighteenth century had created two antagonistic, extremely hostile camps warring under the banners of political parties that contested local and parliamentary elections alike. That their focuses were often more concerned with local than national issues mattered less than the intensity of local

---

[52] NRO, Rumbold MSS, L14/7, 10 Feb. 1821.
[53] *Norwich Mercury*, 8 Jan. 1835.
[54] NRO, Y/TC19/1/20–1.   [55] *Age of Peel*, 154.

feeling. The concerns of each electoral group at many unreformed elections might have appeared petty and provincial to outside observers, but the resulting polarization of the electorate was so intense that Reform could have little impact.

If Great Yarmouth's voters were affected by Whig reforms at all, it was the Municipal Corporations Act of 1835, not the Great Reform Act, that yielded results. The intensified local elections that resulted from the Act pushed partisanship further, if the enhanced τs and λs of 1835–7 and 1837–41 (Table 5.6) are any indication. And it was the Municipal Corporations Act that pushed another borough unaffected by Reform into partisanship. Lord John Russell's Bill failed to drag Beverley's electorate out of its traditional mould, but the 1835 reforms reshaped electoral behaviour even there.

6

Reform Retardant: Parliamentary and Municipal Reform in Beverley

ANALYSES of boroughs such as Bristol, Northampton, and Shrewsbury have pointed to the powerful effects of Reform. Paradoxically, the indifference to Reform shown by some voters in Lewes and Great Yarmouth revealed deep partisan divisions in some constituencies well in advance of 1832. Thus the evidence of electoral behaviour in all seven boroughs examined so far suggests a very Whiggish interpretation of popular politics in English boroughs in the early nineteenth century. Partisan politics, or something very much like it, already dominated some constituencies, but Reform helped push others into a decidedly more partisan mould. Beverley might be seen as the exception that proves the rule; Reform failed to alter traditional non-partisan voting habits there. Though Beverley was referred to as early as 1818 as 'an open borough and generally contested', its popular politics cannot withstand comparisons to towns such as Bristol, much less Lewes and Yarmouth.[1] Neither the Act nor the era could overcome Beverley's resistance to new modes of thought and behaviour. Other than reducing their numbers by disfranchising non-resident freemen, Reform had no measurable impact on the town's electors. They continued after 1832 to be dominated by considerations that had very little, perhaps nothing, to do with the parliamentary parties, specific issues, or political principles.

---

[1] *The Late Elections*, 13. Martin Casey of the History of Parliament has rescued this chapter from a number of blunders. Two recent accounts of 19th-cent. Beverley describe very different towns. David Neave, citing an 1834 account, characterized Beverley as 'on the threshhold of becoming a minor industrial town'. Conversely, Lucy Brown stressed Beverley's poverty and stagnation as she described a town almost completely dependent upon local agricultural business and 'a place without much money'. K. J. Allison (ed.), *The Victoria County History of Yorkshire* (London, 1990), vi. 118, 136–7.

Ironically, Beverley, like Northampton, never failed to contest a general election to the point of a poll.[2] Though far smaller than Northampton or Shrewsbury, Beverley's resident and non-resident freemen generated an electorate that outnumbered Shrewsbury's.[3] Nearly 1,300 men voted in 1818, and more than 1,400 participated in 1831. The disfranchisement of non-resident freemen in 1832 shrank Beverley's electorate to about 1,000.[4] Frequent electoral activity did nothing to improve Beverley's political reputation. Nor should it have, since the frequency of polls apparently did very little to enhance the political sophistication or awareness of Beverley's voters. They could stage a hotly contested election, but not infrequently money constituted the only fuel for electoral fires. Gold possesses strong catalytic properties in an apolitical medium. Elections bankrupted a number of candidates, including John Wharton. If Shrewsbury and Maidstone were not renowned for the purity of their elections, neither town could challenge Beverley's reputation for exceptional corruption. By 1870 some felt corruption to be so ingrained that 'it is impossible to arrest or counteract it'.[5]

Beverley's 1818 election illustrates the near irrelevance of parliamentary parties and national political issues. Structurally, the

[2] Beverley was unusual in the continuity of its elections in the early 19th-cent., failing to poll only five general elections between 1722 and 1831.

[3] In 1831 Beverley contained just over 8,000 inhabitants, growing from about 6,000 in 1811, and 6,700 in 1821. Three parishes encompassed the town: St Martin's and St Mary's, with large populations of about 3,000 each, and the tiny parish of St Nicholas, with fewer than 600. E. Baines, (ed.), *The History, Directory, and Gazetteer of the County of York* (Leeds, 1823); *The Parliamentary Gazetteer* (Glasgow, 1840).

[4] Nevertheless, most of Beverley's voters after 1832 were freemen. Crosby, *Parliamentary Record*, 141.

[5] Beverley's reputation for corruption, while in many ways deserved, rests to some extent on perfectly legitimate reimbursements of the travel expenses of non-resident freemen. At the election of 1826 e.g. the record of moneys disbursed by the Tory election agent Matthew Empson indicates a rate paid to voters that varied only according to the type of conveyance and distance travelled, with occasional *per diem* expenses included. For example, three men from the same town received different amounts because one travelled by steam packet (£1 10s.), another by outside mail coach (£1. 15s.), and another by inside mail coach (£3). Yet another hired a private coach and received £3 17s. The permissible expenses appear to have been well established in advance, and the payment of the money appears straightforward. HumRO, DDBC/22/10, 11, 29. Also *Parl. Pap.* 15 (1870), pp. vii, xxiii–xxxi. Burn, citing the investigation following the 1868 election that led to Beverley's disfranchisement, noted that of 104 found guilty of bribery, not one received money during the parliamentary election, 'but during the elections for the Town Council on the supposition that the convinced voters would remember their duty on a greater occasion'. W. L. Burn, 'Electoral Corruption in the Nineteenth Century', *Parliamentary Affairs* 4 (1951), 439.

election could not have been more conducive to strictly partisan voting. Two candidates from each party stood, but mere chance led to such propitious structural conditions. Beverley contained no organized parties. Individual decisions resulted in four candidates offering themselves who happened to represent equally the parliamentary parties. John Wharton, incumbent since 1790, returned from an extended trip abroad just in time to pay his debts from the previous election and announce his candidacy. Beverley's other incumbent resigned, and Robert Christie Burton, the son of General N. C. Burton (MP for Beverley in 1802 and unsuccessful candidate in 1806), announced for the seat. The younger Burton's candidacy cannot have been enhanced by his incarceration in the Fleet prison for debt at the time of his announcement, but a family member represented his interests pending the imprisoned candidate's release, possibly as a result of his election.[6]

Recognizing the dual vulnerability resulting from Burton's imprisonment and his failure to purchase his freedom from the Beverley Corporation (for the not inconsiderable sum of 200 guineas), Dymoke Wells quickly bought his own freedom and announced his candidacy for the seat Burton wished to occupy.[7] Wells happened to be a Whig and Burton happened to be a Tory, but pragmatism rather than party spirit led to Wells's decision to challenge his political opposite rather than his fellow Whig Wharton. The fourth candidate, alderman William Beverley, like Burton, never appeared personally, and like Burton, was a Tory.[8] Beverley's absence from the proceedings diminished his chances, but he provided a theoretical political balance, though neither Whigs nor Tories attempted to link the candidates of their ostensible parties. The candidates conducted completely separate and independent campaigns. Still, both votes could be cast for either party without penalty.

---

[6] *The Late Elections*, 13.

[7] Burton paid no money and was indeed elected without having the freeman status required of candidates, but he was sworn a free burgess two days after the election on 19 June 1818, again without the payment of fees. K. A. Macmahon (ed.), *Beverley Corporation Minute Books, 1707–1835* (London, 1958), 119. Henry Burton, R. C. Burton's relative, and Capel Cure were the last candidates to submit to such corporate robbery. The third candidate in 1830, Daniel Sykes, refused to pay, knowing that the Corporation could not enforce the payment. Sykes, who sat for Hull between 1820 and 1830, won the Beverley seat, but died in 1832. Ibid., pp. xii, 139.

[8] Beverley served as deputy mayor in 1815.

In such a political vaccuum the non-partisan behaviour of Beverley's electorate followed naturally. Nine of ten voters in 1818 recorded votes unaffected by partisan considerations. Nearly half split for the two original candidates, Wharton and Burton, despite their obvious political disparities (see Table 6.1). More revealing and far more damning in a partisan sense, most of the remaining voters plumped without partisan justification. In most boroughs the prospect of casting a plumper, however politically justifiable, created a serious dilemma. Conversely and surprisingly, voters in Beverley plumped by the hundreds without cause. The more than 200 who cast plumpers for the incumbent Wharton are more easily explained than the other 100 who plumped for either Burton or Wells. Some of those who plumped for Wharton might have been confused by the relative newness of the other candidates, but so many unnecessary plumpers strongly suggests that gold motivated a substantial number. Ironically, Burton may have owed his success to the selective application of the money that he lacked personally. The two unsuccessful candidates may not have had shallower pockets, but they failed to finance their campaigns sufficiently. Wells neglected to follow his original 200-guinea outlay (to purchase his freedom) with enough additional money to ensure victory since he relied heavily on Burton's ineligibility for a seat. And William Beverley's friends pursued his candidacy *in absentia* with less money than Burton's relatives.[9]

Nor could the remainder of Beverley's unreformed elections claim any more successfully to have been shaped by partisan political behaviour. Quite the contrary. Table 6.1 reveals a striking record of non-partisan electoral behaviour. The remainder of Beverley's unreformed contests involved three candidates, but the voters in 1818 had achieved such nearly unanimous non-partisan behaviour that the subsequent absence of a balanced ticket could hardly have led to a decline in partisanship. The shift to three-man contests, however, enhances the analytical perspective because three candidates theoretically gave voters an opportunity to cast politically motivated plumpers. Beverley's voters responded by casting far more non-partisan than partisan plumpers. Standard political labels fit some of the candidates so poorly that determining partisan plumpers is not

[9] Having won and lost a Beverley election, Burton died in 1822, leaving two new Tories to stand in 1826. G. P. Judd, *Members of Parliament, 1734–1832* (New Haven, Conn., 1955).

TABLE 6.1. *Split-Voting and Plumping in Beverley* (%)

Election year	1818	1820*	1826	1830**	1831	1832	1835	1837	1841
Split-voting	48.2	3.4	28.1	44.0	22.6	24.2	22.4	5.5	6.0
Partisan plumps	4-man	1.3	10.5	4.1	9.6	26.6	32.4	4-man	37.8
Unnecessary plumps	40.3	60.8	21.4	16.9	42.1	19.7	34.7	1.8	0.5

4-man Four candidates; politically motivated plumping not required.
* The poll book for 1820 recorded an unusual election at which the incumbent, R. C. Burton, attracted only 71 votes from the 1,203 men voting before the polls closed.
** For computational purposes, Henry Burton counted as a Whig in all elections.
Sources: Poll books.

always a simple matter, but even straightforward cases failed to evoke them. About 10 per cent of the voters plumped for the Whig, John Wharton, in 1826 when he stood alone, but half again as many (15 per cent) had plumped for him at the previous election when there was absolutely no partisan reason for doing so. Voters often simply ignored party ties, as did the candidates at many contests. Almost half of the electorate plumped unnecessarily for George Lane Fox in 1820, far more than cast Whig doubles.[10] At the other end of the political spectrum, electors behaved with no more partisan zeal. R. C. Burton attracted a pathetic total of seventeen plumpers from more than 1,300 voters when he stood as the lone Tory candidate in 1820.

This non-partisan behaviour reflected non-partisan electioneering. The first election to include more than a token discussion of political issues was 1826, when John Stewart's supporters printed flyers that referred to national political leaders and suggested that voters might be interested in a candidate's stand on slavery or religion.[11] Yet Stewart's relatively tolerant view of Catholicism, while not absolutely clear in 1826, alienated many Tories, and while he invoked famous political names, his candidacy also perpetuated partisan confusion by using blue ink for posters and by flying blue banners when crimson was Beverley's nominal Tory hue. If colours failed to serve their long-accepted function as a guide to party, it is easy to understand the confusion that might have dominated early elections in Beverley.

The behaviour of the Corporation suggests that religion helped blur partisan boundaries in Beverley. From the time of the formation of the Friends of the Established Church of England in 1790, a group sworn to oppose all efforts to repeal the Test and Corporation Acts, many residents of Beverley made their unyielding devotion to the Church known. Beginning in 1813, the Corporation's hostility shifted from Protestant Dissenters to a relentless petitioning campaign against 'the unceasing efforts of His Majesty's Roman Catholic subjects to be admitted into offices of the highest Trust and Power and even to sit in the Imperial Parliament to legislate for a

---

[10] Neave counted G. L. Fox as a Tory in 1820, but the standard parliamentary guides list him as a Whig. D. Neave, 'Beverley, 1700–1835', in Allison (ed.), *Yorkshire*, vi. 130. If Neave is correct, voters in Beverley were even more oblivious to party, since more than 400 doubled for Fox and Wharton while only 31 doubled for Fox and Burton. H. S. Smith, *Register*, 11.

[11] HumRO, DDBC/11/81/1, 4–6.

Protestant Church and State'.[12] Petitions to both Commons and Lords in 1813 initiated a series of vehement demands that Parliament 'resist those claims of His Majesty's Roman Catholic Subjects and continue those safeguards by which our invaluable constitution in Church and State has hitherto been preserved'. The Corporation seldom let a year pass without another expression of their concern; six additional petitions were sent before the double blow of repeal and Catholic emancipation rendered them moot.[13]

In this vehemently anti-Catholic milieu the religious attitudes of candidates might take precedence over all other considerations in the minds of many voters. Otherwise acceptable Tories could run afoul of their constituents in this area.[14] Henry Burton's views on this volatile issue also caused confusion and some consternation. Religion impeded partisanship, and the relative paucity of other issues exacerbated the effects of disunity and disorganization. Tory candidates stood independently and looked to their friends, not a local party, for victory. A blue-edged flyer issued from John Stewart's committee room stressed his solicitation of 'support *solely* for him, and unconnected with any other candidate'.[15] Tories won both seats in 1826, but their joint victory resulted from Beverley's rejection of the incumbent but financially embarrassed John Wharton rather than from Tory party activity.[16] Too many voters

[12] Macmahon (ed.), *Minute Books*, 109.

[13] Beverley submitted petitions against Roman Catholic demands and in favour of retaining the Test and Corporation Acts in 1813, 1819, 1821, 1822, 1823, 1825, 1827, and finally in Apr. 1828. The only other petitions generated by the town were a not very timely one concerning the abolition of the slave trade (11 July 1814) and a series of loyal addresses prompted by events in the lives of the royal family. The attacks on the monarch in 1817 and 1832 provoked particularly effusive missives, as did the disturbing events of 1819 and 1820. Ibid. 109, 120–6, 131, 135–7.

[14] Stewart's support of Sir Francis Burdett's motion for the relief of Ireland in 1827 may have helped create Beverley's confused electoral milieu despite the fact that Burdett's bill actually proposed the disfranchisement of Ireland's 40-shilling freeholders.

[15] HumRO, DDBC/11/81/4. Seven different Stewart election posters have survived. The refrain of a typical Stewart song is strongly reminiscent of an earlier, simpler, non-partisan political system:

> Drink to Liverpool, Huskisson, Canning and Peel,
> And to all who have hearts warm with patriot zeal,
> And TRUE BLUE with STEWART, our friend, that's your sort,
> We'll steer him right safe within the Parliamentary Port.

[16] A letter soliciting the candidacy of Capel Cure in Sept. 1830 is the first hint of what may have been Tory party activity in Beverley. The letter made it clear that Cure would be expected to support retrenchment and reduction of governmental

plumped unnecessarily for one or the other to believe that anyone saw the election in terms other than those specified by Stewart himself. Each candidate attracted whatever support he could in whatever manner he could attract it. Partisan consciousness and party activity seemed equally absent.

Beverley's non-partisan behaviour persisted at the next contest, and the two that followed. The results of the 1830 election should be difficult to interpret because of the politically enigmatic Henry Burton, whose candidacy may have helped perpetuate non-partisan voting in Beverley by blurring the distinctions between the national parties.[17] Standard parliamentary guidebooks listed Burton as a Whig, which he probably was after the Reform Act, but in 1830 his political preferences were not clear. The summary statistics included in Tables 6.1 and 6.2 have counted Burton as a Whig, but fortunately, Burton's partisan ambiguity does not impede an analysis of electoral behaviour in the least, because equally large numbers of voters doubled Burton/Sykes (Whig) and Burton/Cure (Tory).[18] Another sizeable contingent plumped for one of the three candidates, leaving the unmistakable conclusion that non-partisan voting dominated the election, wherever Burton should be placed. A contemporary observer claimed in 1829 that Beverley contained 'two conflicting parties', but the voters seemed unaware of their existence.[19]

Burton, now an incumbent, can be counted more assuredly as a Whig in 1831, but as in 1830 Beverley's voters behaved in such a determinedly non-partisan fashion that Burton's party matters very little analytically. Fewer voters joined Burton with the Tory candidate, than with the Whig in 1831, but non-partisan voting

expenditure, but it did not use the term 'party', nor identify the 46 signatories (including Conservative electoral agent Matthew Empson) as other than 'friends'. HumRO, DDBC/22/36–7. An election cartoon portrayed Wharton's former campaign manager John Barnby as a treacherous cur for deserting his master. Bankrupted at last by Beverley's insatiable avarice, Wharton ended his life imprisoned for debt. The cartoon may have been the original for an election poster, but if so no published version has survived. HumRO, DDBC/11/71.

[17] David Neave counts Burton as a Tory in 1830. The standard guides list him as a Whig, which he undoubtedly became, even if he had not always been so. Neave, 'Beverley, 1700–1835', 130.

[18] At the 1830 election 456 voters joined Burton with Sykes while 502 joined Burton with Cure. Another 197 voters plumped for Sykes, 69 plumped for Cure, and 93 plumped for Burton.

[19] G. Oliver, *The History of Beverley* (Beverley, 1829), 413. See also G. Poulson, *Beverlac* (London, 1829).

continued to dominate the election.[20] The last election of the old order is indistinguishable from the first examined. The debate over the Reform Bill generated no more partisanship than other issues. In the midst of a national demand for Reform and a general election that had turned into a pure referendum in many constituencies, most voters in Beverley maintained old patterns.

Not until the first reformed election did any sign of partisan political life emerge among the electorate in Beverley, and even then the signs were anaemic. The Great Reform Act's meagre impact appears in Table 6.1 as an increase in the number of partisan plumpers in 1832, as a sizeable group of electors cast plumpers for the solitary Tory candidate Charles Winn, who had lost the previous year. Winn's Tory supporters spared no efforts to capture the seat. Intense canvassing ensured that no potential supporter was over-looked. Attesting the thoroughness of their efforts are surviving lists of (1) unpromised voters, (2) half-unpromised voters, (3) outvoters who lived within the statutory seven-mile limit, (4) householders to be registered, (5) names against which objections were to be raised when they attempted to register, (6) names of non-voters who might still reside in Beverley, and (7) Whig plumpers who might be called upon to give their other vote to the Tories.[21] Rather than allowing the Reform Act to dominate the election completely, the Tories circulated rabidly anti-Catholic broadsheets that described one of the Whigs as a Catholic candidate who subscribed to the old persecuting principles of 'Lateran, Constance, and Trent'. These broadsheets denounced the role of the Pope in English affairs and described in detail the Pope's oath, bishop's oath, and priest's oath in an effort to persuade the voters that Roman Catholicism severely jeopardized English liberties. Also taking a paternalist, agrarian stance, the Tories argued that in addition to defending the Protestant religion, their candidate, Winn, could be counted upon to ameliorate the lot

[20] Three hundred and thirty-eight voters in 1831 joined Burton with Marshall, both nominal Whigs; 171 combined Burton with Winn, the clear Tory; 54 joined Marshall, undoubtedly a Whig, with Winn, while no fewer than 623 plumped for one of the three candidates. It could be argued, perhaps, that Marshall's 327 plumpers came from voters who wanted to be sure that they were supporting reformers exclusively. Burton's vote on the first Reform Bill is not clear from the record.

[21] Voter list after voter list containing notes on non-voters, names against which objections were to be raised, householders to be registered, and promises (either full or half) given indicate the intensity of the Tory electioneering that failed, as it had in 1831. HumRO, DDBC/22/72–114. Orange became the Radical Reform colour in both Beverley and Hull. Johnson, *The Man with Forty Crowns*, 197.

of factory children, maintain the county's agricultural interests (since Winn himself was a landed proprietor), and abolish slavery.

The Tory appeal to other issues met with limited success. More than twice as many voters were willing to plump for Winn in the first reformed election than had been willing to do so under virtually identical structural circumstances just a year earlier. The elimination of non-resident freemen in 1832 made the absolute increase in Winn's plumper support more difficult to achieve. Only 116 voters (10 per cent) plumped for him in 1831, and while the total number of voters actually declined by 20 per cent (1,204 to 971), more than 250 (27 per cent) plumped for Winn in 1832. The increase was as significant as it was substantial; this election finally broke the apolitical pattern of so many previous elections, at least in one area.

Turning from the static assessments of voting behaviour in Table 6.1 to a diachronic view reinforces the impression created by the increased level of partisan plumping in 1832. Clearly, the Beverley electorate did not escape the Reform era entirely unaffected. The two measures of electoral behaviour reported in Table 6.2 do not present a completely congruent picture of electoral change, but both measures suggest increasing consistency as a result of Reform. λ indicates a much stronger and perhaps more suddenly developed relationship between electoral choices after 1832. The achievement of at least a weak relationship (>0.2 but <0.3) twice before 1832 is discounted by the negligible relationship (0.06) of voting choices at the elections of 1830 and 1831. Conversely, according to λ, the Reform Act seems to have established a persistent though only moderate relationship (>0.3) between a voter's choices at successive elections until the much more dramatic change after 1837, when scores for Beverley finally resembled their counterparts in Maidstone, Shrewsbury, and elsewhere. Table 6.1 indicated a striking shift in electoral behaviour beginning not in 1832, but in 1837. λ reinforces that image.

Kendall's τ_b indicates a more gradual change in Beverley's electorate, the beginnings of which are visible as early as 1830 and the end of which is not visible since these τs continued to increase with the last pair of elections examined. Beverley's voters clearly failed to develop the very strong, persistent partisan link evident in the other boroughs, but the scores in the >0.6 range found at the first three reformed elections suggest that voters were not behaving in a political vacuum. Their counterparts in Maidstone were

TABLE 6.2. *Electoral Behaviour across Elections in Beverley:* λ *(Asymmetric) and* τ_b

Election Years	1818–20	1820–6	1826–30	1830–1	1831–2	1832–5	1835–7	1837–41
λ	0.17	0.19	0.24	0.06	0.27	0.38	0.37	0.61
τ_b	0.22	0.21	0.34	0.43	0.51	0.63	0.60	0.73

behaving in a similar fashion as early as 1830, and most other towns achieved 𝜏s in that range by 1831. Moreover, voters in other boroughs moved on to substantially stronger relationships very quickly. Despite this, the relationship between successive voting choices in Beverley showed some improvement after 1832, and at these levels of political consistency, party considerations cannot be discounted completely. If partisan development was delayed in Beverley, it was not missing altogether.

The clarification of Beverley's political environment that accompanied Henry Burton's solid attachment to the Whig party after Reform helped to some extent. Two voters help illustrate this change. One of them, John Abbott, an innkeeper in Beckside, split his votes in 1830 and 1831 between Henry Burton and the unmistakable Tory candidate. In 1832 Abbott could have continued to split for Burton and Winn as he had done in 1831, but instead he plumped for the lone Tory, Winn. He followed this politically correct vote with another Tory plump in 1835 when he helped place James Wier Hogg atop the poll. Abbott may have been politicized by the Reform Act, but he may also have been a moderate Tory for some time who was unsure about Burton's position. Another Beverley voter, entirely inappropriately named Charles James Fox, a watchmaker who lived in Saturday-Market, behaved identically. Like Abbott, he also supported Burton along with the Tory candidate at each of Beverley's last two unreformed elections. After 1832 Fox, like Abbott, plumped for the sole Tory. Fox's post-Reform 'partisan' behaviour may have stemmed from a new awareness of partisan demands when a party nominated a single candidate, or it may have indicated an end to his uncertainty about Burton. In either case, the behaviour of Abbott and Fox reflected the general change in the electorate after 1832 which suggests a heightened political awareness on the part of a rather large portion of Beverley's electorate.

These comparative figures for election sequences, therefore, must be interpreted cautiously. Some of the increased 'continuity' stems from the problematic measurement of political choices in Beverley. Also, some of the political 'consistency' across elections in Beverley resulted from electors consistently making apolitical choices.[22] Until

---

[22] Oddly enough, Seymour identified Beverley as one of only eight towns after 1832 in which artisans accounted for an absolute majority of the population. *Electoral Reform*, 89. Householders comprised only 14% of the new electorate.

several years after Reform, Beverley contained too few men like John Abbott and Charles James Fox and too many men like Joseph Baitson (or Bateson), a miller living in Butcher Row. Baitson failed the test of partisanship by casting three successive unnecessary plumpers for Henry Burton in 1830, 1831, and 1832. Only in 1835, when he cast a non-partisan split for Burton and James Wier Hogg, was Baitson's behaviour reflected accurately in Table 6.2. Yet because Baitson's first three votes were consistent, his behaviour artificially enhanced the overall partisan appearance of Beverley's electorate.

However striking the increase in partisan plumping in 1832, as reported in Table 6.1, and however noticeable the increase in levels of consistent behaviour reported after 1832 in Table 6.2, much about Beverley's first reformed election reflected the non-partisan atmosphere so evident before 1832. The voters faced a straightforward choice which almost duplicated the previous election. The Tory, Winn, stood against two Whigs who refused to stand together. Winn seized every opportunity to tar both of his opponents with the same brush, and he applied the tar indiscriminately. By playing the anti-Catholic and agricultural protection cards, Winn set his candidacy well apart from those of his Whig opponents and presented voters with a stark contrast between himself and the reformers. It should not have mattered that the Whigs, Henry Burton and Charles Langdale, refused to stand together on a united Reform ticket. The voters should have been able to distinguish Winn's position easily enough. And under these explicitly partisan conditions, if more by default than by design, Beverley's voters might have been expected to fall into party voting.

But it did matter in Beverley that Burton and Langdale stood separately, and many voters did not cast party votes. Almost a quarter of the electorate split while another fifth plumped without partisan justification. Reform itself passed almost without notice.[23] Ancient-right voters dominated the electorate well into the reign of Victoria. In stark contrast to Maidstone, where the new voters outnumbered the old as soon as Reform Bill became the Reform Act, only about 14 per cent of the Beverley electorate voted in the 1832 election as a direct result of the Act, and their relative proportion grew only marginally to 18 per cent by 1841. Thus the electors of

---

[23] Allison (ed.), *Yorkshire*, vi. 118, 136–7.

1832 were, for the most part, the electors of 1831, and their behaviour in 1832 could almost be mistaken for their behaviour in 1831. Voters casting both votes for the Whigs returned Langdale and Burton, but a quarter of Beverley's voters continued to split.

Party organizers had even greater cause to be exasperated with voters who plumped in defiance of slates. Particularly in the enhanced partisan environment of reformed England, plumping without cause implied that voters actively rejected the demands of the party that they otherwise gave the appearance of supporting. Their support was tainted, quite possibly fatally, because the vote they chose to waste could otherwise have been put to good use. Having made what often amounted to extraordinary efforts to field two candidates, party leaders could not afford to have their potential partisans ignore one candidate or the other. It was essential that each elector tender both votes. As a result, a more revealing measure of the determined persistence of non-partisan behaviour in Beverley is the 20 per cent of the electorate who plumped indefensibly and inexplicably for one of the Whig candidates. Langdale attracted more single votes than the incumbent Burton, for some reason unconnected with party, but neither group of plumpers could have defended their decisions politically. Despite Reform, one in five participants at the 1832 contest failed to recognize the irrationality of a Whig plump, and another one in four refused to choose one party or the other. Counting all non-partisan choices together, almost half of the electorate did not respond to the new political environment. Though Reform altered some political behaviour in Beverley, far too many 'reformed' electors retained unreformed attitudes and persisted in the patterns of voting behaviour learned over many hotly contested but usually apolitical elections. Old habits died a harder death in Beverley than in many other boroughs.

So ingrained were these habits that they continued to dominate electoral behaviour at Beverley's second reformed election in 1835. The proportion of the electorate choosing to cast partisan votes actually declined slightly between the first and second reformed elections despite the new Beverley Political Union and the new Reform Association.[24] A new but solitary Tory candidate, James

---

[24] Beverley's Political Union preceded a Reform Association by two years. T. Perronet Thompson attended the formation of the Beverley Reform Association shortly after his narrow victory at the Hull election of 1835. Johnson, *The Man with Forty Crowns*, 197. In an effort to attract the lesser sort, the Beverley Conservative

Wier Hogg, managed to persuade nearly a third of the electorate to vote only for him, yet Hogg's necessary plumpers were outnumbered slightly by unnecessary Whig plumpers. The apparent competence and determination of the Tory electoral agent, solicitor Matt Empson, helps explain Tory success in attracting plumpers in both 1832 and 1835.[25] At the same time, though, the extravagant spending habits of Hogg, a nabob just returned from India, casts a suspicious hue over many of the Tory plumps of 1835.[26] Whatever their reasons, the supporters of this sole Tory candidate gave the appearance of behaving in a partisan fashion while much of the remainder of the electorate failed the test. Still, more than one in five Beverley electors split their votes, and even worse, more than one in three plumped without cause. This plethora of plumps placed Hogg at the head of the poll, followed relatively closely by Henry Burton, who retained his seat. The second Whig candidate, Joseph Sykes, lost because most of Beverley's splitters coupled Hogg with Burton.

MUNICIPAL REFORM: THE MERGER OF PARLIAMENTARY AND MUNICIPAL POLITICS

The real transformation of electoral behaviour in Beverley occurred between the elections of 1835 and 1837. Finally, Beverley's electorate began to behave in every respect like the voters in Maidstone and elsewhere as voters discarded almost completely their non-partisan habits in favour of party voting. After sitting in four Parliaments, the Whig incumbent, Henry Burton, abandoned Beverley. The other incumbent, Hogg, stood again, with another Tory, George Lane Fox, giving Beverley two Tory candidates for the

Association required a subscription of only a shilling per quarter, but the great majority of those on the rolls contributed a half-guinea or more. HumRO, DDBC/10/ 1, 2.

[25] HumRO, DDBC/22/6–142.

[26] Hogg studied for the Irish Bar at Gray's Inn. He left for India in 1814, practised before the Calcutta Bar until 1822, and served as registrar of the Supreme Court of Calcutta from 1822 until his return to England in 1833. Hogg's net worth cannot be calculated easily, but the profits accruing from his continuing involvement in the India trade stagger the imagination. His credit in Fergusson Brothers in 1844 from the manufacture and sale of indigo amounted to 277,348 Calcutta rupees (approximately £30,000 sterling). India Office, MSS EUR. E.342.19. According to the accounts of Sir George Robinson, Sicca rupees exchanged at 2s. 6d. Ibid., F. 142. 10.

first time since 1826. Two Whigs, both strangers, also announced, creating an unusually balanced contest. The return of both Tories at this election was never in much doubt. Part of the continuing national shift to the Tories that had begun with a vengeance in 1835, Hogg and Fox took an early lead and kept it.

Far more important than the result was the nature of the vote. As Table 6.1 indicates, partisanship emerged for the first time in 1837. Voters appeared to recognize the previously rejected link between candidates of the same parliamentary party. Balanced slates eliminated the necessity of partisan plumpers, the only area in which Beverley had shown any partisan feeling previously, but the other evidence is overwhelming. Reform may have been enough to make partisans out of men like Charles James Fox and John Abbott, but it failed to affect the behaviour of too many others. Frederick Campbell, an attorney living in Lady Gate who gained his franchise in 1832 as a householder, plumped unnecessarily in 1832 and 1835, as did John Crosskill, a whitesmith of Lairgate. Crosskill's neighbour, Robert Constable, a labourer, continued to split his votes at those elections, as did Robert Cressey, a breechesmaker who, like Campbell, lived in Lady Gate. All four men, and many others like them, whether householders or ancient-right voters, cast their first strictly partisan parliamentary votes in 1837.

Only forty-five men linked Hogg with one of the Whigs while nine others joined a vote for Fox and one of the Whigs. These voters accounted for less than 6 per cent of the electorate. More impressive yet was the near elimination of unnecessary plumpers. In 1835 no fewer than 331 men, more than a third of the electorate, cast plumpers for one of the two Whig candidates. In 1837, one man cast a Whig plumper. Eleven others voted for Hogg alone and six for Fox, for a grand total of eighteen, fewer than 2 per cent of all voters. The voters of 1837 hardly resembled the voters of 1835, yet they were the same men. Something had pushed Beverley into the partisan mould evident elsewhere five to six years earlier.

This transformation did not stem from the rare four-candidate structure of the election. Such a contest had not been fought since 1818, and certainly a balanced ticket made it easier for the voters to support either party fully, but Beverley's electors had never shared the loathing of plumpers so common in England's other boroughs. Quite the contrary. Their penchant for casting politically indefensible plumpers had proven perhaps the most tenacious obstacle to partisan behaviour. Moreover, the change apparent in 1837 persisted when Beverley reverted to a three-man contest in 1841. No one cast unnecessary plumpers while almost 40 per cent of the entire electorate cast partisan plumpers, demonstrating convincingly that something other than structure changed Beverley at this late date.

Beverley's political awakening can be traced to the fundamental alteration of local politics as a result of the Municipal Corporations Act. The political line of demarcation so noticeably absent in Beverley prior to 1835 was drawn through the community by the opening up of the Corporation. Impervious to the demands of party in the years before, during, and immediately after the passage of the Great Reform Act, this second political reform changed the attitudes of many voters towards political parties in municipal and parliamentary politics simultaneously. Nor would this result of municipal reform have come as a surprise to Joseph Parkes, the principal architect and orchestrator of the 1835 bill, or his enemies. The Tories believed that the bill was generally 'ruinous to Conservative interests'. Municipal reform was nothing more than a 'party job, intended . . . to destroy the Conservative party in this country. It was a Whig measure—Whig in its principle, Whig in its character, and Whig in its object.' Moreover, the bill 'would exclude in a great measure the Tories . . . from borough representation'.[27]

The most dire predictions about the impact of municipal reform were made before the Lords rescued the freeman franchise from destruction, but their failure to prevent the enfranchisement of all householders paying rates for three years somewhat tarnished their success in rescuing the freemen. Parkes himself found the householder suffrage provision more than an ample trade-off for the survival of the freemen. The broader borough franchise augured well for Whig/Radical candidates standing for the new councils, and the augury proved accurate. Radicals were 'in the seventh heaven of delight at the success of their comrades' when the results of the first reformed municipal elections became known in January 1836.[28]

---

[27] B. G. A. M. Finlayson, 'The Politics of Municipal Reform', *English Historical Review*, 81 (1966), 677–8, 680. Though not able to win an outright majority and permit the continuation of Peel's ministry, Peel's supporters gained almost 100 additional seats in the Commons, frightening many Whigs who saw sweeping municipal reform, written as a Whig measure for Whig ends, as a means of preventing a Tory resurgence.

[28] Ibid. 689, cited from *The Times*, 4 Jan. 1836.

Beverley was one of the reasons for Whig jubilation: Whigs controlled Beverley's new town council in 1836. Though their success was fleeting, and Whig inferences of perpetual success from their huge national victory in 1835 proved to be badly mistaken, the general impact of municipal reform could hardly be exaggerated. It transformed the relationship between townsmen and the political parties in both their parliamentary and local guises. On the other hand, the influence of municipal reform on the future success of party ventures was more complicated and less predictable than the Whigs thought. Municipal reform politicized the electorate, but as much as the Whigs (and Radicals) wanted to believe otherwise, the politicization was bipartisan. The second round of reform benefited Whigs in the first municipal elections in many boroughs where inhabitants had been either actually or effectively disfranchised for generations, but the initial spate of victories had little predictive value.[29] After their initial disaster in open elections for the first town council, the Tories quickly recovered and reaped a positive long-term-effect reward.[30] Tories and Whigs alike benefited from municipal partisanship.

The dramatic effect of the Municipal Reform Act upon Beverley is easily explained. Unlike Maidstone, where well-organized political parties actively contested local as well as parliamentary elections for decades before the Whig reforms of the 1830s, Beverley had no significant experience with local partisan political battles until 1835. Without doubt, the Great Reform Act stimulated party development to some degree, but even the critical registration process, which could determine an election before it happened, failed to shake the borough out of its old habits. Too much remained the same. The only available political prizes, the two parliamentary seats, were an insufficient inducement for the kind of frenetic activity that made politics meaningful to ordinary voters. The prospect of a general election that might lie several years in the future was too insubstantial on the one hand, and too ephemeral on the other, to generate meaningful party activity in the interstices. The lack of a

---

[29] Whigs and Radicals have been equated for this analysis.

[30] No poll book exists for the 1835 council election, but a broadsheet issued the day after the election listed all the candidates and the results of the poll. No fewer than 156 candidates appear on the list, and nearly 40 men received at least 50 votes in an election at which just over 80 votes won a seat. At the other extreme, 15 candidates received a single vote apiece, and another 64 won fewer than 10 votes each. HumRO, DDBC/11/86, Broadsheet published 26 Dec. 1835.

local partisan press also retarded the development of local conflicts that could be translated easily into votes. In order to unlearn the behavioural patterns acquired during decades of non-partisan contests, Beverley's voters needed better prizes and more opportunities. Parliamentary reform generated neither; municipal reform generated both.

Though not completely closed prior to 1835, Beverley's Corporation hardly served as a model of participatory politics. Freemen theoretically possessed the right to elect a mayor each year from the town's thirteen aldermen and the privilege of 'shouting in' by acclamation the thirteen capital burgesses who comprised the other part of the Corporation from a list of twenty-six names proposed by the mayor and aldermen. In practice, neither process much resembled an election. The mayor selected the thirteen sitting capital burgesses, or chambermen. Since all municipal 'elections' could be conducted only by that portion of the commonalty who happened to be present, without any provision for a formal poll that would have broadened the base of participation, municipal elections in Beverley hardly deserved to be called such. The Corporation encountered little opposition to its wishes and would not have tolerated more than token electoral involvement. Those few instances in which issues arose do not seem to have deviated substantially from the standard 'selection' façade.[31] Growing dissatisfaction with the Corporation led to a few unpleasant incidents as early as 1828.[32] The mayoral election of 1830, for example, involved handbills that raised the anti-Catholic banner as clearly as it was raised in parliamentary elections.[33] Parliamentary reform heightened the potential for conflict. The creation of a Reform Society shortly after the 1832 election played a role in the unusually strong protest against the traditional selection process during the annual 'elections' in September 1833.[34] But the Reform Society could not hope to achieve much at the annual municipal ritual until the destruction of the old Corporation.

[31] HumRO, DDBC/27/113; *Squibs and Handbills relating to Mayor Choosing at Beverley* (Beverley, 1824).

[32] The incumbent mayor in 1828, John Williams, attempted to limit the choice of mayor to two names rather than all 13 aldermen. A crowd of freemen protested without success. HumRO, DDBC/11/83–4.

[33] An 1830 handbill for Samuel Hall, mayor in 1829, identified Hall as an ardent supporter of the 'true Protestant Church, and the British Constitution'. HumRO, DDBC/11/85. See also *Parl. Pap.* 5 (1835), 1454–9.

[34] HumRO, DDBC/27/5–6.

The parliamentary election of 1835 occurred months before the demise of the old Corporation. Reform was being pursued by the Whig Ministry through the accumulation of damning evidence about the Corporations, but Beverley's Corporation still appeared intact and inviolate in January. Whatever the voters missed in the way of propaganda and polemic early in 1835, however, they received, and more, in the last six months of the year. A voluminous assortment of handbills, open letters, placards, and the like, reminiscent of the most viciously contested parliamentary election, blanketed Beverley from June until December. The town's MPs stood on opposite sides of the issue, as would be expected from a split delegation, and their names and positions took pride of place in the propaganda war. Reform now assumed a local flavour, but local Tories attacked reform in both its 1832 and 1835 manifestations. Arguing that anyone who supported either bill stood squarely against the interests of Beverley's freemen, a vivid red and black poster argued that the Municipal Corporations Bill added 'INSULT to ROBBERY'. Unlike his Whig colleague, Hogg would not stand for it:

> No trifling reform Mr Hogg does pretend,
> He'll be firm to your interest and true to each friend.[35]

The Tories had not bothered particularly to tar Burton with the Reform brush in either 1831 or 1832, but they now condemned his role in passing the Great Reform Act and in supporting this new, more pernicious, Whig effort. When Parliament passed the Municipal Corporations Act, leaving no alternative but compliance, the existing Corporation decided to cancel its regular September selection since elections for the new council would be held in December.[36] It was this extended political fight over and stemming from municipal reform, not the debate over parliamentary reform or the Reform Act itself, that politicized the electorate and forced them into step with their counterparts in so many other towns. From December 1835 onward, Beverley's two parties competed constantly. The parliamentary parties now had important, permanent, local manifestations.

Changes not directly attributable to municipal reform took on new meaning once the 1835 Act engendered local partisan battles. For example, voter registration requirements preceded the creation of the town council by three years, but now the effort to register (at a

---

[35] HumRO, DDBC/11/87, 90.   [36] Macmahon (ed.), *Minute Books*, 149.

cost of 1 shilling) all supporters well in advance of an actual election took on new meaning. The registration requirement created some party activity as early as 1832 because most partisans understood that failure to register voters could mean that a party could lose an election by default. In order to ensure their candidate (or candidates) a reasonable chance once the polling began, party agents had to endeavour to register every potential supporter. No matter how comfortable a party's lead at any election, failure to attract and register enough potential new supporters to offset the registration of potential opponents could mean political disaster at a subsequent contest. The annual revision of the electoral register, therefore, could be as important as the actual poll. Diligence and persistence were essential. But in the years immediately after 1832, neither party in Beverley possessed the necessary experience and drive to take advantage of the revisions. The added incentive of municipal reform meant that struggles over revisions quickly developed a new level of sophistication. After municipal reform, both parties immediately began using printed forms for registering voters. By 1838, both parties had begun to use pre-printed forms for objections.[37] Reformed municipal elections created a constant demand for party activity. Calls for annual Parliaments had always fallen on deaf ears, but the Municipal Corporations Act achieved locally what would never be established nationally. Every winter the parties faced another election, and intense efforts to register sympathetic voters were continuous. Municipal elections were as certain and as regular as Guy Fawkes Day. Any delay, any lapse, could spell defeat. The certainty and complexity of municipal elections required constant attention.

The use of printed forms in registering and opposing new electors illustrates the new sophistication and organization of the parties, but another kind of printed form played a crucial role in the reorientation of politics after 1835. Both the frequency and certainty of municipal elections helped politicize the electorate and contributed to the rapid development of party organizations, but municipal elections also affected politics fundamentally because of their complexity. At parliamentary contests before 1835, Beverley's voters could not seem to remember which candidates stood for which party, much less which candidates stood together.[38] With no experience in voting at

---

[37] HumRO, DDBC/11/90–90a; DDBC/27/368–75; DDBC/22/105–07.

[38] Studies of municipal voting in Maidstone have shown the partisan ease with

elections involving many candidates, their ability to cope with the demands of complicated ballots was very much in doubt. If parliamentary elections with their maximum of two seats and three or four candidates posed problems, the mind boggled at the voters' likely response to the new council's eighteen seats (nine from each of two wards) and, in the first contest, no fewer than 156 candidates. The 1835 council election was a party organizer's worst nightmare come true.

Many of those who stood for the council had absolutely no chance of success. Fifteen of them received but a single vote, probably their own. Yet no distinct line of demarcation separated the serious candidates from the others. A wide gulf separated the top of the poll from the middle, but a surprisingly large number of votes also separated successful candidates. William Brigham, a reformer, topped the poll in St Mary's ward with 215 votes, while Edward Page, also a reformer, managed to win the last seat in the ward with only eighty-eight votes, barely edging out his closest opponent, a Conservative, with eighty-seven votes. The reformers swept St Mary's and won most (at least six) of the seats in Minster ward at this first election. Yet the Whigs could take little comfort from a victory in an event that resembled a circus more than an election.[39] Their success was a gift, not an achievement.

Both parties responded to these extraordinary new circumstances by restructuring their approaches to elections. The second set of municipal elections (to elect three councillors per ward) elicited slates of clearly identified candidates for all three seats falling vacant. Theoretically, voters retained as much political mobility as they had possessed at the first of these new elections. In practice, however, the identification of party slates reshaped municipal elections. Now electors could not help but be aware of opposing candidates being offered by each of the local parties. In this new environment a

which voters could respond to large numbers of candidates and seats even in the 18th cent. if slates were clearly identified. The organization of poll books often facilitated the casting of straight party ballots. J. A. Phillips, 'Municipal Matters'; id., 'Electoral Polarization'.

[39] The announcement of election results in 1835 did not specify party affiliations. The affiliations of the successful candidates were determined by examining their votes at the parliamentary elections of 1835 and 1837, a perfectly satisfactory solution for most of those involved. The party preferences of William Hodgson and William Farrah, however, cannot be determined with certainty since more than one person with those names lived and voted in Beverley.

straight party ballot was expected and may have been the easiest course of action. Party voting may not have been mandated, but certainly it was greatly facilitated by the need to create some order out of the potential electoral chaos. Partisan awareness must have been greatly enhanced by the entire process.

Beverley's electorate responded immediately and overwhelmingly. The figures for parliamentary elections in Table 6.1 and the cross-election comparisons on Table 6.2 leave little doubt about the transforming impact of municipal reform on the electorate. Following the divisive and bitter struggle over municipal reform, the voting choices of the electors at the parliamentary contest hardly resembled their choices just months earlier. The number of splitters in 1837 fell by three-quarters. One-nineteenth as many voters cast unnecessary plumps. Most of the voters had followed non-partisan ways less than three years earlier, yet they now resembled their counterparts in boroughs like Maidstone and Shrewsbury. And their new partisan postures persisted.

The issues involved in local and parliamentary elections were, with some exceptions, perceived to be the same. Candidates standing for the council espoused a party line virtually indistinguishable from that taken by candidates for Parliament. Pennock Tigar used his status as a vehement advocate of parliamentary reform to boost his successful candidacy for the council in 1835. Though William Oxley stood only for a council seat in St Mary's ward in 1837, he claimed to be a 'Genuine Radical Reformer'.[40] Both parties set up ward committees to supervise local registration, and central committees to plan for parliamentary as well as council elections. Equally remarkably, voters in Beverley also turned in determinedly partisan performances at the municipal elections of 1837. Though not quite reaching the partisan heights attained at the parliamentary election, 84 per cent of the municipal electors voted exclusively and fully for the Conservative or Radical slate.

Moreover, remarkable party loyalty linked the parliamentary election of July 1837 and the city elections in December. Almost all (96 per cent) of those casting party votes at the municipal election who can be found on the earlier parliamentary poll book cast consistent straight party votes. Only a tiny handful of the men who were municipal partisans had either split or voted for the opposite

[40] HumRO, DDBC/11/86; DDBC/27/97.

party in July.[41] The only other extant municipal poll book for this period confirms the pattern so strikingly in evidence in 1837.[42] More than 90 per cent of the municipal electorate cast strictly partisan votes in 1841, and of those who can be traced to the parliamentary poll books that year, the overwhelming majority (over 75 per cent) cast party ballots for the party they supported in the municipal contest of that year. Clearly, the newly partisan choices of Beverley's electors were closely related at both types of elections, across elections of each type, and across types as well as across elections. Indeed, by any measure of partisan behaviour, the impact on the electorate of the elimination of the old Corporation far exceeded the impact of reforming Parliament.

SOCIAL AND ECCLESIASTICAL CONSIDERATIONS

Among the eight successful Radical candidates standing for Minster ward in Beverley's initial council elections was Gillyat Sumner, described in the poll book as a 'gentleman'. The only Conservative candidate to win a seat, John Brownrigg, also called himself a 'gentleman'. Did these self-ascribed titles by two victorious candidates of opposing political views reflect socio-economic parity between the two late-developing parties? Sumner actually made a far more convincing claim to gentle status than his Conservative opponent, Brownrigg. Both Gillyat Sumners, snr. and jnr., had used the title 'gentleman' in the poll book of 1818. The senior Sumner ceased to participate in elections by 1830, but his son continued to call himself a gentleman at election after election. The two John Brownriggs,

[41] Approximately 85% of the straight party municipal voters can be traced to the parliamentary poll book. Given that straight party voters also accounted for 84% of all municipal votes cast, the straight party municipal voters constituted nearly three-quarters of the parliamentary electorate.

[42] Shrewsbury showed even greater sophistication by using paper ballots upon which the names of the entire party slate had been printed in advance. Voters were not compelled to use these printed slate ballots. Other paper ballots were available upon which no candidates' names appeared, allowing voters to write in each of the six names they preferred. Alternatively, a voter could choose to use a printed ballot if it was more convenient, and alter its entries as he saw fit. The prospective voter could strike out any names, or indeed all the names, printed on a ballot and write in the name of the candidate or candidates of his choice. He then had only to sign the ballot and deliver it at the polling station for his vote to be recorded. SRO, Shrewsbury Borough MSS 3465/IV/7; 1060/454.

senior and junior, on the other hand, claim only to be wheelwrights in 1818. The junior Brownrigg then called himself a joiner at each subsequent election until 1835. His self-ascribed 'gentle' status was new when he stood for office on the council at the first municipal elections.

Several of the other Radicals also called themselves gentlemen, many with good reason. Pennock Tigar, a grocer and porter merchant, had run a substantial commercial establishment for more than a decade. James Mowld Robinson, newly added to the parliamentary electorate through his residence valued at more than £10, was a surgeon, as was Thomas Sandwich who topped the poll. Virtually all of the Radicals who swept the seats in St Mary's ward held positions in the merchant élite. None of them used the title 'gentleman', but the list included an alderman, a merchant, two grocers, a currier, a land surveyor, and a tallow chandler. These men almost certainly could match their fellows in Minster ward guinea for guinea. Were the political affiliations of individuals unaffected by their social, occupational, or economic status? Was class not a factor in Beverley? And what of Bristol, Maidstone, Northampton, and the other towns? What role, if any, did social stratification play in political developments before, during, and after Reform? Completely satisfactory answers cannot be found to such extremely difficult questions, but these electorates offer some clues.

The same year that Radicals swept the town council Joseph Coltman, an Anglican clergyman, voted for the Tories, just as he had done at the parliamentary election in 1832. Coltman's Tory voting began before the Reform Act when he cast a Tory plump in 1831. On the other hand, the very next year, rather than repeating his Tory plump, Coltman also voted for Henry Burton, the ambiguous Whig he had ignored at the 1831 election when Burton's partisanship was more uncertain. Coltman had also split his vote in 1818. While Coltman split in 1832, another Anglican clergymen, George Sampson, plumped Tory, and continued to vote exclusively Tory in 1835 and 1837. Countering the Tory votes cast by these two Anglican gentlemen, John Mather, a Nonconformist minister, voted strictly for Whig candidates in 1835, as he was to do in 1837, and as all Beverley's other Nonconformist ministers had done in 1832 and 1841. If the occupations of Beverley's councilmen provide no reason to assume that politics reflected class antagonisms, the behaviour of some religious leaders suggests that religion may have played a vital role in determining partisan loyalties. The political influence of religious groupings among the electorates of these towns demands to be considered along with class.

Recently, two distinguished students of electoral behaviour dismissed 'discussions of whether class, religion, regions, party identification, or the pursuit of individual self-interest are most important in determining voting behaviour' as theoretically un-enlightening.[43] Their contention may well be true. What is worse, the data available for nineteenth-century electors will not permit testing that would generate definitive answers to such theoretically unenlightening questions, should one be so unenlightened as to ask them. Nevertheless, in assessing the impact of Reform on some of England's borough voters, some attention must be given to this host of questions about class and religion. Raising these issues complicates further the already complex question of the popular impact of Reform, but they are too potentially important to ignore.

---

[43] A. Przeworski and J. Sprague, *Paper Stones* (Chicago, 1986), 143–4.

PART IV
CLASS, RELIGION, AND REFORM

7

Reform Refracted 1:
Working and Voting

HOWEVER much the preceding chapters may suggest the opposite, measuring the voting behaviour of thousands of individuals is a relatively straightforward, albeit arduous task. An assessment of the social composition of the electorate runs foul of far more daunting obstacles. An analysis of the relationship between political behaviour and socio-economic status is hardest of all. Many other scholars have wrestled with these complex problems, and Frank O'Gorman's recent description of the occupational composition of the Hanoverian electorate has left little more to be said. Combined with work on the Victorian electorate by Nossiter, Vincent, Neale, Morris, and others, the overall structure of the electorate, unreformed or reformed, borough or county, freeman or householder, has been considered in all of its remarkable diversity.[1] As O'Gorman notes, 'There is, in practice, massive common ground between the classifications' used by those examining socio-economic status.[2]

This examination of occupation, relative economic status, and political preference corroborates much preceding work from a somewhat different perspective and with a more comprehensive database. The available evidence is both complex and confusing, but it seems clear that while 1832 heralded a wider transition to partisan

[1] Nossiter, *Influence, Opinion, and Political Idioms*; J. Vincent, *Pollbooks: How Victorians Voted* (Cambridge, 1967); R. S. Neale, *Class and Ideology in the Nineteenth Century* (London, 1972); R. J. Morris, 'The Leeds Middle Class, 1820 to 1850', Report to the Committee of Economic Affairs, SSRC, June 1983; id., 'Property Titles and the Use of British Urban Poll Books for Social Analysis', *Urban History Yearbook* (1983).

[2] O'Gorman, *Voters*, 202. Much of what might seem to be disagreement often reflects differences more evident than real. The conceptualization of Sewell's study of 19th-cent. Marseilles, e.g. appears to use quite a different set of categories reflecting differences in French and English social structure, but his classifications resemble the ones used in this study, which in turn reflect the work by O'Gorman, Nossiter, and others who have worked on 18th- and 19th-cent. populations. W. Sewell, jnr., *Structure and Mobility* (Cambridge, 1985). See also O'Gorman, 'Electoral Behaviour'.

politics tied to national rather than local issues, it did not mark a transition to the politics of class. Students of modern English politics have chronicled the emergence, triumph, and (in the past decade) decline of what has been termed 'pure class politics'. Similar concerns are not apparent in English elections during the first decades of the nineteenth century despite the growing national awareness of class. Neither occupation nor relative economic status was generally and systematically related to the political preferences of the enfranchised either before or after Reform. Socio-economically related voting patterns occurred spasmodically, but consistent patterns emerged neither over time nor across constituencies.

OCCUPATIONAL AND SOCIAL STRATIFICATION

Decades before Edward Cox detailed the voting habits of England's upper, middle, and working classes shortly after the second Reform Act, some variety of class had entered the political and social vocabularies of many.[3] Shrewsbury's R. A. Slaney was by no means the only candidate in 1830 who claimed to have demonstrated his 'zealous attention to the interest and prosperity of the working classes'.[4] A writer in Norfolk claimed that year's general election 'demonstrated a rising spirit of independence among the middle and lower classes' and 'showed us that the struggle now going forward is between the popular and aristocratic powers'.[5] That year the Liberal editor of the *Norwich Mercury*, R. M. Bacon, believed that all classes had been converted into 'complainants' by a system in which 'every intercourse, every connection of life is estimated by its money value'.[6] The Liberal *Northampton Free Press* sounded anachronistically Marxist in 1832 when they hailed the support of the reformers by 'mechanics, whose daily labour is their only property, cheerfully

---

[3] E. W. Cox, *Hints to Solicitors for the Conduct of Elections* (London, 1868). Cox believed in decided opinions or party connections among the upper class, sectarian influences among the middle class, and strong prejudices coupled with weak party attachments among the working class. See also A. Briggs, 'The Language of "Class" in Early Nineteenth-Century England', in id. and J. Saville (eds.), *Essays in Labour History* (London, 1960).

[4] *A Correct Alphabetical List of the Burgesses who Voted* (Shrewsbury, 1830), p. vii.

[5] *East Anglian*, 12 Oct. 1830.   [6] *Norwich Mercury*, 23 Oct. 1830.

sacrificing it, to support their political principles'.[7] Party propaganda in Bristol sounded a similar note three years later in urging 'Whigs of all classes' and particularly all 'working men' to unite behind the Whig candidates Baillie and Hobhouse.[8] In various guises class awareness was not uncommon by the decade of Reform, though many references to social structure reflected the persistence of older conceptions. Building a working model of socio-economic stratification within these boroughs is a difficult task not made easier by evidence of a growing awareness of something like class in the early decades of the century. Some have attempted to avoid the problems associated with class by relying upon occupation as a practical alternative.[9] Strictly occupational analyses, however, also encounter severe problems, particularly economic disparities within specific occupations. The failure of most historical records to distinguish between master and man, employer and employee, or retailer and craftsman, may have been less important in the nineteenth-century world of work because 'people engaged in making the same kind of thing were the same kind of people', but that remains to be demonstrated. Some have flatly denied it.[10] R. S. Neale, for example, has demonstrated extreme economic heterogeneity among shoemakers in Bath and has questioned the meaningfulness of a category as simultaneously broad and narrow as 'shoemaker'.[11] Moreover, Neale examined only the upper end of the economic spectrum; all of Bath's enfranchised shoemakers were £10 householders. Shoemakers in many other towns, particularly Northampton, occupied the opposite end of the economic scale, paying on average less than £3 rent for their dwellings. An occupational category assumes too much if it equates a shoemaker in Maidstone occupying a dwelling assessed at £3 with a Bath shoemaker living in a house assessed at £141. It is difficult to imagine the ways in which a journeyman shoemaker in Northampton resembled a well-established

---

[7] *Northampton Free Press*, 1 Nov. 1832. On the other hand, the *Free Press* published a letter in that same issue from one of those very mechanics aimed at persuading the 'working classes' to support unions, not necessarily the Birmingham Political Union of which he was a member, but 'all Unions of the working classes, which are rapidly expanding throughout the three Kingdoms'.

[8] CRO, Vyvyan MSS, DDV/BO/62/12.

[9] P. Calvert, *The Concept of Class* (London, 1982). For an interesting combination of poll books and supplementary data far richer than most see Edmund M. Green, 'Social Structure and Political Behaviour in Westminster, 1784–1788', in P. Denley et al. (eds.), *History and Computing II* (Manchester, 1989), 239–42.

[10] Vincent, *Pollbooks*, 52, 53, 68–9.   [11] *Class and Ideology*, 62–74.

master shoemaker of Colchester other than in their common interest in shoes. Thus it seems impossibly exclusionary at one level to use a category as limited as 'shoemakers' to analyse voters, yet at the same time 'shoemaker' seems to be far too inclusive unless economic status is also considered. The problem is not a new one.

Messrs Gore & Son, printers, occasionally appended occupational lists of voters to their Liverpool poll books. The rationale underlying these lists is far from obvious.[12] In 1818, after beginning rather conventionally with 'Gentlemen, Merchants, and Brokers' taken together, the Gores used thirty-six other occupational categories containing sometimes a single occupation, sometimes several. Coopers appeared alone, as did masons, hatters, and jewellers, while painters were lumped with plumbers and glaziers. Bricklayers were forced into the company of slaters and plasterers. The Gores may have conceived of their list as a hierarchical structuring of occupations since it began with 'gentlemen' and almost ended with 'labourers', but if so the hierarchy is not always apparent. The Gores must have believed the information to be of value, because categorizing nearly 3,000 voters in such detail could not have been easy, but for any systematic analysis of occupations and votes the list is virtually useless. Knowing the political preferences of tobacconists or enamellers or musicians advances our knowledge of electoral behaviour very little.

Exhibiting the trait that has resulted in virtually every census differing markedly from its predecessor, the Gores adopted a new list in 1830 that began identically with 'Gentlemen, Merchants, and Brokers', but immediately took a different tack with new categories and a new ordering. Accounts and book-keepers, twenty-sixth on the 1818 list, jumped to second place. Shipwrights and boat-builders moved from second to fourth. Categories expanded and contracted without rhyme or reason. Making up for the elimination of the single 'musician' in 1818 was a new final category, 'sword-bearer and mace-bearer', of which there were two. Veterinary surgeons (also two) joined the list in 1830, while tobacconists, brush-makers, and cork-cutters, each of whom had enjoyed an independent entry in 1818 found themselves united. Joiners, turners, and carvers were added

---

[12] *The Poll for the Election* (Liverpool, 1818), 62. This listing of occupations is by no means unique. The Yorkshire poll book of 1807 lists the votes of 24 specific occupations. R. I. Wilberforce (ed.), *The Life of William Wilberforce*, 5 vols. (London, 1838), iii. 329.

to cabinet-makers and upholsterers.[13] The forty new categories bore little resemblance to the thirty-seven of 1818. The new listing was so unsatisfying that a contemporary observer calculated another version in his copy of the printed poll book. This anonymous analyst simply divided voters into 'first class' (including followers of the liberal professions, gentlemen, merchants and brokers), and 'second class' (accountants, book-keepers, master tradesmen, and the like). Assessed in this fashion, Denison, the losing candidate, could be shown to have had a majority of fifty-six votes among voters of the first class, and a fatal deficit of eighty-eight votes among second-class electors.[14]

The new editors of Liverpool's poll books followed the anonymous analyst's lead in 1832 and scrapped the whole complicated occupational listing in favour of only three categories. The first included the 'Gentry, Clergy, Bankers, Merchants and Brokers, including the Medical and Legal Professions, Wine Merchants, and Wholesale Dealers'. The second contained 'Tradesmen in general, including Innkeepers, Victuallers, Pawnbrokers', while the third added 'Mechanics, viz. Shipwrights, Sailmakers, Coopers, Ropemakers, etc.' The new listing was used to show that William Ewart and Lord Sandon enjoyed a majority among two of Liverpool's three occupational groups. Only the tradesmen would have returned two Whigs instead of a split delegation.[15]

Similarly, the editors of the *Sussex Advertiser* introduced an occupational scheme for the 1818 Lewes election containing only two divisions: 'clergy, gentry, yeomanry, and tradesmen', and 'clerks, journeymen, handicraftsmen, and labourers'.[16] The *Advertiser* believed that this division proved that the incumbent Tory candidates had greater support from 'respectable' voters.[17] Despite the *Advertiser*'s hierarchical rationale, however, the composition of

---

[13] *The Poll for the Election* (Liverpool, 1830), 81. William Ewart won the by-election from John E. Denison with a margin of only 19 votes out of 4,335 accepted as valid.

[14] BL 10349e/10. Manuscript notes in front sheet of poll book taking account of occupational listing on last page.

[15] *The Poll for the Election* (Liverpool, 1833), 162.

[16] *Sussex Advertiser*, 18 June 1818. Such a concern was of long standing in Lewes. In 1628 'the gentry . . . refused to have themselves numbered with the meaner sort at the poll, presumably considering their names should not be rated on paper on an equal basis with those of the commons, and in consequence saw the candidate they supported suffer'. D. Hirst, *Representative of the People?* (Cambridge, 1975), 14.

[17] *Sussex Advertiser*, 18 June 1818.

the 'respectable' element of the population varied widely in the opinions of contemporaries.[18] The publishers of a Shrewsbury poll book eleven years earlier had tried to impose a similar concept when they listed 'Persons in Trade upon their own Account' to demonstrate that if the votes of 'respectable' tradesmen alone had been counted, a losing candidate would have won again with a majority of twelve. The publishers asked electors in future to:

> Justly scorn the mean inglorious soul,
> Which creeps and winds beneath the mob's control,
> Which courts the rabble's smile, the rabble's nod,
> And makes, like Egypt, every beast its God.[19]

R. A. Slaney repeated this theme when he told the Commons that 'in all my experience I have never seen a more respectable body of men than that which' drew up the petition from Shrewsbury supporting Reform in 1831. Slaney went on to say that Shrewsbury's petitioners 'belonged chiefly to the middle classes of society'.[20] But the limits of respectability were flexible. Political exigency could widen considerably the circle of support sought. That same year the *Manchester Guardian* counted on 'the great mass of the property, the knowledge, the moral energy, and the respectability of the country' to achieve Reform.[21] Their definition of respectability may have been far more inclusive than most, though Richard Howes's circular letter against the Reform Bill specifically asked those to whom he turned for help to ensure that the petition be signed by all 'except the lowest class of the poor'.[22] But Howes was desperate for assistance in a losing cause when he cast his net so widely, though the editors of the *Trial of Charles Pinney* also cast a wide net in distinguishing 'respectable' artisans as 'men earning their livelihood', which included 'porters, carpenters, journeymen bakers, and labourers'.[23]

---

[18] The *East Anglian* appeared to conflate similar categories when contrasting 'the small landed proprietors, in short the Yeomanry of the King, as well as artisans, tradesmen, and shopkeepers' with 'the rabble, the mere guzzling "potwallopers" which are always to be found at an election booth'. *East Anglian*, 12 Oct. 1830.

[19] *Considerations on the Principles of Representation with a Review of the Late Contest* (Shrewsbury, 1807).

[20] *MoP* (21 Mar. 1831), 1033.

[21] A. Briggs, *The Collected Essays of Asa Briggs*, 2 vols. (Brighton, 1985), i. 37.

[22] NEO, Northampton Borough Records, Box x5469, Circular of 18 Apr. 1831.

[23] C. Pinney, *The Trial of Charles Pinney* (London, 1833), 126. Gutch also edited Bristol's Conservative *Felix Farley's Bristol Journal*.

Deciding on the 'respectable' among those on the *Advertiser* list or those on Liverpool's list is simply impossible. Nor are these groupings analytically useful in other ways. Without knowing the specific occupations that made up each occupational grouping, each remains *sui generis*. And just as certainly as historians would refuse to use these divisions of voters in Lewes and Liverpool, historians are virtually certain to disagree over any alternative division of specific occupations into larger occupational categories, often for good reasons.

These categorizations illustrate some of the dilemmas regarding class, but the problems facing all attempts to divide the electorate along occupational lines are actually far worse. Some occupational titles pose few problems. Whatever an alderman's particular trade, he fell somewhere near the upper end of a town's commercial élite. However successful a 'labourer', he fell somewhere at the other end of that continuum. Despite the economic heterogeneity of shoe-makers, surely as a group shoemakers can be distinguished economically and socially from bankers as a group. Worsted weavers were not likely to rate at all well in comparison to large merchants or wool-staplers. There is integrity in all work, but Edmund Burke argued decades earlier that 'the occupation of an hairdresser, or of a tallow-chandler, cannot be a matter of honour to any person'.[24]

Many specific job titles, on the other hand, are less unambiguous that they appear initially. Assessing the rank of a 'clergyman' involves a variety of judgements, not the least of which is whether the claim was made by a member of the Church of England or a Nonconformist. Poll books often distinguished clergymen from lay clerks of various kinds, and poll books could be quite specific about the various kinds of secular clerks. Equally often, a clergyman's denomination cannot be determined without further research. John Vincent's belief that Anglican clergymen appear in the poll books designated as 'clerks' or 'clergymen' while their Dissenting brethren are found under the title 'minister' is sometimes correct, but exceptions are too commonplace to apply the distinction as a rule. Compilers of poll books displayed no consideration for twentieth-century researchers. They recorded clergymen by a variety of titles including simply 'Reverend', which applied to Dissenter and Anglican alike.[25] The most common title, 'clerk', included Dissenters

---

[24] E. Burke, *Reflections on the Revolution in France* (London, 1790), 58.

[25] Some of the general difficulties involved in stratifying occupations are conveyed

in many constituencies. After Reform, poll books often identified Dissenting or Catholic clergy, but clerical titles are not easily categorized.

If secular clerks can be separated from clergymen and Anglican clergy from other clergy, vexing questions then arise about the relative status of Nonconformist and Anglican ministers. Should Dissenters be grouped with their Anglican brethren, or were the social differences between them too great to permit such a clustering, particularly in the light of the ephemeral nature of some Nonconformist titles. Anglican clergymen persisted; Nonconformists often did not. The Revd. C. P. Valentine of Lewes considered himself a Dissenting Clergyman in 1830, but had given it up for farming by 1841. James Boden of Beverley also seems to have left the pulpit after his initial listing as a Dissenting minister in 1830. Samuel Wigg of Great Yarmouth, a butcher in 1818, called himself a Dissenting clerk in 1820, only to revert to his previous occupation, in 1826. Joseph Patrick, who called himself a Dissenting minister at Northampton's 1820 election, kept a shop in 1826. Thus, while Anglican clergymen invariably kept their titles, occupational mobility among the Dissenters raises questions about their position in society both during and after their claims to ecclesiastical status. The added dilemma of the Roman Catholic clergy presents itself after 1829, though priests posed fewer difficult questions for the purposes of social stratification than the Protestant Dissenting clergy.

Similarly, in this context the label 'gentleman' becomes problematic. Few voters who described themselves as 'gentlemen' would have liked a contemporary definition that 'a gentleman is one who is not under the necessity of doing anything, and whose ancestors for several generations have done nothing'.[26] Nor is it safe to believe Alexis de Tocqueville's assertion that the word applied to any well-

---

by the more than 20 titles used by the clergy including clerk, parish clerk, Revd., clergyman, Dissenting minister, Baptist minister, Unitarian minister, clergyman of the Church of Scotland, Methodist minister, Roman Catholic priest, clerk of the Welsh chapel, Presbyterian minister, and DD.

[26] *Westminster Review*, Apr. 1831, 482; Henry Southern's review of Augustus St John, *Anatomy of Society* (London, 1830). The Northamptonshire poll book of 1831 lists schoolmasters with gentlemen and others as among 'the most prominent classes', but this decision appears to be a rare historical agreement with the determination of many academics to rank themselves among the élite despite all the evidence that calls such a ranking into question.

educated man 'whatever his birth'.[27] What these voters did mean in using the title, on the other hand, is difficult to fathom. Successful artists often found themselves in 'genteel' circumstances since 'princely and patrician munificence has frequently enabled the artist to live like a gentleman and mix in the first societies', but at the same time the earnings of artists often fell hopelessly below the requirements of a gentle life.[28] Were artists gentlemen? Might a gentleman call himself an artist at the hustings?

The principal townsmen of Great Yarmouth exhibited a very refined sense of the term 'gentleman'. The Yarmouth Harbour Committee, established to prepare a parliamentary bill in 1835, included only prosperous, politically active, influential men who all certainly had some claim to the title of gentlemen, and who are all virtually indistinguishable in other historical records. Chairman Sir Edmund K. Lacon's title understandably placed him apart, but the committee list made other distinctions among its members based upon unspecified and undiscoverable criteria. John Shelly, Benjamin Dowson, James Clark, and William Barber all called themselves merchants on the 1835 poll book, and all four were freemen rather than £10 householders. Nevertheless, the formal committee report listed Shelly and Dowson as 'Esquires' while their poll book equals Clark and Barber had to settle for a mere 'Mr' in front of their names. 'Esquires' John Brightwen and Benjamin Dowson had contributed £100 sterling to the Whig party war chest in 1831, while 'Esquires' John Shelly and H. V. Worship had been willing or able to afford only £50, the exact amount donated by 'Mr'. Simon Cobb. The line that Shelly, Dowson, and Worship had somehow crossed, leaving Clark, Barber, and Cobb behind, is now invisible. However similar they appear a century and a half later, these men perceived social divisions within their ranks.[29]

Virtually every attempt to construct meaningful occupational categories for eighteenth- and nineteenth-century populations has

[27] A. de Tocqueville, *Journeys to England and Ireland*, ed. J. P. Mayer (London, 1958 [1833]), 67.

[28] Sir R. Phillips, *The Book of English Trades and Library of the Useful Arts* (London, 1818), 368. Complicating matters is the difficulty of distinguishing artists from house-painters and the impossibility of separating successful from failed artists. Painting houses successfully could be far more rewarding financially than painting people unsuccessfully. Another of many suggested occupational divisions is T. Mortimer, *A General Commercial Dictionary* (London, 1819), particularly app. 2.

[29] *Statement on Behalf of the Promoters of . . . the Haven of Great Yarmouth* (Yarmouth, 1834).

failed as badly to meet with general acceptance as these now obscure contemporary efforts. The reason, of course, is what appears to be a universal inability to grapple effectively with the infinitely complicated questions raised in discussing social relationships. Ultimately, the problem becomes one of defining 'class', a task that seems to have baffled Marx himself.[30] Quite a few students of English history have assumed the importance of class in determining many things. Linda Colley recently observed that 'no period of British history has been more ruthlessly anatomized in the search for social tensions and class consciousness than the years between the mid-eighteenth century and the first Reform Act in 1832'.[31] Nor, it might be said, has so much effort ever resulted in so little agreement. The various anatomies have failed to achieve anything resembling consensus. Those engaged in the social post-mortem have not been able to agree on the proper genus of the corpus they have examined with such care, much less its species. Class has been accurately described as an 'essentially contested concept' over which agreement between two researchers seems highly unlikely, if not truly impossible.[32]

At the beginning of this century Charles Seymour wrote that 'whatever might be said as to the party affiliations of the artisans, it would not be fairly argued that their tendencies were strongly conservative'.[33] There has not been a more categorical assertion than E. P. Thompson's claim that 'in the years between 1780 and 1832 most English working people came to feel an identity of interest as between themselves and as against their rulers and employers'.[34] An equivalently large number dismiss class defined theoretically or empirically. In addition to rejecting class, many historians have specifically denied any relationship between occupation and the voting choices of nineteenth-century electors. None has been more

---

[30] P. N. Furbank, *Unholy Pleasure: The Idea of Social Class* (Oxford, 1985), 40–50. See also J. Massie, *Calculations of the Present Taxes Yearly Paid by a Family of Each Rank, Degree, or Class* (London, 1761); P. Colquhoun, *A Treatise on Wealth, Power, and Resources of the British Empire* (London, 1814). Two recent useful discussions of class are J. Rule, *The Labouring Classes in Early Industrial England, 1750–1850* (London, 1986), and R. J. Morris (ed.), *Class, Power, and Social Structure in British Nineteenth-Century Towns* (Leicester, 1986).

[31] 'Whose Nation?', 98.   [32] Calvert, *Class*, 209.

[33] *Electoral Reform*, 90.

[34] *English Working Class*, 110. On the other hand, Glen's recent look at urban workers in the Industrial Revolution found little to support 'class' interpretations. R. Glen, *Urban Workers in the Industrial Revolution* (London, 1984); see also R. S. Neale, *Class in English History, 1680–1850* (London, 1981), 98.

dismissive than D. C. Moore and John Vincent who agree that 'class as stratum . . . class in the colloquial sense cannot really be used to describe voting patterns or to explain them'.[35] Moore, whose assertions rest heavily upon the evidence provided by John Vincent's pioneering survey of printed poll books, asserted flatly that nineteenth-century 'voters did not vote as members of occupational categories. Indeed, the principal significance of the occupational identifications which many poll books provide lies in what they reveal of the usual lack of correlation between electoral behaviour and occupation.'[36] Patrick Joyce has extended the rejection of class well beyond the second Reform Act.[37]

The fluidity of nineteenth-century society exacerbates the problem. The census-takers themselves, who constantly wrestled with occupational categories, failed to achieve either consistency or precision.[38] In fact, the key to an analysis of social stratification might be a recognition of the fluidity of the existing occupational stratification as well as its complexity. Thomas Erskine expressed such a view of English society when he argued rather optimistically that 'nothing has more contributed to the stability of this . . . kingdom than the innumerable shades in which all her people are blended. Our community is like a changing coloured silk—the eye can perceive that there are different colours, but cannot distinctly

---

[35] Vincent, *Pollbooks*, 27. Speight concluded that 'there was certainly no hint of class conflict [in Colchester] at any time during the period'. 'Colchester', 129, *passim*. A recent study of weavers in Gloucestershire in 1825 found only a 'hint of modern class conflict', and then only at the very end of a long set of circumstances occasioned by a strike. A. Urdank, 'The Gloucestershire Weaver Strike', *Journal of British Studies*, 25 (1986), 193–226.

[36] Moore, *Politics of Deference*, 5; Moore goes on to say 'criteria of wealth, status, or relationship to the means of production are effectively useless as a means of distinguishing the men who voted together' (p. 23).

[37] Furbank, *Unholy Pleasure*, 21.

[38] Neale, *Class in English History*, 100–153; R. J. Morris (ed.), 'Introduction', *Class, Power, and Social Structure in British Nineteenth-Century Towns* (Leicester, 1986), 2–22; W. C. Runciman, 'Explaining Social Stratification', in T. J. Nossiter (ed.), *Imagination and Precision in the Social Sciences* (London, 1972). Armstrong has suggested the use of other kinds of information, such as the employment of servants, as a means of discriminating within specific occupations, but the relevant information was not available for these populations. W. A. Armstrong, 'The Use of Information about Occupations', in E. A. Wrigley (ed.), *Nineteenth Century Society* (Cambridge, 1972), 191–310. Sarlvik and Crewe have argued that English society in the 1970s was less polarized around the issue of class than it was scattered along a continuum. B. Sarlvik and I. Crewe, *Decade of Dealignment* (Cambridge, 1983), 7–35. Nevertheless, they believe that 'class has long been pre–eminent', and seems to have accounted for the bulk of the votes of the working class as late as 1964.

trace where any one of them ends or another begins.'[39] Erskine's description seems particularly apt for voters who used more than 900 different titles to describe themselves when the polling clerk asked their occupations immediately prior to voting.[40]

The potentially insurmountable difficulties associated with measuring social stratification in the best of circumstances are compounded enormously by deficiencies in the data available for early nineteenth-century towns. Occupational title is often the only socio-economic datum available for any individual. Poll books rarely distinguish journeymen from masters. Census-takers in the later nineteenth century struggled with the same problem, complaining that 'out of the 26 millions, . . . there were not 1,000 who returned themselves as journeymen anything'.[41] Fortunately, the self-ascription of these occupational titles and the relatively short intervals between ascriptions mitigate some of the problems and increase the confidence with which they can be used. A few months or at most a few years separated these elections, and occupational descriptions of the same individuals were recorded as many as nine times between 1819 and 1841.[42] The quantity and frequency of these descriptions improves our perspective considerably. Many studies of class and voting in England have concluded that a variety of definitions of class is preferable to a single definition because all existing definitions are imperfect. By looking often, and by occasionally changing perspective, these data can be put to good use despite their inherent flaws.

Socio-economic Stratification: Another Attempt

Finding no generally acceptable solution to the problem of 929 distinct occupational titles and not wishing to break with a long tradition of idiosyncrasy, this chapter employs occupational categories intended only as crude indices of relative socio-economic status sufficient to permit tests for differences among groups of voters. Many of the greatest difficulties raised by occupations

[39] Thomas Erskine, *The Second Part of Armata* (London, 1817), 89–90.

[40] A polling clerk with a strange sense of humour systematically recorded a number of very humble voters as 'gentlemen' at the Northampton election of 1831. His private joke was revealed only in the process of linking the records of these men over time.

[41] Vincent, *Pollbooks*, 53.

[42] As few as 10 (1830–31) and as many as 75 months (1820–26) separated these general elections, with an average for the period of just under three years.

stemmed from a small subset of the entire range.[43] The specific placement of men claiming to be beadles, quack doctors, poachers, warners, bird and dog fanciers, or comedians, might provoke interesting debates, but happily they contributed small numbers to the electorate. The men who claimed to be shoemakers, innkeepers, mercers, and brokers can be ranked more readily, and they made up the bulk of the voters. Therefore, while the individual occupations in these towns were divided initially into eleven strata, the overwhelming majority (> 90 per cent) of all occupations fell into only five categories, leaving all the rest lumped together into a sixth, insignificant, residual category ('Other').[44]

The first of the five meaningful categories (professional/gentle) included relatively few titles, such as attorney, gentleman, esquire, Anglican clergyman, and medical doctor, that identified the voter as a member of one of the established professions or the gentry.[45] The second (merchant élite) included titles, such as banker, merchant, broker, factor agent, or dealer, that clearly placed the claimant at the top of a town's commercial economic scale.[46] Not small retailers, these men engaged in business at the wholesale or larger volume retail level in their towns. Some men, like apothecaries, earned their place among the merchant élite as a result of profits likely to accrue to a reasonably successful practitioner.[47] Following behind these commercial leaders were butchers, bakers, and shopkeepers (retail)

---

[43] Of the many handbooks that sort through the complex commercial landscape of 19th-cent. England, the most helpful is Sir R. Phillips, *English Trades*. Mortimer, *A General Commercial Dictionary* is also useful.

[44] O'Gorman, *Voters*, 202–23. Sewell's study of 19th-cent. Marseilles used 10 categories: business/professional, rentier, sales/clerical, small business, artisan, service, unskilled, maritime, argiculture, and miscellaneous. *Structure and Mobility*, 327–33.

[45] Nonconformist clergy were relegated first to 'lesser' professions, and ultimately to 'Other'. Other categories lumped under 'Other' were clerical (e.g. writing-clerks), Government employees (gaoler, collector of dues, etc.), skilled service workers (wharfinger, boatman), agriculturalists (farmer, cowleech), and the truly unclassifiable (almsman).

[46] According to R. Phillips, 'Factors or Brokers are a species of Merchant who deal by commission.' *English Trades*, 250–5. Holyoake called these men a 'numerous class of capitalists under the denomination of Importers, Merchants, Brokers, Shipowners, and Wholesale Dealers'. G. Holyoake, *Sixty Years of an Agitator's Life* (London, 1906), 171.

[47] Good apothecaries (or chemists) could clear £200 to £500 p.a., 'frequently only a just remuneration for skill and labour. They are almost invariably medical advisors of the poor, and not infrequently of the rich.' Wade, *History*, 188. R. Phillips agreed that apothecaries stood at the top of the commercial heap. *English Trades*, 98.

of all sorts who called themselves by dozens of titles. All varieties of mongers and sellers were included among these lesser business figures.

The fourth and largest category by far (artisan/craftsman) included 'skilled' workers. Distinguishing a working tailor from someone who ran a haberdashery often proved difficult, but this category attempted to separate men who spent most of their energy making goods from those who spent most of their time selling them.[48] The unskilled (labour) finished off the five categories to which the bulk of the electorate belonged. Many of those listed as labourers followed occupations that may not have required much less skill than those in the fourth category. In general, though, labourers claimed jobs demanding little more than muscle. Cartmen, haulers, labourers, servants, porters, and the like fell into this last group.

A sample of towns and elections using these six categories is presented in Table 7.1. A comparison of these figures with O'Gorman's recent account of the unreformed borough electorate simultaneously corroborates their general accuracy and points to variations that emerge from different definitions. O'Gorman's assessment of Shrewsbury placed more men in the professional/ gentle category, and somewhat more in retail, but many of the discrepancies between O'Gorman's figures and Table 7.1 stem from the voters contained in the 'other' category.[49] Variations notwithstanding, there is little doubt about the general structure of the electorate. Both O'Gorman's tables and Table 7.1 indicate borough electorates in which the élite constituted perhaps 15 per cent, retailers made up a quarter, and craftsmen (a steadily declining category) and the unskilled constituted the remaining 60 per cent. The proportions varied from town to town and from election to election, but endless tampering with specific occupations probably would not change the overall image substantially.

---

[48] Holyoake described his early days in a house 'amid which was a hatter's working shop'. Hatters were placed with craftsmen, as were glovers, breechesmakers, and the like. *Sixty Years*, 17. R. Phillips reported e.g. that a master tailor needed 'considerable capital' and had to be able to manage credit well since he lived on his capacity to manipulate relatively large sums. A journeyman tailor, on the other hand, was little more than a wage labourer earning a parliamentarily decreed 4s. 6d. *per diem*. *English Trades*, 397.

[49] O'Gorman, *Voters*, 202–23.

TABLE 7.1. *Occupational Composition in Unreformed and Reformed Boroughs (Franchise Type)* (%)

	1818	1830	1832	1841
Bristol (freeman/freeholder)				
Professional/gentle	8.1*	8.2	8.2	10.8
Merchant élite	7.8	7.2	10.6	10.8
Retail	12.2	10.7	16.4	18.5
Artisan/craftsman	56.9	57.6	48.6	38.7
Labour	6.2	7.5	6.8	9.5
Other	8.8	8.8	9.4	11.7
Northampton (potwalloper)				
Professional/gentle	7.2	5.0	4.6	5.8
Merchant élite	7.2	5.8	8.2	9.2
Retail	15.4	8.8	10.2	16.8
Artisan/craftsman	55.1	64.0	56.3	50.7
Labour	8.9	9.3	11.8	9.9
Other	6.2	7.1	8.9	7.6
Shrewsbury (freeman—scot and lot)				
Professional/gentle	7.2**	5.8	8.3	9.4
Merchant élite	6.6	5.7	8.8	6.2
Retail	20.7	17.6	22.0	20.2
Artisan/craftsman	51.3	55.8	43.6	45.2
Labour	7.8	7.4	5.7	7.9
Other	6.4	7.7	11.6	11.1
Lewes (inhabitant householder—scot and lot)				
Professional/gentle	8.7	9.0	10.7	11.9
Merchant élite	4.5	5.9	5.4	6.4
Retail	19.9	19.1	19.3	20.0
Artisan/craftsman	41.3	38.8	43.6	37.1
Labour	19.1	18.5	12.0	12.8
Other	6.5	8.7	9.0	11.8

* Bristol election of 1812.
** Shrewsbury election of 1819.
Sources: Published poll books for relevant elections.

Some confirmation of the efficacy of these occupational strata is provided by Table 7.2 which measures the degree to which the strata were related to identifiable economic variations in the electorates. Economic data for these individuals are both extremely rare and severely flawed, but they tend to underscore the utility and reliability of the occupational groups. Neither wealth nor income data exist for any group, but poor-rate levies can be dragooned into service as a substitute for a reasonably large number of voters. Elizabeth Baigent's close study of eighteenth-century Bristol has identified serious problems with poor-rate data.[50] They can appear orderly and reliable when they are in fact spurious. At best, poor rates indicate only estimated rental values of property, and as such pose an extremely nebulous and inflexible guide to the economic status of individuals. Moreover, regardless of the relative accuracy of each individual's assessment in one rate-book for a specific property, that individual's overall relative economic status can be measured only if all relevant assessments can be recovered. Despite these problems, however, poor-rate assessments can be used to make extremely broad distinctions between rich and poor, and it is this very limited task to which they are turned in Table 7.2.[51]

Two mid nineteenth-century publishers used poor rates unapologetically as a guide to individual economic status. Printed poll books for Banbury (1859) and Bath (1855) included rate assessments for each voter and used them to analyse the relative 'respectability' of the support for the candidates involved. By simply totalling the rateable values of the voters for each candidate, the Banbury publishers demonstrated what they believed to be the inequity involved in the one-vote victory of Bernhard Samuelson over John Hardy in the face of an 'excess of assessment of Mr Hardy's voters

[50] Ginter has shown that land-tax assessments cannot be used for these purposes. D. Ginter, 'The Incidence of Revaluation', in M. Turner and D. Mills (eds.), *Land and Property: The English Land Tax, 1692–1832* (Gloucester, 1986). See also D. Ginter, *A Measure of Wealth: The English Land Tax in Historical Analysis* (Montreal, 1991); E. Baigent, 'Bristol Society in the Later Eighteenth Century', D.Phil. (Oxford, 1985).

[51] To avoid some of the problems raised by unequal comparisons, rental values were included for consideration only if a figure for a house could be found. This strategy did not eliminate possible under-assessment from incomplete data, but provided a minimal comparability for each rated person. The economic analysis of Lewes and Shrewsbury employs all surviving poor-rate data. See also J. T. Jackson, 'Housing Areas in Mid-Victorian Wigan and St Helens', *Transactions of the Institute of British Geographers*, 6 (1981), 413–32.

TABLE 7.2. *Shrewsbury: Assessed Rental Values and Occupational Strata* (%)

Year	Stratum	Assessed Rental Value (Quartiles)				N
		First	Second	Third	Fourth	
1826	Professional/gentle	100	—	—	—	
	Merchant élite	100	—	—	—	
	Retail	51	20	21	8	
	Artisan/					
	craftsman	11	27	30	32	
	Labour	—	28	29	43	
						173
1830	Professional/					
	gentle	80	20	—	—	
	Merchant élite	63	25	12	—	
	Retail	31	38	16	15	
	Artisan/					
	craftsman	13	20	31	36	
	Labour	6	18	35	41	
						198
1835	Professional/					
	gentle	85	15	—	—	
	Merchant élite	66	23	8	3	
	Retail	24	36	31	9	
	Artisan/					
	craftsman	9	16	30	45	
	Labour	—	10	35	55	
						251
1841	Professional/					
	gentle	83	17	—	—	
	Merchant élite	68	32	—	—	
	Retail	39	28	26	7	
	Artisan/					
	craftsman	19	31	32	19	
	Labour	—	25	37	38	
						122

Sources: Shrewsbury Parliamentary Poll books 1826–41; SRO, Parish Poor-Rate Assessments for St Mary's, 1041/1n/11, 1041/ch31–49; St Julian's, 2711/p/4, 2711/p/5b; St Alkmund's, 1049/A, 1049/B, 1049/9; St Chad's, 1048–84.

over Mr Samuelson's' of nearly £5,000, and an 'excess of assessment of Mr Hardy's voters over *all* the other electors', of almost £68.[52] Similarly, the printers of a Bath poll book in 1855 proved that even though he lost, the rates of William Whateley's supporters exceeded his opponent's by more than £22,000.[53]

Poor-rate assessments are not put to such an unusual and unconvincing task here. Instead, Table 7.2 presents the results of a comparison of the assessed rental values contained in all extant Shrewsbury poor-rate lists (divided into quartiles) and the occupational group of each individual for whom economic data could be found.[54] The results broadly support the suggested occupational stratification. Considerable economic variation existed in the 'retail' and 'skilled' categories used, as might be expected, but the relationship between occupational stratum and economic position is strongly positive in each of the years examined. These strata appear to serve as crude indices of socio-economic status.

Such rough socio-economic strata do not entirely side-step the question of class. Moreover, economic heterogeneity existed within socio-economic strata, virtually by definition. Nevertheless, Table 7.2 suggests that roughly identifiable socio-economic lines of demarcation can be drawn around the five occupational categories.[55] They will serve crudely in the search for any socio-economic differences that might have underpinned the political divisions so apparent in these boroughs.

[52] *The Banbury Poll Book* (Banbury, Rusher, 1859).

[53] *The Bath Poll-Book* (Bath, 1855). The only other poll book to report each voter's rateable value was Banbury in 1859.

[54] The greatest problem with the data involved steadily rising median rentals coupled, usually, with stable rate assessments. Thomas Johnson's house in All Saints, Lewes, e.g. was rated at £14 in 1818 and 1826, £33 12s. in 1830, and £104 in 1837. He paid the same taxes of £2. 16s. on the property each time, however, indicating that the rental assessment cannot be trusted. But if estimated rental values in these two towns had little to do with real worth, they can be used for relative comparisons. By comparing only quartiles for each year the effect of the upward movement in recorded rental values is eliminated. The upper ranges of the bottom three quartiles in Shrewsbury for each year considered were (in decimalized pounds sterling): 1826—2, 3.5, 7; 1830—2.5, 4.5, 11; 1835—3.5, 7.5, 14; 1841—5, 12, 23.75.

[55] Neither Bristol nor Shrewsbury would be the place to look for class warfare, and Foster has shown how poorly Northampton would serve as a testing-ground for class struggle. *Class Struggle*, 84–127.

WORKING AND VOTING

Crudely put, the issue is the relationship between party *as* it existed and class *if* it existed. Or, without an acceptable definition of class, the issue is the relationship between party and socio-economic status, variously defined. Did Reform alter any relationship that might have existed, or did the separation between politics and economics suggested by some as characteristic of this period persist in the face of the patently economic arguments that often accompanied the debate over the Reform Bill?

Nineteenth-century data are ill-suited to the construction of complex models, so the remainder of this chapter simply tests for relationships between socio-economic status and partisan affiliations, recognizing that the both occupational strata and economic data may hide as much as they reveal. When the *Sussex Advertiser* published a break-down of the supporters of the Tory and Whig candidates at the election of 1818, the editors believed they had uncovered a significant difference in the voting choices of the two groups of voters they had identified. Roughly three-quarters of the more 'respectable' category voted Tory while only 60 per cent of the less respectable voters did so.[56] On the other hand, either socio-economic category acting in isolation would have yielded a Tory victory. Did the difference in the votes of these two groups reflect a meaningful socio-economic political division (or divisions) in the Lewes electorate? Was this division, if it existed, evident elsewhere?

Circumstances often made meaningful socio-economic divisions within the electorate unlikely. Almost immediately after the Bristol riots in 1831, for example, Tories strenuously cultivated the political support of working men by creating the Operative Conservative Association to assist the White Lion Club in combating what they believed to be the pernicious influence of rabble-rousers such as the Bristol Political Union. The Operative Conservative Association

---

[56] Though double votes and plumps were not recorded by the *Advertiser*, the élite group cast votes in a somewhat distinctive pattern.

	Gentry	Others
Shelly	168	106
Shiffner	161	97
Erskine	46	66
Baring	12	15

used money and influence to win working men away from Reform and espoused the need for constitutional continuity in order to guarantee the rights of the poorest freeman to the richest peer. Many members of the Association may have been responding to pure bribery. Alluring prizes ranging from free coal to the payment of 10 shillings to the wives of members confined by pregnancy may have been nearly irresistible for poor freemen, but some may have believed in the avowed 'principles' of the Association, particularly after the destruction of much of Queen Square at the hands of the more radical elements of the population.[57] Moreover, as Sykes has shown for Oldham, the incompetence of the two major parties coupled with the guilt of their candidates on the critical issues of religion and slavery often prevented Whigs from acquiring an affinity among the voters further down the social scale.[58] Existing socio-economic rifts in the electorate meant little unless local parties could mobilize the issue convincingly.

The broadest test of the degree to which electorates responded to these sorts of issues is presented in Table 7.3. Using the five occupational categories already described, occupational groupings and party choices were compared at each election in five boroughs using the simplest test for significant cross-sectional differences, χ^2. The results of this initial test were mixed. The two towns with the most frequent political differences in occupational strata, Lewes and Northampton, could hardly have been more dissimilar. They stood at opposite ends of the economic spectrum as towns and as electorates. As evident Table 7.1 shows, Lewes's electorate contained twice as many professional/gentle voters and far fewer artisans than Northampton's. Poverty dominated Northampton, the shoemaking town, just as relative prosperity dominated Lewes, a diversified, non-industrial commercial and agrarian town.

What is more, political developments in the two towns took entirely different routes. Lewes's electorate was divided into extremely rigid partisan camps well in advance of Reform. The unwillingness of Tories to plump masked the strength of partisan ties in Lewes, but as Chapter 5 demonstrated the town had a long history of partisan voting. Lewes's voters did not need Reform to stimulate partisan growth; Northampton's voters did. After a long period in which elections had not been contested, Northampton

---

[57] CRO, Vyvyan MSS, DDV/BO/62/21; Seymour, *Electoral Reform*, 173.
[58] 'Working-Class Consciousness', 171–4.

TABLE 7.3. *Occupations and Voting Choices: Cross–Sectional Comparisons using* χ^2

	1818	1820	1826	1830	1831	1832	1835	1837	1841
Lewes	0.000*	NC	0.000*	0.000*	NC	NC	0.059	0.000*	0.331
Northampton	0.000*	0.014	0.000*	0.000*	0.001*	0.153	0.000*	0.000*	0.201
Maidstone	0.941	0.009*	0.015	0.003*	0.680	0.245	0.342	0.204	0.581
Beverley	0.020	NC	0.618	0.521	0.194	0.750	0.009*	0.843	0.069
Colchester	0.001*	0.022	NC	0.104	0.204	0.253	0.001*	0.458	NC
Shrewsbury	0.000*	NC	0.017	0.001*	0.015	0.009*	0.007*	0.051	0.012

Note: Comparisons based on five occupational categories containing more than 90 per cent of all electors.
★ Statistically significant at 0.01.
NC No contest.

began to experiment with electoral politics only in 1818. Reform dramatically affected Northampton's electorate by bringing their behaviour in line after 1832 with the sort of partisanship Lewes's voters exemplified as early as 1818.

Yet significant occupational differences underlay voting choices at four out of six Lewes elections and six out of eight in Northampton. Confusing matters further, the elections at which significant differences emerged followed no pattern. Occupation was not significant at Northampton's elections of 1820 and 1832, and proved irrelevant in Lewes in 1835 and 1841. In other words, elections at which occupational strata proved significant appeared to be distributed randomly, just as the few instances of statistical significance in the other four towns reported in Table 7.1 also appeared and disappeared in a meaningless scatter. Maidstone almost reversed the overall pattern in Northampton for no apparent reason. Colchester's first (1818) and penultimate (1835) elections proved significant; all the rest were not. Beverley's 1835 election, like Colchester's, was significant, but no others were. Shrewsbury's pattern, like the others, is best described as hit and miss.

Somewhat fewer elections after Reform exhibited significant occupational differences. The ratio at elections prior to 1832 stood at roughly 50:50 and shrank to one in three afterwards. Whether this reduction was related to Reform or perhaps the Poor Law of 1834 is not clear, but occupation could be tied to voting choices at only two of the last ten elections tested. The Poor Law may well have proven fatal to the not very successful Whig efforts prior to 1834 to portray the Whig party as the champion of the poorer voters.

Examining more closely the two towns in which occupational strata were most often related to voting patterns, Tables 7.4 and 7.5 display the relative conservatism of the five occupational strata in Lewes and Northampton, with one Beverley election appended for comparison. A relatively clear pattern marks these two tables; they tend to replicate politically the 'sandwich' that Harold Perkin saw as characterizing religion in nineteenth-century England. Anglicans occupied the top and the bottom of the social spectrum, sandwiching three layers of Nonconformists of middling social standing between them. A roughly similar description fits Northampton generally and the post-1830 pattern in Lewes. While Tories captured the top and bottom occupational strata, those in the artisan/craftsman stratum were less likely to vote Tory. As Table 7.4 demonstrates, voters

TABLE 7.4. *Political Rankings of Occupational Strata in Northampton: Most Conservative to Least Conservative* (Actual Odds)⋆

Rank	Election year						
	1826	1830	1831	1832	1835	1837	1841
1	M (1.5)	L (7.5)	L (0.65)	NS	R (17.5)	L (2.8)	NS
2	R (1.3)	R (7.4)	P (0.61)	NS	L (14.9)	P (2.6)	NS
3	P (1.0)	P (7.0)	R (0.56)	NS	P (9.5)	R (1.3)	NS
4	L (0.75)	A (3.0)	A (0.25)	NS	A (6.5)	A (0.54)	NS
5	A (0.48)	M (1.0)	M (0.15)	NS	M (4.6)	M (0.28)	NS

NS Variations between occupational strata not significant.

P Professional/gentle. M Merchant élite. R Retail. A Artisan/craftsman. L Labour.

⋆ All occupational groups voted Whig in 1818, and differences for 1820 were not significant.

TABLE 7.5. *Political Rankings of Occupational Strata in Lewes and Beverley: Most Conservative to Least Conservative (Actual Odds)**

Rank	Election Year				
	Lewes				Beverley
	1818	1826	1830	1837	1835
1	M(5.6)*	P (1.6)	P (0.35)	L(1.6)	P (2.0)
2	P (4.5)	M(0.52)	M(0.23)	P (0.98)	M(1.0)
3	L(3.2)	R(0.04)	L(0.17)	R(0.83)	R(0.53)
4	A(2.6)	L(0.03)	A(0.07)	A(0.59)	A(0.39)
5	R(1.8)	A(0.02)	R(0.03)	M(0.42)	L(0.25)

Note: No contest in Lewes in 1820, 1831, 1832; patterns in 1835 and 1841 not significant. Election of 1835 sole significant pattern in Beverley.
 P Professional/gentle. M Merchant élite R Retail. A Artisan/craftsman. L Labour.
 * See Table 7.4.

in Northampton's professional/gentle and labouring strata ordinarily displayed the strongest Tory tendencies, though retailers were almost as conservative. Labouring men were most conservative 1830, 1831, and 1837. Professional/gentle voters were the second most likely to vote Tory in 1831 and 1837, and labourers filled the second slot in 1835. Except for their pronounced Tory hue in 1826, the merchant élite, on the other hand, usually turned in the least conservative performance; they were last on the scale at six of seven elections. Artisans/craftsmen shared the bottom of the scale with them; they ranked last once and next to last in five elections.

Voters in Lewes behaved similarly in some respects, though the pattern was far from identical. At the four Lewes elections with statistically significant variations, Professional/gentle voters were most conservative twice and once the runner-up, conforming nicely to the Northampton pattern. Artisans in Lewes also conformed closely to Northampton's model; they typically showed little enthusiasm for Tory candidates and remained near the bottom of the scale at all four elections (Table 7.5). Lewes's lowest occupational stratum wound up as most conservative, just as they were in Northampton, but they arrived at that post reluctantly, having been not particularly well disposed towards conservative candidates before Poor Law reform. Similarly, the merchant élite in Lewes became the least conservative group, but they also had to reverse their original position to get there. Prior to Reform, the merchant élite had been the most, or among the most, supportive Tory voters. Complicating matters further, the odds at Beverley's one significant election did not fit the pattern very closely. As in the other two towns, the professional/gentle stratum was most conservative while retailers occupied a middle and artisans a lower rank. Unlike Northampton and Lewes, however, Beverley's labourers were the least conservative of all, and Beverley's merchant élite stood shoulder to shoulder with the gentlemen and professionals at the top. What does all this mean?

The sporadic nature of statistically significant political differences between occupational strata suggests that at most elections in most constituencies occupational strata played a minor role in determining votes. With that important caveat in mind, the general tendency of professional and gentle voters to be more conservative than their fellows is supported by the equally strong tendency of artisans/ craftsmen to be among the least conservative in their communities. Evidence from across elections and across constituencies reinforces this pattern, but members of the merchant class, retailers, and labourers avoided a precise fit. Labourers often tended to join with gentlemen as most conservative, particularly after 1835, but the data will not support a generalization. Labourers exhibited a strong tendency towards the Conservatives at the 1835 Lewes election, and they stood at or near the top in Northampton's later elections, both before and after the passage of Reform. If their political alliance was weighted towards the Tories, they were also the group most susceptible to Whig charges of venality and were most at risk to outright bribery since they were more likely to view their franchises as private property to be treated with an eye towards maximizing income rather than accomplishing political ends.

The balanced performance of retailers also says very little about their political tendencies. Their middle rank did not prevent massive swings in the probabilities of their voting for Tory candidates, either across elections or across boroughs. In Northampton retailers were strongly Tory in 1830, mildly so in 1831, and rabidly Tory in 1835. Retailers in Lewes, on the other hand, were never actually likely to vote for Tory candidates, and often were quite unlikely to do so.

While retailers voted massively for Tories in Northampton in 1830, virtually none of them voted Tory in Lewes. Nor were Beverley's retailers ardent Tory voters in their one showing in 1835.

Turning from occupational strata as indices of socio-economic status to a more direct economic assessment of voters helps to clarify the confused image emerging from Tables 7.3 and 7.4. The relatively reliable economic data that have survived for Lewes quite clearly argues against a significant relationship between economics and politics, either before or after 1832. Looking at Lewes's voters as members of partisan groups, which they were, Table 7.6 demonstrates (with a little interpretation) that Whigs and Tories did not belong to two separate economic strata. The mean assessed rents and poor rates for the two groups of voters appeared to identify distinct differences between them, but in fact extremely high rental values and tax assessments for a few Tory voters generated the substantial differences in means every year between 1818 and 1835. The medians for voters adhering to one of the two parties more reliably indicated their basic economic similarity. There was nothing to choose economically between the Whig and Tory voters in Lewes except for a possibly spurious statistic for 1826. Fewer voters could be identified on tax rolls that year, and with a sample size of fewer than 150 and every other figure suggesting economic equality, the 1826 difference must be discounted. By 1837, even the means reported in Table 7.6 have merged. Fewer extremely wealthy Tory voters eliminated the positive skewing of the mean, allowing it to join the median. According to rents and poor-rate levies, Whigs and Tories belonged to the same socio-economic population.

If the economic data available for Lewes's voters is compared with individual voting choices instead of through party aggregates, a similar picture emerges. The negative values for τ_b in Table 7.7 in 1818, 1826, and 1830 imply that relative economic status measured through rents or rates was very mildly and inversely related to Tory voting; the further down the economic spectrum, the less likely a Tory vote. These tendencies, however, were too weak to be taken very seriously. Only the relationship between rental and vote at the election of 1830 proved to be statistically significant. After 1830 the inverse relationship disappeared as the absolute values of the τs declined to 1837's extremely weak scores. Thus Table 7.7 leads to the same conclusion as Table 7.6. Economic status was not strongly related to political choice. As Tables 7.3 and 7.4 indicated, voters

TABLE 7.7. *Economic Status and Tory Voting in Lewes 1818–1837*: τ_b *(Probability)*

Year	1818	1826	1830	1835	1837
Rent	−0.050	−0.179	−0.102	0.016	0.070
	p = 0.014	p = 0.011	p = 0.008*	p = 0.403	p = 0.158
Poor rate	−0.147	−0.145	−0.122	0.085	0.019
	p = 0.229	p = 0.035	p = 0.012	p = 0.099*	p = 0.398
N	196	141	426	188	177

* significant at 0.01.

TABLE 7.6. *Rents, Rates, and Voting Choices in Lewes:*[59] *Mean (Median) (pence)*

	Assessed rental value				
	1818*	1826*	1830*	1835	1837*
Tory	603 (240)	801 (480)	2,147 (656)	5,774 (1,560)	6,900 (4,320)
Whig	346 (180)	475 (300)	1,024 (648)	2,736 (1,680)	7,439 (4,800)
	Poor rate levied				
Tory	142 (54)	162 (96)	197 (56)	356 (98)	213 (138)
Whig	79 (54)	96 (60)	94 (54)	201 (108)	206 (140)
N	196	141	426	188	177

* Statistically significant stratum/vote comparison; see Table 7.3.

[59] Lewes's rent and tax data were dividing into three groups suggested by the natural clustering of the data, coupled with some consideration of meaningful monetary differences. Cell sizes in each category varied considerably, but overall the divisions seem defensible. The totals for tax and rent for each year do not necessarily coincide because of variations in the data. As would be expected, the data demonstrate very strong multicolinearity. Indeed, with a Pearson's r in excess of +0.9, the two measures represent the same variable. The samples were not random, of course, but include all extant information. Fortunately, τ_b requires no assumptions about randomness.

		Category			
Year	Variable	Lowest	Middle	Highest	N
1818	Tax	187	49	89	325
	Rent	50	139	136	
1826	Tax	103	33	73	209
	Rent	28	83	98	
1830	Tax	330	132	188	650
	Rent	101	249	303	
1835	Tax	144	49	77	270
	Rent	64	75	146	
1837	Tax	103	48	63	214

who claimed professional or gentle status, voters who were likely to be wealthier than the norm, tended to support Tory candidates. With that one possible exception, relative economic success did little to determine political affiliations.

At the very beginning of the century the *Annual Register* lamented the conduct of voters at general elections in places such as Nottingham and Middlesex because 'in those struggles . . . the dangerous spirit of opposition between high and low, rich and poor, gentleman and mob, was extremely conspicous', and dangerous.[60] The occupational analyses published in Liverpool, Lewes, and elsewhere also suggest, albeit less forcefully, that some observers perceived social differention as an important, or potentially important, issue in a number of elections. Nevertheless, the voting behaviour of various social strata in these towns did not support these views. Relationships can be identified between some socio-economic strata and partisan choices at some elections, but the evidence is far too variable and too weak to support any generalization other than a negative one.

Nor should this state of affairs be surprising in the light of other studies of Victorian electoral behaviour. T. J. Nossiter believed 'there was much less basis for a class war between capital and labour at the polls than for a status struggle between the lower and upper middle class'. He found that 'influence never entirely destroys the impact of occupation as a social determinant', but could discover no evidence of 'constituency-wide support for either party among any but the highest occupational group'.[61] These data were somewhat more suggestive, yet they support Nossiter's general scepticism about the political influence of occupation or social stratum. Neither seemed to be other than occasional and unpredictable influences. There is nothing to support Nossiter's claim that the lower down the social scale, the more an elector was likely to vote as his district, but there is some evidence that less well-off electors were most susceptible to bribery and more likely to vote for a well-funded party.

What is more, if there is a trend at all in these data, it is a lessening of the relationship between socio-economic strata and party preference. If the Whigs were able to generate some additional support among humbler voters in these towns in the years leading up to

---

[60] *AR* (1802), 184.   [61] *Influence, Opinion, and Political Idioms*, 167–70.

Reform, they seem to have lost their appeal rather quickly. Whig administrations were no more popular with poorer voters than Tory administrations, particularly after 1834. A reviewer for *Leigh Hunt's London Journal* in 1835 agreed with John Leslie's argument against the new Poor Law being 'looked upon as a subject of party politics'. Leslie tried to disabuse Englishmen of the idea that it was the responsibility of the Whig Ministry because 'the measure has been, and still is, both supported and opposed by men of all parties'.[62] Whigs in Shrewsbury and elsewhere tried and failed to make the point locally that Leslie tried and failed to make nationally. The Whigs could not escape the onus of the measure that had proven to be such a powerful source of propaganda. Its enemies portrayed the new Poor Law as perhaps the most noxious measure ever taken by an English Government against its citizens.

Shrewsbury's Tories were not alone in their attempt to turn 1837 and 1841 into referendums over the Poor Law, but their efforts were particularly intense. A look at the relative success of the Tories among Shrewsbury's occupational strata suggests that the Tories may have made gains among the poor by taking this *post hoc* stance against the Law, but equally clearly, Table 7.8 reinforces the impression created by Tables 7.3 and 7.4. The political preferences of Shrewsbury's occupational strata could not be predicted easily, and whatever powers of prediction strata permitted tended to

TABLE 7.8. *Proportional Tory Vote among Shrewsbury Occupational Strata* (%)

Year	Professional/ gentle	Merchant élite	Retail	Artisan/ craftsman	Labour
1819	69	57	30	42	35
1826	64	37	48	36	44
1830	72	62	44	35	31
1831	53	57	40	40	44
1832	58	44	36	36	46
1835	70	52	53	45	48
1837	66	44	41	45	44
1841	75	61	50	53	51

[62] Review of John Leslie, *A Letter to the Industrious Classes on the Poor Laws* (London, 1835) in *Leigh Hunt's London Journal*, 2 (1835), 439.

disappear over time. Various occupational strata in Shrewsbury supported Tory candidates in substantially different degrees, and the members of the highest stratum supported Tory candidates as a rule. Tories always won a majority of the professional/gentle stratum, and often managed a two-thirds majority. Artisans and craftsmen, on the other hand, tended not to vote for the Tories, though that tendency faded quickly after 1832 and disappeared in 1841.

Shrewsbury's other strata, however, followed no pattern or a far less evident pattern. Merchants vacillated wildly from election to election. They refused *en masse* to vote Tory in 1826, only to flock to the Tory colours in 1830. They supported the anti-reformers in 1831, only to back the reformers in 1832. They reverted to the Tories in 1835, but again turned coat in 1837. They finished as they began, but the road to their 1841 Tory majority had been far from smooth. Shrewsbury's business giants adhered to the pattern identified in modern English elections which 'all confirm that there is no consistent tendency . . . for partisanship to alter with rising incomes'.[63] Nor did retailers in Shrewsbury appear entirely comfortable waving either party's colours. Their swings were less extreme than their commercial superiors, but swing they did, particularly after 1832. Unlike their counterparts in Northampton, enfranchised labourers in Shrewsbury did not support Tory candidates across the board, but like their counterparts in Lewes, they did finally join the Tory camp. These variations bring to mind Kenneth Wald's conclusion about the later nineteenth-century electorate. After a lengthy quantitative analysis based on aggregate voting statistics, Wald asserted that 'broad claims about the electoral significance of class divisions' could not be sustained.[64]

Shifting from measurements of occupations to pure economics reinforces the image of voting in Shrewsbury responding to other stimuli. Relatively reliable data on residential and commercial rental values can be found for many of Shrewsbury's voters.[65] Dividing the electorate into quartiles on the basis of their total assessed property

---

[63] Their behaviour did not, however, support the other part of the conclusion, that 'there may be a threshold, but if so, it seems to be manual/non-manual, not economic'. If a threshold was in operation here, it took a different form. R. Rose, *Electoral Behaviour* (London, 1974), 504.

[64] K. Wald, *Crosses on the Ballot* (Princeton, NJ, 1983), 150.

[65] See n. 54. These economic data coupled steadily rising median rentals with stable rate assessments.

valuations permits a test of the likelihood of voters at the top and bottom of the economic spectrum voting Tory. The notable lack of a pattern in Table 7.9 confirms the evidence of Table 7.8 and again suggests a conclusion for Shrewsbury's voters similar to Richard Rose's conclusion for modern English voters. Greater wealth did not necessarily translate into greater affinity for Tory candidates. The wealthiest quartile always voted Tory, but their tendency to do so differed hardly at all from the second quartile. The third rather than the lowest quartile leaned most heavily away from the Tory party. There is also no indication of change across time, or change related to Reform in this evidence. Shrewsbury's powerful response to Reform had little to do with the socio-economic situations of voters.

TABLE 7.9 *Proportional Tory Voting: Shrewsbury Economic Quartiles* (%)

Year	Quartiles			
	1 (highest)	2	3	4 (lowest)
1826	59	59	47	51
1830	63	63	45	33
1835	56	49	48	58
1841	58	52	47	56

Sources: See Table 7.2.

Most studies of England's later twentieth-century electorate have concluded that 'whatever theory or method is used to define class, the result is the same: most British voters do not have their vote determined by occupational class'.[66] The same might be said of the early nineteenth-century electorate. J. P. Parry recently noted that the evidence of voting by occupation in the early nineteenth century suggests 'that under certain circumstances social status could affect voting patterns'.[67] The evidence from these towns confirms that suggestion, but those 'certain circumstances' were locally specific. In this area more than any other, O'Gorman's dictum rings true: 'The study of electoral politics becomes the study of local communities.'[68]

[66] H. T. Himmelweit, P. Humphreys, and M. Jaeger, *How Voters Decide* (Milton Keynes, 1985), 37, 50.
[67] 'Constituencies, Elections', 155.   [68] *Voters*, 9–10.

If not socio-economic status, might religion be a key to electoral behaviour, unreformed or reformed? Wald, for instance, has argued forcefully that 'class . . . was secondary to religion in its capacity to structure the vote'.[69] If recent studies of the electorate in Thatcherite England can describe voting as the 'last religious act in a secular age', what was the likely nature of voting during what Boyd Hilton has called the Age of Atonement?[70]

[69] *Crosses on the Ballot*, 161.
[70] Himmelweit, Humphreys, and Jaeger, *How Voters Decide*, 37; Hilton, *Age of Atonement*.

8

Reform Refracted 2:
Praying and Voting

THE politics of class dominated neither unreformed nor reformed politics, but a strong, consistent pattern of religious differentiation marked the partisans at every election tested in each of these constituencies both before and after Reform. The link forged in the eighteenth century between Nonconformists and Whigs persisted into the nineteenth century and survived 1832. If anything, the affinity of Nonconformists for the Whig party may have increased with Reform.

In contrast to the discord that dominates discussions of class, assessments of the political role of religion have been surprisingly harmonious. Again and again contemporaries and historians have pointed to the vital role of Protestant, non-Anglican Christianity in the development of political parties over the eighteenth and nineteenth centuries. Lecky, Macaulay, and Trevelyan all assumed the connection between the Whig party (in its earlier and later manifestations) and the Nonconformist community, and they found much support for their assumptions in contemporary opinion. Burke, Fox, and many of their later contemporaries often acted upon their belief that Dissenters supported Whigs. Most observers have shared similar assumptions about both unreformed and reformed England.[1] Robert Southey was clear in his own mind about the politics of Dissenters both in the era of Burke and Fox and in his own time: 'they [the Dissenters] were wholly with the Americans; and, during . . . the French Revolution their wishes were not with the government.' Writing in 1829, Southey assumed that 'at contested elections their weight is uniformly thrown into the

[1] Catholic emancipation and the Reform Act may have altered the normal relationship between Dissenters and the Whig party. Sellers argued that Nonconformity 'patched up its alliance with the Whigs' in 1835 following a temporary breakdown after 1828/9. I. Sellers, *Nineteenth–Century Nonconformity* (London, 1977), 69.

opposition scale'.[2] About 'old' Dissenters, then, there has been virtually no question; Dissenters were, always had been, and had no choice but always to be Whigs. Equally obvious to many was the relationship between the Church of England and the Tories. Indeed, many have assumed that the stronger the tie to the Established Church, the stronger the affiliation with the Tory party. Macaulay put it most succinctly in calling the Church of England 'the Tory party at prayer', but most other accounts have assumed the correctness of Macaulay's aphorism.[3]

Most observers, contemporary and otherwise, did not believe that Reform altered the existing relationship between religious and party preference. The House of Commons heard testimony in 1833 characterizing Dissenters as 'Reformers'.[4] James Florance believed 'the dissenters in Essex, almost to a man, adopt one line of politics, they are all of the Yellow [Whig] party'.[5] If, as many have argued, religion and not economics was 'probably the best demarcation line' in nineteenth-century England, the partisan rift between Dissenters and Anglicans should have continued despite the Reform Act's alterations in the political landscape.[6] P. F. Clarke has argued that religion rather than class defined the salient reference group in Victorian England, a view echoed by Patrick Joyce's view that 'a man's religion was the surest guide to his politics' in the later decades of the nineteenth century.[7] Norman Gash has pointed out that some Dissenters voted for Radicals, but that aside, the basic political division remained: 'the bulk of the dissenters . . . supported left wing politics'.[8] O. F. Christie agreed that the middle classes were divided into 'dissenters, who were generally Liberal or Radical, and Churchmen, who were generally Conservative'.[9] Very recent studies have concluded that 'Nonconformists were overwhelmingly

[2] Southey, *Sir Thomas More*, ii. 44.

[3] P. G. Pulzer, *Political Representation and Elections* (London, 1967), 108.

[4] *Parl. Pap.* 9 (1833), 238.

[5] As for the Catholics, J. Willcocks, chief magistrate of police in Tipperary, argued that Roman Catholics were not influenced by their priests to vote against their consciences. Ibid. 8 (1835), 675–7, 5560–1; E. R. Norman, *Church and Society in England* (Oxford, 1976), 186–7.

[6] D. G. Wright, 'Politics and Opinion', 34.

[7] 'Electoral Sociology', 42. Joyce argued 'religion was probably of the first importance in politics', but also that 'for the mass electorate work was undoubtedly the primary matrix of political consciousness'. *Work, Society*, 223.

[8] Gash also believed that the connection linking Wesleyans and the Tory party diminished after 1832. *Age of Peel*, 111.

[9] *Transition from Aristocracy*, 71–4.

Liberal, usually by ratios of between eight and twelve to one'.[10] A quantitatively sophisticated study of the *fin de siècle* has argued that religion was the major electoral factor in elections from 1885 to 1910 since 'Nonconformity was a strong, significant, negative predictor of Conservatism'.[11]

Much qualitative evidence from these towns supports the view that religion weighed heavily in political matters. The local opposition party in Great Yarmouth emerged at the end of the eighteenth century primarily as a result of the political exclusion of Yarmouth's large and wealthy Dissenting community which contained relatively large groups of Congregationalists and Baptists as well as a smaller but no less powerful set of Quakers. Nonconformists were 'the nucleus of every opposition interest in Yarmouth'.[12] Similarly in Lewes, 'opposition was synonymous with dissent'.[13] Colchester's opposition party also leaned heavily on Dissenters, whose apostasy in 1790 proved the exception rather than the rule.[14] Since Dissenters constituted approximately a quarter of the borough by 1829, their behaviour could tip the scales in an election. In Colchester as in many places, 'the *odium theologicum* permeated almost every aspect of the political life of the borough', because 'the alignment of Church and Tory and Liberal Dissent was normally adhered to by the majority of the politically committed in the town'.[15] Northampton's Baptist MP, R. V. Smith, feared in 1837

[10] J. P. Parry, *Democracy and Religion* (Cambridge, 1985), 11; D. H. Close, 'The General Elections of 1835 and 1837', D.Phil. (Oxford, 1967), 141.

[11] Anglicanism, on the other hand, was not equally positively associated with Conservatism. Wald, *Crosses on the Ballot*, 151, 161, 150.

[12] C. J. Palmer, *The Perlustration of Great Yarmouth*, 3 vols. (Great Yarmouth, 1872–5), i. 197, 325. Hayes used virtually the same phrase for the 1820s: 'the Yarmouth dissenters were the nucleus of every opposition interests.' 'Politics in Norfolk', 124. See also L. Namier and J. Brooke, *The House of Commons, 1754–1790*, 3 vols. (London, 1964).

[13] Brent, 'Second Reform Act. See also W. K. Rector, 'Lewes Quakers in the Seventeenth and Eighteenth Centuries', *Sussex Archeological Collections*, 116 (1978), 31–40.

[14] George Tierney attributed his defeat in 1790 'to the cool, deliberate treachery of the Dissenters who formerly supported me. To them alone I owe my defeat, and to their conduct I can give no other name than that of treachery, because it never showed itself in the shape of open hostility, but wore the mask of friendship to the last.' *Chelmsford and Colchester Chronicle*, 4 June 1790.

[15] The parliamentary return of 1829 listed 4,330 Dissenters in Colchester of a total population of about 16,000, broken down into 2,200 Independents, 1,100 Baptists, 930 Methodists, and 100 Quakers. Speight, 'Colchester', 250. Speight's characterization of the town is a restatement of the *Essex Standard*'s comment that the general election 'is Church and Tory against Dissent and Whig'. *Essex Standard*, 30 July 1847.

that Northamptonshire's Dissenters might be deflected from their normal support of the Whigs by Lord Milton's abstention on the Church Rates Abolition Bill, but he clearly assumed that Dissenters would support any Whig candidate *ordinarily*. In the eyes of Northampton's Whigs, the publication of the *Herald* was a desperate effort to 'support the tottering Tory party in this county and especially that part of it belonging to the Church establishment'.[16]

Bristol echoed these views. A letter to Sir Richard Vyvyan before the 1832 election suggested that 'scattered chiefly among all classes of the Dissenters' was a 'numerous body of respectable Voters, who are intelligent, moral and strictly religious', and Whig.[17] Political commentators in Maidstone also equated post-Reform Whig and Dissenting fortunes. The editor of the Whig *Maidstone Gazette* condemned the Nonconformist editor of the Tory *Maidstone Journal* as a modern-day Judas Iscariot who 'would sell every non-conformist in the Kingdom for thirty pieces of silver'. William Bentliff reminded Maidstone's Dissenters in 1835 that 'the only chance they had of procuring relief from their disabilities was by acting energetically' for Whig candidates.[18] Playing upon that theme, Whig candidates often called for Church reform and for fully opening England's universities to Dissenters.[19] While few commentators went as far as the contributor to the *Northampton Free Press* who in 1841 'wished heartily every Methodist, or indeed every Dissenter, who voted for Conservative candidates, might, when dead, be refused a Christian burial!!!—that his body be burnt!!! and his ashes kicked about in the public streets', contemporary political observers in these towns assumed that Dissenters should not, and ordinarily would not, cast Tory votes.[20]

Despite the certainty with which opinions about Dissenters' affinity for the Whigs were voiced, other observers occasionally qualified or denied the existence of the relationship, at least for specific times and places. Reflecting on English history, Sir John Dillon believed that 'Mr Pitt defeated the Whigs through his

[16] Smith, a Baptist, represented Northampton at each Parliament from 1831 until 1859. NtRO, Gotch MSS 582, 23 June 1837; *Northampton Free Press*, 29 Sept., 17 Nov. 1832; Ayers (ed.), *Paupers and Pig Killers*, 223.
[17] CRO, Vyvyan MSS, DDV/BO/61/7, Curnick to Vyvyan, 3 Nov. 1832; DDV/BO/62/12, 3 Jan. 1835.
[18] *Maidstone Gazette*, 4 Nov., 9 Dec. 1834; 6 Jan. 1835.
[19] Ibid. 16 Dec. 1834; 25 July 1837.
[20] *Northampton Herald*, 12 June 1841.

popularity at the time with the Dissenters'.[21] Few commentators can be found to agree with Dillon's blunt rejection of the Whig/Dissent link, but many have at least hedged their bets. In some towns Roland Thorne found that 'the dissenting interest was drawn into political animosity', but as late as 1818 only seventeen boroughs contained Dissenters who were a 'force to be reckoned with'.[22] Others have warned that religion's role could be vastly altered by particular circumstances. When at Oldham's first parliamentary election John Bright was accused of being as bad as a Tory on the slavery issue, 'it proved', in the words of a diarist, 'their [the Whigs'] death blow amongst the religious portion of the constituency'.[23] The other religious issue, Catholicism, was seen as particularly likely to alter the normal partisan balance among Anglicans and Non-conformists. John Allen believed that fear of popery could easily drive the Dissenters into the arms of the Church since he had 'heard of Dissenters and even Quakers declaring that they look to the Church as the only security against the Papists'.[24] Anti-Catholic mania such as was found in Beverley lends some credence to views like Allen's. Antipathy towards Catholicism may have determined more votes than rifts between different varieties of non-Catholics.[25] The kind of unanimity achieved against Catholicism in Colchester in 1829, when Sir G. H. Smyth presented a petition against emancipation signed by 3,000 men, points to Catholicism's potential power to override Protestant sectarian differences.[26] The inhabitants of Bristol who demanded in 1835 that Peel and the King defend Protestantism above all made it clear that they regarded 'the contest between Protestantism and Popery, as a struggle between Truth and Falsehood', and therefore could 'agree to no compromise'.[27] Non-negotiable issues can generate unusual political alliances.

[21] Sir J. Dillon, *Horae Icenae* (London, 1835), 35.

[22] Thorne, *House of Commons*, i. 258. 62.

[23] Sykes, 'Working-Class Consciousness'.

[24] A. Kriegel (ed.), *The Holland House Diaries, 1831–40* (London, 1977), 373, citing the diary of John Allen, 25 Aug. 1837.

[25] By mid-century Catholics constituted no more than 4% of the population, and that represented a tenfold increase over the later 18th cent. E. R. Norman, *The English Catholic Church in the Nineteenth Century* (Oxford, 1984).

[26] CLHL, E. COL. 1/324.26/DG29196. In 1829 Harvey reneged on his pledge and voted 'as a representative of the people and not merely as a deputy of some borough'. *Colchester Gazette*, 3 June 1826, 17 Mar. 1827; *MoP* (1829), 443, 515.

[27] CRO, Vyvyan MSS, DDV/BO/63/88, 6 Apr. 1835.

The degree to which other constituencies shared the rabid anti-Catholicism of Beverley and Colchester is less clear. Dawson Turner, long-time political activist and reformer in Great Yarmouth, explained in 1821 that the 'Catholic Question' had all but vanished. Men like Turner's father and grandfather thirty-five years earlier who could still remember the Jacobite rebellion of 1745 'entertained the utmost horror of papacy', but Dawson claimed 'the breed is now quite extinct; Nobody seems now to care a doit about the matter except the clergy'.[28] Those who did care might have been confused about the most appropriate party choice for defeating Catholic claims. Both parties had at times acted in ways likely to antagonize fervent anti-Catholics. Moreover, many Dissenters had regarded Liverpool as a friend, particularly after he reduced penalties against Nonconformists in 1812.[29] Under these circumstances, it would have been difficult for Dissent to maintain a united political front even if, as Cowherd insists, they had 'acquired the solidarity of a religious minority'.[30]

Frank O'Gorman has recently questioned the Whig/Dissent connection and warned against the automatic assumption of a connection between Dissenters and Foxite Whigs. Although he noted that 'in the revival of party distinctions at the constituency level the function of religion can hardly be overestimated', and admitted that Nonconformists exhibited an 'acute municipal consciousness' in thirty or forty larger and smaller market towns that cut two large swathes through the English countryside, he characterized the political influence of religion as possibly more perception than reality. No one, he has argued, has shown religion to be 'the critical element in the political and social perceptions' of the unreformed electorate, and religion was only one of many group interests that affected electoral behaviour. It may have wielded less punch because 'it was less frequently mobilized' than many others. There is, besides, 'no evidence that Dissenters had Whig tendencies or that Anglicans had Tory preferences' at elections in four Northern counties in the 1820s. Nottingham's Dissenters also appear to have failed to vote as a group in 1780. Abingdon's Nonconformists

[28] NRO, Rumbold MSS, L14/7, Dawson Turner to Charles Rumbold, 10 Feb. 1821.

[29] Gash, *Lord Liverpool*, 94–5.

[30] R. G. Cowherd, *The Politics of English Dissent* (New York, 1956), 22; Thorne, *House of Commons*, i. 258, citing *The Late Elections*.

supported Tory candidates before 1774 (though they switched *en bloc* to the Whigs that year). And Preston's Methodists in 1807 failed to vote in lock-step for the independent candidate (though 39 per cent did plump necessarily to support the lone independent).[31] If these Nonconformists refused the Whig yoke, might not others have done so?

Thus, however often and however confidently the relationship between religion and politics has been asserted, it has seldom been demonstrated, at least in part because of the constraints imposed by the availability of data. While it is frequently possible to identify members of particular congregations either from membership rolls or from records of births, baptisms, and deaths, most researchers have concluded with Nossiter that 'the painstaking correlation of poll books with church records would be possible with sufficient time, but it is doubtful if the effort would be adequately repaid'.[32] Nossiter's caution seems reasonable, but as it happens, such 'painstaking correlation' does repay the effort sufficiently often. Discerning the actual political behaviour of Dissenters, particularly across time, permits demonstration to take the place of mere surmise. Before tackling entire electorates, though, an analysis of clerical behaviour permits a limited test of the relationship between religion and politics. Positively identified clergymen leave little doubt about the political preferences of the Anglican, Dissenting, and Catholic establishments.

Dissenting ministers and Roman Catholic priests were so remarkably uniform in their preference for Whig/Liberal/reforming candidates that it is impossible for their behaviour to be mistaken. As Vincent notes, 'no other occupation was so partisan, so militant, so unfloating, as the Dissenting ministers', and, one might add, Catholic priests.[33] With a few rare aberrations, such as William Thorpe's plump for the arch-Tory Sir Richard Vyvyan at the Bristol election of 1832, or the Tory double cast in 1837 by the Revd. John Stevens, a Dissenting minister in Lewes, the behaviour of the Nonconformist clergy was so uniformly Whiggish in orientation that

[31] O'Gorman, *Voters*, 363–8; id., *The British Two-Party System*, 78–80.

[32] 'Elections and Political Behaviour', 524. O'Gorman did not correlate poll books and church records, noting instead with regard to Abingdon what might be generalized to all of the boroughs he examined, that 'The paucity of information regarding religious affiliation in most poll books makes it very difficult to estimate' the relationship. *Voters*, 364 n. 169.

[33] Vincent, *Pollbooks*, 57, 67–9.

it is easy to understand the *Maidstone Gazette*'s outraged attack on the Tory votes and editorials of John Vynall, Dissenting minister and editor of the *Maidstone Journal*. Dissenting clergymen adhered so closely to the stereotype that Vynall's behaviour appeared nothing short of treacherous.[34] Dissenters were almost never willing even to split their support. Henry Reece, minister to Shrewsbury's Welsh chapel, split his votes between the parties for three successive elections beginning in 1832, and he was joined in 1835 by Thomas Weaver, an Independent minister. These two men stood virtually alone among all the Dissenting or Catholic clergy identifiable in all contested elections examined here. Lock-step behaviour of this sort well justifies Vincent's metaphorical identification of Dissenting ministers as the 'sort of Communist hard core to the Popular Front'.[35]

The Anglican clergy are sometimes less easily identified, but their behaviour is no less easily summarized. Vincent has confidently argued that unlike their 'militant' Nonconformist counterparts, Anglican clergymen, along with their retinues of sextons, organists, and gravediggers, were 'more evenly split between the parties, by a long way'.[36] One study of the general elections of 1830 and 1831 has lent support to this generalization by identifying 1,735 Anglican ministers opposed to Reform and another 796 in favour of it, a Tory majority of only 70 per cent.[37] These arguments for mixed political views from the Anglican pulpit, however, are not corroborated by the evidence from the eight towns. Anglican clergymen at these elections were anything but mixed. Vincent's arguments notwithstanding, Anglicans in these towns were Tories.

Richard Astley, Unitarian minister of Shrewsbury, plumped for the sole Whig candidate in 1832, as did James Craig, a minister of the Church of Scotland, Samuel Jones, a Roman Catholic priest, and Manoah Kent, a local Baptist minister. Conversely, that same year, Richard Lawrence, the curate of St Chad's parish church in Shrewsbury, voted for the two Tory candidates, and he was joined in

---

[34] At the Bristol election of 1820 one of five Dissenting ministers (the Methodist, John Rowe) cast a plumper for the mild Whig, Henry Bright, while the others, along with the bulk of their fellow electors, cast double votes for Bright and Protheroe. Bristol Central Library, Manuscript Poll Book, 1820, B4419. Williams, 'Bristol in the General Elections of 1818 and 1820', 193 n. 3.

[35] *Pollbooks*, 27.   [36] Ibid. 18.

[37] J. N. Odurkene, 'The British General Elections of 1830 and 1831', B.Litt. (Oxford, 1976), 148–50 cited in O'Gorman, *Voters*, 368.

the Tory ranks by his fellow Established clergymen G. A. Maddock and Benjamin Maddy. In fact, not one of the twenty-six men who belonged to the Established Church in Shrewsbury during all of the elections considered here cast a Whig vote. Only two of them even split their support. Shrewsbury's clergymen often declined to vote, but if they did vote, they voted Tory. An equally sharp political division separated the Anglican clergy from their Dissenting counterparts in other towns. Poll books from Colchester list only one Dissenter. The other, presumably Anglican, clergymen cast their votes exclusively for Tory candidates with the sole exception of James T. Round, who cast a double Whig vote in 1832 before joining his brethren among the Tories in succeeding years. At Lewes elections the Established clergy followed the idiosyncratic but no less definite Tory pattern common to the years before 1837. Lewes Tories simply did not cast plumpers. Therefore, Lewes's Anglican clergymen appear to have been splitting when in fact they were strictly adhering to the Tory line.[38] Faced with two Tories standing in 1837 and 1841, the parsons uniformly cast double Tory votes. A rare exception to the rule, the parish clerk of St John's split his vote in 1841, but the remainder of the incumbents cast doubles correctly in both elections.

Bristol's clergymen voted overwhelmingly for the White Lion choices of Davis and Protheroe in 1818. Only one resident and one non-resident parson cast a vote for the radical Whig, Sir Samuel Romilly. The Anglican establishment turned out as forcefully for the Tory/West Indian Whig duo of Vyvyan and Baillie at Bristol's first reformed election. Again, only one of dozens of Anglicans cast a vote for the reformers Protheroe and Williams. The only recorded exception to a Vyvyan-Miles double Tory vote among the clerics in 1835 came from the Revd. C. P. Bullock, who split his support by voting for Vyvyan and Baillie. Bullock's rebellion is not very impressive since Baillie had been the 'acceptable' Whig candidate three years earlier when he stood with Vyvyan against the reformers. Parson Bullock had reason to be somewhat confused because occasionally the picture in Bristol was confused by nominally Whig candidates who created the misleading appearance of split-voting among the clergy. Clergymen who appear to have been voting for Whigs, however, were in fact adhering strictly to White Lion policy.

[38] J. A. Phillips, 'Partisan Behaviour in Adversity: Lewes and Reform', *Parliamentary History*, 6 (1987), 262–79.

In 1832, for example, Anglican clergymen, like all Bristol Tories, voted for a nominal Whig as the lesser evil to accompany their solitary Tory candidate, Sir Richard Vyvyan.

Poll books in Maidstone and Beverley contained relatively few clergymen, and their overt political strength was reduced further in Maidstone by several who chose not to vote at all. The few clerks who did record their choices, however, voted Tory. Typically, the Revd. Henry J. Parker plumped necessarily for Wyndham Lewis in 1832 and cast a double for Lewis along with his partner, Benjamin Disraeli in 1837. Beverley's Revd. Joseph Coltman turned in a slightly less reliable performance; he split his vote between the parties in 1818 and again in 1832. Ordinarily, though, he could be counted upon to fill Conservative ranks, even when asked to plump for a single Tory candidate. He plumped for Capel Cure in 1830, Charles Winn in 1831, and James Wier Hogg in 1835. His colleague Ebenezer Robertson split his support by coupling Henry Burton with his vote for Hogg in 1835, but most other Established clergymen such as G. B. Blythe and W. R. Gilby passed the party test consistently.

In some towns like Great Yarmouth, poll books indicate a substantial number of 'clergymen' voting for Whig candidates. If one assumes that 'the terms "clerk" and "clergyman" always referred to an Anglican, and the term 'minister' always identified a Nonconformist', Yarmouth's poll books appear to demonstrate a partisan split among the Anglicans.[39] Many of those described as 'clerk' in this extremely partisan town voted for Whig candidates. This apparent demonstration is merely a mirage. Yarmouth's 'clerks' were not necessarily Anglicans, and Yarmouth's 'ministers' were not always Nonconformists. For example, Richard Turner, listed in 1826 as 'minister', was an Anglican parson who voted Tory year after year. After 1820, Yarmouth's poll books used the title 'clerk' indiscriminately. Thus the votes of Thomas Sayers, W. T. Worship, T. C. Fowler, Thomas Clowes, and C. J. Cheeper, all 'clerks', appear to indicate an Anglican phalanx in the Yarmouth electorate that in fact did not exist.

Towns with better poll-book keepers such as Northampton presented a very different image. Northampton's poll books left no questions about institutional affiliations; parish clerks were never

---

[39] Vincent, *Pollbooks*, 52.

confused with vicars, Dissenting ministers were separated from their Anglican counterparts and usually had their particular denomination identified. With this sort of unmistakable attribution, the deep rift between Anglican clergymen and the rest was immediately visible. Of thirty-eight identifiable clergymen between 1818 and 1841, all but one fit the pattern precisely. The fourteen Nonconformist ministers and the two Catholic priests voted exclusively for Whig/reformer/Liberal candidates at every election, while twenty-one of twenty-two Anglicans voted each time for Tory candidates only, though usually this meant casting plumpers. Only Parson T. C. Haddon failed the party test when he cast Whig doubles in 1832 and in 1837, the only two polls at which he exercised his franchise.

Thus in these towns Anglican ministers voted Tory, Nonconformist ministers voted Whig. And as they voted, often so did they preach. Despite the Church of England's 'discouragement of party-political behaviour' that stood 'very centrally in the tradition of the nineteenth-century Church', many Anglican clergymen assumed an overtly political role.[40] Most observers perceived the pulpit as 'an important instrument of propaganda', agreeing with Lord Holland that 'A sermon on the subject is worth two pamphlets.'[41] Certainly, many clergymen made every effort to ensure their effectiveness.[42] The Bristol clergy made their political views absolutely clear in 1832 by locking all the belfrys in town to prevent ringing in celebration of the passage of the Reform Act, though, it must be said, these actions were particularly ineffective.[43] Testimony before a Commons

[40] R. Hole, *Pulpits, Politics, and Public Order in England, 1760–1832* (Cambridge, 1989). Sydney Smith, for one, stayed clear of the first reformed election, partly to make up for his essay on Mrs Partington. He remarked that he was instead 'behaving quite like a dignitary of the Church; that is, [he was] confining himself to digestion'. Lady Holland, *Memoir*, 501. Henry Hunt pointed out that in 1812 a majority of England's incumbents were non-resident, a condition that might have impaired their efficacy, but more than 4,000 did reside with their parishioners, and many of the non-residents lived very near. *Memoirs*, iii. 123. Hunt cited the parliamentary return listing 4,421 resident and 5,840 non-resident incumbents. Some non-residents, however, interacted closely with the parishes in their care. See Ayers (ed.), *Paupers and Pig Killers* for a description of the relationship between William Holland and his parishioners in Monkton Farley.

[41] E. A. Smith, 'Election Agent', *English Historical Review* (1969), 13.

[42] Richard Howes of Northampton sent a circular letter to the clergy in 1831 enclosing a copy of a 'Declamation against the violent Reform Measure', with the request that the clergy 'be kind enough to get it signed by as many of your Parishioners as are willing to sign the same'. NtRO, Northampton Borough Records, Box x5469, Circular of 18 Apr. 1831.

[43] Latimer, *Annals*, 184.

committee in 1835 branded the clergy as 'the most persevering and unscrupulous canvassers' and 'also the best keepers of their promises in not continuing their custom or otherwise'.[44] A report from Yarmouth in 1818 pointed out the degree to which clergymen often exerted themselves. Trying their best to defeat the True Blue (Whig) candidates in Yarmouth:

the Clergy in our latest struggle for independence not only supported the Ministerial candidates by their personal exertions on the canvass, the influence their cloth gave, and the pen which many of them wield so clumsily, but one Revd. Gentleman furnished a troop of 16 horse, which he mounted from the boldest of his tenantry and labourers for the purpose of acting in a body on the day of the election in the support of the Ministerialist Candidates in the market. They actually made their appearance on the Quay [in Yarmouth] and mounted their ORANGE cockades.[45]

The *Brighton Guardian* attributed Tory victories in 1835 to 'the influence of parsons' gained from their control over tithes.[46] Yarmouth's reformers tacitly recognized the potential power of the Established clergy when they promised that same year to 'fight the Tories and Parsons into fits'.[47] Some Whigs attributed their losses in 1837 to 'the violence and activity of the Clergy, who with very few exceptions have been indefatigable in their exertions to influence the farmers and landed gentry against the ministerial [Whig] candidates'.[48]

Nor were ministers of the Established Church the only ones trying to sway votes. In 1841 Lord Fitzwilliam noted that a Baptist minister named Giles in Leeds 'has been recommending to the flocks to put a great number of questions vis tests—such as abolition of church rates, —of Eccles.1 Courts—liberation of the tithes'. Fitzwilliam objected because 'the effect of this will be to play the game of the Tories, for tho some of the questions might be answered favourably, others could not'. The result 'must be most injurious to those who have a favourable feeling towards the Dissenters, though they do not see every question which interests them in precisely the same light in which they view it themselves'.[49] That same year one of Northampton's Independent

---

[44] *Parl. Pap.* 8 (1835), 45–55.

[45] *Norwich, Yarmouth, and Lynn Courier*, 27 June 1818.

[46] 28 Jan. 1835.

[47] BL, Dawson Turner MSS, N. TAB 2012/6/17.

[48] Kriegel (ed.), *Holland House Diaries*, 373.

[49] NtRO, Gotch MSS 613, Fitzwilliam to Gotch, 7 June 1841.

ministers nominated Raikes Currie at the hustings and worked actively in his successful Liberal campaign.[50]

But if the votes of the clergy leave few doubts about their political affiliation, there is considerable doubt about their political efficacy. The effects of ecclesiastical electioneering cannot be easily measured, but many questioned the political efficacy of the clergy. Thomas Erskine warned that the clergy should take care not to let themselves be seen by the 'common orders . . . as oppressors', and warned particularly that they 'ought never to be personally seen' as secular advocates.[51] The problem was likely to be compounded because many among the 'common orders' were almost certain to perceive the Established clergy as oppressive because Anglicans were usually 'men of birth and refined education'. This disparity between parsons and their flocks often resulted in a 'want of sympathy betwixt . . . pastors' and their congregations. The Earl of Mulgrave thought that political influence was more likely to be wielded by 'the illiterate and extemporizing artisan' than by a clergyman.[52] In 1835 James Florance agreed; he did 'not think that [the laity] are unduly influenced by their ministers, who in general are of the same kind of politics as the body of the congregation'.[53]

Anticlericalism further confuses the issue.[54] While it is not perhaps widespread, enough evidence of it exists to raise serious questions about the potential political efficacy of the Established clergy, if not all clergymen. A broadside from the Yarmouth election of 1831 entitled *The Parson's Lament* belittled

> Those pious sons of Church and State
> Reform they dread, reform they hate,
> Can they but of the fleece partake,
> The Devil may the carcase take,
> But they too long have borne the sway
> The people now must have their way.

Admonishing the reader to remember that 'the voice of Conscience is the Voice of God', the author of this piece looked to the day when each person 'like a Briton then will fight, ¦ Flooring the Parsons, left

[50] *Northampton Herald*, 3 July 1841.

[51] *Armata*, 128.   [52] Normanby, *The English at Home*, 241, 244.

[53] *Parl. Pap.* 8 (1835), 675–7, 41. This comment is much in line with Norman's view that 'the clergy did not advise the laity about their political conduct'. *Church and Society*, 186.

[54] E. J. Evans, 'Some Reasons for the Growth of English Rural Anti-Clericalism', *Past and Present*, 66 (1975), 84–109; id., *The Contentious Tithe* (London, 1976).

and right'.[55] A poem published in Keighley in 1834 voiced the 'Weaver's Complaint' against parsons who would, 'while folks are starving . . . sit down to dine, | On plenty of roast beef, plum pudding and wine'. The political opinions of those who were thought to 'learn like actors to speak from the stage, | Then follow the trade for the sake of the wage' might not be expected to carry much weight.[56]

Poll books do not really permit a test of assertions about the efficacy of ecclesiastical electioneering, but they allow an assessment of the political behaviour of ordinary Nonconformists. This research has heeded Nossiter's warning that 'the painstaking correlation of poll books with church records' probably would not repay the effort in one respect: the great bulk of the population who were at least nominally Anglican have been omitted from this examination. Nossiter is undoubtedly correct about the difficulties of the task, but more critically, Anglicanism is a difficult concept to measure among the rank and file. Nonconformity may have meant very different things to different people, a problem aggravated by the variety of Nonconformist denominations, but the 'meaning' of subscribing to the Established Church, at least nominally, is too nebulous to be addressed behaviourally. Agreement would never be reached about who the Anglicans were, much less what it meant to call them that.[57] Therefore, altering the focus from shepherds to their flocks will be necessarily a one-sided affair as Anglicans are ignored in favour of Dissenters, who present substantial problems of their own but lend themselves more readily to reasonably certain identification and interpretation.[58]

Finding Nonconformist voters is not always possible. They could not be identified in Bristol's electorate, for example, because the town was too large and names too widely duplicated for Dissenters to be traced effectively. Bristol voters could be identified in a series of poll books because occupation and address made it possible to distinguish most of the various men sharing names. Changes in one or other of these descriptors could also be handled in many instances

[55] BL, N. TAB 2012/6/1, 42.

[56] *The Weaver's Complaint* (Keighley, 1834).

[57] J. A. Phillips, 'The Social Calculus: Deference and Defiance in Later Georgian England', *Albion*, 21 (1989), 426–49.

[58] Robert Morris, cleverly using parish church rebuilding lists for 1837, found that an 'important minority' (15–32%) of Leeds's Anglicans voted Whig at the elections of 1832 and 1834.

without the individual being lost from view, particularly if poll books used two (or more) given names. Chapel records, on the other hand, usually identified individuals only by name because parish clerks used the combinations of given names of husbands and wives to keep their records straight. Since wives' names did not appear on poll books, Nonconformists could not be detected. Nonconformist electors in Beverley and Maidstone also largely escaped detection simply because the names appearing on chapel records of various kinds could not be found in poll books. The baptismal roll of the Week Street Independent Chapel in Maidstone recorded the names of 270 men from 1817 to 1832, most of them presumably of voting age, yet only twelve of these names also appeared on poll books.[59] Maidstone's Methodists, Presbyterians, and Baptists were just as elusive. Of the 155 names found on baptismal records that asked for occupation as well as name, only fourteen men could be traced to Maidstone's electorate. Beverley actually permitted the identification of more Nonconformist electors from far sparser chapel records, but the combination of scanty records and few matches generated only a few dozen Dissenters in Beverley whose votes could be examined.[60]

Conversely, nearly 10 per cent of the Lewes electorate could be identified as Dissenters. Their support for Whig/reformer and Tory candidates is presented in Table 8.1, along with overall Whig voting for comparison. A relatively strong, and notably consistent pattern, is evident. While not as adamant as Maidstone's few identifiable Dissenting voters, a solid majority of Lewes's chapel-goers voted Whig. The electorate overall gave Whig candidates more than half of their votes in 1835, and nearly half in 1826 and 1837 as well, yet the Dissenters still accorded Whigs significantly greater support.[61] The remainder of the Dissenters divided between Tory candidates or split their votes. If Lewes's Dissenters are any indication of the norm, the Whig party would have benefited from an electorate

---

[59] Ordinarily, a link from Dissenting register to poll book should be made for essentially coterminus records because membership in a congregation often was temporary. Individuals switched to other chapels or denominations or reverted to the Established Church. After failing to find many Maidstone Dissenters in the electorate using the normal procedures, however, an effort was made to expand their numbers by searching through all poll books, also without success.

[60] When found, Maidstone's Dissenters were zealous Whigs. Conversely, Beverley's few identifiable Dissenters supported neither party.

[61] Excess support for Whig candidates among Dissenters was only marginally significant in 1826.

TABLE 8.1. *Lewes Dissenters and Electors* (%)

Election year	Dissenters voting Whig	Dissenters voting Tory	All electors voting Whig
1818	56.3	43.8	26.6
1826	59.6	0	48.1
1830	60.1	3.3	40.9
1835	67.5	18.4	50.1
1837	73.2	24.2	49.3
1841	70.5	21.6	48.1

Note: Dissenting N = 188. Overall electorate N = 2011.
Sources: PRO, RG4/2063, 2623, 2850, 2967; locally printed poll books for the six elections.

composed exclusively of Nonconformists. Even in an electorate dominated by Anglicans, the Nonconformist vote could be critical.

Dissenters in Colchester and Great Yarmouth demonstrated a similar preference for Whig (or Radical) candidates (Table 8.2). Colchester's elections were simplified before 1835 by the constantly successful candidacy of the Radical Whig Daniel Whittle Harvey, who accomplished something just short of a miracle for consistently winning a seat in an overwhelmingly Conservative town. After his initial victory in 1818 Harvey persuaded 31 per cent of all voters to cast plumpers for him and another 20 per cent to disregard his political views and couple his name with one of the two Tories, placing him at the top of the poll.[62] Yet even with this much general support, Nonconformists supported Harvey far more fervently. Nearly two-thirds plumped for Harvey (more than twice the overall rate) in 1820 while only one in ten cast a double Tory vote.

Colchester's Dissenting voters helped return Harvey for the fifth time in 1832 by casting nearly three-quarters of their votes for the two reforming candidates, just as they had helped return both reformers the year before. And they continued, despite the absence of Daniel Whittle Harvey, to cast Whig votes in subsequent elections, though without Harvey's charisma, Whigs had no chance of winning a seat.

[62] Harvey's victory in 1818 followed a defeat by fewer than 30 votes in 1812, and an overwhelming defeat at the 1818 by-election to fill the seat of Richard Hart Davis. The third time proved a charm.

TABLE 8.2. *Dissenters in Colchester and Great Yarmouth* (%)

| | | Election Year | | | |
		1820	1832	1837	N
Colchester					
	Whig	64.1	72.1	74.8	193
	Tory	11.5	16.3	25.2	
	Split	24.4	11.6	0	
Great Yarmouth					
	Whig	76.4	78.1	80.3	119
	Tory	23.6	21.9	19.7	
	Split	0	0	0	

Sources: PRO, RG4/357–8, 1099, 1508–9, 1973–5, 2163, 2473, 2907; printed poll books for elections of 1820, 1832, and 1837.

The figures for Great Yarmouth's Dissenters in Table 8.2 also points unmistakably to their affinity for Whig candidates. The complete domination of Great Yarmouth at election after election by three Whig MPs, George Anson, C. E. Rumbold, and William Wilshere, helps clarify Dissenting electoral choices. Anson and Rumbold won each election between 1818 and their narrow defeat in 1835.[63] Rumbold and his new partner, William Wilshere, then resumed the string of victories in 1837 and 1841. Table 8.2 reports two victories by the Anson/Rumbold ticket and one by its successor Rumbold/Wilshere. In all three the attractiveness of the ticket to Dissenters far outweighed its strong appeal to the entire electorate. At the three reported elections Whig candidates managed to attract approximately 54 per cent of the overall vote, but won three-quarters or more of the Nonconformists.[64] Virtually all of Great Yarmouth's voters cast strictly partisan ballots at all of these contests, making comparisons straightforward. A sizeable minority of the town's Dissenters cast strictly Tory votes, year in and year out, but the

[63] George Anson actually replaced his brother T. W. Anson after the 1818 victory.

[64] At the elections in question the Whigs won by attracting 55.2%, 53.7%, and 53.6% of the overall vote. Since no one in Great Yarmouth split, the Tories attracted the remaining 45–6% of the total vote. When the Tories turned the tide and won both seats in their solitary victory of 1835, they also won by attracting 53% of the vote. The only election at which more than two-thirds of all voters supported Whig candidates, a feat that should have been all but impossible, occurred at the abbreviated and poorly attended election of 1826. For a summary see H. S. Smith, *Register*, 177–8.

preponderant Dissenting influence fell consistently and powerfully in the Whig camp.

These two tabular presentations of dissenting voting patterns share a generic perspective; each counts all Nonconformists together. Relatively sparse records and the need to keep a sufficiently large number of Dissenters in view at any one time necessitated this aggregation. Fortunately, these necessarily crude measurements of Nonconformist behaviour are supported by a more detailed examination of Northampton, a town that bred a better class of record-keepers. Its poll books described the denominational affiliations of clergymen far better than many other towns, and its Nonconformist ministers also kept exemplary records of their congregations, resulting in the identification of more Dissenters in Northampton than in the other towns of this study. These superior records permit members of specific congregations to be examined individually, with interesting results that broadly corroborate the patterns in Lewes, Colchester, and Great Yarmouth (see Table 8.3).

TABLE 8.3. *Northampton Nonconformists (%)*

Congregation		Election year			N
		1818	1832	1837	
King's Head Lane	Whig	62.5	75.1	73.9	107
Independent	Tory	14.6	10.4	17.4	
	Split	22.9	14.5	8.7	
Commercial Street	Whig	69.8	77.1	76.3	113
Independent	Tory	18.7	15.8	18.6	
	Split	11.5	7.1	5.1	
King Street Chapel	Whig	NA	81.0	96.2	43
Presbyterian	Tory	NA	13.5	3.8	
	Split	NA	5.5	0	
College Street	Whig	94.3	96.1	91.8	86
Baptist	Tory	0	1.8	6.1	
	Split	5.7	2.1	2.1	
All Saints Methodist	Whig	45.5	64.3	75.5	259
	Tory	34.8	24.7	16.0	
	Split	19.7	11.0	8.5	

NA Not applicable.
Sources: PRO, RG4/902, 903, 1141, 1275, 1277, 1347, 1348; printed poll books for elections of 1818, 1832, and 1837.

Dissenters of all kinds and at nearly all times in Northampton preferred Whig candidates by a wide margin. Thomas Roberts, a Presbyterian builder who attended King Street Chapel, plumped for Sir George Robinson, the only Whig candidate, in 1818. He cast two Whig votes in 1820 and 1826, supporting Robinson and the other Whig, W. L. Maberly, both times. He continued to vote for Robinson along with his two new companions, C. Hill in 1830 and R. V. Smith in 1831, and followed this exclusively Whig behaviour in the unreformed period with a series of equally Whig votes after Northampton's reform by supporting Smith and the person with whom he stood at the next four contests. Thomas Roberts was hardly alone. Too few of his fellow Presbyterians could be identified to justify a report of percentages in Table 8.3, but all five voted Whig. At subsequent elections, when more Presbyterians could be found, they voted overwhelmingly Whig. The 81 per cent of 1832 and the 96.2 per cent of 1837 reported here were not atypical. A few renegades lived among them. William Hollowell, a shoemaker, voted for the two Tory candidates in 1832. James Mason, also a shoemaker, split his support in 1837 despite two Whig candidates. But these men were exceptional; on the whole, Northampton's Presbyterians had little use for Tory candidates.

Northampton's Baptists managed to be more determinedly Whig. Nine out of ten Baptists voted exclusively Whig at each of these elections, and at times the College Street congregation almost achieved Whig unanimity. The few who departed the fold were rare, and usually rejoined the flock quickly. Russell Piddington of Fetter Lane voted Tory in 1818, then split from 1820 to 1830 before rejoining the rest of Northampton's Baptists in voting Whig in 1832, 1835, and 1837. Henry Samwell split his vote in 1837, but all the elections leading up to 1837 found him in the Whig fold. He continued to split in 1841, but his votes may have stemmed from antagonism towards one of the Whig candidates rather than a shift in his political sentiments.[65] Both Independent congregations contributed heavily to Whig victories in Northampton. The voters affiliated with the King's Head Lane chapel turned in the lowest Whig proportionate vote of all of the old Dissenters, but that poorest performance was unmistakably Whig as more than 62 per cent of the Independents in 1818 followed the example of Thomas Roberts, the Presbyterian,

---

[65] Samwell's votes in 1837 and 1841 omitted the leading Northampton Whig R. V. Smith, for whom Samwell had voted since 1832.

and cast partisan plumpers for Sir George Robinson. The Independents who worshipped in Commercial Street turned in a slightly better performance in 1818 when nearly 70 per cent cast plumpers for Robinson. Both congregations moved well past 70 per cent, and usually beyond 75 per cent, in subsequent elections.

Only Northampton's Methodists presented a slightly different picture, and that difference all but disappeared over time. Along with a majority of the town's voters, Methodists refused to support Sir George Robinson's initial candidacy in 1818. Though it is not shown in Table 8.3, a majority of Northampton's Methodists switched to Robinson's camp at the election two years later. Their voting pattern was marred by far more splits and unnecessary plumps than adherents to old Dissent, but the swing to the Whigs was well under way before the Reform Act altered the composition of Northampton's electorate. Some Methodists, such as Peter Culcheth, persisted in their support for Tory candidates, but at the election of 1831 a majority of them voted for both Whig candidates, and this support increased the next year to nearly two-thirds while the overall electorate split Northampton's delegation. At subsequent elections most Methodists continued to vote Whig, achieving a proportionate level of support by 1835 and 1837 that was virtually indistinguishable from Northampton's Independent congregations while falling short of the remarkable Whiggery of the Baptists and Presbyterians.

CLASS AND RELIGION AND PARTISAN AFFILIATION

Chapter 7 argued that little measurable influence on electoral behaviour can be attributed to socio-economic variables in those towns where surviving data permit a test. Conversely, this chapter has pointed to quite a strong relationship between religious affiliations and political preferences among voters in most of these towns. One obvious response to this joint information would be to echo the conclusions of several recent studies and argue that religion, not class, was the key variable for political decisions in general and electoral decisions in particular. Unfortunately for the sake of neatness and simplicity, a response of such certainty cannot be upheld with the available evidence. The strong correlation of religious affiliation and partisan choice is interesting and suggestive, but it is impossible to discount socio-economic variables entirely, particularly in the light of the interrelationship of these two variables, class and religion.

Harold Perkin's assertion that Nonconformity was 'the midwife of class' points to the need for the utmost caution in distinguishing the effects of religion as distinct from socio-economic divisions within the electorate.[66] Other opinions about class and religion reveal apparent contradictions that resulted from the complexity of nineteenth-century social and economic realities. Nuttall and Chadwick believed that the Whigs drew support from Nonconformity in all its social gradations while the Tories could count on the votes of Anglicans of all classes.[67] Yet Blondel has argued that 'it is difficult to distinguish the influence of religion from the influence of occupations'.[68] Cowherd thought that 'at the beginning of the nineteenth century, Dissenters were primarily middle class', but others have been less certain about the social status of Nonconformists.[69] Wellington bemoaned the effects of Reform in 1833 as likely to transfer power from 'the Gentlemen of England, professing the faith of the Church of England, to another class of society, the shopkeepers, being dissenters from the Church, many of them Socinians, others Atheists'.[70] In mid-century Independents seemed to take pride in the exclusivity of their appeal. They believed that they attracted 'congregations of tradesmen, but never of artificers'.[71] Most who have written about Independents and other Nonconformists subsequently have assumed the accuracy of these kinds of self-assessments. Thus from Cowherd and Inglis to Ward, Dissenters have been allowed to take on an aura of respectability that may be undeserved. While David Thompson held that Dissenters were mainly of the middle class, he pointed out that the range of occupations followed included 'respectable working men'. Moreover, certain sects, notably the General Baptists of the New Connection and the Primitive Methodists, reached considerably

[66] H. Perkin, *The Origins of Modern English Society, 1780–1880* (London, 1969).
[67] G. F. Nuttall and O. Chadwick, *From Uniformity to Unity* (London, 1962), 257.
[68] J. Blondel, *Voters, Parties, and Leaders* (Harmondsworth, 1963), 61.
[69] *Politics of English Dissent*, 15.
[70] L. J. Jennings (ed.), *The Correspondence and Diaries of John Wilson Croker*, 3 vols. (London, 1885), ii. 205–6, Duke of Wellington to Croker, 6 Mar. 1833.
[71] *Congregational Year Book* (London, 1848), 84, cited in M. R. Watts, *The Dissenters*, ii. (Oxford, forthcoming).

further down the occupational ladder and included artisans, small craftsmen, and manual workers.[72]

More recent studies of nineteenth-century Dissenters go much further than Thompson in rejecting middle-class characterizations of Nonconformity. Rather than the speculation and surmise common in so many earlier studies, A. D. Gilbert examined the evidence contained in the non-parochial registers of births, deaths, and baptisms. Though these records cannot provide a random sample in the technical sense, the nearly 11,000 recorded occupations indicate a relatively homogenous Nonconformist community which may have been somewhat more 'respectable' than the overall population, but which certainly fails any middle-class test. Whether Methodists, Baptists, or Congregationalists, the great bulk of Dissenters on the registers claimed to be artisans or labourers. Well over half of most dissenting congregations were artisans; another 10 per cent claimed to be nothing more than labourers.[73] Gilbert's analyses of Dissenting occupations were, in fact, strikingly similar to the analyses of electorates discussed in Chapter 7. Many at the lower end of the socio-economic spectrum were excluded from both groups, but those appeared as voters or Dissenters represented a broadly based portion of the population.

Michael Watts has now corroborated Gilbert's careful work. The majority of Nonconformists were workers, either craftsmen or labourers, not merchants and shopkeepers.[74] And Watts's extension of Nonconformity far below the reaches of the middle class is supported by the most recent study of eighteenth-century Dissent. James Bradley's quantitatively-based assessment found that many of those affiliated with old Dissent as well as with newer sects came from 'lower-paid, semi-skilled workers and labourers'.[75] Particularly after the American Revolution, Dissent attracted followers from the lower ranks of society at least in proportion to their overall presence, and frequently drew disproportionately from the more humble members of the community.

The greater socio-economic diversity now recognized among the Dissenting community complicates any attempted assessment of

[72] D. Thompson, *Nonconformity in the Nineteenth Century* (London, 1972), 13.
[73] A. D. Gilbert, *Religion and Society in Industrial England* (London, 1976), 63, 67.
[74] *Dissenters*, ii.
[75] *Religion, Revolution*, 17, 30, 413; id., 'Religion and Reform at the Polls', *Journal of British Studies*, 23 (1984); id., 'Nonconformity and the Electorate in Eighteenth-Century England', *Parliamentary History*, 6 (1987).

class and religion. It has been suggested by some theoretically oriented political scientists that 'discussions of whether class, religion, region, party identification, or the pursuit of individual self-interest are most important in determining voting behaviour are not theoretically enlightening'.[76] Perhaps not, but certainly it would be of considerable interest to students of the nineteenth century if some robust test could be undertaken that might permit a generalization about the underpinnings of partisan affiliation, however theoretically unenlightening. Unfortunately, the available individual-level data simply will not allow sophisticated tests of these interrelationships. Multicollinearity cannot be overcome. Too few voters who are also Dissenters can also be identified on tax rolls, and the sample of Dissenters is both too small and too non-random for any attempt at the relatively sophisticated statistical tests that might permit the separation of the occupational and religious components of voting choices.

It is impossible to determine qualitatively whether *laissez-faire* economics or theology provided the dominant impetus for the men guiding many of the changes in English society.[77] Either interpretation, if it excludes the other, rests on faith as much as on evidence. So too with the apparently solid data about working, praying, and voting. Religion emerges in these very simple tests as a dominant feature almost by default, but to elevate religion on the basis of the tests would be as simplistic as the tests have been simple. The figures in these pages point to religion as a critical component in the determination of popular political allegiances, but many other factors undoubtedly entered into the complicated formula that resulted in the voting decisions of both the unreformed and the reformed electorate.

[76] Przeworski and Sprague, *Paper Stones*, 143–4.

[77] Hilton, *Age of Atonement*; Parry, *Democracy and Religion*; Newbould, *Whiggery and Reform*; P. Mandler, *Aristocratic Government in the Age of Reform* (Oxford, 1990).

Conclusion
The Great Reform Bill?

SHORTLY after his daughter Arabella left for church on Sunday morning, 11 September 1831, John Calcraft sat down in his parlour in Whitehall Place, cut his throat with a razor, and died in a pool of blood.[1] His ambivalence about the Reform Bill killed him. Calcraft, a Whig sitting for his personal pocket borough Wareham off and on since 1790, had reluctantly joined Wellington's Government in 1828 as Paymaster General.[2] In that capacity he delivered 'one of the best speeches' against the Reform Bill before its second reading, only to become 'the only one of the Duke's Whig friends who proved faithless' by voting for it, thus providing its one-vote majority.[3]

Calcraft did not bear sole responsibility for the Reform Bill's survival. Another MP who supported the second reading argued quite pointedly that '*every* individual who voted in the majority is personally responsible for the event'. Moreover, Calcraft was not alone either in his ambivalence or in his apostasy. Fifteen MPs who voted with Calcraft for the Bill almost immediately deserted the

[1] J. C. Hobhouse, *Recollections of a Long Life*, ed. Lady Dorchester, 4 vols. (London, 1910), iv. 130–1. Coincidentally, that same morning Gladstone began the sixth volume of his diary with a poem about 'death that endures'.

[2] Calcraft, having inherited a fortune worth an estimated £10,000 p.a. at the premature death of his father in 1772, took his seat initially at 21 in 1786, left it in 1790, sat again from 1800 to 1806, then sat for Rochester until 1818, and returned to Wareham until 1831 when he let his son take borough while he won the county easily as a reformer. Calcraft's father bought the manor of Wareham in 1767, and further extensive purchases made it the family pocket borough by 1818. The younger Calcraft kept the single seat left to Wareham by Schedule B (it having just escaped Schedule A).

[3] Aspinall (ed.), *Diaries*, 17–18; T. Creevey, *The Creevey Papers*, ed. Sir H. Maxwell, 2 vols. (London, 1903), i. 213. Calcraft's suicide was attributed almost universally to his action in March. Lord Ellenborough noted: 'Calcaft . . . thought both Tories and Whigs despised him. He was right.' Aspinall (ed.), *Diaries*, 128. A rare exception was J. C. Hobhouse who believed 'politics had nothing to do with the matter [Calcraft's suicide]. He had lost his head from excessive worrying, I hear.' Hobhouse, *Recollections*, iv. 130–1.

Whigs to vote for Gascoyne's amendment carefully devised to sabotage it. One of them, George Staunton, a self-professed Liberal Tory until joining the Whigs after Canning's death, initially did not believe that Reform would leave England 'disposed to still further change and so on down to the lowest depth of Revolution and anarchy'. While in this optimistic frame of mind, Staunton voted for Reform. Soon, however, he found it 'impossible not to fear that the Parliament now electing [1831] under the influence of the prevailing excitement will prove a Revolutionary Parliament'.[4] Pessimism replacing optimism, Staunton voted against Reform. But if other MPs shared Calcraft's responsibility for the Bill's success on its second reading, and if some proved as unreliable, none shared Calcraft's high profile and anguish. Staunton and the others successfully defended their tergiversation to themselves and their fellows; Calcraft failed in both areas, fatally.

The persistent debate over the Reform Bill since its passage casts a sympathetic light on Calcraft's ambivalence in 1831. If hindsight, ordinarily so acute, has not permitted a clear image of 1832, Calcraft can hardly be faulted for his indecision and inconsistent behaviour. His vote for the Bill might have led to disaster, but his vote against it might have had the same effect. Who could say? If he listened to Wellington's gloomy prediction that Reform would mean that 'in a short time . . . nothing will remain of England but the name and the soil', he could hardly be expected to vote for the Bill. And Wellington's voice was but one of a host who believed England to be on the verge of revolution. In April 1831 the King himself opposed a general election which might throw the country 'into convulsion from Land's End to John O'Groat's house' and lead to 'open rebellion'.[5] Long before major riots such as Bristol's convinced many that the threat of revolution was only too real, much other evidence seemed to corroborate the most exaggerated apprehension. Reading Macaulay in June 1831, Wellington was 'much alarmed by the resemblance between the commencement of the Civil War and

---

[4] O'Neill and Martin, 'Backbencher', 543–8.

[5] Henry, Earl Grey (ed.), *The Correspondence of the late Earl Grey with H.M. King William IV*, 2 vols. (London, 1867), i. 154–83. By Nov. Staunton, the waverer, thought the question was no longer 'how shall we improve the system of our Representation, but how shall we prevent a Revolution'. The *Quarterly Review* made similarly ominous comparisons the following Mar., and Staunton found the 'numerous points of comparison . . . almost appalling'. O'Neill and Martin, 'Backbencher', 548, 554.

the present times'. Lord Brougham raised the same spectre in the minds of many others in his *Friendly Advice* to the Lords.[6] If weavers in Glasgow were openly threatening to 'arm themselves' in order to accomplish Reform, could revolution be far behind?[7]

On the other hand, how could Calcraft, a moderate, well-meaning man, originally a protégé of Charles James Fox, who had 'always' been 'a strong advocate for parliamentary reform', vote against a measure for which Thomas Hardy and so many others harboured such great expectations?[8] William Cobbett had predicted that Reform would restore an England in which it would be possible 'once more to see the labouring man with meat and bread, and a bed to lie on, and a Sunday coat to wear'.[9] Even if Calcraft knew better, and even if he agreed with Creevey that Cobbett was a 'foul-mouthed, malignant dog', could he vote against a measure that promised the nation's improvement?[10] As it happened, Calcraft's moderate, well-meaning side prevailed. He could not vote against Reform, whatever his fears.

Far lesser fears and more moderate hopes might well have been sufficient to sway opinions and votes such as Calcraft's and Staunton's. The *Westminster Review* believed that Reform would forever reduce the Tories to 'a contemptible minority'.[11] Lord Holland thought it might already have done so since Wellington's opposition to Reform had 'lost himself and his party in public estimation, perhaps forever'.[12] Nevertheless, the passage of the Bill threatened to make permanent the damage inflicted by the Duke's stand. The Radicals were arguing that 'no Tory must ever again be permitted to sit in a Reformed Parliament', and this prospect seemed all too likely after the general election of 1831.[13] The country seemed united against them. Only one county, Shropshire, returned two Tories in 1831, and the party could claim only four other county members after the election. With one exception, the Tories had lost

---

[6] Aspinall (ed.), *Diaries*, 93; Henry Brougham, *Friendly Advice Most Respectfully Submitted to the Lords* (London, 1831). See *AR* (1831), 254.

[7] *Westminster Review*, July 1831, 161.

[8] Aspinall (ed.), *Diaries*, 17–18.

[9] *Twopenny Trash*, 241. Ironically, hopes such as Cobbett's were reversed by the Whig Poor Law reforms. It seems certain that the new Poor Law was not just an effort by the aristocracy to reassert paternalistic control, but instead was a response to a new market-oriented vision of reality. See Mandler, *Aristocratic Government*.

[10] Creevey, *Papers*, i. 213, 333.

[11] Buller, 'Bribery and Intimidation at Elections', 485.

[12] BL, Add. MSS 51687, fo. 5.   [13] *Northampton Free Press*, 9 June 1832.

every town with an electorate of more than 600. Such a consequence cannot have appealed to Calcraft, as a member of Wellington's government, albeit a reluctant one, and such an outcome would have suited Staunton even less well. In any case, a substantial portion of the political nation had already made absolutely clear the country's determination to have 'the Bill, the whole Bill, and nothing but the Bill'. It could not have been at all clear to Calcraft or anyone else how Parliament could refuse to pass a measure that enjoyed such overwhelming popular support. The King's image of a convulsion from Land's End to John O'Groat's house was apparently all too true, and his worry about open rebellion seemed reasonable. Far larger groups of men as determined as Glasgow's weavers were not just asking for Reform. They were demanding it.

Calcraft's tortured decision saved the Bill at a critical juncture, but he need not have suffered such anguish over the measure that his vote rescued. The Reform Bill led to the realization of neither the great expectations nor the great fears of so many in 1831. In fact, most modern evaluations have heavily discounted its effects and stressed instead the striking continuities in the political system across the reigns of William IV and Victoria, particularly the corruption and undue influence that survived Reform. Whether or not they accept the arguments of Norman Gash and D. C. Moore, most 'have chosen to emphasize the conservative aspects of the bill, and in neglecting the positive spirit of reform, they have ignored the sense of progress and confidence in man's potential that was an essential part of Whig ideology'.[14] Those who have stressed the many unseemly aspects of electioneering that resisted Reform have sold short both the unreformed electoral system and the Reform Bill. Frank O'Gorman's study of the Hanoverian electorate concluded that 'One electoral system disappeared and gave way, then, to one remarkably like itself'.[15] O'Gorman's emphasis on continuity reflected his essentially positive assessment of the electoral system prior to 1832 rather than a negative view of it afterwards, but even so, he stressed continuity.

Was Calcraft's sacrifice, therefore, ultimately meaningless?[16] The

---

[14] A. D. Kriegel, 'Biography and the Politics of the Early Nineteenth Century', *Journal of British Studies*, 29 (1990), 284; Wasson, *Whig Renaissance* (New York, 1987).

[15] O'Gorman, *Voters*, 389–92.

[16] Calcraft was replaced at Wareham by Anthony Ashley Cooper because 110 of Calcraft's 158 voters supported him. Aspinall (ed.), *Diaries*, 138.

simple answer is no. Calcraft's rescue of the Reform Bill and its ultimate success substantially changed the nature of English popular politics. The closing years of the unreformed electoral system may have witnessed 'the revival of party', and party attachments before 1832 may not have been 'noticeably less assertive nor less popular' than afterwards, but Reform politicized the nation.[17] In some boroughs electoral behaviour changed little with Reform, either positively in the sense that voters in Great Yarmouth were (to use O'Gorman's term) *'party* politicized' well before 1832, or negatively, in the sense that Beverley's voters required more than the Reform Act to bring them into the partisan political arena. Nevertheless, the figures in table after table in these chapters demonstrate clearly Reform's powerful effect on electoral behaviour.

The complex range of popular politics in early nineteenth-century England is apparent from this close study of individual electors at specific elections and across elections. The Great Reform Bill as an issue or as a statute reshaped electoral behaviour in many boroughs, however politically or physically diverse. Towns as large and vibrant as Bristol and as small and stagnant as Colchester felt its effects in remarkably similar ways. Neither the relative political openness of Bristol, a town with a long tradition of political parties and electoral activity, nor the relative political closeness of Colchester, a town without a party machine, much affected the Act's reception. Electoral behaviour in both towns took on a much more consistently and determinedly partisan tone after 1832. Other towns responded similarly to the Reform Act or the nearly two years of occasionally intense agitation leading up to Reform. The size of a parliamentary borough, the size of its electorate, its electoral composition before 1832, and its location, all had little to do with the impact of the Reform Bill. It transcended parochial concerns and conditions.

A summary of the effects of Reform upon a political nation whose protean nature this book has revealed in some detail, however, requires careful and qualified recapitulation. In Bristol, a town long accustomed to political party activity and well-organized political battles, the Reform Bill substituted national political issues for local, idiosyncratic, and complicated political debates. It simplified the political choices facing voters after 1832, and despite an old and powerful party machine, substantially enhanced partisan behaviour.

[17] O'Gorman, *Voters*, 356–7.

At the very least, Reform increased Bristol's partisan voters by 50 per cent.[18] Similarly, Reform had an important impact upon Lewes's electorate which had been split into two hostile political camps from early in the century. There Reform transformed an essentially local rift into a principled disagreement over national political issues while enhancing partisanship.

Voters in Maidstone and Colchester responded as much to the agitation over Reform as to its actual alteration of England's electoral fabric. These two towns illustrated the Reform era's impact on a large segment of the political nation. Significant political changes were unmistakable in both electorates as early as the general election of 1831. Maidstone experienced further profound change in 1832, but at both elections Reform was the instrument of change. Differences in timing related only to the degree of local involvement with the political turmoil of 1831. Voters in Shrewsbury and Northampton more clearly demonstrated the artificiality of distinguishing the effects of the Reform Bill from those of the Reform era. Voting patterns revealed significant changes in both towns in 1831 and 1832. The greatest change in Shrewsbury may have preceded the Bill's passage, but Northampton's voters were affected equally by the debate and the Bill.

Reform generated and strengthened partisanship. Split-voting all but disappeared along with non-partisan plumping, and voters began to support particular parties with much greater regularity. Not only were individual electors likely to cast unmistakably partisan votes at elections after 1832, they were increasingly likely to repeat those partisan votes at subsequent elections. In sharp contrast to their tendency to cast non-partisan votes and to waver between the parties or between party voting and non-party voting earlier in the nineteenth century, voters tended to choose sides during the controversy over Reform and, having chosen, tended to remain loyal in the decade following Reform. The 'Great' Reform Act justified its epithet by altering England's political environment profoundly.[19]

These changes did not signal the emergence of an unshakeably and permanently partisan electorate, however, at least not one

---

[18] As shown in Table 2.2, 50% more voters cast strictly partisan votes in 1832 compared to 1820. A comparison of 1830 and 1832 shows an improvement of 47.5%.

[19] As one example of the ease with which the number of boroughs in this set could be expanded, it might be noted that 97% of Newark's voters cast straight party ballots in 1841. Ten of 1,004 cast non-partisan plumps, and 34% cast partisan plumps. In other words, Newark fits the description. *Newark Poll Books, 1826–47.*

divided along Whig/Tory or Reform/anti-Reform lines. The notable shift to partisanship found in some of these boroughs did not survive the 1840s, and the very altered circumstances of the 1850s must have reshaped some constituencies beyond recognition. The patterns of the 1830s did not persist even in some places where they might have been most expected to survive. The voters of Great Yarmouth, for example, were unusual in the precocity and intensity of their partisanship during the reigns of George and William IV. Their votes, in lock-step from 1818 until 1841, required no tabular presentation. In election after election, almost to a man, Yarmouth's voters turned in exemplary partisan performances. This strong pattern should have been repeated at the election of 1847 since it involved balanced slates of two candidates from each party. And it was: virtually all of Yarmouth's electors continued to cast strictly partisan votes. Yet the very next year, in a by-election required by a successful petition against the general election return, a shocking 42 per cent of the electorate split their votes between a Whig and a Tory. Tarnishing their hitherto glistening partisan record further, another third (32.7 per cent) cast unnecessary plumpers for one of the two Whig candidates.[20]

What happened to Yarmouth? The more appropriate question might be, what happened to the parliamentary parties? The politically meaningful distinctions so frequently made by Yarmouth's voters disappeared. Yarmouth began to resemble Beverley in the days before 1835. If distinctions between Tories and Whigs during the early decades of the century have puzzled some observers, they were clear enough to Yarmouth's voters prior to 1848. Its electorate may not have had a terribly refined vision of party, but however crude, their vision was sufficient to generate rigid partisan voting. In 1848, on the other hand, Yarmouth's party unity collapsed. The fundamental confusion of the voters may have been caused by the weakening of party in Parliament and the consequent disappearance of clearly perceived issues dividing candidates. Party labels were no longer easily tied to the issues of the 1820s and 1830s, particularly Reform. New issues were scarce and many were not clearly partisan. New parties and new issues called for rethinking, reformulation, and

---

[20] Lennox and Coope stood against the perennial Rumbold with a new partner, Goldsmid, in 1847. Forty-nine of 1,562 split. No one cast an unnecessary plump. The next year the Liberal Rumbold won with a new Tory candidate, Sandars, because only 76 voters of 678 cast double Whig votes.

realignment, a process that would require several elections and another Reform Act to complete.

During the debate over its passage, some perceived Reform in economic terms, yet occupational and economic status within the electorate contributed little to political differences despite the twin economic stresses of industrialization and urbanization. Significant socio-economic divisions in the electorate were not measurably reflected in most battles over parliamentary representation, and when such divisions made rare appearances at specific elections, they did not constitute trends. At some elections in some towns occupations were related to voting preferences, but the contribution of either occupation or economic status to partisan alliances within the electorate was ephemeral at best. The paucity of measurable relationships between socio-economic status and political choices either before or after Reform reveal the general failure of Whig appeals to voters from the lower rungs of the socio-economic ladder.

If class played a minor role in determining electoral behaviour, religion appears to have influenced many political decisions. But political differences among religious groups had more to do with group identification than with theology. Dogma may have contributed meaningfully to individual political identities and motivations, particularly among the élite, but among electorates, Nonconformity and Catholicism created communities within constituencies that helped determine political orientations. Neither the repeal of the Test and Corporations Acts nor Catholic emancipation eliminated all penalties against those who refused to conform to the Church of England. Those who were not equal were often made painfully aware of their inequality, and their inferior status, reinforced by social interactions in church and chapel, generated a powerful influence that swayed many votes towards the Whig/Liberals.[21] But religion had played an important role in shaping the contours of the political nation long before 1832 just as it continued to do afterwards. Reform was a Whig issue and therefore it attracted strong support from Nonconformists, who usually supported Whig policies, but the political role of religion was only tangentially related to Reform.

Ultimately, the alteration of the political nation in 1832 had little to do with class or religion. In general, Reform was a strictly political

---

[21] This is not necessarily to agree with those who have recently elevated religion to principal importance in 19th-cent. politics. Parry, *Democracy and Religion*.

issue, debated in exclusively political language, and fought in purely partisan ways. English radicals had conducted their struggles in such fashion since the 1770s. The struggle over Reform adhered to the long-established pattern, and the electorate responded appropriately.

Norman Gash pointed out 'the fallacy . . . in using the Reform Act to symbolize certain trends in politics that started long before', but Veitch was justified in contending that 'though . . . the Reform Bill was not a good Bill, it was a great Bill when it passed. It was a first and necessary step in parliamentary reform.'[22] In fact the Reform Bill was much more. It not only took the necessary first step towards more comprehensive reforms, it also politicized much of the electorate to a degree not possible or even imaginable before. The Act solidified what the Bill provoked. The Great Reform Bill may not have justified the panegyrics that often have surrounded it. Reform left many problems unresolved and some of its more important effects were not intended by the Bill's framers. Remaining problems aside, however, both the Bill and the intense political agitation leading to its passage altered the nature of parties, partisanship, and politics generally. Widespread party voting began to be the electoral norm in the boroughs containing most of England's active voters during the Reform era. As with most historical events, elements of continuity and change complicate an evaluation of Reform, era, Bill, or Act. England contained a vibrant 'political nation' well before 1832, much of it unenfranchised, but continued to suffer from corruption and coercion well after 1832. Nevertheless, the Reform Act expanded the ranks of the enfranchised, catalysed partisan politics, and reshaped the political process in constituency after constituency across the country. Not merely the first, but the Great Reform Act, established a new pattern of politics which began the inexorable movement towards parliamentary democracy.

[22] *Age of Peel*, p. x; Veitch, *Parliamentary Reform*, 355.

BIBLIOGRAPHY

MANUSCRIPT COLLECTIONS

Beverley Local History Library
Gillyat Sumner MSS.

Birmingham University Library
Slaney MSS 9/v/2.1–5.

Bodleian Library, Oxford
Bodleian Library, John Johnson Collection of Printed Ephemera, Elections, Box 6, unfoliated.

Bristol Central Library
Manuscript Poll Book, 1820, B4419.

Bristol Record Office
John Rose Collection, unfoliated.
Stedfast MSS 12144.
Hare MSS 8073.
Dakin Papers, 'Arrangements for the Entry of Sir Charles Wetherell, 29 October 1831', unfoliated.
Bristol MSS 38699 (1–2).
        B6979, 'Bristol Elections 1774–1790'.
        22225, Ward Lists for 1834 used as canvass books for the election of 1835.
        04736.
        04728 (1).
        Election Proceedings, 1806–12.

British Library, London
Dawson Turner MSS, N. TAB 2012/6/vols. 1–10.
Add. MSS 64813/53, Pelham MSS.
Add. MSS 61826, J. C. Hobhouse MSS.
Add. MSS 51867.
Add. MSS 40403, 40310, 40491.
Liverpool Poll Book 10349e/10.

Colchester Local History Library
J. B. Harvey Collection of Local Materials.
Rebow Family Papers (now in Essex Record Office).

William Wiles Notebook and Memorandum Book.
E. COL. 1/9579, 49.
E. COL. 1/324.26, Harvey Papers.
E. COL. DG/29212, 'Book of Colchester and Chelmsford compiled by a Member of the Rebow Family' (now in Essex Record Office).

Colman and Rye Local History Library, Norwich
F. D. Palmer, *Yarmouth Notes* (Great Yarmouth, 1889), clippings of *Norwich Mercury*, 1830.

Cornwall Record Office, Truro
Vyvyan MSS, DDV/BO/60–3.

East Sussex Record Office, Lewes
LEW/C7/1–34.
Shiffner MSS 2998, 305, 170.
Charles Wille, Diaries 1826–78, acc. 1977.
Lewes Poor-Rate Books, 410/30/1–43; 410/30/3.
   All Saints, 1817–35.
   St Peter and St Mary Westout, 1816–37.
   St Ann, 1818–41.
   St John sub Castro, 1818–38.
   St Michael, 1818–40.
   St Thomas at Cliffe, 1817–35.

Essex Record Office, Chelmsford
Magdalen Charity, Letters of D. W. Harvey, D/DU/77/50c, 51–2.
Colchester, All Saints, Rate Books 1763–1870 (2 vols.).
                              1776–1841 (7 vols.).
   Holy Trinity, Rate Books 1818–55 (8 vols.).
   St Botolph, Rate Books 1805–49 (7 vols.).
   St James, Rate Books 1838–46 (3 vols.).
   St Mary Wells, Rate Book 1835–41.
   St Nicholas, Rate Books 1773–1837.
   St Peter, Rate Books.
   St Runwald, Rate Books 1832–58.

Friends Library, London
Gurney MSS.
E. J. Addington Exracts, L002.3/13291.

Hertfordshire Record Office, Hertford
Wilshere MSS, D/EX 14.

Humberside Record Office, Beverley
BC II/7.
DDBC/10.
DDBC/11.
DDBC/22.

DDX 22.
DDX 23.
DDX 24/5.
DDX 27.

India Office, London
MSS EUR. E.342.19.
MSS EUR. F.142.10.

Kent Archives Office, Maidstone
Md/AEb2/25. A Poll for the election of three Common Council Men, 28 Oct. 1817.
Md/AEb2/29. A Poll for the election of five Common Council Men, 23 May 1828.
Md/AEb2/30. A Poll for the election of two Common Council Men, 11 Apr. 1835.

London School of Economics Library
Potter MSS, vols. 3–13b.

Norfolk Record Office, Norwich
Y/C19/31, Yarmouth Corporation Assembly Minute Book.
Rumbold MSS, L14.
D53/3.
Y/TC19/1.
Yarmouth Rate Books, Y/L1/44–60.
Wilshere MSS, L15.

Northampton Public Library
Broadsides relating to Northampton.

Northamptonshire Record Office, Delapre Abbey, Northampton
Gotch MSS.
Northampton Borough Records, Election Papers 1834–5, Y2/4975–86, and Box x5469.
College Street Baptist Chapel, CSB/17, 31(a), 48, 50, 52, 99.
Commercial Street Congregational, CSC/2.
Doddridge Castle Hill Congregational, DCHC/236–310.
Grafton Square Baptist, 6.
Kettering Road Unitarian.
Princes Street Baptist, 2, 15.
Gunning MSS 24045.
Laurie MSS 5405.
Hughenden MSS 0842.
All Saints, 223p/193.
King's Street Chapel, AAC/28(a–b); 54 (later Abington Avenue United Reform Church, AAC/55).
Northampton Union, PL6/16–18.

St Giles, 233p/1–2.
St Peter, 240p/47–51.
St Sepulchre, 241p/275–310.

Public Record Office, Kew
H020.
H040.
H052.

Public Record Office, Portugal Street
Nonconformist Registers, RG4.
   Beverley, 3515, 3646, 3668, 4104.
   Great Yarmouth, 1973–5, 2473.
   Lewes, 2623, 2062, 2967, 2850.
   Maidstone, 935–7, 1010, 1015, 1667–8, 3575.
   Colchester, 357–8, 1099, 1508–9, 2163, 2907.
   Northampton, 10, 902–3, 1141–2, 1275–7, 1347.

Shrewsbury Local History Library
Morris Eyton Collection, MSS 1–9.
DA45/1170.
Dq45/6.
Dq46/acc 2228.
Berwick MSS 6760/362, 363.

Shropshire Record Office, Shrewsbury

Eyton MSS 665/3–4.
Shrewsbury Borough MSS 3465/IV/1835–6.
                                         840, Box 76/2736.
                                         1060/454.
St Julian's, 2711/p/4, 2711/p/5b.
St Chad's, 1048–84.
St Alkmund's, 1049/A, 1049/B, 1049/9.
St Mary's, 1041/1n/11, 1041/ch31–49.

CONTEMPORARY PRINTED MATERIAL

Published Poll Books

Banbury 1859.
Bath 1855.
Beverley 1818, 1820, 1826, 1830, 1831, 1832, 1835, 1837, 1841.
Bristol 1781, 1812, 1830, 1832, 1835, 1837, 1841.

Colchester 1818, 1820, 1830, 1831, 1832, 1835, 1837.
Great Yarmouth 1818, 1820, 1826, 1830, 1831, 1832, 1835, 1837, 1841.
Lewes, 1818, 1826, 1830, 1835, 1837, 1841.
Liverpool 1818, 1830, 1832, 1833.
Maidstone 1818, 1820, 1826, 1830, 1831, 1832, 1835, 1837, 1841.
Newark 1826, 1829, 1830, 1831(2), 1832, 1841, 1847.
Northampton 1818, 1820, 1826, 1830, 1831, 1832, 1835, 1837, 1841.
Shrewsbury 1819, 1826, 1830, 1831, 1832, 1835, 1837, 1841.
The Poll for the Election of Headmen (Colchester, 1821).

Newspapers and Periodicals

Brighton Guardian.
Brighton Patriot.
Bristolian.
Bristol Gazette.
Bristol Mercury.
Bristol Observer.
Bristol Times.
Carpenter's Monthly Political Magazine.
Chelmsford and Colchester Chronicle.
Colchester Gazette.
East Anglian.
Essex Standard.
Felix Farley's Bristol Journal.
Gentleman's Magazine and Historical Chronicle.
Hull Advertiser.
Hull Packet.
Kent and Essex Mercury.
Leigh Hunt's London Journal.
Maidstone Gazette.
Maidstone Journal.
Morning Chronicle.
Northampton Free Press.
Northampton Herald.
Northampton Mercury.
Norwich Mercury.
Norwich, Yarmouth, and Lynn Courier.
Punch.
Salopian Journal.
Shrewsbury Chronicle.
Sussex Advertiser.
Vanity Fair.

Weekly Political Register.
Westminster Review.

Primary Printed Sources

The Annual Register of World Events: A Review of the Year, 105 vols. (London, 1758–1863).

An Authentic Account of the Evidence given to the Committee . . . on the Bristol Election (Bristol, 1819).

An Authentic Report of the Evidence and Proceedings before the Committee on the Bristol Election (London, 1813).

The Bristol Riots by a Citizen (Bristol, 1832).

Charge to the Grand Jury by Sir Nicholas C. Tindal (Bristol, 1832).

The Companion to the Newspapers and a Journal of Facts (London, 1834).

Considerations on the Principles of Representation with a Review of the Late Contest (Shrewsbury, 1807).

The Court Martial of Captain Warrington (Bristol, 1832).

Dreadful Riot. Destruction of Bristol New Gaol, Bridewell, Lawford's Gate Prison, Mansion House, Bishop's Palace, Customs House, Excise, and 42 Other Houses (Bristol, 1831).

A Full Detail of the Facts relative to the Late Election of Edward Protheroe (Bristol, 1819).

Full Particulars of the Dreadful and Tremendous Riots in Bristol (London, 1831).

A Full Report of the Trials of the Bristol Rioters (Bristol, 1832).

Great Britain in 1841, or, The Results of the Reform Bill (London, 1831).

'An Impartial Citizen', *The Magistracy of Bristol Brought to the Bar of Public Opinion* (Bristol, 1832).

An Impartial Statement of All Proceedings Connected with the Progress and Result of the Late Elections (Bristol, 1819).

Incidents in the Life of Joseph Kayes (Bristol, 1832).

Journals of the House of Commons.

Lamentation on those Five Unfortunate Men now Lying under Sentence of Death (Bristol, 1832).

The Late Elections: An Impartial Statement of All Proceedings Connected with the Progress and Results of the Late Elections (London, 1818).

A Leaf From the Future History of England (London, 1831).

A Letter to the Judges . . . upon the Impropriety of Punishing the Rioters with Death (Bristol, 1832).

The Life and History of Swing, the Kent Rick-Burner, Written by Himself (London, 1830).

Narrative of Conversations Held with Christopher Davis (Bristol, 1832).

A Narrative of the Dreadful Riots and Burnings which Occurred in Bristol on 29, 30, 31 October 1831 (Bristol, 1831).

Parliamentary Debates, 3rd ser.

The Parliamentary Gazetteer (Glasgow, 1840).

Parliamentary Papers.

A Peep at the Commons (London, 1820).

Proceedings of the Late Election in Colchester (Colchester, 1820)

Real Character and Tendency of the Proposed Reform (1831).

Squibs and Handbills relating to Mayor Choosing at Beverley (Beverley, 1824).

Statement on Behalf of the Promoters of a Bill Pending in Parliament for Improving the Haven of Great Yarmouth (Yarmouth, 1834).

A Summary View of the Public Conduct of Edward Protheroe, Esq., MP (Bristol, 1818).

A Voice to Bristol (Bristol, 1831).

The Weaver's Complaint (Keighley, 1834).

AINSLIE, ROBERT, *Discourse at the Death of Daniel Whittle Harvey* (London, 1863).

APPERLEY, W. H. (Nimrod), *The Life of John Mytton* (London, 1893).

ARNOULD, SIR JOSEPH, *Lives of the Chief Justices*, 6 vols. (London, 1881).

ASPINALL, ARTHUR (ed.), *Three Early Nineteenth Century Diaries* (London, 1952).

AYERS, JACK (ed.), *Paupers and Pig Killers: The Diary of William Holland* (Harmondsworth, 1986).

BAINES, EDWARD (ed.), *The History, Directory, and Gazetteer of the County of York* (Leeds, 1823).

BAMFORD, F. (ed.), *The Journal of Mrs. Arbuthnot, 1802–32*, 2 vols. (London, 1950).

BARFOOT, P., and WILKES, J. (eds.), *The Universal British Dictionary*, 4 vols. (London, 17, 3–8).

BARROW, J. H. (ed.), *The Mirror of Parliament*, 52 vols. (London, 1828–41).

BRETT, R. L. (ed.), *Barclay Fox's Journal* (Totowa, NJ, 1979).

Bristol, City and Port of, *Letters, Essays, and Tracts Illustrative of the Municipal History of Bristol* (Bristol, 1836).

Bristol Corporation, *An Analysis of the Report of the Commissioners of Corporate Enquiry* (Bristol, 1835).

BROUGHAM, HENRY, *Friendly Advice Most Respectfully Submitted to the Lords* (London, 1831).

BULLER, ARTHUR, 'Bribery and Intimidation at Elections', *Westminster Review*, 25 (1836), 485–513.

BURKE, Sir B., *A Second Series of Vicissitudes of Families* (London, 1860).

BURKE, EDMUND, *Reflections on the Revolution in France* (London, 1790).

CARLYLE, THOMAS, *Chartism* (1839).

CARTER, J., *Memoirs of a Working Man* (London, 1845).

CAVE, K. (ed.), *Diary of Joseph Farington*, 16 vols. (New Haven, 1984).

CLARIDGE, J., *Extracts from the City Cash Book* (Bristol, 1814).

COBBETT, WILLIAM, *Cobbett's Twopenny Trash* (London, 1851).

COCKBURN, A. E., *The Corporations of England and Wales* (London, 1835).

COLQUHOUN, PATRICK., *A Treatise on Wealth, Power, and Resources of the British Empire* (London, 1814).

COX, E. W., *Hints to Solicitors for the Conduct of Elections* (London, 1868).

COX, J. C., and MARKHAM, C. A. (eds.), *The Records of the Borough of Northampton*, 2 vols. (Northampton, 1898).

CRANIDGE, JOHN, *A Mirror for the Burgesses of Bristol* (Bristol, 1818).

CREEVEY, T., *The Creevey Papers*, ed. Sir Herbert Maxwell, 2 vols. (London, 1903).

CROMWELL, THOMAS, *History of the Borough of Colchester*, 2 vols. (London, 1825).

CROSBY, GEORGE, *Crosby's Parliamentary Record* (York, 1841).

CROXALL, CALBEB, *What Will Reform Do?* (Birmingham, 1832).

CURME, T., *The Bristol Riots by a Citizen* (Bristol, 1832).

DILLON, Sir John, *Horae Icenae: Being the Lucubrations of a Winter's Evening on the Result of the General Election of 1835* (London, 1835).

DISRAELI, BENJAMIN, *What is He?* (London, 1833).

—— *Coningsby* (New York, 1962 [1844]).

—— *Sybil, or, The Two Nations* (London, 1845).

—— *Letters*, vols. i–ii, ed. J. A. W. Gunn, vols. iii -iv ed. M. G. Wiebe et al. (Toronto, 1988).

—— and SARAH DISRAELI, *A Year at Hartlebury, or, The Election* (London, 1834).

DISRAELI, R. (ed.), *Lord Beaconsfield's Correspondence with his sister*, (London, 1886).

EDEN, EMILY, *The Semi–Attached Couple* (London, 1831).

EDWARDS, EDWARD, *Parliamentary Elections of the Borough of Shrewsbury* (Shrewbury, 1859).

ELIOT, GEORGE, *Felix Holt* (Harmondsworth, 1972 [1866]).

—— *Middlemarch* (New York, 1985 [1871–2]).

ELTON, C. A., *An Apology for Colonel Hugh Baillie* (Bristol, 1818).

ERSKINE, THOMAS, *The Second Part of Armata* (London, 1817).

GALT, JOHN, *The Member: An Autobiography* (London, 1832).

GORE, MONTAGU, *What Will Be the Practical Effects of the Reform Bill?* (London, 1831).

GREVILLE, C. C. F., *The Greville Memoirs: A Journal of the Reigns of King George IV, King William IV, and Queen Victoria*, ed. Henry Reeve, 8 vols. (London, 1896–9).

GREY, HENRY Earl (ed.), *The Correspondence of the late Earl Grey with H.M. King William IV*, 2 vols. (London, 1867).

HARDY, THOMAS, *Memoir of Thomas Hardy, Written by Himself* (London, 1832).

HOBHOUSE J. C., *Recollections of a Long Life*, ed. Lady Dorchester, 4 vols. (London, 1910).

HOGARTH, W., *Four Prints of an Election* (London, 1755–8).

HOLLAND, LADY, *A Memoir of the Reverend Sydney Smith* (London, 1869).

HOLYOAKE, GEORGE, *Sixty Years of an Agitator's Life* (London, 1906).

HORSFIELD, T. W., *History, Antiquities, and Topography of the County of Sussex* (Lewes, 1835).

HOWELL, THOMAS, (ed.), *State Trials* (London, 1817).

HUNT, HENRY, *Memoirs*, 3 vols. (London, 1821).

JENNINGS, L. J. (ed.), *The Correspondence and Diaries of John Wilson Croker*, 3 vols. (London, 1885).

JONES, JOHN GALE, *Sketch of a Political Tour through Rochester, Chatham, Maidstone, and Gravesend* (London, 1796).

KRIEGEL, ABRAHAM (ed.), *The Holland House Diaries, 1831–40* (London, 1975).

LAMBERT, J., 'Parliamentary Franchises Past and Present', *The Nineteenth Century*, 54 (Dec. 1889).

LATIMER, JOHN, *Annals of Bristol in the Nineteenth Century* (Bristol, 1887).

LAW, EDWARD, Earl of Ellenborough, *A Political Diary, 1828–30*, ed. Lord Colchester, 2 vols. (London, 1881).

LOVELESS, GEORGE, *The Victims of Whiggery* (London, 1837).

McCULLOCH, J. R., *A Statistical Account of the British Empire* (London, 1839).

MACMAHON, K. A. (ed.), *Beverley Corporation Minute Books, 1707–1835* (London, 1958).

MANCHEE, T. J., *Origin of the Riots in Bristol* (Bristol, 1831).

LE MARCHANT, D. (ed.), *Memoir of John Charles, Viscount Althorp, Third Earl Spencer* (London, 1876).

MARSHALL, J., *Statistics of the British Empire* (London, 1831).

MARTINEAU, HARRIET, *Deerbrook* (London, 1839).

MASSIE, JOSEPH, *Calculations of the Present Taxes Yearly Paid by a Family of Each Rank, Degree, or Class* (London, 1761).

MOLESWORTH, W. N., *The History of the Reform Bill of 1832* (London, 1865).

MORTIMER, THOMAS, *A General Commercial Dictionary* (London, 1819).

NEHEMIAH, *Plain Account of the Riot in Bristol* (Bristol, 1832).

NORMANBY, CONSTANTINE H. (Earl Mulgrave), *The English at Home* (London, 1830).

OLDFIELD, T. H. B., *The History of the Boroughs*, 2 vols. (London, 1794).

—— *Representative History of Great Britain and Ireland*, 6 vols. (London, 1816).

OLIVER, GEORGE, *The History of Beverley*, 2 vols. (London, 1829).

PALMER, C. J., *History of Great Yarmouth* (Great Yarmouth, 1856).

—— *The Perlustration of Great Yarmouth*, 3 vols. (Great Yarmouth, 1872–5).

PHILLIPS, SIR RICHARD, *The Book of English Trades and Library of the Useful Arts* (London, 1818).

Pigot's *National and Commercial Dictionary* (London, 1835).

PINNEY, CHARLES, *The Trial of Charles Pinney* (London, 1833).

POULSON, GEORGE, *Beverlac* (Beverley, 1829).

PROTHEROE, Sir Henry, *A Full Account of the Late Election for Bristol Vindicating the Conduct of Edward Protheroe* (Bristol, 1819).

ROMILLY, Sir Samuel, *Memoirs*, 3 vols. (London, 1840).

RUSSELL, R. (ed.), *The Early Correspondence of Lord John Russell, 1805–40*, 2 vols. (London, 1913).

SMITH, HENRY STOOKS, *The Register of Parliamentary Contested Elections* (London, 1841).

SMITH, VERENA (ed.), *The Town Book of Lewes, 1702–1837*, Sussex Record Society, 69; (1972–3).

SOUTHEY, ROBERT, *Sir Thomas More, or A Colloquia on the Progress and Prospects of Society*, 2 vols. (London, 1829).

STEPHENS, F. G., HAWKINS, E., and GEORGE, M. D. (comp.), *A Catalogue of Prints and Drawings in the British Museum. Division 2: Political and Personal Satires*, 11 vols. (London, 1879–1954).

STRACHEY, L. and FULFORD, R. (eds.), *The Greville Memoirs*, 8 vols. (London, 1938).

THELWALL, Mrs. CECIL (BOYLE), *Life of John Thelwall* (London, 1837).

DE TOCQUEVILLE, ALEXIS, *Journeys to England and Ireland*, ed. Jacob Peter Mayer (London, 1958 [1833]).

TWISS, H. (ed.) *Memoirs of Lord Eldon*, 3 vols. (London, 1844).

VINCENT, JOHN, and STENTON, M. (eds.), *McCalmont's Parliamentary Poll Book* (Brighton, 1971).

VINE, J. R. SOMERS, *English Municipal Institutions* (London, 1879).

WADE, JOHN, *The Extraordinary Black Book*, 2 vols. (London, 1820).

—— *History of the Middle and Working Classes* (London, 1833).

WALKER, CHARLES H., *Address to the Electors of Bristol* (Bristol, 1818).

—— '*Address to the Electors of Bristol Showing the Ineligibility of H. Bright to Represent Them*' (Bristol, 1820).

—— *A Second Address to the Electors of Bristol* (Bristol, 1820).

—— *A Third Address to the Electors of Bristol* (Bristol, 1820).

—— *The Petition of William Clark* (London, 1832).

WILBERFORCE, R. I. (ed.), *The Life of William Wilberforce*, 5 vols. (London, 1838).

Bibliography

Books and Dissertations

ALFORD, R., *Party and Society: The Anglo-American Democracies* (Chicago, 1963).

ALLISON, K. J. (ed.), *The Victoria County History of Yorkshire* (London, 1990).

AMEY, GEOFFREY, *City under Fire* (London, 1979).

ARROW, KENNETH J., *Social Choice and Individual Values* (New York, 1951).

BAIGENT, ELIZABETH, 'Bristol Society in the Later Eighteenth Century', D.Phil. (Oxford, 1985).

BELCHEM, J., *'Orator' Hunt: Henry Hunt and English Working–Class Radicalism* (Oxford, 1985).

BENTLEY, MICHAEL, *Politics without Democracy*, 1815–1914 (London, 1984).

BLACK, E. C., *The Association* (Cambridge, Mass., 1963).

BLACK, JEREMY, *The English Press in the Eighteenth Century* (London, 1987).

BLAKE, R., *Disraeli* (New York, 1967).

BLALOCK, H. M., *Social Statistics* (New York, 1979).

BLONDEL, JEAN, *Voters, Parties, and Leaders* (Harmondsworth, 1963).

BOWDER, B. D., and WEISBERG, H. F., *An Introduction to Data Analysis* (San Francisco, 1980).

BRADLEY, JAMES E., *Religion, Revolution, and English Radicalism: Nonconformity in Eighteenth–Century Politics and Society* (Cambridge, 1990).

BRAMS, STEVEN, *Paradoxes in Politics* (New York, 1976).

BRENT, RICHARD, *Liberal Anglican Politics* (Oxford, 1987).

BREWER, JOHN, *Party Ideology and Popular Politics at the Accession of George III* (Cambridge, 1976).

—— *Sinews of Power* (London, 1989).

BRIGGS, ASA, *The Collected Essays of Asa Briggs*, 2 vols., (Brighton, 1985).

BROCK, M., *The Great Reform Act* (London, 1973).

BROWN, A. F. J., *Colchester, 1815–1914* (Chelmsford, 1980).

—— Essex People (Chelmsford, 1972).

BULMER-THOMAS, I., *The Growth of the British Party System* (London, 1953).

BUSH, GRAHAM, *Bristol and its Municipal Government, 1820–1851* (Bristol, 1976).

BUTLER, D., and STOKES, D., *Political Change in Britain* (New York, 1971).

BUTLER, J. R. M., *The Passing of the Reform Bill* (London, 1914).

CALHOUN, C., *The Question of the Class Struggle* (Chicago, 1982).

CALVERT, PETER, *The Concept of Class* (London, 1982).

CANNON, JOHN, *Parliamentary Reform, 1640–1832* (Cambridge, 1973).

CESTRE, CHARLES, *John Thelwall* (London, 1906).

CHRISTIE, O. F. *The Transition from Aristocracy 1832–1867* (London, 1927).

CLARK, J. C. D., *The Dynamics of Change* (Cambridge, 1982).

—— *English Society, 1688–1832* (Cambridge, 1985).

—— *Revolution and Rebellion* (Cambridge, 1986).

CLOSE, D. H., 'The General Elections of 1835 and 1837' Ph.D. (Oxford, 1967).

COOK, CHRIS and KEITH, BRENDAN, *British Historical Facts* (New York, 1975).

COOKSON, J. E., *The Friends of Peace: Anti-war Liberalism in England, 1793–1815* (Cambridge, 1982).

COWHERD, RAYMOND G., *The Politics of English Dissent* (New York, 1956).

DAVIS, R. W., *Political Change and Continuity, 1760–1885* (Newton Abbot, 1972).

DENNIS, R., *English Industrial Cities of the Nineteenth Century* (Cambridge, 1984).

DICKINSON, H. T., *British Radicals and the French Revolution* (Oxford, 1985).

—— *Caricatures and the Constitution, 1760–1832* (Cambridge, 1986).

DOGAN, M., and ROKKAN, S. (eds.), *Quantitative Ecological Analysis* (Cambridge, Mass., 1969).

DRIVER, C., *Tory Radical: The Life of Richard Oastler* (Oxford, 1946).

EDSALL, N. C., *The Anti-Poor Law Movement* (London, 1971).

EVANS, ERIC J., *The Contentious Tithe* (London, 1976).

—— *The Forging of the Modern State* (London, 1983).

FORRESTER, ERIC G., *Northamptonshire County Elections and Electioneering, 1695–1832* (Oxford, 1941).

FOSTER, JOHN, *Class Struggle and the Industrial Revolution* (London, 1974).

FRANKLIN, M. N., *The Decline of Class Voting in Britain: Changes in the Basis of Electoral Choice, 1964–1983* (Oxford, 1985).

FURBANK, P. N., *Unholy Pleasure: the Idea of Social Class* (Oxford, 1985).

GASH, NORMAN, *Politics in the Age of Peel* (London, 1952).

—— *Reaction and Reconstruction in English Politics, 1832–1852* (Oxford, 1965).

—— *Lord Liverpool* (London, 1984).

—— *Pillars of Government* (London, 1986).

GIBSON, JEREMY and ROGERS, COLIN, *Poll Books, 1696–1872* (Birmingham, 1989).

GILBERT, A. D., *Religion and Society in Industrial England* (London, 1976).

GINTER, DONALD, *Whig Organization in the General Election of 1790* (Berkeley, Calif., 1967).

—— *A Measure of Wealth: The English Land Tax in Historical Analysis* (Montreal, 1991).

GIROUARD, MARK, *The Return to Camelot* (New Haven, Conn., 1981).

GLEN, ROBERT, *Urban Workers in the Industrial Revolution* (London, 1984).

GRAY, D., *Spencer Perceval* (Manchester, 1963).

GREAVES, R. W., *The Corporation of Leicester* (Leicester, 1939).

GREGO, JOSEPH, *History of Parliamentary Elections and Electioneering* (London, 1892).

HAGAN, F. A., 'Richard Jenkins and the Residency of Nagpur', Ph.D. (California, 1960).

HANHAM, H. J. (ed.), *Dod's Electoral Facts* (Brighton, 1972).

HARRISON, MARK, *Crowds and History* (Cambridge, 1988).

HARVEY, A. D., *Britain in the Early Nineteenth Century* (New York, 1978).

HAYES, B. D., 'Politics in Norfolk, 1750–1832', Ph.D. (Cambridge, 1958).

HEATH, A., JOWELL, R., and CURTICE, J., *How Britain Votes* (Oxford, 1985).

HERSHBERG, T. (ed.), *Philadelphia: Work, Space, Family, and Group Experience in the Nineteenth Century* (Oxford, 1981).

HILL, B. W., *British Parliamentary Parties, 1742–1832* (London, 1985).

HILLS, Wallace B., *The Parliamentary History of the Borough of Lewes* (Lewes, 1908).

HILTON, BOYD, *The Age of Atonement* (Oxford, 1988).

HIMMELWEIT, H. T., HUMPHREYS, P., and JAEGER, M., *How Voters Decide* (Milton Keynes, 1985).

HIRST, Derek, *Representative of the People?* (Cambridge, 1975).

HOBSBAWM, ERIC and RUDE, GEORGE, *Captain Swing* (New York, 1968).

HOFFMAN, PAUL, *Archimedes' Revenge* (New York, 1988).

HOLE, ROBERT, *Pulpits, Politics, and Public Order in England, 1760–1832* (Cambridge, 1989).

HOLLAMS, Sir JOHN, *Jottings of an Old Solicitor* (London, 1906).

HOLMES, GEOFFREY, *British Politics in the Age of Anne* (London, 1967).

HOPPEN, T. K., *Elections, Politics, and Society in Ireland, 1832–1885* (Oxford, 1984).

HOUGHTON, W. E., *The Wellesley Index to Victorian Periodicals, 1824–1900*, 5 vols. (Toronto, 1966–89).

JOHNSON, L. G., *The Man with Forty Crowns a Year: General T. Perronet Thompson* (London, 1957).

JONES, G. S., *Languages of Class* (Cambridge, 1983).

JOYCE, PATRICK, *Work, Society, and Politics* (New Brunswick, NJ, 1980).

JUDD, GERRIT P., *Members of Parliament, 1734–1832* (New Haven, Conn., 1955).

KATZ, M. B., *The People of Hamilton, Canada West* (Cambridge, Mass., 1975).

KISHLANSKY, MARK, *Parliamentary Selection* (Cambridge, 1986).

LANGFORD, PAUL, *The Excise Crisis* (London, 1975).

LAQUEUR, THOMAS, *Religion and Respectability* (New Haven, Conn., 1976).

LITTLE, BRYAN, *The City and County of Bristol* (Bristol, 1967).

MACCOBY, S., *English Radicalism, 1832–52* (London, 1935).

MCGRATH, P., and CANNON, J. (eds.), *Essays in Bristol and Gloucestershire History* (Bristol, 1976).

MANDLER, PETER, *Aristocratic Government in the Age of Reform: Whigs and Liberals, 1830–1852* (Oxford, 1990).

MARLOW, JOYCE, *The Tolpuddle Martyrs* (London, 1985).

MITCHELL, JEREMY, 'Electoral Change and the Party System in England', Ph.D. (Harvard, 1977).

MONYPENNY, W. F. and BUCKLE, G. E., *The Life of Benjamin Disraeli*, 6 vols. (London, 1910–20).

MOORE, D. C., *The Politics of Deference* (Hassocks, 1976).

MORRIS, R. J. (ed.), *Class, Power and Social Structure in British Nineteenth-Century Towns* (Leicester, 1986).

—— *Class, Sect, and Party: The Making of the British Middle Class, Leeds 1820–50* (Manchester, 1990).

NAMIER, LEWIS, *The Structure of Politics at the Accession of George III* (London, 1929).

—— *England in the Age of the American Revolution* (London, 1930).

—— *Monarchy and the Party System* (Oxford, 1952).

—— and BROOKE, JOHN, *The House of Commons, 1754–1790*, 3 vols. (London, 1964).

NEALE, R. S., *Class and Ideology in the Nineteenth Century* (London, 1972).

—— *Class in English History, 1680–1850* (London, 1981).

NEWBOULD, IAN D. C., *Whiggery and Reform 1830–1841: The Politics of Government* (Stanford, Calif., 1990).

NORMAN, EDWARD R., *Anti-Catholicism in Victorian England* (London, 1968).

—— *Church and Society in England* (Oxford, 1976).

—— *The English Catholic Church in the Nineteenth Century* (Oxford, 1984).

NOSSITER, T. J., *Influence, Opinion, and Political Idioms in Reformed England* (Hassocks, 1975).

NUTTALL, G. F. and CHADWICK, O., *From Uniformity to Unity* (London, 1962).

OBELKEVICH, J., *Religion and Rural Society: South Lindsey, 1825–1875* (Oxford, 1976).

ODURKENE, J. N., 'The British General Elections of 1830 and 1831', B.Litt. (Oxford, 1976).

O'GORMAN, FRANK, *The Whig Party and the French Revolution* (London, 1967).

—— *The Rise of Party in England* (London, 1975).

O'GORMAN, FRANK *The Emergence of the British Two-Party System, 1760–1832* (London, 1982).

—— *Voters, Patrons, and Parties: The Unreformed Electorate of Hanoverian England, 1734–1832* (Oxford, 1989).

OMAN, C. (ed.), *The Gasgoyne Heiress* (London, 1968).

PARRY, J. P., *Democracy and Religion* (Cambridge, 1985).

PERKIN, H., *The Origins of Modern English Society 1780–1880* (London, 1969).

PHILBIN, J. H., *Parliamentary Representation 1832* (New Haven, Conn., 1965).

PHILLIPS, JOHN A., *Electoral Behaviour in Unreformed England* (Princeton, NJ, 1982).

PLUMB, J. H., *The Growth of Political Stability in England, 1675–1725* (London, 1967).

PORRITT, EDWARD and ANNIE PORRITT, *The Unreformed House of Commons*, 2 vols. (Cambridge, 1909).

PORTER, R., *English Society in the Eighteenth Century* (Harmondsworth, 1982).

PREST, J., *Politics in the Age of Cobden* (London, 1977).

—— *Liberty and Locality: Parliament, Permissive Legislation, and Ratepayers' Democracies in the Nineteenth Century* (Oxford, 1990).

PRZEWORSKI, ADAM and SPRAGUE, J., *Paper Stones* (Chicago, 1986).

PULZER, PETER G., *Political Representation and Elections: Parties and Voting in Great Britain* (London, 1967).

RICHARDSON, RUTH, *Death, Dissection, and the Destitute* (London, 1988).

ROGERS, NICHOLAS, *Whigs and Cities: Popular Politics in the Age of Walpole and Pitt* (Oxford, 1989).

ROSE, RICHARD, *Electoral Behaviour* (London, 1974).

—— and MCALLISTER, I., *Voters Begin to Choose* (London, 1986).

ROUTLEY, E., *English Religious Dissent* (Cambridge, 1960).

RUDE, GEORGE, *Wilkes and Liberty* (Oxford, 1962).

RULE, JOHN, *The Labouring Classes in Early Industrial England, 1750–1850* (London, 1986).

SAMBROOK, JAMES, *William Cobbett* (London, 1973).

SARLVIK, B., and CREWE, I., *Decade of Dealignment* (Cambridge, 1983).

SELLAR, W. C., and YEATMAN, R. J., *1066 and All That* (London, 1931).

SELLERS, IAN, *Nineteenth-Century Nonconformity* (London, 1977).

SEWELL, W., jnr., *Structure and Mobility* (Cambridge, 1985).

SEYMOUR, CHARLES, *Electoral Reform in England and Wales* (New Haven, Conn., 1915).

SHARPE, J. A., *Crime and the Law in English Satirical Prints, 1660–1832* (Cambridge, 1986).

SILBEY, J. H., et al. (eds.), *The History of American Electoral Behaviour* (Princeton, NJ, 1978).

SIMS, JOHN (ed.), *A Handlist of British Parliamentary Poll Books* (Leicester, 1984).

SMITH, E. A., *Lord Grey, 1764–1845* (Oxford, 1990).

SOUTHGATE, D., *The Passing of the Whigs, 1832–1886* (London, 1962).

SPECK, W. A., *Tory and Whig* (London, 1970).

SPEIGHT, M. E., 'Politics in the Borough of Colchester, 1812–47', Ph.D. (London, 1969).

STEWART, R., *The Politics of Protection* (Cambridge, 1971).

STEWART, ROBERT MACKENZIE, *Henry Brougham, 1778–1868: His Public Career* (London, 1985).

SUTHERLAND, DOUGLAS, *The Mad Hatters: Great Sporting Eccentrics of the Nineteenth Century* (London, 1987).

THOMPSON, D., *Nonconformity in the Nineteenth Century* (London, 1972).

THOMPSON, E. P., *The Making of the English Working Class* (London, 1963).

THORNE, ROLAND G. (ed.), *The House of Commons, 1790–1820*, 5 vols. (London, 1986).

TREVELYAN, G. M., *Lord Grey of the Reform Bill* (New York, 1920).

TRINDER, B., *Victorian Banbury* (Chichester, 1982).

TURBERVILLE, A. S., *The House of Lords in the Age of Reform 1784–1837* (London, 1958).

VEITCH, G. S., *The Genesis of Parliamentary Reform* (London, 1913).

VINCENT, DAVID, *Literacy and Popular Culture* (Cambridge, 1990).

VINCENT, JOHN, *Pollbooks: How Victorians Voted* (Cambridge, 1967).

WALCOTT, ROBERT, *English Politics in the Early Eighteenth Century* (Oxford, 1956).

WALD, KENNETH, *Crosses on the Ballot* (Princeton, NJ, 1983).

WALLAS, GRAHAM, *The Life of Francis Place* (New York, 1919).

WARD, J. R., *British West Indian Slavery, 1750–1834* (Oxford, 1988).

WASSON, ELLIS A., *Whig Renaissance: Lord Althorp and the Whig Party 1782–1845* (New York, 1987).

WATTS, MICHAEL R., *The Dissenters*, 2 vols. (Oxford, 1978–   ).

WEAVER, STEWART A., *John Fielden and the Politics of Popular Radicalism* (Oxford, 1987).

WEBB, SIDNEY and BEATRICE WEBB., *English Local Government* (London, 1913).

WRIGHT, D. G., 'Politics and Opinion in Bradford, 1832–1860', Ph.D. (Leeds, 1966).

ZEGGER, R. E., *John Cam Hobhouse* (Columbia, Mo., 1973).

ZIMMECK, META, 'Chartered Rights and Vested Interests: Reform Era Politics in Three Sussex Boroughs', MA (Sussex, 1972).

320   *Bibliography*

Articles

ABBOTT, ANDREW, and FORREST, JOHN, 'Optimal Matching Methods for Historical Sequences', *Journal of Interdisciplinary History*, 16 (1986), 471–94.

ARMSTRONG, W. A., 'The Use of Information about Occupations', in E. A. Wrigley (ed.), *Nineteenth Century Society* (Cambridge, 1972), 191–310.

ASPINALL, A., 'English Party Organization in the Nineteenth Century, *English Historical Review*, 41 (1926), 389–411.

BASKERVILLE, S. W., '"Preferred Linkage" and the Analysis of Voter Behaviour in Eighteenth–Century England', *History and Computing*, 1 (1989), 112–20.

BOHMER, D., 'The Maryland Electorate and the Concept of a Party System in the Early National Period', in J. H. Silbey, et al, (eds.), *The History of American Electoral Behaviour* (Princeton, NJ, 1978), 146–73.

BRADLEY, J. E., 'Religion and Reform at the Polls', *Journal of British Studies*, (23 (1984), 55–78.

—— 'Nonconformity and the Electorate in Eighteenth-Century England', *Parliamentary History*, 6 (1987), 236–61.

BRENT, C. E., 'The Immmediate Impact of the Second Reform Act on a Southern County Town: Voting Patterns at Lewes Borough in 1865 and 1868', *Southern History*, 2 (1980), 129–78.

BRIGGS, ASA, 'The Language of "Class" in Early Nineteenth-Century England', in id. and J. Saville (eds), *Essays in Labour History*, 2 vols. (London, 1960), i. 43–73.

BUCHANAN, W., 'Nominal and Ordinal Bivariate Statistics', *American Journal of Political Science*, 18 (1974), 625–46.

BURN, W. L., 'Electoral Corruption in the Nineteenth Century', *Parliamentary Affairs*, 4 (1951), 398–446.

CANNON, JOHN, 'Poll Books', *History*, 47 (1962), 166–9.

CHAMBERS, W. N., and DAVIS, C., 'Party, Competition, and Mass Participation', in J. H. Silbey et al. (eds.) *The History of American Electoral Behaviour* (Princeton, NJ, 1978), 174–97.

CLAEYS, GREGORY, 'A Utopian Tory Revolutionary at Cambridge', *Historical Journal*, 25 (1982), 583–603.

CLARK, J. C. D, 'A General Theory of Party, Opposition, and Government, 1688–1832', *Historical Journal*, 23 (1980), 295–325.

CLARKE, P. F., 'Electoral Sociology of Modern Britain', *History*, 57 (1972), 31–55.

COLLEY, LINDA, 'The Apotheosis of George III: Loyalty, Royalty, and the British Nation', *Past and Present*, 102 (1984), 94–129.

—— 'Whose Nation? Class and National Consciousness in Britain 1750–1830', *Past and Present*, 113 (1986), 97–117.

DAALDER, H. 'Parties, Elites, and Political Developments in Western Europe', in J. LaPalombara and M. Weiner (eds.), *Political Parties and Political Development* (Princeton, NJ, 1966), 43–78.

DAVIS, R. W., 'Toryism to Tamworth: The Triumph of Reform, 1827–1835', *Albion*, 12 (1980), 132–46.

DENNIS, R. J., 'Intercensal Mobility in a Victorian City', *Transactions of the Institute of British Geographers*, 2 (1977), 349–63.

DICKINSON, H. T., 'Party, Principle, and Public Opinion in Eighteenth Century Politics', *History*, 61 (1976), 28–45.

DUNBABIN, J. P. D., 'Parliamentary Elections in Great Britain, 1868–1900', *English Historical Review*, 81 (1966), 82–99.

DUTTON, H. I. and KING, J. E., 'The Limits of Paternalism: The Cotton Tyrants of North Lancashire, 1836–54', *Social History*, 7 (1982), 59–74.

EASTWOOD, DAVID, 'Toryism, Reform, and Political Culture in Oxfordshire, 1826–1837', *Parliamentary History*, 7 (1988), 98–121.

—— '"Amplifying the Province of the Legislature": The Flow of Information and the English State in the Early Nineteenth Century', *Historical Research*, 62 (1989), 276–94.

ELKIT, JORGEN, 'Nominal Record Linkage and the Study of Non-Secret Voting', *Journal of Interdisciplinary History*, 16 (1985), 419–43.

ELVIN, MARK, 'A Working Definition of "Modernity"?', *Past and Present* 113 (1986), 209–13.

EVANS, ERIC J., 'Some Reasons for the Growth of English Rural Anti–Clericalism', *Past and Present*, 66 (1975), 84–109.

FINLAYSON, B. G. A. M., 'The Politics of Municipal Reform', *English Historical Review*, 81 (1966), 673–92.

FISHER, J. R., 'Issues and Influence: Two By–Elections in South Nottinghamshire in the Mid–Nineteenth Century', *Historical Journal*, 24 (1981), 155–63.

FRASER, PETER, 'Party Voting in the House of Commons, 1812–1827', *English Historical Review*, 98 (1983), 764–5.

GADIAN, D. S., 'Class consciousness in Oldham and Other North-West Industrial Towns, 1830–1850', *Historical Journal*, 21 (1978), 161–72.

GASH, NORMAN, 'Bonham and the Conservative Party, 1830–1857', in id., *Pillars of Government* (London, 1986), 108–35.

GINTER, DONALD, 'The Incidence of Revaluation', in M. Turner and D. Mills (eds.), *Land and Property: The English Land Tax, 1692–1832* (Gloucester, 1986), 180–8.

GREAVES, R. W., 'Roman Catholic Relief and the Leicester Election of 1826', *Transactions of the Royal Historical Society*, 22 (1940), 199–224.

GREEN, EDMUND M., 'Social Structure and Political Behaviour in West-minster, 1784–1788', in Peter Denley, et al. (eds.), *History and Computing II* (Manchester, 1989), 239–42.

HARRISON, MARK, '"To Raise and Dare Resentment": The Bristol Bridge Riot of 1793 Re-examined', *Historical Journal*, 26 (1983), 557–86.

—— 'Time, Work, and the Occurrence of Crowds, 1790–1835', *Past and Present*, 110 (1986), 134–68.

HATLEY, V. A., 'Some Aspects of Northampton's History, 1815–51', *Northamptonshire Past and Present*, 3 (1965), 243–53.

—— 'Literacy at Northampton, Some Interim Figures', *Northamptonshire Past and Present*, 9 (1971), 347–8.

—— 'Literacy at Northampton, 1761–1900', *Northamptonshire Past and Present*, 5 (1976), 379–81.

HAWKINS, ANGUS, '"Parliamentary Government" and Victorian Political Parties, c.1830–c.1880', *English Historical Review*, 104 (1989), 638–49.

HERSHBERG, T. and DOCKHORN, R., 'Occupational Classification', *Historical Methods Newsletter* 9 (1976), 59–98.

—— et al., 'Occupation and Ethnicity in Five Nineteenth–Century Cities: A Collaborative Inquiry', *Historical Methods Newsletter* 7 (1974), 174–216.

JACKSON, J. T., 'Housing areas in Mid-Victorian Wigan and St. Helens', *Transactions of the Institute of British Geographers*, 6 (1981), 413–32.

JAGGARD, EDWIN, 'Cornwall Politics, 1826–1832: Another Face of Reform?', *Journal of British Studies*, 22 (1983), 80–97.

—— 'The Parliamentary Reform Movement in Cornwall, 1805–1826', *Parliamentary History*, 2 (1983), 113–29.

JONES, PHILIP D. 'The Bristol Bridge Riot and its Antecedents: Eighteenth-Century Perception of the Crowd', *Journal of British Studies*, 19 (1980), 74–92.

JOYCE, PATRICK, 'The Factory Politics of Lancashire in the Later Nineteenth Century', *Historical Journal*, 18 (1975), 525–54.

KATZ, M., 'Occupational Classification in History', *Journal of Interdisciplinary History*, 1 (1972), 63–88.

KOUSSER, J. M., 'Toward "Total Political History": A Rational–Choice Research Program', *Journal of Interdisciplinary History*, 20 (1990), 521–60.

KRIEGEL, A. D., 'Biography and the Politics of the Early Nineteenth Century', *Journal of British Studies*, 29 (1990), 284.

LANDAU, N., 'Independence, Deference, and Voter Participation: The Behaviour of the Electorate in Early Eighteenth–Century Kent', *Historical Journal*, 22 (1979), 561–84.

'Lewes Election, 1818', *Sussex Notes and Queries*, 12 (1949), 132–5.

LINDERT, PETER and WILLIAMSON, JEFFREY G., 'Reply to N. F. R. Crafts', *Journal of Economic History*, 45 (1985), 145–53.

McCORMICK, RICHARD L., 'New Perspectives on Jacksonian Politics', *American Historical Review*, 65 (1960), 288–301.

—— 'Ethno-Cultural Interdependence of Nineteenth Century American Voting Behaviour', *Political Science Quarterly*, 89 (1974), 351–78.

McINNES, A., 'The Emergence of a Leisure Town: Shrewsbury, 1660–1760', *Past and Present*, 120 (1988), 53–87.

MALCOMSOM, ROBERT, '"A Set of Ungovernable People": The Kingswood Colliers in the Eighteenth Century', in John Brewer and John Styles (eds.), *An Ungovernable People*, (London, 1980), 85–127.

MARX, K., 'Lord John Russell', in *Karl Marx and Frederick Engels on Britain* (Moscow, 1962), 426–45.

MASON, J. F. A., 'Parliamentary Representation in Shrewsbury', in G. C. Baugh (ed.), *VCH Shropshire*, iii (London, 1979), 232–358.

MILTON-SMITH, J., 'Earl Grey's Cabinet and the Objects of Parliamentary Reform', *Historical Journal*, 15 (1972), 55–74.

MITCHELL, J. C., 'Electoral Strategy under Open Voting', *Public Choice*, 28 (1976), 17–35.

—— and CORNFORD, J., 'The Political Demography of Cambridge, 1832–68', *Albion*, 9 (1977), 242–72.

MOORE, D. C., 'The Other Face of Reform', *Victorian Studies*, 4 (1961), 7–34.

—— 'Concession or Cure: The Sociological Premises of the First Reform Act', *Historical Journal*, 9 (1966), 34–59.

MOORE, SALLY F., 'Political Meetings and the Simulations of Unanimity', in ead. and Barbara Myerhoff (eds.), *Secular Ritual* (Amsterdam, 1977), 151–72.

MORRIS, R. J., 'The Leeds Middle Class, 1820 to 1850', Report to the Committee of Economic Affairs, SSRC, June 1983.

—— 'Property Titles and the Use of British Urban Poll Books for Social Analysis', *Urban History Yearbook* (1983).

NEWBOULD, IAN, 'The Emergence of a Two-Party System in England from 1830 to 1841', *Parliaments, Estates, and Representation*, 5 (1985), 25–32.

NOBLE, MARGARET, 'The Land Tax Assessment in the Study of the Physical Development of Country Towns', in M. Turner and D. Mills (eds.), *Land and Property: The English Land Tax 1692–1832* (Gloucester, 1986).

O'GORMAN, FRANK, 'Electoral Deference in Unreformed England, 1760–1832', *Journal of Modern History*, 56 (1984), 391–429.

—— 'Party Politics in the Early Nineteenth Century', *English Historical Review*, 102 (1987), 63–84.

—— 'Election Ritual', *Past and Present* (forthcoming).

—— 'Electoral behaviour in England, 1700–1872', in Peter Denley, et al. (eds.), *History and Computing II* (Manchester, 1989), 220–38.

O'NEILL, MARK and MARTIN, GED, 'A Backbencher on Parliamentary Reform, 1831–1832', *Historical Journal*, 23 (1980), 539–64.

PARRY, J. P., 'Constituencies, Elections, and Members of Parliament, 1790–1820', *Parliamentary History*, 7 (1988), 147–60.

PHILLIPS, J. A., 'Nominal Record Linkage and the Study of Individual-Level Electoral Behaviour', *Laboratory for Political Research* (Iowa City, Ia., 1976), 1–71.

—— 'Achieving a Critical Mass while Avoiding an Explosion', *Journal of Interdisciplinary History*, 9 (1979), 493–508.

—— 'Popular Politics in Unreformed England', *Journal of Modern History*, 52 (1980), 599–625.

—— 'The Many Faces of Reform: The Reform Bill and the Electorate', *Parliamentary History*, 1 (1982), 115–35.

—— 'Poll Books and English Electoral Behaviour', in J. Sims (ed.), *A Handlist of British Parliamentary Poll Books*, (Leicester, 1984), pp. i–xx.

—— 'Partisan Behaviour in Adversity: Lewes and Reform', *Parliamentary History*, 6 (1987), 262–79.

—— 'From Municipal Matters to Parliamentary Principles', *Journal of British Studies*, 27 (1988), 327–51.

—— 'The Social Calculus: Deference and Defiance in Later Georgian England', *Albion*, 21 (1989), 426–49.

—— 'Electoral Polarization in the Reign of George III', in Eckhart Hellmuth (ed.), *The Transformation of Political Culture* (Oxford, 1990), 185–203.

—— and Thompson, T. C., 'Jurors v. Judges in Later-Stuart England', *Law and Inequality*, 4 (1986), 189–229.

PLUMB, J. H., 'Political Man', in J. Clifford, (ed.), *Man vs. Society in the Eighteenth Century* (Cambridge, 1968), 1–21.

RECTOR, W. K., 'Lewes Quakers in the Seventeenth and Eighteenth Centuries', *Sussex Archaeological Collections*, 116 (1978), 31–40.

RICHARDS, PAUL, 'R. A. Slaney, the Industrial Town, and Early Victorian Social Policy', *Social History*, 4 (1979), 85–101.

RUNCIMAN, W. C., 'Explaining Social Stratification', in T. J. Nossiter (ed.), *Imagination and Precision in the Social Sciences* (London, 1972), 157–80.

SMITH, E. A., 'Election Agent', *English Historical Review*, 84 (1969), 12–35.

SPECK, W. A., 'The Electorate in the First Age of Party', in Clyve Jones (ed.), *Britian in the First Age of Party, 1680–1750* (London, 1987), 45–62.

—— and GRAY, W. A., 'A Computer Analysis of Poll books: an Initial Report', *Bulletin of the Institute of Historical Research*, 43 (1970), 105–12.

—— *et al.*, 'Computer Analysis of Poll Books: A Further Report', *Bulletin of the Institute of Historical Research*, 48 (1975), 64–90.

SYKES, R. A., 'Some Aspects of Working-Class Consciousness in Oldham, 1830–1842', *Historical Journal*, 23 (1980), 167–79.

THOMAS, KEITH, 'The Brilliant Misfit', *New York Review of Books*, 37 (1990), 46–8.

TURNER, VICTOR, 'Variations on a Theme of Liminality', in Sally F. Moore and Barbara Myerhoff (eds.), *Secular Ritual* (Amsterdam, 1977), 36–52.

URDANK, ALBION, 'The Gloucestershire Weaver Strike', *Journal of British Studies*, 25 (1986), 193–226.

WASSON, E. A., 'The Great Whigs and Parliamentary Reform, 1809–1830', *Journal of British Studies*, 24 (1985), 434–64.

WELLS, ROGER, 'Rural Rebels in Southern England in the 1830s', in Clive Emsley and James Walvin (eds.), *Artisans, Peasants, and Proletarians* (London, 1985), 122–65.

WEYMAN, HENRY T., 'Shrewsbury Members of Parliament', *Transactions of the Shropshire Archaeological Society*, 4th ser., 12 (1929–30), 69–276.

WILLIAMS, J., 'Bristol in the General Elections of 1818 and 1820', *Transactions of the Bristol and Gloucestershire Archaeological Society*, 87 (1968), 173–201.

WOOLLEY, S. F., 'The Personnel of the Parliament of 1833', *English Historical Review*, 53 (1938), 240–62.

INDEX